Game Theory and its Applications

INTERNATIONAL SERIES IN SOCIAL PSYCHOLOGY

Series Editor: W. Peter Robinson, University of Bristol

Assertion and its Social Context
Children's Social Competence in Context
Emotion and Social Judgements
Genius and Eminence
Making Sense of Television
Psychology of Gambling
Social Dilemmas: Theoretical Issues and Research Findings
The Theory of Reasoned Action

Game Theory and its Applications in the Social and Biological Sciences

Second Edition

Andrew M. Colman

LONDON AND NEW YORK

First published 1982 as *Game Theory and Experimental Games*

Published 1995 by Butterworth-Heinemann Ltd

Published 1999
by Routledge
11 New Fetter Lane, London EC4P 4EE

Simultaneously published in the USA and Canada
by Routledge
29 West 35th Street, New York, NY 10001

Routledge is an imprint of the Taylor & Francis group

© 1982, 1995, 1999 Andrew M. Colman

The right of Andrew M. Colman to be identified as the author of this work
has been asserted by him in accordance with the Copyright, Designs and
Patents Act 1988

British Library Cataloguing in Publication Data
A catalogue record for this book is available from the British Library

Library of Congress Cataloging in Publication Data
A catalogue record for this book is available from the Library of Congress

ISBN 0–7506–2369–1

Printed and bound in the UK by Clays Ltd, St Ives plc

Contents

Preface to the First Edition   ix

Preface to the Second Edition   xi

Part I Background

1 Introduction   3
  1.1 Intuitive background   3
    1.1.1 Head On   4
    1.1.2 Price War   5
    1.1.3 Angelo and Isabella   5
  1.2 Abstract models: basic terminology   6
  1.3 Skill, chance, and strategy   10
  1.4 Historical background   12
  1.5 Summary   14

2 One-person games   15
  2.1 Games against Nature   15
  2.2 Certainty   15
  2.3 Risk   17
  2.4 Expected utility theory   19
  2.5 Uncertainty   23
    2.5.1 Insufficient reason   25
    2.5.2 Maximax   26
    2.5.3 Maximin   26
    2.5.4 Minimax regret   28
  2.6 Summary   32

3 Coordination games and the minimal social situation   33
  3.1 Strategic collaboration   33
  3.2 Coordination games   33
  3.3 The minimal social situation   40
  3.4 The multi-person minimal social situation   48
  3.5 Summary   50

Part II Theory and empirical evidence

4 Two-person zero-sum games   53
  4.1 Strictly competitive games   53
  4.2 Extensive and normal forms   54
  4.3 Games with saddle points: Nash equilibria   57
  4.4 Games without saddle points   62
  4.5 Dominance and admissibility   69
  4.6 Methods for finding solutions   71
  4.7 Ordinal payoffs and incomplete information   78
  4.8 Summary   83

5 Experiments with strictly competitive games   85
  5.1 Ideas behind experimental games   85
  5.2 Empirical research on non-saddle-point games   87
  5.3 Empirical research on saddle-point games   91
  5.4 Framing effects   94
  5.5 Critique of experimental gaming   97
  5.6 Summary   99

6 Two-person mixed-motive games: informal game theory   100
  6.1 Mixed-motive games   100
  6.2 Subgame perfect and trembling-hand equilibria   101
  6.3 Classification of 2 × 2 mixed-motive games   107
  6.4 Leader   108
  6.5 Battle of the Sexes   110
  6.6 Chicken   111
  6.7 Prisoner's Dilemma   115
  6.8 Comparison of archetypal 2 × 2 games   118
  6.9 Theory of metagames   121
  6.10 Two-person cooperative games: bargaining solutions   126
       6.10.1 Maximin bargaining solution   129
       6.10.2 Nash bargaining solution   130
       6.10.3 Raiffa–Kalai–Smorodinsky bargaining solution   131
  6.11 Summary   132

7 Experiments with Prisoner's Dilemma and related games   134
  7.1 The experimental gaming literature   134
  7.2 Strategic structure   135
  7.3 Payoffs and incentives   139
  7.4 Communication effects   141
  7.5 Programmed strategies   142
  7.6 Axelrod's computer tournaments   144
  7.7 Sex differences and cross-cultural studies   149

7.8 Attribution effects   152
7.9 Framing effects   154
7.10 Summary   160

8 Multi-person cooperative games: coalition formation   161
8.1 *N*-person cooperative games   161
8.2 Characteristic function and imputation   163
8.3 Core and stable set   167
8.4 Harold Pinter's *The Caretaker*   169
8.5 Shapley value   172
8.6 Kernel, nucleolus, and least core   174
8.7 Coalition-predicting theories   177
    8.7.1 Equal excess theory   177
    8.7.2 Caplow's theory   179
    8.7.3 Minimal winning coalition theory   179
    8.7.4 Minimum resource theory   180
8.8 Experiments on coalition formation   180
8.9 Summary   185

9 Multi-person non-cooperative games and social dilemmas   186
9.1 *N*-person non-cooperative games: Nash equilibria   186
9.2 The Chain-store paradox and backward induction   187
9.3 Auction games and psychological traps   191
9.4 Social dilemmas: intuitive background   201
    9.4.1 The "invisible hand" and voluntary wage restraint   202
    9.4.2 Conservation of natural resources   203
    9.4.3 The tragedy of the commons   204
9.5 Formalization of social dilemmas   205
9.6 Theory of compound games   209
9.7 Empirical research on social dilemmas   212
    9.7.1 Group size effects   215
    9.7.2 Communication effects   218
    9.7.3 Individual differences and attribution effects   221
    9.7.4 Payoff and incentive effects   223
    9.7.5 Framing effects   224
9.8 Summary   226

Part III Applications

10 Social choice and strategic voting   229
10.1 Background   229
10.2 Alternatives, voters, preferences   230
10.3 Voting procedures   233

10.4 Voting paradoxes   237
10.5 Arrow's impossibility theorem   244
10.6 Proportional representation: single transferable vote   246
10.7 Strategic (tactical) voting   250
10.8 Sophisticated voting   258
10.9 Empirical evidence of strategic voting   267
10.10 Summary   270

11 Theory of evolution: strategic aspects   272
11.1 Historical background   272
11.2 Strategic evolution and behavioural ecology   272
11.3 Animal conflicts and evolutionarily stable strategies   276
11.4 An improved multi-person game model   281
11.5 Empirical evidence   288
11.6 Summary   293

12 Game theory and philosophy   294
12.1 Relevance of game theory to practical problems   294
12.2 Rationality in games   297
     12.2.1 Coordination games   297
     12.2.2 Prisoner's Dilemma games   300
12.3 Newcomb's problem   304
12.4 Kant's categorical imperative   308
12.5 Plato, Hobbes, Rousseau: social contract theories   310
12.6 Evolution and stability of moral principles   314
12.7 Summary   316

Appendix A simple proof of the minimax theorem   317
A.1 Introductory remarks   317
A.2 Preliminary formalization   317
A.3 The minimax theorem   318
A.4 Proof   319
A.5 Remark   324

References   325

Index   363

Preface to the First Edition

The primary aim of this book is to provide a critical survey of the essential ideas of game theory and the findings of experimental research on strategic interaction. In addition, I have reported some new experiments using lifelike simulations of familiar kinds of strategic interactions, and included discussions of recent applications of game theory to the study of voting, the theory of evolution, and moral philosophy. The time has (alas) long since passed when a single person could reasonably hope to be an expert on all branches of game theory or on all of its applications, and I have not attempted to achieve the impossible. But I thought it worthwhile, none the less, to aim for a fairly comprehensive coverage of important topics, with particular emphasis on those that seemed to be most relevant to naturally occurring strategic interactions.

Game theory and the experimental gaming tradition have grown up in relative isolation from each other. Game theorists, in general, remain largely oblivious of the empirical studies that have been inspired by the theory, and experimental investigators have tended to assume that the nuts and bolts of the theory do not concern them. Both parties are the losers from this divorce, and I have therefore tried to contribute towards a reconciliation by examining in detail, for the first time in a single volume, both sides of the story.

My goal has been to introduce and evaluate the fundamental theoretical ideas, empirical findings, and applications as clearly as possible without over-simplifying or side-stepping important difficulties. In so far as I have succeeded, this is the kind of book that I should have liked to have read when I first became interested in game theory and experimental games, or better still, before I developed any interest in these matters. Wherever possible, I have attributed seminal contributions to their originators and cited the original sources: ideas are almost invariably expressed more clearly and forcefully by their inventors or discoverers than by subsequent commentators. But I have also cited many useful review articles, which will be of assistance to readers wishing to pursue particular topics in depth.

The most important chapters [the numbering of chapters has been amended here to correspond with the second edition] for social psychologists and others whose primary interest is in such strategic phenomena as cooperation, competition, collective equilibria, self-defeating effects of individual rationality, coalition formation, threats, altruism, spite, escalation, social entrapment, and so forth, are chapters 1, 2, 3, 6, 7, 8, and 9. Mathematically inclined readers should pay special attention to chapters 3, 4, 6, 8, 10, and to the Appendix in which the minimax theorem is rigorously proved. The chapters most relevant to sociology, economics, and politics are chapters 1, 2, 3, 6, 8, 9, and 10. Biological applications are discussed in chapter 11, but chapters 1, 2, 6, 7, and 9 provide a necessary background. Philosophical applications are dealt with primarily in chapter 12, to which chapters 1, 2, 3, 6, 9, and 11 provide the necessary background. Most of the translations from original French and German sources in chapter 12 and elsewhere are my own.

I am indebted to a number of people who contributed to this book in various indirect ways. In particular, I am grateful to Michael Argyle, Alan Baker, Barbara Barrett, Dorothy Brydges, Roy Davies, Julia Gibbs, Gabriele Griffin, John Lazarus, Nicholas Measor, Richard Niemi, Ian Pountney, Albert W. Tucker, Diane Williams, Bill Williamson, and the Research Board of the University of Leicester. I should be delighted to receive comments from readers, indicating their reactions to the final product.

Andrew M. Colman

Preface to the Second Edition

The first edition of this book was entitled *Game Theory and Experimental Games: The Study of Strategic Interaction* and was published by Pergamon Press in 1982. It aimed to bridge the gap between game theory and its applications by providing an introduction to the theory and a reasonably comprehensive survey of some of its major applications and associated experimental research. Its more specific objectives were to explain the fundamental ideas of mathematical game theory from first principles and to provide an introductory survey of experimental games and other applications of the theory in social psychology, decision theory, evolutionary biology, economics, politics, sociology, operational research, and philosophy.

The first edition was favourably received and generously reviewed on both sides of the Atlantic and adopted as a text for a number of specialist courses. Demand for the book, though modest, remained remarkably steady for many years, but theoretical developments and new empirical findings accumulated over the years, making the need for a revision of the original text increasingly difficult to ignore. This second edition is so radically revised as to be hardly the same book, and I believe it to be a significant improvement on the first. The principal changes that I have introduced are as follows. I have modified the title, at the suggestion of the publisher, to indicate the scope of the book more accurately. I have corrected the errors and plugged the gaps that have been pointed out to me, and I have introduced numerous amendments and improvements to every chapter. I have thoroughly updated the contents of the book to include significant or interesting theoretical developments and empirical research findings related to coordination games, social dilemmas, strategic aspects of evolutionary biology, framing effects, strategic voting, and many other areas of research. In the light of comments from readers and reviewers I have introduced a little more formal mathematics where omitting it seems to have created more problems than it solved.

In addition, I have improved the book's coverage by incorporating into this second edition a number of important topics that have developed recently or were missing from the first edition for other reasons. Chapter 3 now includes a great deal more theoretical and empirical work on coordination games and the minimal social situation. Chapter 6 includes a section on subgame perfect and trembling-hand equilibria and a further section on bargaining solutions for two-person cooperative games; chapter 7 includes a discussion of Axelrod's tournaments of Prisoner's Dilemma game computer programs and a brief review of cross-cultural comparisons of cooperativeness; chapter 8 is renamed and largely rewritten to include a detailed review of the major theories of coalition formation; chapter 9 is renamed and restructured and includes a discussion of the Chain-store paradox and backward induction; chapter 10 is renamed and restructured and incorporates material on strategic voting, which was in a separate chapter of its own in the first edition, and a discussion (requested by a number of readers) of proportional representation voting procedures, chapter 11 is renamed and includes a refutation of the notion that the strongest always survive in evolutionary games, and chapter 12 is renamed and restructured and includes discussions of philosophical problems related to coordination games and Newcomb's problem.

I no longer believe that "ideas are almost invariably expressed more clearly and forcefully by their inventors or discoverers than by subsequent commentators", as I said in the preface to the first edition. I now believe, on the contrary, that innovators sometimes struggle to understand their own inventions or discoveries and that their successors often understand and explain them better. I have therefore been more liberal with my citations of secondary sources in this edition.

I remain indebted to the people who helped me with the first edition and were acknowledged in its preface. Preparation of this edition was facilitated by Grant No. L122251002 from the Economic and Social Research Council as part of the research programme on Economic Beliefs and Behaviour. Numerous thoughtful readers in Britain, the United States, the Netherlands, and elsewhere have made helpful suggestions that have been incorporated into this second edition, and I am grateful to them all. They are too numerous to list exhaustively, but special thanks are due to Jerome Chertkoff, whose thoughtful review in *Contemporary Psychology* included constructive suggestions for improvement that I have implemented fully, to Werner Tack and Manfred Vorwerg, who also offered important practical advice that I have followed, to Michael Bacharach of Oxford University and other colleagues involved in the Framing, Salience and Product Images research project for inspiration and advice, to Brian Parkinson and David Stretch, who provided useful comments, to Roy Davies, who helped me to improve the mathematical appendix and the general presentation of this edition, to Zhu Zhifang of Wuhan University in the People's Republic of China, who discovered an important though deeply hidden error while working on a Chinese translation of the book, and to Kathy Smith for preparing many of the payoff matrices. But in spite of everyone's help and my own best efforts, this book is not free of errors. It cannot be error-free, because if it were, then the sentence immediately preceding this one would be an error, which would mean that it was not error-free after all. I should be grateful to readers who spot any more serious defects or who have any other comments to make.

Andrew M. Colman

— *Part I* —
Background

— *1* —

Introduction

1.1 Intuitive background

Game theory is a branch of mathematics devoted to the logic of decision making in social interactions. It is applicable to any social interaction with the following three properties:

(a) there are two or more decision makers, called *players*;
(b) each player has a choice of two or more ways of acting, called *strategies*, such that the outcome of the interaction depends on the strategy choices of all the players;
(c) the players have well-defined preferences among the possible outcomes, so that numerical *payoffs* reflecting these preferences can be assigned to all players for all outcomes.

Any social interaction with these three properties is a game in the terminology of game theory – or to be more precise could be modelled by a game, which is really an abstract mathematical invention.

An essential feature of these social interactions is that each decision maker has only partial control over the outcome. It is immediately obvious that games like chess and poker are games in the technical sense, but that other activities such as patience (solitaire), doll play, hopscotch, and solitary computer games such as Nintendo or Sega, in spite of being games in the popular sense of the word, are not. More importantly, many economic, political, military, and interpersonal conflicts that are seldom if ever referred to as games in everyday speech nevertheless have the three properties that define them as games in the terminology of game theory. In spite of its name, game theory is not specifically concerned with recreations and pastimes, and a less misleading name for it would have been the *theory of interdependent decision making*, but it is too late to rename game theory without risking even worse confusion.

The principal objective of mathematical game theory is to determine, through formal reasoning alone, what strategies the players ought to choose in order to pursue their own interests rationally and what outcomes will result if they do so. Formal game theory is therefore *normative* rather than *positive* or *descriptive* inasmuch as it seeks to discover how players *ought* to

3

behave in order to pursue their own interests most effectively but makes no predictions about how they *will* behave in any actual interaction, and for that reason it cannot be tested by experimental methods. But in non-mathematical applications in the social and biological sciences, game theory has provided a useful framework for explaining and predicting behaviour in a wide range of situations involving interdependent decision making, and predictions derived from informal game theory have been tested through empirical research. Even in cases in which satisfactory formal solutions cannot be found, informal game theory has often provided deep and illuminating insights. Certain important features of individual and collective rationality, cooperation and competition, trust and suspicion, threats and commitments cannot even be clearly described, let alone explained, without the framework of game theory.

Traditional theories in social psychology and related fields lack the necessary concepts with which to deal rigorously with interdependent decision making. They have tended to emulate the theoretical models that are used in classical physics, in which the behaviour of objects is explained in terms of responses to external forces. But inanimate objects do not make deliberate choices, and their behaviour is not governed by any assumptions about how other objects will behave. One-way causal models may be appropriate for explaining certain involuntary human responses, such as kicking the air in response to a doctor's tap on the patellar tendon or blinking the eye in response to the intrusion of a speck of dust. But a person may kick the air voluntarily as an act of symbolic aggression in the hope of gaining some strategic advantage during a competitive interaction, or may deliberately wink an eye in an attempt to increase the intimacy of a personal relationship. These are deliberate actions whose outcomes depend on the decisions of other people as well, and one-way causal models of the kind that have proved so successful in the physical sciences are unlikely to explain them adequately. Psychologically interesting and significant forms of social behaviour almost all involve deliberate decisions, and they are sometimes amenable to game theory analysis. A few simple examples will help to provide an intuitive understanding of the kinds of social interactions involving interdependent decision making that fall within the compass of game theory.

1.1.1 Head On

Two people are walking briskly towards each other along a narrow corridor. They are heading for a collision, which they would both prefer to avoid. To simplify the analysis, let us assume that the walkers have to make their decisions immediately, and therefore simultaneously, and that each has just three strategies from which to choose: swerve left, swerve right, or keep going straight ahead. If both keep going straight ahead, or if both swerve to the same side of the corridor, then they will collide; all other strategy combinations lead to non-collision outcomes, which they both prefer. The outcome of the game depends on the decisions of both walkers, whose interests coincide exactly inasmuch as their preferences among the outcomes are identical.

1.1.2 Price War

Three retail companies are each trying to carve out a larger slice of a market for which they all compete. Each has to decide, in ignorance of the decisions of the others, whether or not to advertise its product. If all three companies advertise simultaneously, none will gain or lose market share, but all will lose the cost of their advertisements. The status quo market shares will also be preserved, slightly more cheaply, if all three decide not to advertise. Other strategy combinations result in increased market share for one or two of the companies at the expense of the other(s). In this example, the players' interests are mutually opposed, because one company's gain necessitates a loss for at least one of the others.

1.1.3 Angelo and Isabella

This poignant example is taken from Shakespeare's *Measure for Measure* (II. iv). Angelo is holding a prisoner whom he intends to execute. The prisoner's sister, Isabella, comes to plead for her brother's life. Angelo is sexually attracted to her and at length proposes the following ungentlemanly bargain: "You must lay down the treasures of your body" to save your brother. Isabella initially declines the offer: "More than our brother is our chastity". Angelo then complicates the game by threatening not merely to kill the prisoner, as he had originally intended, but to subject him to a *lingering* death unless Isabella submits. At this point Isabella faces a choice between submitting and refusing, and whichever option she chooses there are three courses open to Angelo: to spare the prisoner's life, to execute him humanely, or to subject him to a lingering death. The outcome depends on the choices of both Angelo and Isabella, and all but one of the possible outcomes lead to unattractive payoffs for Isabella (the exception being Isabella's refusal coupled with a reprieve from Angelo), although some are clearly worse than others. Both protagonists would prefer to see the prisoner executed humanely rather than cruelly, other things being equal, so the players' interests are partly opposed and partly coincident (Schelling, 1960, p. 140).

1.2 Abstract models: basic terminology

Game theory deals with social interactions like the ones described above by abstracting their formal, logical properties. A game is a purely imaginary idealization of a social interaction. A real social interaction is invariably too complex and transitory to be clearly perceived and perfectly understood, so it is replaced by a deliberately simplified abstract structure whose rules and basic elements – players, strategies, and payoffs – are explicitly defined and from which other properties can be deduced by formal reasoning. These deductions apply not to the social interaction itself but to the game that models it, and they are true, provided only that the reasoning does not contain errors, whether or not the game corresponds accurately to the original social interaction. But if the game does not correspond to social reality in important particulars, then its practical value is at best limited; and if it does not yield insights that transcend a common-sense understanding of the social interaction, then it serves no useful purpose at all.

The formal models devised by game theorists are sometimes criticised for their lack of concreteness and their failure to capture the full complexity of the social realities that they are designed to represent. This criticism stems from a profound misunderstanding of the purpose of a formal model, which is to reduce reality to its bare essentials by deliberately excluding non-essential details. In some fields of investigation formal models have proved so successful that many people forget that they are merely abstractions and confuse them with reality itself. Euclidian geometry is a striking (and indeed a classical) example, which was eventually shown to correspond imperfectly to reality, although it remains adequate for most ordinary purposes.

The examples in the previous section illustrate the fact that the decision makers or players (to use the technical term) may be individual human beings or corporate decision-making bodies, and there are even applications discussed elsewhere in this book in which they represent non-human animals. The essential attribute of a player is the capacity to choose or, in other words, to make decisions. These decisions are called *moves* or *strategies* – the distinction between these two concepts will be explained shortly.

In some games, the outcome depends partly on the invisible hand of chance, and consequently the moves or actions of the (other) players do not, on their own, fully determine the outcomes that follow. In order to handle games like these, a fictional player called Nature is brought into the game, and it is assumed that Nature chooses her moves according to the laws of probability. Poker is a typical example: Nature makes the first move by arranging the deck in a particular (random) order, and from that point on she plays no part in the game until the next hand is to be dealt. In many economic, political, military, and interpersonal games of everyday life, Nature also plays an important part.

A game must involve at least two players, otherwise there could be no interdependence of choice, but in the widest interpretation of game theory this includes interactions between one ordinary player and Nature. Furthermore, each player must have at least two courses of action from which to choose, because an agent with only one way of acting would have no effect on the outcome of the game and could therefore be ignored. In defining the set of strategies facing a player, as in everyday life, it is necessary to remind oneself that doing nothing is often one of the available options.

The rules of the game specify what moves or actions are available to each player, how the moves are made, including what the players are permitted to know when they choose their moves, and what *outcome* is associated with each possible combination of decisions by all the players. The rules of chess, for example, specify three possible outcomes: White wins, Black wins, or a draw. The rules governing the games outlined in the previous section were specified informally in their descriptions. The outcome of Head On is either a collision or a non-collision. In Price War, the outcomes are various distributions of market share among the three companies. Angelo and Isabella is a slightly more complicated case, which will help to clarify the subtle though important distinction between moves (or actions) and strategies.

One possible outcome of Angelo and Isabella is this: Isabella surrenders her chastity to Angelo and her brother is subjected to a lingering death. From Isabella's point of view, this is the worst possible outcome. It is assumed in general that players have consistent preferences across the set of possible outcomes. At the very least, each player must be able, in principle, to arrange the outcomes in order of preference from best to worst with equal ranks assigned to those between which the player is indifferent. It is then possible to assign numerical *payoffs* to the outcomes, indicating the players' relative preferences among them. In Angelo and Isabella, it is possible to assign Isabella's lowest payoff, say 1, to her least preferred outcome, 2 to her next-to-worst outcome – presumably a surrender of her chastity to Angelo coupled with a humane execution of her brother – and so on up to her favourite outcome, namely a preservation of her chastity and a reprieve for her brother. Angelo's lowest payoff may (reasonably) be assigned to the outcome in which Isabella withholds her sexual favours and her brother is reprieved, and his highest to the one in which Isabella submits and her brother is humanely executed as originally planned. Ordinal payoffs like these are all that are needed for solving some games, but in others the payoffs must be measured on interval scales. In other words, it is sometimes necessary to know not merely which outcomes a player prefers to which others, but also how strong the preferences are relative to one another.

In either event, a *payoff function* is defined for every player in the game. Mathematically speaking, an individual player's payoff function is a relation that associates each possible outcome of the game with a unique (ordinal or interval) payoff to that player; in other words it specifies what payoff the player receives for every conceivable outcome of the game. A complete payoff function for all of the players is simply an amalgamation of the individual players' payoff functions; it specifies the payoffs to all players for every conceivable outcome of the game.

A *strategy* is a complete plan of action, specifying in advance what moves a player will make in every possible situation that might arise in the course of the game. If each player has only one move to make, and if the moves are made simultaneously or (what amounts to the same thing) in ignorance of the moves chosen by the other player(s), then the available strategies are simply the moves, and there is no distinction between the two concepts. In Head On, for example, each player has only one move to make, namely swerve left, swerve right, or keep going straight ahead, and the moves are made simultaneously, so they are also the strategies available to the players. Similarly in Price War, the players' strategies or moves are simply to advertise or not to advertise. But in other cases, the players' strategies are more complicated than the individual moves of the game. In Angelo and Isabella, Isabella has just two moves, namely submit (*S*) or don't submit (*DS*), and these are also her strategies. But the rules of this game stipulate that Angelo makes his move after – and in full knowledge of – Isabella's. He has just three available moves, namely reprieve (*R*), execute humanely (*E*), or torture (*T*), but his strategy choice must specify in advance which move he will choose in response to each of Isabella's possible moves. Although he has only three moves or actions, it turns out that he has nine possible strategies, as follows:

(1) If *S*, choose *R*; if *DS*, choose *R*.
(2) If *S*, choose *R*; if *DS*, choose *E*.
(3) If *S*, choose *R*; if *DS*, choose *T*.
(4) If *S*, choose *E*; if *DS*, choose *R*.
(5) If *S*, choose *E*; if *DS*, choose *E*.
(6) If *S*, choose *E*; if *DS*, choose *T*.
(7) If *S*, choose *T*; if *DS*, choose *R*.
(8) If *S*, choose *T*; if *DS*, choose *E*.
(9) If *S*, choose *T*; if *DS*, choose *T*.

Angelo's promise (or threat, depending on one's point of view) is to choose his third strategy, but he is not bound by the rules of the game to honour it if his bluff is called. In Shakespeare's play, Angelo's untrustworthiness becomes tragically clear as the story unfolds and it transpires that he has in fact chosen his fifth strategy in spite of his promise.

By choosing a strategy that specifies in advance what particular moves a player will make in all possible contingencies, a player does not sacrifice any freedom of action. All moves that are available to a player in the *extensive form* of the game, which sets out the full sequence of moves in the order in which they are made, are preserved in the *normal form*, which collapses each player's sequence of moves into just one strategy choice. In the normal form, a game involving a sequence of moves can be represented statically, as though the outcome were determined by a single choice on the part of each player, and this does not affect the strategic properties inherent in the situation. The strategies chosen by the players determine a unique sequence of moves and a definite outcome. On the basis of their strategy choices, a referee could in principle make all the moves in accordance with the players' plans and discover the outcome. But this is a practical impossibility except in very simple games. In chess, some 160 000 different positions can arise after only two moves by each player, and all the paper or all the computer disks in the world would not have the storage capacity to record a player's strategy for an entire game. Only much simpler games can be represented in normal form, and even in these cases the way players actually think is often more usefully displayed in extensive form, which is usually represented by a branching tree. The normal form, though logically equivalent, is often less useful for practical analysis, and it impedes the identification of subgame perfect equilibria, which will be explained in section 6.2 (Myerson, 1991, chap. 5; Rasmusen, 1989, chap. 2).

Two technical terms, which need to be carefully distinguished, are used to describe what the players know during the course of the game. In a game of *complete information*, the players know not only the rules of the game and their own payoff functions but also the payoff functions of the other player(s). In other words, they know the available strategies and preferences of all of the players. There is also an important assumption that each player knows that the other(s) have complete information, and that they know that the other player(s) know this, and so on; this is the assumption that the description of the game is *common knowledge* (Heal, 1978; Lewis, 1969; see also Bicchieri, 1993, *passim*; Sugden, 1991, pp. 764–765). Most games that have been studied by game theorists, and most that have been used in applications in the social and biological sciences, have been games of complete information, but some important work has also been done on games of incomplete information.

A game of *perfect information* is something rather different from one of complete information. Informally, it is a game in which the players move one at a time, rather than simultaneously, and a player choosing a move always has full knowledge of all moves that have preceded it. Chess is a game of perfect information, and so is Angelo and Isabella, but Head On and Price War are not, because in these last two games moves are not made one at a time and with the benefit of knowing what moves the other players have chosen. All of these games are, however, games of complete information.

1.3 Skill, chance, and strategy

It is possible to classify games according to certain family resemblances. This is useful because the method used to analyse a particular game can often be applied without modification of its underlying ideas to other games belonging to the same general class; only a relatively few need therefore to be studied in order to understand a much larger number. Perhaps the most fundamental criterion of classification concerns the factors that influence the outcomes of the games. It is accordingly useful to distinguish between games of skill, games of chance, and games of strategy.

Games of skill and chance are species of one-person games, whereas games of strategy involve two or more decision makers in addition to Nature. Games of skill are often referred to as *individual decision making under certainty*. Games of chance are called *individual decision making under risk or uncertainty* or *one-person games against Nature*. These important distinctions deserve the less cumbersome terminology of skill, chance, and strategy.

The defining property of a game of skill is the involvement of just one player who has complete control over the outcomes so that each of the player's strategy choices leads to a single certain outcome. Responding to an IQ test might possibly be modelled by a game of skill, provided that there is no significant element of luck: every possible combination of answers that a testee might give to the questions constitutes a strategy, each strategy choice leads to a definite outcome in the form of an IQ score, and it is reasonable to assume that the player prefers some outcomes to some others. In view of the fact that other players have no effect on the outcomes of games of skill – not even Nature plays any part – these games constitute a degenerate class from which the element of interdependence of choice is lacking, and they do not, strictly speaking, qualify as games in the technical sense outlined in section 1.2. But for the sake of completeness, and also to place other one-person games in theoretical perspective, a brief discussion of games of skill is included in section 2.2.

Games of chance are models of one-person decisions whose outcomes are influenced by Nature. In a game of chance, the decision maker does not control the outcomes completely, and strategy choices do not lead to outcomes that can be guaranteed. The outcomes depend partly on the choices of the decision maker – the agent to whom the adjective "one-person" refers – and partly on the choices of the fictitious player, Nature. Although these are one-*person* games, they involve two *players*, and they can therefore be included within the domain of game theory.

Depending on how Nature's strategies are interpreted, games of chance can be further subdivided into those involving *risk* and those involving *uncertainty*. (This distinction was made explicit by Keynes, 1937; see also Bicchieri, 1993, pp. 25–27; Lucas, 1981, p. 15.) In risky decision making, the decision makers know the probabilities associated with each of Nature's strategies and therefore of the outcomes associated with each of their own strategy choices. Russian roulette is a good example of a game of chance involving risk. For any number of live bullets that one chooses to load into a revolver before pointing it at one's temple and pulling the trigger, the probabilities associated with the two possible outcomes – life and death – are obvious, but unless all of the bullet chambers are filled or all are empty, the outcome cannot be predicted with certainty. The theory of games of chance is essentially the theory of probability, which arose out of a mathematical analysis of gambling. All games of this type can be satisfactorily solved, as will be shown in chapter 2, provided that the player's preferences among the outcomes are consistent.

There are other games of chance in which meaningful probabilities cannot be assigned to Nature's strategies, and these are called decisions under uncertainty. A doctor needing to choose a treatment for a patient with a rare complaint may, for example, have no basis on which to judge the relevant probabilities. Nature obviously has a hand in this game, because the outcomes of the doctor's decisions are not certain, but in this case even the probabilities are unknown. Ingenious solutions have been devised for games of this type, but it will be argued in chapter 2 that none of them is entirely sound.

Games of strategy model social interactions in which the outcomes depend on the choices of two or more decision makers, each of whom has partial control of the outcome. The players cannot meaningfully assign probabilities to one another's choices, and therefore the decisions are said to be made under uncertainty rather than risk. The bulk of the literature on game theory is devoted to games of strategy, and it is fair to say that the theory came into its own only when methods were discovered for solving these games.

Games of strategy are especially useful for explaining social interactions, and most of the chapters that follow are concerned with them. They can be subdivided into two-person and multi-person games according to the number of players (excluding Nature) involved. Both two-person and multi-person games can be further subdivided according to their structural properties. One important structural property is the way in which the players' payoff functions are related to one another. The players' preferences may coincide perfectly as in Head On, they may be mutually opposed as in Price War, or they may be partly coincident and partly opposed as in Angelo and Isabella. Games in which the players' preferences coincide are called *co-ordination games*, and research into such interactions is discussed in section 3.2. Games in which the players' preferences are mutually opposed are called *zero-sum games*; they are dealt with in chapters 4, 5, and (part of) 8. Most recreational games between two players or two teams are zero-sum in the sense that what one player or team wins, the other must lose, and the payoffs to the two players therefore add up to zero in each outcome, but most social interactions of everyday life lack this property. The rest of this book is concerned mainly with two-person and multi-person games in which the preferences of the players are neither perfectly coincident nor entirely opposed. They are known technically as *mixed-motive games*.

Two-person zero-sum games are also called *strictly competitive games*. They can be convincingly solved, provided that each player has only a finite number of strategies, and empirical research has thrown some light on the way in which people behave in strictly competitive interactions. Other types of games, including multi-person zero-sum games and both two-person and multi-person mixed-motive games, are not generally soluble in the formal sense, but they provide important insights into some aspects of social interaction, and some of them are more relevant to the social and biological sciences than strictly competitive games.

1.4 Historical background

The forerunner of the theory of games of strategy was the theory of games of chance. This earlier theory originated in the seventeenth century from attempts to solve practical problems of gambling raised by members of the dissolute French nobility before the revolution. From those frivolous origins sprang the theory of probability, which provided a foundation for the later development of statistics, quantum physics, and population genetics.

The theory of games of chance – or the theory of probability – is traced by most historians to 1654, when an exchange of letters took place between Blaise Pascal and Pierre de Fermat concerning the misfortunes of the French nobleman, the Chevalier de Méré. De Méré had written to Pascal explaining that he had won a considerable sum of money over a period of time by betting even odds that at least one six would come up in four throws of a die, only to lose it all by betting that at least two sixes would come up in 24 throws. According to de Méré's faulty calculations, his second bet ought to have been at least as favourable as his first. The correct probabilities, however, are in fact .5177 and .4914 respectively, that is, the first is favourable but the second is not. De Méré must have been an extraordinarily industrious and deep-pocketed gambler to have discovered by dint of sheer bitter experience that the second bet was unfavourable, in other words to have distinguished empirically between probabilities of .4914 and .5000. The fundamental principles of probability theory were developed in order to solve De Méré's and other similar problems. The story is entertainingly told, with extracts from the Pascal–Fermat letters, by Florence N. David (1962).

The first important contribution to the theory of games of strategy was made by the German mathematician, Ernst Zermelo, in 1912. Zermelo managed to prove that every strictly competitive game of perfect information that has a finite number of moves is *strictly determined*, that is, it possesses either a guaranteed winning strategy for one of the players or guaranteed drawing strategies for both. This result applies to games such as noughts and crosses (ticktacktoe) and chess in which each player knows what moves have been made previously, but it provides no method for finding the winning or drawing strategies. Noughts and crosses has drawing strategies for both players – if it is played rationally it must end in a draw – but in the case of chess it is still not known whether White (or conceivably Black) has a winning strategy or whether both players have drawing strategies, although the latter is most likely.

Much of the groundwork of the theory of games of strategy was laid in a series of papers by the French mathematician Emile Borel between 1921 and 1927 (see Fréchet, 1953; Leonard, 1992), although Borel was anticipated more than two centuries earlier by the Englishman James Waldegrave, who later became the Earl Waldegrave (Dimand and Dimand, 1992). But Borel was unable to prove the minimax theorem (see chapter 4 and the appendix) that lies at the heart of formal game theory; in fact, he rashly conjectured that the no such theorem could be proved. The minimax theorem was promptly proved by the Austro-Hungarian mathematician John von Neumann in 1928. In 1934, independently of von Neumann, the British mathematician Ronald Aylmer Fisher, who is remembered chiefly for his colossal contribution to experimental design and statistics, proved the minimax theorem for the special case in which each player has just two strategies. Game theory became more widely known after the publication in the United States of von Neumann and Morgenstern's classic *Theory of Games and Economic Behavior* in 1944. This book stimulated a great deal of interest among mathematicians and mathematically sophisticated economists, but it was a later text entitled *Games and Decisions: Introduction and Critical Survey* by Duncan Luce and Howard Raiffa (1957) that made the theory accessible to a wide range of social scientists and psychologists.

Only a handful of empirical investigations of interdependent decision making appeared before 1957, but the publication of Luce and Raiffa's book was followed by a steady growth of experimental gaming as a field of research (Smith, 1992). The first comprehensive review of experimental games was written by Rapoport and Orwant in 1962, by which time 30 experiments had been published. By 1965, experimental games had become sufficiently popular for the *Journal of Conflict Resolution* to begin devoting a separate section of each issue to it, and by 1972 more than 1000 empirical studies had appeared in that journal and elsewhere (Guyer and Perkel, 1972; Wrightsman, O'Connor, and Baker, 1972). Towards the mid-1970s, many researchers began to express dissatisfaction with experimental gaming research, which was then dominated by extremely abstract versions of one particular two-person game called the Prisoner's Dilemma game (see chapters 6 and 7). This crisis of confidence in experimental games was highlighted by an acrimonious debate in the *European Journal of Social*

Psychology initiated by Plon (1974). The flow of experimental gaming research nevertheless continued to increase, but less emphasis was placed on the Prisoner's Dilemma game and more on newly developed multi-person games. By the mid-1990s some 2000 experimental gaming studies had been published and empirical research continues to flourish.

Theoretical work on games of strategy also accelerated from the 1960s onwards. The *International Journal of Game Theory* was founded in 1971 and the journal *Games and Economic Behavior* in 1989. Russian scholars began to make significant contributions to game theory in the late 1960s (see Robinson, 1970; Vorob'ev, 1977). In 1972 the Nobel Prize for Economics was shared by Kenneth J. Arrow, whose work is closely related to game theory and will be discussed in section 10.5, and in 1994 the prize was awarded to the game theorists John Nash, John Harsanyi, and Reinhard Selten, whose contributions are discussed at various points in the chapters that follow. Numerous applications of the theory to economics were published from the 1950s, but applications to politics, biology, and philosophy, some of which will be discussed in later chapters of this book, are more recent and are developing rapidly.

1.5 Summary

Section 1.1 opened with an informal definition of game theory and an outline of the types of social interactions to which it applies. An essential property of these interactions is interdependent decision making, and it was argued that game theory is more appropriate than the conventional one-way causal models of social psychology and related fields for understanding such interactions. Three hypothetical examples were given of social interactions to which game theory could be applied. In section 1.2, the important properties of games as abstract models, and basic technical terminology, were explained with the help of the examples given earlier. Section 1.3 focused on the various categories into which games can be grouped. Games of skill, which constitute a degenerate class without true interdependence, games of chance, which involve either risky gambles or uncertainty, and games of strategy were distinguished. Games of strategy were further subdivided into coordination, zero-sum, and mixed-motive varieties. Section 1.4 was devoted to a synopsis of the historical develop-ment of game theory and its principal applications from the mid-seventeenth century to the present.

___ 2 ___

One-person games

2.1 Games against Nature

This chapter introduces the theory of one-person games. These are decision-making problems that are sometimes called one-person games against Nature, and because of their non-social properties some theorists do not consider them to be genuine games. The dilemmas discussed in section 2.2, in which Nature plays no part, are certainly not games in the strict sense, because they do not involve interdependent decisions, but they represent a limiting case that serves as a convenient and logical point of departure. In contrast, risky decisions, which will be discussed in sections 2.3 and 2.4, are interdependent in the formal sense, although they involve no social interaction, because Nature functions as an additional player, and some of the techniques that are used to analyse them will reappear in more sophisticated forms in the solution of two-person and multi-person games in later chapters. In particular, the fundamental ideas underlying probability theory and expected utility theory provide essential tools for the solution of more complex games. Section 2.5 will deal with individual decision making under uncertainty rather than risk, and the ideas developed in that section will also reappear in later chapters in which two-person and multi-person games, which invariably involve decisions under uncertainty, are introduced.

2.2 Certainty

Individual decisions under certainty are games of skill in which the solitary player knows exactly what the outcome of any strategy choice will be. The player has complete control of the outcomes, which are not affected by the actions of any other interested parties or Nature.

It is worth pointing out that sports such as golf and archery are not games of skill in this strict sense, because an element of chance limits the players' control over the outcomes, which are never certain. To put it another way, Nature influences the outcomes to a degree that depends to some extent on the player's level of skill. Solving a crossword puzzle, on the other hand, is a game of skill, and so is writing a computer program to perform certain logical operations most economically, and so too is shopping for various foods in order to minimize the overall cost while ensuring a supply of certain basic nutrients – this is a classic game of skill called the *diet problem*.

Mathematically, games of skill are simply optimization problems, and from a game theory point of view they are uninteresting, because the solution in all cases is simply to choose the strategy that maximizes the payoff, that is, the option that leads to the best outcome. But in spite of this, a branch of mathematics called linear programming and large tracts of operational research, management science, welfare economics, and behavioural science are devoted to these non-games. The reason is that optimal strategies are often difficult and sometimes impossible to find. The decision maker may wish to maximize the payoff but be unable to determine which strategy to choose in order to do so.

The following infamous problem of the *travelling salesman* illustrates the unexpected difficulties that can arise in decision making under certainty. A travelling salesman needs to visit a number of specified cities exactly once, using the shortest possible route, before returning to base. The options or strategies are the various orders in which the cities may be visited during the tour, and the distance between any pair of cities can be looked up on a map. Optimizing the payoff amounts to minimizing the distance, and the salesman's deceptively simple objective is to choose the shortest tour. In the language of linear programming, the salesman needs to minimize the objective function that defines the length of the tour.

The problem is that the number of options rises astronomically with the number of cities. For 10 cities, there are 3 628 800 different tours from which to choose. This is easy to prove. There is obviously a choice of ten cities for the first visit, and for each of these there are nine possibilities left for the second. There are therefore $10 \times 9 = 90$ different ways in which the salesman can begin the tour by visiting two cities. For each of these 90 opening pairs, there are eight possibilities left for the third visit, and so on. The total number of options is therefore $10 \times 9 \times 8 \times 7 \times 6 \times 5 \times 4 \times 3 \times 2 \times 1 =$ 3 628 800. For 20 cities, the number of options is 2 432 902 008 176 640 000, and for 30 cities it exceeds 265 thousand billion billion billion. It would test the patience of the most industrious travelling salesman to compare the length of each tour with that of each of the others, and even the world's fastest supercomputer would take many billions of years to solve the travelling salesman problem for a tour of the 52 county towns of England and Wales or the 50 state capitals of the United States. But no satisfactory alternative method has been found, and this simple game of skill turns out to be an intractable problem. Mathematicians have come very close to proving that efficient solutions to problems of this type are impossible *in principle* (see Papadimitriou and Steiglitz, 1982, for a full account of this intriguing branch of mathematics).

Although games of skill, or decisions under certainty, constitute a vast and thriving area of research, nothing more will be said about them here because they lack the interdependence of choice that is characteristic of game theory in the strict sense.

2.3 Risk

A risky decision is a game of chance in which the solitary decision maker is pitted against the fictitious player, Nature. The decision maker does not know with certainty what moves Nature will make but can nevertheless assign meaningful probabilities to them and therefore to the various possible outcomes. It was pointed out in chapter 1 that this is precisely the problem facing a player of Russian roulette.

On the face of it, a decision involving only risk presents few problems. It can apparently be solved by working out, according to the principles of probability theory, the *expected value* of each available strategy choice and then choosing the one that is best according to this criterion. The following imaginary game of chance will illustrate the basic ideas. A competitor in a television quiz game, after answering several trivia questions correctly, is offered a choice between two alternatives:

(1) A coin will be tossed; if it lands heads, the competitor will receive a prize of £1000, but if it lands tails, no prize will be given.
(2) The competitor must select one of three envelopes, which are known to contain prizes of £900, £300, and £150 respectively, although there is no way of knowing which prizes are in which envelopes.

What is the rational strategy in this game? Intuitively, and also according to elementary principles of probability theory, the expected value of (1) is $1000/2 + 0/2 = £500$, and the expected value of (2) is $900/3 + 300/3 + 150/3 = £450$. To maximize the expected value, the competitor should therefore choose (1): it pays better than (2) "on average", in the sense that if the game were repeated many times, a player would tend to win more money by choosing (1) than (2). It therefore seems obvious to many people that the principle of maximizing expected value can be generalized to all purely risky decisions.

There are two serious objections to this straightforward type of solution, however. First, it is well known that rational human beings do not always maximize expected value. Roulette (the French, not the Russian variety) is a classic game of chance in which Nature's moves and their associated probabilities are transparently obvious, yet millions of people play this game in the full knowledge that the expected value is always negative, otherwise the house would not make a profit. The same applies to pools and lotteries, and to one-armed bandits, fruit machines, and other gambling devices found in amusement arcades. In all such games, the expected monetary value of not playing at all, which is zero, is higher than that of playing for any stakes. One might respond by classifying gambling as an irrational form of behaviour in which neglect of the principle of expected value maximization is merely evidence of mental pathology, but in that case what is one to make of insurance policies, which sane and prudent citizens buy regularly? The expected monetary value of insurance is negative for essentially the same reason: insurance companies are out to make profits, and they calculate their premiums according to probability estimates so that their clients are bound to lose out "on average". To call the purchase of insurance policies irrational would be to warp the notion of rationality unreasonably.

A second objection arises from situations in which the principle of expected value maximization appears to break down by generating obviously absurd solutions. Perhaps the most famous example of this is the St Petersburg paradox which the Swiss mathematician Daniel Bernoulli first presented to the St Petersburg Academy in the early eighteenth century. The rules of the St Petersburg game are as follows. A coin is tossed, and if it falls heads, then the player is paid one rouble and the game ends. If it falls tails, then it is tossed again, and this time if it falls heads the player is paid two roubles and the game ends, otherwise it is tossed again. This process continues for as long as necessary, with the payoff doubling each time, until the player wins something, and then it stops. Assuming that the house has unlimited funds, what is the expected value of playing this game? Or to put the question another way, how much should a rational person be willing to pay for the privilege of playing it?

The expected value can be calculated very simply. The player wins one rouble with probability $1/2$, two roubles with probability $1/4$, four roubles with probability $1/8$, and so on. The expected value of playing this game is therefore

$$(1/2)(1) + (1/4)(2) + (1/8)(4) + \ldots,$$

and it is easy to see that the sum of this endless series is infinite, because each of its terms is equal to $1/2$. According to the principle of expected value maximization, it would therefore be rational to offer one's entire fortune, such as it is, to play the St Petersburg game once, because "on average" the payoff is worth more than any fortune. But this conclusion is self-evidently absurd, because there is a high probability of losing everything: to begin with, there is a 50 per cent chance of reducing one's entire fortune to one rouble on the very first toss. According to the expected value principle, this is more than counterbalanced by the very small probability of winning a vastly greater fortune if there is a long series of tails. But the St Petersburg game is fatally damaging to the principle of expected value maximization, as Bernoulli was the first to realize, because it would clearly be irrational to stake one's fortune on it. The question that arises naturally from this is whether a better principle can be found for solving games of chance involving pure risk.

2.4 Expected utility theory

The risky choices of rational decision makers are guided by their preferences among the possible outcomes, but the examples of section 2.3 show clearly that the superficially plausible principle of expected value maximization cannot satisfactorily distinguish common sense from foolishness in risky decision making.

Daniel Bernoulli's great contribution was the suggestion, which seems obvious with hindsight, that the values of things to a person are not simply equivalent to their monetary values. A small sum of money could be precious to a pauper but almost worthless to a millionaire, even if the pauper and the millionaire were one and the same person, for example the day before and the day after winning a fortune in a lottery. People's decisions are guided more by what the outcomes are worth to them than by the cash value of the outcomes. Bernoulli (1738) called the subjective desirability of an outcome its "moral worth", and this hypothetical quantity later became known as *utility*.

Utilities must obviously be closely related to monetary values in cases in which the outcomes of decisions are merely varying amounts of money or can be straightforwardly translated into money. A large amount of money cannot have less utility for a rational person than a small amount, because it is easy to convert a large sum into a smaller sum by disposing of some of it. Utility must therefore be a *monotonically increasing* function, but it may not be a *linear* function of monetary value, which means that an increase in x units of money may not increase its recipient's utility by the same amount irrespective of the starting point. Bernoulli suggested a "law of diminishing marginal utility", as it was later called, according to which the greater a person's starting capital, the smaller the utility (or disutility) of any fixed monetary gain (or loss). Bernoulli went further and claimed that the functional relation between money and utility is logarithmic, which implies that equal increases in utility correspond to equal proportional increases in money, just as logarithms increase by equal steps as their corresponding numbers increase by equal proportions. Historians of psychology (e.g. Boring, 1950) seldom if ever point out that Bernoulli anticipated by more than a century the famous psychophysical law of Gustav Theodor Fechner, which propounds the same logarithmic relation between sensation and stimulus intensity in general.

Bernoulli's theory of utility fell into disrepute for two main reasons. The first was its arbitrariness: there seemed to be no logical or empirical reason why the relation should be logarithmic or why it should be the same for all people in all circumstances. The second major limitation of Bernoulli's theory was that it provided no method for assigning utilities to non-monetary outcomes. How, for example, can the logarithmic function be used to assign utilities to the outcomes of a game of Russian roulette? The answer is that it cannot. Similarly, recalling the examples presented in chapter 1, Bernoulli's theory provides no way of assigning interval-scale utilities to preserving one's chastity and saving one's brother's life, increasing a market share, or even to avoiding a collision in a corridor. But in order to solve such games we often need utilities that are measured quantitatively on an interval scale, and we shall also be needing interval-scale utilities for solving certain classes of two-person and multi-person games. Fortunately, a brilliant solution is at hand.

John von Neumann and Oskar Morgenstern (1947) rehabilitated the concept of utility by proposing a completely new theory that suffered from neither of the defects of the old one. The essential ideas are simple, and the theory is remarkably flexible (for a review of later theoretical developments, see Fishburn, 1988). Von Neumann and Morgenstern's utility theory is based on the assumption that a player can express a preference (or indifference), not only between any pair of outcomes, but also between one outcome and a lottery between a different pair of outcomes. To give a concrete interpretation of these ideas, consider once again the imaginary television quiz game outlined in section 2.3. For von Neumann and Morgenstern's utility theory to work, a player must be able to express a preference (or indifference) between any pair of outcomes – prizes of £1000, £900, £300, £150, and nothing – and also between such pairs as the following:

(1) £300 for certain; *or*
(2) a 50:50 lottery between £1000 and nothing.

If the player turns out to prefer (2) to (1), then a new choice can be offered between a fixed amount of money larger than £300 and (2). It is reasonable to assume that there is *some* amount that the player will consider no less and no more desirable than (2). It is then possible to convert the monetary outcomes of the game into utilities, provided only that the player's preferences are consistent. If the amounts involved are not too large, then it is very likely that the player's utilities will be directly proportional to the monetary values, because most people value £4 twice as much as £2, and £3 three times as much as £1, and this linear relation will be reflected in their preferences between fixed amounts and lotteries. When large amounts are involved, however, this linear relationship between utility and cash value is likely to break down or at least bend, because £100 million does not seem twice as desirable as £50 million to most people.

Von Neumann and Morgenstern succeeded in proving two things about utilities that are determined in this way. First, it is always possible in principle to convert a player's consistent preferences into utilities. Second, if players apply the principle of maximization outlined in section 2.3 to expected utilities rather than to expected monetary values, then they are in fact choosing according to their preferences. This method of decision making is called the *principle of expected utility maximization*.

Expected utilities, which are simply weighted average utilities (weighted according to the corresponding probabilities), are purely psychological quantities, and in the light of this principle it is not necessarily irrational to gamble or to buy insurance policies. The expected utility of a lottery involving the probable loss of a small stake and the improbable gain of a huge prize may be positive even if the expected monetary value is negative; and for most people the expected utility of a lottery involving the probable loss of an insurance premium and the improbable repayment of the value of one's property after a burglary, for example, may be considerably greater than that of the premium, even if the expected monetary value of the lottery is worth much less than the premium. It is equally clear that the paradoxical quality of the St Petersburg game dissolves in this new light. There is no reason why a person should prefer to stake everything on gambling with a high probability of losing it all just because the expected monetary value of the game is theoretically infinite.

Expected utility (EU) theory has another important consequence. It enables numerical utilities, corresponding to degrees of preference, to be assigned to games whose outcomes are inherently qualitative. The method of quantifying preferences on an interval scale of utilities can be explained with the help of the game of Angelo and Isabella, which was outlined in chapter 1. We begin by assigning arbitrary utilities, say 1 and 10, to each player's least and most preferred outcomes respectively. (In more familiar interval scales such as the centigrade or Celsius scales of temperature, two values corresponding, for example, to the freezing and boiling points of water, are also assigned entirely arbitrarily.) It is then possible to determine the utilities of the other outcomes by finding lotteries involving the two extreme outcomes that the player considers equally preferable to each of the other outcomes. Let us consider one possible outcome from Isabella's point of view. It may turn out that she is indifferent between the outcome labelled (1) below, and the lottery involving her least and most preferred outcomes labelled (2):

(1) She preserves her chastity and her brother is executed humanely; *or*
(2) A die will be rolled. If it comes up six she will surrender her chastity to Angelo and her brother will be tortured to death; if any other number comes up she will preserve her chastity and her brother will be reprieved.

Isabella is indifferent between one of the intermediate outcomes and a 1/6:5/6 lottery involving her least and most preferred outcomes. If her least preferred outcome is arbitrarily assigned a utility of 1 and her favourite outcome a utility of 10, then the utility of the outcome under consideration is

$$(1/6)(1) + (5/6)(10) = 8.5.$$

This utility is much closer to 10 than to 1, which reflects the fact that the outcome is a relatively attractive one for Isabella – compared to the worst and the best that can happen. Every possible outcome of the game can be assigned a utility in this way, and the utilities represent Isabella's true preferences. The same can be done from Angelo's point of view, and thus the payoffs of this game can be expressed numerically. This method can be used in any other game, provided that the players can express consistent preferences between outcomes and hypothetical lotteries involving out-comes. Utilities derived in this way are measured on interval scales. This means that the zero points and units of measurement are arbitrary – they are fixed by the numbers chosen for the least and most preferred outcomes – so that if they are all multiplied by a positive constant, or if a constant is added to each of them, the information that they contain is unaffected. The information concerns *relative* preferences. It is important to bear in mind that a player's utilities, thus defined, may be influenced by any factors that have a psychological bearing on the player's satisfaction or dissatisfaction with the outcomes, including spiteful or altruistic feelings towards the other players, religious beliefs, idiosyncratic tastes, phobias, masochistic tenden-cies, and so on. Expected utility (EU) theory is neutral with regard to the roots of a player's preferences.

Von Neumann and Morgenstern's utility theory has not solved all problems concerning the assignment of numerical payoffs to the outcomes of games, and some of the residual problems will surface in later chapters. The theory does, on the other hand, provide a convincing method for solving games of chance involving pure risk. It follows almost tautologically from the theory that in any game of this type a rational decision maker will choose the strategy that maximizes expected utility. When the outcomes are relatively small amounts of money, or can be readily interpreted as such, the principle of maximizing expected monetary value outlined in section 2.3 will generally yield solutions that closely approximate those generated by the principle of maximizing expected utility, because utility in such cases will usually be a linear function of monetary value.

Utility functions can be constructed quite successfully for a wide range of risky choices – for critical reviews of the relevant theory and empirical research, see Bell, Raiffa, and Tversky (1988, chaps 4–9, 15–21), Dawes (1988), and Rapoport (1989). When these functions are based on subjective rather than objective probabilities, they are called *subjective expected utility (SEU)* functions. Investigations of the behaviour of people in games of chance involving pure risk have produced rather surprising results. In some very simple games of this type, experimental subjects have tended to choose strategies that are manifestly non-optimal. Humphreys's (1939) light-guessing experiment is a classic in the field, and many later experiments were modelled on it (e.g. Goodnow, 1955; Ofshe and Ofshe, 1970; Siegel and Goldstein, 1959; Siegel, Siegel, and Andrews, 1964). In these experiments, the subjects were typically seated in front of two light bulbs and asked to try to predict which of the two would light up on each trial. The bulbs were, in fact, lit up in a random pattern according to probabilities fixed in advance, for example, 80 per cent for the left-hand bulb and 20 per cent for the right-hand bulb. Subjects typically began by distributing their guesses roughly equally between the two options. After a number of trials they usually began to increase the frequency of choosing the bulb that was being lit up more often. After very many trials, by which time the subjects had enough information to judge the probabilities reasonably accurately and were therefore playing a game of chance involving pure risk, most subjects settled into a non-optimal *matching strategy.* In other words, they tended to choose strategies with probabilities approximately equal to the probabilities with which the bulbs lit up, for example 80 per cent left and 20 per cent right in the case mention above. This is clearly non-optimal because the probability of a correct guess is maximized by choosing the more frequently illuminated bulb on every single trial. This optimal strategy obviously yields 80 per cent correct guesses, whereas the matching strategy yields a probability of only (.8)(.8) + (.2)(.2) of being correct, that is, 68 per cent correct guesses. These and other similar experiments provide vivid illustrations of irrational human behaviour in games of chance involving pure risk. A thought-provoking critical review of expected utility (EU) theory has been provided by Frisch and Clemen (1994); see also the reviews of behavioural decision research by Einhorn and Hogarth (1988), Kahneman and Tversky (1982), Rapoport (1989), Slovic, Fischhoff, and Lichtenstein (1977) and Poulton (1994).

2.5 Uncertainty

Games of chance involving uncertainty rather than risk crop up frequently in everyday life. In these cases the player does not know for certain the outcomes of the available strategy choices and cannot even assign meaningful probabilities to them. Uncertainty and risk both imply a degree of ignorance about the future, but uncertainty is a profounder type of ignorance than risk.

The following example of a journalist's dilemma will illustrate the general ideas. A freelance journalist wishes to send an article through the post to a magazine in a foreign country. If the article is delivered safely, she will receive a fee of £200. It is possible, however, that the article will be lost in the post. The cost of normal postage is negligible, but for an additional £5 she can register the parcel; if it is then lost, the Post Office will reimburse the £200 that she would have been paid for the article.

If the journalist chooses to register the parcel, then she loses £5 in postal registration charges but receives £200 either from the Post Office (if the parcel is lost) or from the magazine (if it is delivered safely). If she chooses not to register it, she receives nothing if it is lost and £200 with no postal registration charge to pay if it is delivered safely. The journalist's monetary payoffs in each of the four possible outcomes, determined by her own and Nature's strategy choices, are most neatly displayed in what is called a *payoff matrix* (Matrix 2.1).

It is possible, of course, that the figures in the payoff matrix do not accurately reflect the journalist's utilities, because there may be other

Matrix 2.1
Journalist's Dilemma

Nature

		Lose	Deliver
	Register	195	195
Journalist			
	Don't register	0	200

psychologically significant aspects of the outcomes apart from their monetary values that affect her preferences. Her reputation for reliability, for example, or her satisfaction at seeing her article in print, may be worth more to her than the figures in the payoff matrix suggest. But the discussion in section 2.4 showed that considerations like these present no problems in principle, and we may therefore assume that the payoff matrix accurately reflects the journalist's utilities, or rather that they have been adjusted to do so.

What principles of rational choice can be offered in a case like this? If the journalist knows the probability of the parcel being lost, then the game is a straightforward risky decision, and the principle of expected utility maximization explained in section 2.4 is indicated. If, for example, she knows that the chances are one in ten that it will be lost, then the expected utility of registering it is

$$(1/10)(195) + (9/10)(195) = 195,$$

and the expected utility of not registering it is

$$(1/10)(0) + (9/10)(200) = 180,$$

and if she were to choose rationally according to her preferences she would accordingly register the parcel. But suppose that she has no knowledge of Nature's probabilities; in other words, she has not the faintest idea of how likely it is that the parcel will be lost. The country for which it is destined, let us say, is going through a period of industrial unrest and no one knows whether or not the postal services are affected, in fact no one is even willing to hazard a guess. In that case, we have on our hands a decision involving uncertainty rather than risk, and a number of principles of rational choice have been suggested for solving them.

2.5.1 Insufficient reason

In practice, a decision involving uncertainty can always be transformed into a risky one by assigning probabilities to Nature's strategies arbitrarily. The *principle of insufficient reason*, advanced by the English clergyman and mathematician Thomas Bayes in the middle of the eighteenth century, and later championed by Laplace and many other influential figures, is based on this idea. According to the principle of insufficient reason, one is supposed to be justified in assigning equal probabilities to events in the absence of any sufficient reason to believe that they are unequal.

Using this principle, the journalist in the example could cut the Gordian knot by simply assuming that the probability of the parcel being lost is 1/2, and having made that assumption she could apply the principle of expected utility maximization straightforwardly. This method of solving – or, I should prefer to say, side-stepping – the problem of uncertainty is, in my opinion, illusory. If the probabilities are unknown, then they are simply unknown, and there is no logical justification for calling them equal. "Subjective probabilities", or degrees of belief, which are popular with many modern Bayesian statisticians, have not provided a firm foundation for the principle of insufficient reason. In spite of the useful distinction between risk and uncertainty made long ago by John Maynard Keynes (1937), there are nevertheless still those who believe that "a player always has some idea of what the payoffs are, so we can always assign him a subjective probability for each possible payoff" (Rasmusen, 1989, p. 66) and that "*all* decision problems may be treated, subjectively at least, as risky choice" (Shepsle, 1972, p. 278, italics in original).

The principle of insufficient reason can be shown to lead to contradictions as follows. Suppose the journalist in the example constructs a slightly different abstract model of her dilemma, by incorporating *three* possible states of Nature, namely loss of the parcel, safe and timely delivery of the parcel, and delayed delivery of the parcel. She would presumably be entitled to assign equal probabilities of 1/3 to each of these events. But we have already seen that she is entitled to assign probabilities of 1/2 to two of them. By modelling the game in various other logically unassailable ways, she could assign virtually whatever probabilities she chose to Nature's strategies. The principle of expected utility maximization, if applied to these fanciful probabilities, would yield different "solutions" depending on the models that happen to have been chosen. Treating uncertainty as though it were merely risk is an illusory solution to the problem, although some game theorists disagree with this view.

2.5.2 Maximax

This principle of choice can hardly be considered rational, but it is worth discussing, partly as a basis for discussions of more sophisticated principles based on similar ideas, and partly because it is often used in practice by naive decision makers such as children and by voters in elections (see chapter 10). The maximax principle counsels the decision maker to choose the strategy that yields the best of all possible payoffs. In the case of the journalist's dilemma, the highest possible payoff if the parcel is registered is 195, and the highest possible payoff if it is not registered is 200. These two figures are the two row maxima of the payoff matrix. The maximum of the two maxima is 200, and it corresponds to the journalist's decision not to register her parcel. If she follows the maximax principle, she will therefore neglect to register it.

The maximax principle amounts to angling for the best possible outcome of the game without any consideration of the less favourable outcomes that are possible. It is an ultra-optimistic approach to decisions under uncertainty, because it implicitly assumes that the less favourable outcomes will not arise. Although it possesses a certain innocent charm, and although it is widely adopted in certain classes of situations (see section 10.9), it is transparently silly and cannot be said to characterize the behaviour of rational decision makers.

2.5.3 Maximin

Inspired by von Neumann and Morgenstern's (1944) classic text on game theory, the statistician Abraham Wald (1945) suggested this principle. The decision maker is advised to begin by identifying the lowest payoff in each row of the payoff matrix, in other words to look for the worst possible payoff that can result from each possible strategy choice. The final step involves choosing the strategy associated with the best of these worst possible outcomes, thereby *maximizing* the *minimum* payoff, hence the name. In the journalist's dilemma, the maximin principle obviously leads her to choose the strategy of registering the parcel, because the minimum payoff in that row is 195, which is better than the minimum of 0 if she does not register it.

Whereas the maximax principle is ultra-optimistic, the maximin principle could be said to be ultra-pessimistic, because it amounts to choosing the best of the worst possible outcomes based on the assumption that whatever strategy is chosen, the worst will happen. It is essentially a conservative method of maximizing security rather than of trying to get the most out of the game by taking chances. This can be seen most clearly in a payoff matrix such as Matrix 2.2.

Matrix 2.2

Nature

		X	Y
	A	0	1000
Player			
	B	1	1

According to the maximin principle, the player should in this case choose the strategy corresponding to the second row, labelled *B*, which guarantees a minimum payoff of 1 unit, rather than *A*, which risks a zero payoff but offers the possibility of a huge reward. In fact, no matter how large the top right-hand matrix element might be, a player guided by the maximin principle would never choose *A*.

The pessimistic policy of anticipating the worst may be quite sensible when a great deal is at stake, or where the player's prime consideration is to avoid the worst outcomes at any cost. It is the principle governing statistical decision-making, where the primary consideration is to avoid a Type I error (concluding that an effect is real when it may be due to chance) rather than a Type II error (concluding that it is due to chance when it is in fact real). But it does not seem intuitively reasonable to adopt this policy for *all* decisions under uncertainty, as we shall now see.

Consider the maxim "Nothing ventured, nothing gained". An interpretation of this maxim in game theory terms is provided by a consideration of what would happen if it were applied in industry to decide when to devote funds to research and product development (see Moore, 1980, pp.

284–286). The possible strategies are to support a research and development (R&D) project or to neglect it. Nature's moves determine whether or not the R&D will succeed it is supported. If the cost of the R&D project is represented by c and the potential return if it is successful by r, then the decision is represented by Matrix 2.3.

Matrix 2.3 *Research and*
Development

Nature

	R&D Succeeds	R&D Fails
Support R&D	$r - c$	$-c$
Neglect R&D	0	0

Player

The minimum payoff if the research and development is supported (row 1) is clearly -c, and the minimum if it is neglected (row 2) is zero. The maximum of these two minima is zero no matter what the values of r and c might be. Thus, by adopting the ultra-pessimistic maximin principle, industry would *never* support research and development that might fail, no matter how small the cost and how profitable the potential rewards. This would be an absurdly unenterprising approach to business management, and it highlights the limitations of the maximin principle. From a logical point of view, the principle is unassailable in so far as it attains the clearly specified goal of ensuring the best of the worst possible outcomes in any contingency that might arise. But, whereas this is a reasonable goal in some circumstances, it does not correspond to intuitive notions of rationality in others.

2.5.4 Minimax regret

This principle was first advanced by Savage (1951). Many decision theorists consider it to be the soundest method of solving problems involving decisions under uncertainty, because it is neither too optimistic nor too pessimistic, and it combines the best aspects of other approaches, but it contains a subtle though fatal flaw.

Savage's ingenious idea was to transform the original payoff matrix into a *regret matrix* (sometimes called a *loss matrix*). Each element of the regret matrix represents the positive difference between the corresponding payoff in the payoff matrix and the highest payoff that could occur under the same state of Nature. These new numbers reflect the decision maker's "opportunity loss" or degree of regret, if Nature's strategy were to be revealed, for not having chosen differently in those circumstances. Each element of the payoff matrix is converted into an element of the regret matrix by asking: Could the player have obtained a higher payoff by choosing differently if Nature's strategy had been known in advance? If not, then the corresponding regret is zero. If the player could have done better, then the regret is equal to the amount by which the payoff could have been improved by choosing the most profitable strategy given advance knowledge of Nature's intentions.

To illustrate these ideas, consider once again the journalist's dilemma introduced earlier, and suppose that she chooses to register the parcel. If it is delivered safely, her regret for having wasted money registering it amounts to £5, because in those circumstances she could have achieved a payoff £5 higher by not registering it. If the parcel is lost, on the other hand, then she has no cause for regret because, given that state of Nature, she could not have done better by not registering it. Arithmetically, the regret matrix is calculated by subtracting each element of the payoff matrix from the largest element in its column (Matrices 2.4).

Matrices 2.4 *Journalist's Dilemma*

		Nature			Nature	
		Lose	Deliver		Lose	Deliver
Journalist	Register	195	195		0	5
	Unregistered	0	200		195	0
		Payoff matrix			Regret matrix	

Notice that every element of the regret matrix is either positive or zero. This is the case even if some or all of the original payoffs are negative – there is no such thing as negative regret. The minimax regret principle for making decisions under uncertainty is as follows. Choose the strategy that minimizes the maximum possible regret. If the journalist registers the parcel, then the maximum regret (the largest element in the top row of the regret matrix) is £5, and if she does not register it, then the maximum regret (in the bottom row) is £195. According to the minimax regret principle, she should choose the strategy corresponding to the minimum of these two maxima, in other words she should register the parcel.

It is worth examining the minimax regret solution to the game of research and development mentioned earlier. The payoff matrix is reproduced in Matrices 2.5, together with its regret matrix, which has been calculated in the usual way by subtracting each matrix element from the largest in its column.

Matrices 2.5 *Research and Development*

		Nature			Nature	
		R&D succeeds	R&D fails		R&D succeeds	R&D fails
	Support R&D	$r - c$	$-c$		0	c
Player						
	Neglect R&D	0	0		$r - c$	0

Payoff matrix	Regret matrix

According to the minimax regret principle, the player should examine the maximum in each row of the regret matrix and select the row with the least of these maxima. The maximum in the top row of the regret matrix is c, because the cost must be greater than zero, and the maximum in the bottom row is $r-c$ on the reasonable assumption that the cost of R&D (c) is less than the return if it succeeds (r) so that $r-c$ is greater than zero. The player should therefore support R&D if c is less than $r-c$, which is equivalent to c being less than $r/2$, and neglect R&D otherwise. In other words, industry should support research and development if and only if the cost of it is less than half the potential return. This rule of thumb is, in fact, quite commonly applied in research management (Moore, 1980, p. 286), although it is usually justified by experience and intuition rather than game theory analysis.

Unfortunately, the minimax regret principle suffers from a fatal flaw, which was exposed by Chernoff (1954). In some cases it violates a condition of rationality called the *independence of irrelevant alternatives*. (This condition reappears in a slightly modified guise in section 6.10 in connection with bargaining solutions to two-person cooperative games and in section 10.5 in connection with social choice theory.) The following example is based on Luce and Raiffa (1957, p. 288). Suppose a customer in a restaurant consults the menu and finally decides to order poached salmon. The waiter then points out helpfully that, although it is not on the menu, roast chicken is also available. "In that case", says the customer, "I'll have the lamb chops". This behaviour seems irrational, because the addition to the list of the option of roast chicken seems irrelevant to the customer's preference for poached salmon over lamb chops. But this strange phenomenon can arise from the application of the minimax regret principle, as we can see by returning for the last time to the journalist's dilemma.

The minimax regret principle suggests that the journalist will register the parcel if she is rational. But suppose that she contemplates a third strategy, namely to register the parcel and simultaneously to bet a colleague £200 at even odds that it will be delivered safely. If the parcel is lost, she will then lose the £5 postal registration charge and will also have to pay her colleague £200, but the Post Office will reimburse her £200, so she will lose £5 overall. If the parcel is delivered safely, she will lose the £5 registration charge but will receive £200 from the magazine and will win another £200 from her colleague, so that her net gain will be £395. The addition of this new strategy enlarges the game without affecting the payoffs associated with the original strategies; the new payoff matrix is the same as the old one with an additional row joined on to it. The new regret matrix can be calculated in the usual way, but all the regret values turn out to be quite different. The new payoff matrix and its regret matrix are shown in Matrices 2.6.

The maximum in the first row of the regret matrix is 200, the maximum in the second row is 195, and the maximum in the third row is 200. The minimum of these maxima is 195, and it corresponds to the strategy "Don't register"! Something very curious indeed has happened, because in the original formulation of the problem, the journalist's preferred strategy according to the minimax regret principle was to register the parcel. Once an

Matrices 2.6 *Journalist's Dilemma*

| | | Nature | | | Nature | |
		Lose	Deliver		Lose	Deliver
	Register	195	195		0	200
Journalist	Don't register	0	200		195	195
	Register & bet	−5	395		200	0

Payoff matrix   Regret matrix

additional strategy was added to the list, the strategy that was rejected in the original analysis emerged as the rational choice.

At an abstract level, this is similar to what happened to the customer in the restaurant who ordered poached salmon rather than lamb chops but changed the order to lamb chops on being told that roast chicken was also available. If this reversal by the restaurant customer seems irrational on the grounds that the availability of the third alternative is irrelevant to the customer's relative preferences between the other two, then exactly the same can be said of the journalist. The minimax regret principle has fallen foul of the independence of irrelevant alternatives, and it is therefore considered to be suspect by many decision theorists.

Games of chance involving uncertainty are evidently more intractable than those involving mere risk. When probabilities cannot be assigned to the outcomes, the principle of expected utility maximization, which provides compelling solutions to risky decisions, cannot be applied meaningfully. Four decision rules designed to generate rational decisions under uncertainty have been examined, and they have all been found wanting. Others have been advanced from time to time, but none is entirely watertight. In fact it was proved many years ago (Milnor, 1954) that no decision rule can satisfy all of the criteria, of which the independence of irrelevant alternatives is one, that one would require of a completely convincing solution to the problem.

2.6 Summary

Section 2.1 drew attention to the existence of the class of one-person games in which a solitary decision maker is pitted against Nature, and it was pointed out that analyses of these games are based on ideas that crop up in the solution of more complicated games involving two or more decision makers. Section 2.2 discussed decisions under certainty, which are called games of skill, and section 2.3 decisions under risk. The superficially plausible principle of expected value maximization was shown to lead to difficulties, and in section 2.4 it was shown how the worst of these difficulties can be overcome by the application of von Neumann and Morgenstern's expected utility (EU) theory. A method was outlined for assigning numerical utilities on an interval scale of measurement to games whose outcomes are essentially qualitative in character. Section 2.5 was devoted to one-person decisions involving uncertainty rather than risk. Various decision rules – the principle of insufficient reason, maximax, maximin, and minimax regret – were examined critically, and all were found to violate intuitive notions of common sense, although the last two were found to have some merits. It was pointed out that no entirely satisfactory decision rule is possible.

— 3 —

Coordination games and the minimal social situation

3.1 Strategic collaboration

This chapter is devoted to two classes of games involving players whose interests are best served through strategic collaboration. The first is the class of coordination games, which are characterized by coincidence of the players' interests, and the second is the minimal social situation, which has intrigued game theorists and experimental investigators for some time. The minimal social situation is a class of games involving incomplete information; in its strict form, the players are ignorant not only of the nature but even of the fact of their strategic interdependence.

In a coordination game, it is in every player's interest to try to anticipate the others' choices in order to obtain a mutually beneficial outcome, and they all know that the other players are similarly motivated. If the social situation makes communication between the players impossible, then subtle and interesting psychological problems arise, and the outcome often depends on the level of strategic intuition of the players. In the minimal social situation it is once again in the players' mutual interest to collaborate. But the problems confronting the players are quite different in this case, because they arise from a lack of information about the rules of the game. The central question in the minimal social situation is whether the players can learn, through playing the game a number of times, to cooperate without conscious awareness of the need for cooperation and without even being aware of each other's existence.

In the following section the general strategic properties of coordination games will be examined. Theoretical and empirical work on the minimal social situation will be discussed in section 3.3, a multi-person generalization of the minimal social situation will be outlined in section 3.4, and a brief summary of the chapter will be given in section 3.5.

3.2 Coordination games

The defining property of a *coordination game* is agreement among the players as to their preferences among the possible outcomes; in particular, an outcome that is considered best by one player is considered best by the others. A *pure coordination game* is one in which *all* of the players' preferences are identical. In a coordination game there is no conflict of interest between the players: their sole objective is to coordinate their strategies in such a way as to obtain an outcome that they all favour. The game Head On, introduced in section 1.1.1, is an example of a coordination game, because the outcome is either a collision or the avoidance of a collision and both players prefer the avoidance of a collision. In Head On, two people are walking briskly towards each other along a narrow corridor. Each player chooses one of three strategies – swerve left, swerve right, or continue straight ahead – in an effort to avoid colliding with the other player, and an outcome that is good (or bad) for one is similarly good (or bad) for the other.

Coordination games are clearly games of strategy according to the definition given in chapter 1. In treating them as such, I am following Schelling's (1960) "reorientation of game theory", although many authorities do not regard them as genuinely strategic games. In their classic textbook, Luce and Raiffa (1957), for example, asserted that any group of decision makers "which can be thought of as having a unitary interest motivating its decisions can be treated as an individual in the theory" (p. 13), and furthermore that if the players have the same preference pattern over the outcomes "then everything is trivial" (p. 59); "certainly in the extreme case where there is perfect agreement the analysis is trivial" (p. 88). There are, none the less, at least three good reasons for taking coordination games seriously. First, although they may appear trivial from the point of view of formal game theory, informal analysis and empirical evidence discussed in this chapter shows that the problems confronting decision makers in these games are far from inconsequential (see also Bacharach, 1994; Crawford and Haller, 1990; Kandori, Mailath, and Rob, 1993; Young, 1993). Second, there is a growing body of experimental evidence that coordination failures often occur in these games, even in some cases in which communication is allowed (e.g., Cooper, De Jong, Forsythe, and Ross, 1992a, 1992b; Van Huyck, Battalio, and Beil, 1990). Third, it is aesthetically appealing to treat pure coordination games as one extreme of a classification in which strictly competitive structures (two-person zero-sum games) are at the opposite extreme and mixed-motive games occupy the middle ground.

The theoretical symmetry between zero-sum and coordination games can be illustrated by a pair of simple examples that share certain superficial features in common. Two-person hide-and-seek is a classic example of a zero-sum game: one player chooses a hiding place from among a number of locations, and the other chooses a location to search. Each outcome – discovery or non-discovery – represents a victory for one player and a defeat for the other, so the game is strictly competitive. By way of contrast, if two people are accidentally separated in a crowded shopping centre, they usually end up playing a game that I shall call Rendezvous. Once again they choose particular locations where they may or may not be reunited, but in this case each possible outcome is either good for both or bad for both, in other words they are playing a strictly cooperative coordination game.

Most sports and indoor games are zero-sum, but Schelling (1960, p. 85) pointed out that the game usually known as charades is really a coordination game, and the same could be said of the game called sardines. An interesting example is the game "Mr and Mrs" played by married couples on British television. The husband and wife are each presented with the same set of questions about their marriage and neither is allowed to hear the other's answers; if their answers coincide, they win a substantial cash prize. A typical question that has been used is this: "If your kitchen needed redecorating, who would do the work? The husband? The wife? The husband and wife together? A hired professional?" The options are presented to the players in different orders to prevent them from coordinating their answers artificially by agreeing beforehand to choose the first (or the last, or some other option specified in advance).

A coordination game may involve just two players as in the above examples or it may be a multi-person game, and the rules may specify perfect or imperfect information. The two-person perfect information case is the simplest, and it presents no difficulties to the players. It was explained in chapter 1 that in a two-person game of perfect information the players move one at a time, and when choosing a move each player knows the move(s) that have preceded it, including any made by the other player. In Rendezvous, for example, if the players carry portable telephones or walkie-talkies, then they can easily inform each other of their moves, thus transforming it into a game of perfect information, and they can then meet up without difficulty; in fact this is how Rendezvous is often solved by police officers. If there were a convention or law governing which side pedestrians should pass one another in corridors, then Head On would have to be modelled by a game of perfect information, because in that case each player would know in advance which strategy the other would choose, and successful coordination of strategies would be virtually assured; the "rule of the road" governing road traffic exists for precisely that reason.

A multi-person coordination game of perfect information is not as straightforward as its two-person counterpart. The following example highlights the difficulties that can arise. During a revolution, soldiers are often faced with the problem of deciding whether or not to defect to the rebel faction, and the majority decision may determine the success or failure of the revolution. Assuming that most soldiers are less concerned about who wins than they are about being on the winning side, their dilemma is aptly summarized in Benjamin Franklin's famous words: "We must all hang together or, most assuredly, we shall all hang separately." Even if the soldiers make their decisions one at a time in full knowledge of all decisions that have gone before, in other words if the game is one of perfect information, the optimal strategy remains unclear until the point at which it becomes evident which way the majority will decide. As more and more soldiers defect to the rebels or decide to remain loyal, a "bandwagon" effect tends to develop. There is a psychologically critical point in the sequence of moves, long before a clear majority has emerged in favour of either strategy, when the outcome begins to seem inevitable. From that point on the soldiers' optimal strategy is obvious, because they know that most of the others will recognize this inevitability and choose accordingly. The expectations develop a motive power of their own, which helps to determine the eventual outcome.

This type of self-fulfilling prophecy, which is called *tipping*, accounts for a variety of social phenomena that correspond to multi-person coordination games of perfect information. The spontaneous segregation of multi-racial cities into exclusively white and black areas when the critical ratio is reached, for example, was first analysed by Grodzins (1957). Schelling (1971a, 1971b, 1972, 1978, chap. 4) used a simple demonstration with a handful of coins on a chess board to show that extreme segregation is inevitable even if everyone has the relatively mild demand that no more that 50 per cent of their *immediately adjacent* neighbours should belong to the opposite group and they all move to different locations whenever they find themselves outnumbered. Extreme segregation results even if every individual would actually prefer to live in a mixed neighbourhood and no one desires extreme segregation. A similar type of *amplifying aggregation effect* governs the dissemination of various other fads, fashions, and vogues.

Coordination games of imperfect information have quite different strategic properties. In these games, the players have to act in ignorance of one another's moves. They have to try to anticipate what the others will do, and this involves anticipating the others' anticipations of their own choices. There is an endless regress of "I think that they think that I think . . ." inherent in the analysis. The television game "Mr and Mrs", for example, can be played at various levels of strategic depth. At the shallowest level the players choose their "best" strategies according to non-strategic criteria. At a slightly deeper level the husband chooses the options that he thinks his wife will choose, and perhaps she chooses according to the same principle. A deeper level involves the husband choosing the options that he thinks his wife will expect him to choose – and perhaps the wife reasoning similarly. Even more profound levels of strategic sophistication are, of course, possible in this apparently trivial game; in fact the scope for depth in games of this type is potentially limitless (Bacharach, 1992).

The same strategic problem crops up in numerous everyday situations requiring strategic cooperation. The discovery of the endless regress created by imperfect information can be traced to a famous passage in John Maynard Keynes's (1936) *General Theory of Employment Interest and Money.*

Keynes discussed the strategy of buying and selling stocks and shares and compared it to a multi-person coordination game of imperfect information with which most people are familiar:

> Professional investment may be likened to those newspaper competitions in which the competitors have to pick out the prettiest faces from a hundred photographs, the prize being awarded to the competitor whose choice most nearly corresponds to the average preferences of the competitors as a whole; so that each competitor has to pick, not those faces which he himself finds prettiest, but those which he thinks likeliest to catch the fancy of the other competitors, all of whom are looking at the problem from the same point of view. It is not a case of choosing those which, to the best of one's judgement, are really the prettiest, nor even those which average opinion genuinely thinks the prettiest. We have reached the third degree where we devote our intelligences to anticipating what average opinion expects the average opinion to be. And there are some, I believe, who practise the fourth, fifth and higher degrees. (p. 156)

Some coordination games are usually solved without difficulty by the players even if the rules prescribe imperfect information. In practice, coordination is easy if (a) one particular combination of strategies is associated with an outcome that all players consider best; (b) all players know the rules of the game and the preferences of the others, in other words the game is one of complete (though imperfect) information; and (c) all players know that all the others know the rules of the game and the preferences of the others, and all players know that the others know this, and so on – this is the condition of *common knowledge* of the description of the game (Heal, 1978; Lewis, 1969; see also Bicchieri, 1993, *passim*; Sugden, 1991, pp. 764–765). If all three conditions are satisfied, then players usually anticipate that the others will choose the strategies that produce the optimal outcome, assuming that they will expect one another to do the same, but in practice coordination failures are not uncommon (e.g., Cooper, De Jong, Forsythe, and Ross, 1992a, 1992b; Van Huyck, Battalio, and Beil, 1990). In other cases, such as those that have been outlined in this section, no uniquely optimal combinations of strategies exist, and solutions must be sought through informal analysis based on factors outside the abstract structures of the games.

Schelling (1960) showed that, in the absence of any uniquely optimal combination of strategies in a coordination game, informal analysis often reveals a *focal point* (nowadays sometimes called a Schelling point) that possesses qualities of *salience* (or prominence). If the players cannot communicate explicitly with one another, tacit coordination is often possible, provided that each notices the focal point and assumes that the others will also recognize it as the "obvious" solution. In Head On, for example, British players may recognize that for both to keep to the left is salient because of the analogy with road traffic, and in most other countries keeping to the right may be salient for the same reason. It is surprisingly difficult to think of any lifelike coordination game that contains *no* clues pointing towards a salient focal point solution, even when the players have an infinity of options to choose from.

The following coordination games, which were first investigated empirically by Schelling (1960, chap. 3), and later by Mehta, Starmer, and Sugden (1994), illustrate the processes of tacit coordination and "telepathic" communication:

(1) Two people are invited to choose "heads" or "tails" independently, knowing that if they both call "heads" or both call "tails", then they both win; otherwise they will both lose. Is there a sensible way to choose in this game? Is either of the strategies salient? Does an obvious focal point exist? Schelling found that 86 per cent of his subjects chose "heads" when confronted with this game. Mehta, Starmer, and Sugden (1994) replicated this finding in England, where 87 per cent of subjects chose "heads". I have discovered in casual investigations in England that smaller percentages tend to call "heads" when they are simply invited to call "heads" or "tails" under non-strategic conditions. People who would normally calls "tails" to decide who should bath the baby, for example, may none the less call "heads" in this game because of a realization that their partners will probably recognize its conventional precedence over "tails" and expect them to recognize it also, and so on. "Heads" becomes especially salient when the endless loop of expectations is taken into consideration.

(2) Several people are assembled, and paper and pencils are distributed among them. Each person is invited to write down any amount of money in the knowledge that if everyone nominates the same amount, then they will each receive that amount as a prize, otherwise no one will receive anything. In this game, each player has an infinite set of strategies to choose from. Are any of them salient? Is there a focal point? Is this game soluble through informal strategic reasoning? Schelling reported that 93 per cent of his subjects chose a round sum that was a power of 10, and no fewer than 30 per cent succeeded in converging on one million dollars. Choices other than powers of 10 included 64 dollars and 64000 dollars, which were culturally salient in the United States because of their use as prizes in radio and television quizzes. I have found British students to be comparatively unambitious in their choices, with a significant proportion nominating the modest sum of £1. Mehta, Starmer, and Sugden (1994) found that when British subjects were asked simply to "write down any positive number" with the aim of writing down the same number as their partners, without the numbers representing prize values, the favourite choice was 1 (chosen by 29 per cent), and the second favourite was 10 (chosen by 19 per cent).

(3) Two people who know nothing about each other are instructed to meet in New York at a particular time, but no specific meeting place has been nominated. They would both like to keep the appointment, but they cannot get in touch with each other before the appointed time. Where should they meet? What strategies would sensible players adopt in this awkward situation, which is merely a version of the familiar game, Rendezvous? Schelling reported that an absolute majority of his subjects, who were students in New Haven, Connecticut, managed to converge on the information booth at the Grand Central Station. In Mehta, Starmer, and Sugden's (1994) British replication based on London rather than New York, the top choice was Trafalgar Square (38 per cent). It is remarkable that people should have a 38 per cent probability (or better) of coordinating in these difficult circumstances.

(4) The players in No. 3 are told the place and date but not the time of the meeting. Neither is able to waste time; they must both choose the same time to within a minute. What time would people with sound strategic intuition choose to visit the meeting place? Despite the fact that each player has over a thousand strategies from which to choose (there are 1440 minutes in a day), Schelling found that virtually all his subjects chose 12 noon, and Mehta, Starmer, and Sugden (1994), using a slightly different problem, also found that the leading choice was 12 noon (28 per cent), followed by 12 midnight (16 per cent). It is worth pointing out that 12 noon is salient not merely because of its centrality in the day but also for cultural reasons: 12 midnight is arguably even more central, but far fewer subjects chose it.

What is noteworthy about these results is the fact that players often succeed in coordinating their strategies against overwhelming odds in spite of the absence of any formal solutions or prescriptions for choice based on the abstract structures of the games. The psychological ability to recognize the salience of certain combinations of strategies in games like these derives from strategic intuition about how human beings are likely to interpret the problems, how they are likely to expect others to interpret them, and what expectations they are likely to hold about the expectations of others. It is difficult to imagine how a computer could be programmed to solve coordination games of these types, because the method of analysis is difficult or impossible to formalize and depends on a largely unconscious background knowledge of culture and human psychology. It takes a human strategist to anticipate the thinking of another human strategist in games like these. Gilbert (1989) provided an argument that showed, to her own surprise, that coordination cannot be the result of any *rational* decisions by the players: "If human beings are – happily – guided by salience, it appears that this is not a consequence of their rationality" (p. 61). This problem will be examined in greater depth in section 12.2.1.

Mehta, Starmer, and Sugden (1994) argued that the properties of focal points that make them salient in coordination games are often aspects of their *labelling* rather than of their mathematical structures, and they reported some interesting results from an experiment designed to investigate the informal rules used by subjects to solve coordination games. The significance of labelling, and I would add of other incidental properties of strategies apart from their labels (the accessibility of the information booth at the Grand Central Station in New York and of Trafalgar Square in London and their popularity as a rallying points, for example), depends on the common culture and experience of the players, and these properties are invisible to mathematical analysis or formal game theory. In fact, games that differ only in respect of their labelling or other incidental properties of their strategies are regarded as isomorphic – that is, mathematically identical – in formal game theory (see, e.g., Harsanyi and Selten, 1988, pp. 70–74).

More than two centuries ago, the Scottish philosopher David Hume (1739–1740, Bk. III, Part II, Sect. iii) gave a pleasing hypothetical example of a German, a Frenchman, and a Spaniard who enter a room in which there are three bottles of wine, namely Rhenish, Burgundy, and port. Among the six different ways in which three bottles could be distributed among three people, to avoid a quarrel, Hume pointed out that the obvious solution would be to "give every one the product of his own country" (p. 510*n*). This solution emerges from the description of the game, or what Crawford and Haller (1990) call the *common language* shared by the players. In its abstract form (choosing one way of arranging three objects in order) there is clearly nothing to choose between the six available strategies. Crawford and Haller point out that removing players' common language, including the labelling and incidental properties of their strategies, would have the effect of filtering out salient focal points based on descriptions of coordination games.

In real life, people contemplating choices always conceptualize them in terms of some but not all of their attributes; in other words, they describe the problems to themselves in particular ways. This process is called *framing*, and Bacharach (1994) developed a theory according to which the degree of salience of a strategy for a player depends on how rare it is and how noticeable its attributes are likely to be in the player's interpretive frame. Hume's suggested strategy, discussed in the previous paragraph, for assigning three bottles of wine to three people is unique (and thus maximally rare) but its choice by the players depends also on the probability that its uniqueness is in the players' frames. The effects of framing will be addressed in more detail in sections 5.4, 7.9, and 9.7.5.

3.3 The minimal social situation

The minimal social situation, which was first investigated by Sidowski, Wyckoff, and Tabory (1956) and Sidowski (1957), is a class of games of incomplete information. In these games, the players are ignorant of their own payoff functions and those of the other player(s); each player knows merely what strategies are available. In the extreme case, which I shall call the *strictly minimal social situation*, the players are ignorant even of one another's existence: they know that they are making decisions under uncertainty, but they do not know that the uncertainty arises from their involvement in a game of strategy. In a situation such as this, the intriguing possibility arises that cooperative behaviour may develop without the players even realizing that there is anyone with whom to cooperate.

The following example of the cross-wired train (Colman, 1982a, pp. 289–91) illustrates the type of interdependent decision making that can be modelled by a minimal social situation. Two people commute to work on the same train every weekday. They always sit in adjacent compartments, and during the winter both compartments are uncomfortably cold. Each compartment has a lever marked "heater", but it is unclear whether turning it to the left or to the right will increase the temperature. (So far, this story is not entirely fanciful: some of British Rail's rolling stock used to exhibit this frustrating property.) There is a fault in the electrical wiring of the train the effect of which is that moving either lever to the left increases the temperature and moving it to the right decreases the temperature in the *adjacent* compartment.

The two commuters obviously cannot influence their own physical comfort directly by manipulating the levers in their compartments. Their comfort is entirely in each other's hands, although neither of them knows this. But they would none the less both benefit if both turned their levers to the left at the beginning of every journey. The following intriguing question arises: Can they learn to cooperate in this way in spite of being ignorant of their mutual dependence or even of each other's existence? If so, cooperative behaviour can evolve without conscious intention or awareness.

The problem of the cross-wired train is isomorphic with the minimal social situation originally devised by Sidowski and his colleagues (Sidowski, 1957; Sidowski, Wyckoff, and Tabory, 1956) who coined the term *minimal social situation*. Experimental evidence has shown that people can, and generally do, learn to cooperate by choosing "left" on all or most occasions.

The strategies available to the commuters in the cross-wired train may be labelled L and R, and each outcome involves a positive payoff (warm) or a negative payoff (cold) to each commuter. The payoff structure of the game is shown in Matrix 3.1.

It is unnecessary to attach any numerical significance to the matrix elements; we need assume only that each commuter prefers a warm journey (+) to a cold (–). One commuter chooses row L or R, and the other chooses column L or R. By convention, the first symbol in each cell represents the

Matrix 3.1 *Mutual Fate Control*

	L	R
L	+, +	−, +
R	+, −	−, −

payoff to the row chooser, and the second the payoff to the column chooser. If both choose L, then the outcome is shown in the upper-left cell, and both commuters receive positive payoffs (both have warm journeys). If both choose R, then both suffer cold journeys. If one chooses L and the other R, then the L-chooser suffers a cold and the R-chooser a warm journey. The players' payoffs in this game are quite unaffected by their own strategy choices; their destinies are entirely in the hands of their partners, whose existence they do not even recognize. This type of payoff structure, called (for obvious reasons) *mutual fate control* by Thibaut and Kelley (1959), has most commonly been used in research on the minimal social situation. Although it is not a coordination game, because no outcome is uniquely best for both players – and some outcomes are favourable for one player and unfavourable for the other – it obviously calls for strategic collaboration: the solution is for both players to choose L every time the game is played.

Empirical research using this payoff structure under conditions of incomplete information was pioneered by Sidowski and his colleagues. Subsequent experiments were reported by Kelley, Thibaut, Radloff, and Mundy (1962); Rabinowitz, Kelley, and Rosenblatt (1966); Arickx and Van Avermaet (1981); Molm (1981); Bertilson and Lien (1982); Bertilson, Wonderlich, and Blum (1983, 1984); and others. The earliest experiments were devoted to the strictly minimal social situation, and in later experiments the information conditions have sometimes been relaxed.

In the original experiments of the Sidowski group, the appropriate conditions of strategic interdependence were engineered as follows. Pairs of subjects were seated in separate rooms, unaware of each other's existence, and electrodes were attached to their bodies. Each subject faced an apparatus on which was mounted a pair of buttons labelled L and R respectively and a digital display showing the cumulative number of points scored. The subjects were instructed to press one button at a time as often as they wished with the twin goals of obtaining rewards (points) and avoiding punishments (electric shocks). The rewards and punishments were arranged according to the mutual fate control payoff structure shown in Matrix 3.1. Whenever either of the subjects pressed the button labelled L, the other was rewarded with points, and when either pressed *R*, the other was punished with electric shock. From a game theory point of view, the experimental situation is strategically equivalent to that of the cross-wired train outlined above.

Sidowski, Wyckoff, and Tabory (1956) showed that, when the game is repeated many times, pairs of subjects generally learn to coordinate their choices although they are unaware of their strategic interdependence. They usually assume that their strategy choices are connected in some obscure way with their own payoffs, and the frequency of mutually rewarding outcomes tends to increase gradually over time. In the long run, both subjects normally settle down to choosing *L* on every occasion. The subjects behave as if they were learning to cooperate, although as far as they are concerned the situation is entirely non-social. How can these findings be explained? Kelley et al. (1962) proposed a simple principle of rational choice for games of incomplete information that might explain the phenomenon. It is an adaptation of the well known *law of effect* in psychology, and is called the *win-stay, lose-change* principle.

Thorndike's (1911) original statement of the law of effect was as follows:

> Of several responses made to the same situation, those which are accompanied or closely followed by satisfaction [are] more firmly connected with the situation . . .; those which are accompanied or closely followed by discomfort . . . have their connections with the situation weakened. (p. 244)

In the minimal social situation, a person who adopts the win-stay, lose-change principle may be thought of as conforming to a version of Thorndike's law of effect. The principle does not generate any prediction about which strategies the players will choose on the first trial. But if the game is repeated a number of times, the prediction is that each subject will repeat any strategy choice that is followed by a positive payoff and will switch to the other after receiving a negative payoff. On the face of it, this seems to be an eminently sensible policy for a player to adopt in any game of incomplete information that is repeated a number of times, and it seems to be a widespread principle of behaviour in nature (Domjan and Burkhard, 1986; Nowak and Sigmund, 1993). In spite of its almost childlike simplicity, it not only successfully explains the development of strategic collaboration in the minimal social situation, but also generates several non-obvious predictions that can be tested experimentally.

In Sidowski, Wyckoff, and Tabory's (1956) original experiments, the subjects were free to press their buttons whenever they wished. The following theoretical analyses of Kelley et al. (1962) are applicable to experiments in which the subjects are required to choose either simultaneously or alternately. It will be easiest to examine the case of simultaneous choices first.

The outcomes of successive repetitions of the game may be represented by a sequence of ordered pairs corresponding to the row-player's and column-player's choices respectively. Because the players' choices on the first trial are arbitrary, there are three initial outcomes to be considered. First, both players may initially choose L, with the result that both receive positive payoffs. If each adopts the win-stay, lose-change principle, they will then both repeat the same choice indefinitely:

$$(L, L), (L, L), (L, L), \ldots.$$

Secondly, both may initially choose R. They will both receive negative payoffs, and so both will switch to L on the second trial. The payoffs will then be positive, so both will repeat the same choice on all subsequent trials:

$$(R, R), (L, L), (L, L), (L, L), \ldots.$$

Finally, one player may initially choose L while the other chooses R. The first outcome (L, R) or (R, L) will then involve a positive payoff to one player and a negative payoff to the other. Following the win-stay, lose-change principle, the player who is rewarded – the R-chooser – will repeat the same choice on the second trial, and the L-chooser will switch to R. The outcome on the second trial will therefore involve negative payoffs to both players, and the situation will therefore be identical to the beginning of the series shown above. The complete analysis of this case is as follows:

$$(L, R), (R, R), (L, L), (L, L), \ldots$$

or

$$(R, L), (R, R), (L, L), (L, L), \ldots.$$

The players will thus converge on the mutually rewarding combination of strategies in three trials and repeat these L-choices on all subsequent trials.

The theoretical analysis of simultaneous choices under the win-stay, lose-change principle has established, rather surprisingly, that successful coordination of strategies occurs within three trials at most, and as soon as the mutually rewarding strategies occur simultaneously the players continue to repeat them indefinitely. A further unexpected or counter-intuitive conclusion of the theoretical analysis is this: except in the relatively unlikely event that the players hit upon the (L, L) combination on the very first trial, they are bound to pass through a mutually punishing outcome (R, R) before they can reach a mutually rewarding one (L, L). They have to hurt each other simultaneously before they can help each other simultaneously, unless they are lucky enough to help each other at the very outset. This suggests a possible strategic basis to the common belief in the criminal underworld that two people cannot develop a relationship of mutual trust until they have quarrelled or fought with each other: an unpleasant conflict may "clear the air" for more harmonious interaction. The idea that conflict can help to promote intimacy has been advanced from a different theoretical perspective by Braiker and Kelley (1979).

Quite different conclusions flow from an analysis of alternating choices under the win-stay, lose-change principle. In the alternating procedure, the players move one at a time. One player chooses L or R, thereby delivering a reward or punishment to the other, and only then does the second player respond by choosing L or R, effectively rewarding or punishing the first. A second choice is then made by the first player, and this is followed by a second choice by the second player, and so on. The initial choices of both players are again arbitrary, but all succeeding choices are strictly determined by the win-stay, lose-change principle.

If the first player initially chooses L, rewarding the second, and the second player also chooses L, rewarding the first, then the sequence will resemble the analogous process under the simultaneous procedure:

$$(L, L), (L, L), (L, L), \ldots.$$

If both initially choose R, however, the consequences are quite different. The first player punishes the second, and is then punished in return. The first player therefore switches to L, rewarding the second player, who therefore chooses R again, punishing the first. The first player therefore switches back to R, punishing the second, and the second accordingly switches to L, rewarding the first. The first player then chooses R once again, punishing the second, and the second responds by switching to R. We have returned after four exchanges to the pair of choices with which the sequence began. This means that the whole cycle is bound to repeat itself indefinitely without ever generating a single consecutive pair of rewarding choices. The complete analysis is summarized below:

$$(R, R), (L, R), (R, L), (R, R), \ldots.$$

If the first player initially chooses L and the second R or vice versa, the sequences will be as follows:

$$(L, R), (R, L), (R, R), (L, R), \ldots$$

or

$$(R, L), (R, R), (L, R), (R, L), \ldots.$$

Once again, the sequences of choices cycle indefinitely without ever producing a consecutive pair of rewarding choices. The cycles are in fact identical to each other and to the one initiated by a pair of R choices; they merely begin at different points in the same endless loop.

The theoretical analysis of alternating choices has produced results that contrast sharply with those of simultaneous choices. When the choices are made simultaneously, the win-stay, lose-change principle leads inexorably to mutually rewarding coordination of strategies within a very few trials. But when the players choose alternately, the same principle never leads to a coordinated solution, or even to transient mutual reward, unless the players stumble by chance on the rewarding strategies at the very beginning. These conclusions deprive the win-stay, lose-change principle of some of its intuitive appeal as a general rule for the rational conduct of games of incomplete information. It would be difficult to formulate a principle that yields *worse* results in the cases we have just examined; it is easy to verify that even a perverse win-change, lose-stay principle fares better in two of the four cases.

Several unambiguous and testable though curiously non-obvious predictions flow from the theoretical analyses outlined above. Assuming that the players' initial choices are arbitrary but that they thereafter adhere to the win-stay, lose-change principle, which seems reasonable in the light of the well-attested law of effect, then the first prediction from the theory is that rewarding (L) choices and successful coordination will occur more frequently under conditions of simultaneous choice than in the alternating procedure. Kelley et al. (1962) confirmed this prediction in an experiment specifically designed to allow the relevant comparison to be made. Under the alternation procedure, the frequency of rewarding choices was no greater than chance expectation and showed no tendency to increase when the game was repeated over 140 trials. This is precisely what the theory predicts. Under the simultaneous procedure, in contrast, rewarding choices began to exceed chance expectation after relatively few trials and continued to increase in frequency, reaching 75 per cent after about 100 repetitions. Stabilized coordination of mutually rewarding strategies was achieved by many pairs of players under the simultaneous procedure but by only two pairs under the alternating procedure. These results were replicated by Rabinowitz, Kelley, and Rosenblatt (1966), who also reported results in line with theory from minimal social situations involving different payoff structures.

Although these findings strongly confirm the prediction mentioned in the previous paragraph, they also reveal that most pairs of subjects did not adhere rigidly to the win-stay, lose-change principle. This is clear from the fact that most pairs did not succeed in achieving stabilized mutual reward within the first few trials in the simultaneous choice procedure; successful coordination typically took numerous trials to develop. Molm (1981) also showed that disruption of the social interaction upsets coordination in a (non-strictly) minimal social situation more easily and more irrevocably than it does in other strategic situations.

A second prediction from the theoretical analyses is that, under the simultaneous choice procedure, rewarding strategies will be chosen simultaneously only after a mutually punishing outcome, unless the very first outcome happens by chance to be mutually rewarding. Kelley et al. (1962) presented evidence that tends to confirm this prediction. In their simultaneous choice condition, every occurrence of a long run of mutually rewarding outcomes was immediately preceded by a mutually punishing outcome.

A third prediction centres on the difference between strictly and non-strictly minimal social situations. In many everyday situations, the players are aware of the fact, though not the nature, of their mutual interdependence: they are informed of each other's existence and they realize that their choices influence each other's payoffs, but they do not know the payoff structure of the game. If the players adhere to the win-stay, lose-change principle under these circumstances, then their choices will be exactly the same as those in the strictly minimal social situation. But if the players know that they are involved in a game of strategy, even though they do not know its payoff structure, it may be easier for them to coordinate their strategy choices. Thibaut and Kelley (1959) predicted that the frequency of rewarding choices and successful coordination would be greater in these circumstances. The players may be able to guess the payoff matrix of the game by "trying out" their own available strategies and inferring the payoff structure from their partners' responses.

Kelley et al. (1962) therefore compared the behaviour of informed pairs of subjects (in a quasi-minimal social situation) with that of uninformed pairs (in a strictly minimal social situation). The results strongly confirmed the predictions: rewarding choices and mutually rewarding outcomes were much more frequent in informed pairs. When choices were made simultaneously, the relative frequency of rewarding choices in informed pairs rose to 96 per cent after about 150 trials. Even under the alternating procedure, the frequency of rewarding choices gradually increased over trials and greatly exceeded chance expectation. The results under the alternating procedure are particularly impressive in view of the fact that rigid application of the win-stay, lose-change principle generates no more rewarding choices than chance expectation and shows no tendency towards improvement over time, as shown above.

It is appropriate to draw the threads of this section together by returning to the example of the cross-wired train. It was assumed that the commuters travel simultaneously and are oblivious of each other's existence. The following conclusions are therefore justified by theory and empirical evidence. First, it is very likely that after a number of days they would both have learned to move their levers to the left. Second, they would probably not achieve this mutually beneficial pattern of behaviour until they had punished each other by moving their levers to the right on the same day, unless they chanced on the mutually rewarding solution – against which the odds are three to one – on the very first day.

With slight modifications to the example, further conclusions can be drawn. We may assume that the commuters travel on alternate journeys of the same train, and that the heaters are slow-acting so that moving one of the levers to the left or right causes the adjacent compartment to be warm or cold on the *following* journey. Under these conditions, the commuters would probably *never* learn to coordinate their choices in a mutually beneficial way – to move their levers consistently to the left – unless they both happened to choose that strategy on their initial journeys, against which the odds are again three to one. Whether they travel on the train simultaneously or on alternate journeys, their chances of learning to coordinate their strategies satisfactorily would be greatly increased if they became aware of each other's existence and of the fact that the operation of the heaters depends in some way on the controls in the adjacent compartment.

These conclusions are far from obvious, and some are even counter-intuitive. On the basis of common sense alone or, to put it differently, without the benefit of game theory analysis, strategy choices and outcomes in the minimal social situation would be difficult or impossible to predict. But elementary strategic analysis enables clear-cut predictions to be made, and experimental results have tended generally to confirm these predictions in very general terms, although it is clear that people do not follow the dictates of the theory very closely (e.g., Bertilson and Lien, 1982; Bertilson, Wonderlich, and Blum, 1983, 1984; Kelley et al., 1962; Molm, 1981; Rabinowitz, Kelley, and Rosenblatt, 1966). Mutual cooperation *tends* to evolve, which suggests that people *tend* to follow the win-stay, lose-change principle. This implies a stochastic learning process in which the probability of a player's choice on trial t being repeated on trial $t + 1$ increases if the player is rewarded and decreases if the player is punished on trial t (Arickx and Van Avermaet, 1981). There is evidence that something approximating win-stay, lose-change is common in the animal kingdom (Domjan and Burkhard, 1986).

3.4 The multi-person minimal social situation

A multi-person generalization of the two-person minimal social situation was developed by Coleman, Colman, and Thomas (1990). In a group of arbitrary size, on any specified trial the choices of n players may be represented by an n-vector of Ls and Rs, each element having a predecessor and a successor. It is useful to imagine the n players sitting round a table, so that 1's predecessor is n and n's successor is 1. For any such vector there is a unique vector that follows it according to the win-stay, lose-change principle.

A vector consisting entirely of Ls will be repeated on all subsequent trials, and any vector that leads ultimately to this L vector is called *cooperative* in the analysis. It was shown earlier that in the two-person minimal social situation, which is merely a special case of the general n-person game, all vectors are cooperative under simultaneous choice because they all lead to joint cooperation under the win-stay, lose-change principle. This is not true in general. In a six-person minimal social situation, for example, the vector (R, L, R, L, R, L) is followed on the next trial by (R, R, R, R, R, R), and then by (L, L, L, L, L, L). The initial vector (R, L, R, L, R, L) is therefore cooperative. But it is easy to verify that the vector (R, L, R, L, L, L) is followed by (R, R, R, R, L, L), (R, L, L, L, R, L), (R, R, L, L, R, R), (L, L, R, L, R, L), (L, L, R, R, R, R), (R, L, R, L, L, L), which has cycled back to the starting vector. This sequence will therefore repeat itself for ever, never reaching (L, L, L, L, L, L), which shows that the starting vector was not cooperative.

Coleman, Colman, and Thomas (1990) proved the following theorems about the multi-person minimal social situation, under the assumption that the win-stay, lose-change principle is applied strictly:

(1) The only vectors that are followed on the very next trial by joint cooperation are those in which all players make the same choice (all L or all R). In other words, joint cooperation is invariably preceded either by joint cooperation or by joint non-cooperation.
(2) If the number of players is a power of 2 (if n is 2, 4, 8, 16, etc.), then all vectors are cooperative, that is, from any starting pattern of choices joint cooperation follows eventually. The two-person minimal social situation is a special case of this.
(3) If the number of players is odd (if n is 1, 3, 5, etc.), then joint cooperation is achieved only if all players make the same initial choice (all L or all R on the first trial), in which case the very next trial is jointly cooperative. The larger an odd-sized group, the less likely it is that all players will happen by chance to make the same choice on the very first trial (if the number of players is n, this probability is 0.5^{n-1}), and thus the less likely it is that the odd-sized group will ever achieve joint cooperation.
(4) If the number of players is even but is not a power of 2 (if n is even but not 2 or 4 or 8 or 16, etc.), then some vectors are cooperative and others are not. This means that cooperation may or may not follow after a number of trials, depending on the starting pattern of choices. In general, if k is the highest power of 2 that divides n evenly, k players may choose arbitrarily, but the choices of the remaining players are strictly determined for the game to lead eventually to joint cooperation.
(5) In any multi-person minimal social situation, the number of cooperative initial vectors is therefore 2^k. (Odd-sized groups are a special case of this in which $k = 1$, because the highest power of 2 that divides an odd number evenly is $2^0 = 1$.) Because the total number of possible vectors in an n-person group is 2^n, the probability that cooperation will eventually follow under the win-stay, lose-change principle assuming that initial choices are random is $2^k/2^n$. In a seven-person minimal social situation,

for example, the probability is only $2/128 = .016$.

The analysis of the multi-person minimal social situation generated some counter-intuitive conclusions. First, although the frequencies of rewarding choices and joint cooperation tend to increase over trials under simultaneous choices in the two-person minimal social situation, the theory predicts no such increase in odd-sized groups. Second, multi-person minimal social situations in which the number of players is a power of two should behave like the two-person minimal social situation: irrespective of the pattern of choices made on the first trial, there should be steady progress towards joint cooperation. Third, when the number of players is even but not a power of two, progress towards joint cooperation may or may not occur depending on the pattern of initial choices.

3.5 Summary

This chapter began with an introduction to two classes of games in which the players' interests are best served by strategic cooperation. Section 3.2 focused on coordination games characterized by coincidence of the players' interests. Although many of these games elude formal analysis, informal game theory usually uncovers salient strategies and focal points that allow players with well-developed strategic intuition to coordinate tacitly. Such empirical evidence as there is strongly confirms the prediction that successful coordination often occurs even in the absence of "logical" solutions. Section 3.3 was devoted to theory and experimental evidence concerning the minimal social situation, which was interpreted as a class of games of incomplete information. In the strictly minimal social situation the players are unaware, not only of the payoff structure of the game, but even of each other's existence. Theory and experimental evidence none the less reveal that strategic collaboration can develop when these games are repeated a number of times. The win-stay, lose-change principle, derived from the law of effect, permits unambiguous though non-obvious predictions to be made about choices in the minimal social situation, and experimental evidence has generally confirmed these predictions. In section 3.4, a multi-person generalization of the minimal social situation and some surprising theoretical results were discussed.

— Part II —

Theory and empirical evidence

—— *4* ——

Two-person zero-sum games

4.1 Strictly competitive games

A *zero-sum* game, as its name suggests, is one in which, whatever the outcome, the payoffs to the players add up to zero, which means that what one player gains, the other(s) must necessarily lose. A *constant-sum* game is strategically equivalent to a zero-sum game, and the two terms are used almost interchangeably by some writers. The strategic equivalence becomes obvious as soon as one realizes that any constant-sum game can be interpreted as a situation in which each player is first fined or rewarded by a fixed amount for playing the game, depending on whether the constant sum is negative or positive, and the players are then allowed to play the resulting zero-sum game. A zero-sum or constant-sum game, in other words, is a closed system within which nothing of value to the players is created or destroyed: utilities merely change hands when the game is played. If there are just two players, this means that their interests are diametrically opposed, because an outcome that is favourable for one is bound to be correspondingly unfavourable for the other. Because each player can gain only at the expense of the other, there are no prospects of mutually profitable collaboration, and two-person zero-sum conflicts are therefore called *strictly competitive games*. They have proved especially amenable to formal analysis, and the most significant contributions to mathematical game theory relate to them. Zero-sum games with more than two players are not strictly competitive or straightforwardly soluble, as will be explained in chapter 8.

Some economic, political, military, and interpersonal conflicts correspond to strictly competitive games. Most two-person sporting contests and indoor games are strictly competitive, and examples from other spheres of life are not too difficult to find. Two television or radio networks competing for audiences, two retailers or service providers competing for market shares, two politicians or political parties competing for votes, two armies competing for territory, or two parents competing for the custody of their child after a divorce may have diametrically opposed interests that can reasonably be modelled by two-person zero-sum games. But it is a serious mistake to regard *all* competitive interactions as zero-sum, because in everyday life the protagonists' interests are seldom strictly opposed. In most wars, for example, an outcome involving mutual annihilation, or even a protracted stalemate, may represent losses for both sides, so wars are seldom zero-sum – although isolated battles may be, as I shall presently show. Strictly competitive games certainly occur in everyday life, but mixed-motive games are undoubtedly more common.

There are two major classes of strictly competitive games. First, strictly competitive games in which each player has a finite number of strategies are called *finite, two-person zero-sum games*, and convincing methods are available for solving them. A solution consists of a specification of a rational way in which the players should choose among their available strategies, and a payoff, known as the value of the game, which results if both play rationally according to the dictates of the theory. The second class contains *infinite, two-person zero-sum games*, in which at least one of the players has an infinite number of strategies to choose from. Some of these games have formal solutions and some do not. The theory relating to them, which is outlined in Myerson (1991, pp. 140–148), and at a more elementary level in Rapoport (1989, chap. 10) and Owen (1968, chap. 4), is rather obscure and inconclusive, and rarely applied, so these games will not be dealt with in detail in this chapter, although some relevant empirical evidence will be presented in chapter 5.

The essential ideas behind two-person zero-sum game theory will be outlined in the following sections. Two ways of representing the abstract structures of these games will be explained with concrete examples in section 4.2. The following two sections will centre on the fundamental ideas behind the minimax solution. Sections 4.5 and 4.6 will be concerned with special techniques for solving games. Section 4.7 will confront the problem of games in which information about the players' preferences is incomplete or not fully numerical, and section 4.8 will present a brief summary of the chapter.

4.2 Extensive and normal forms

An incident from the Second World War, known by military historians as the Battle of Bismarck Sea, can be modelled by the simplest type of two-person zero-sum game. The following account is based on a classic paper by Haywood (1954; see also Rasmusen, 1989, pp. 30–32).

In February 1943, during the critical phase of the struggle in the south-western Pacific, the Allies received intelligence reports indicating that the Japanese were planning a troop and supply convoy to reinforce their army in New Guinea. The convoy could sail either north of the island of New Britain where rain and poor visibility were almost certain, or south of the island, where the weather would probably be fair. By either route, the trip would take three days. General George C. Kenney, commander of Allied forces in the South Pacific, was ordered by his supreme commander, General MacArthur, to attack the convoy with the objective of inflicting maximum destruction. General Kenney had to decide whether to concentrate the bulk of his reconnaissance aircraft on the northern or the southern route. Once the convoy was sighted, it would be bombed continuously until its arrival in New Guinea.

The players in this game were General Kenney and the Japanese commander, Hitoshi Imamura. The strategies from which each had to choose were the northern and southern routes. The outcomes were the numbers of days of bombing that would result from each possible combination of choices. Kenney's staff estimated that if the reconnaissance aircraft were concentrated mainly on the northern route, then the convoy would probably be sighted after one day, whether it sailed north or south, and would therefore be subjected to two days of bombing in either case. If the aircraft were concentrated mainly on the southern route, on the other hand, then either one or three days of bombing would result depending on whether the Japanese sailed north or south respectively. The number of days of bombing may be interpreted as Kenney's gains and the Japanese commander's losses. Because the Japanese payoffs are just the negatives of Kenney's, the game is obviously zero-sum. The essential information is summarized in Figure 4.1.

In Figure 4.1 the *extensive form* of the game is represented in the most convenient way, by means of a *game tree*. The nodes of the game tree correspond to choice points and are labelled with the names of the players whose choices they represent, and the branches represent the strategies between which the players must choose. The initial (topmost) node is labelled "Imamura", indicating that the Japanese commander has the first

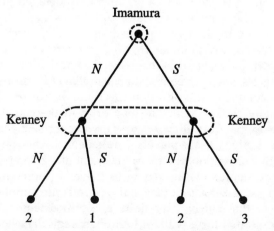

Figure 4.1 *Extensive form of the Battle of Bismarck Sea game*

move, and the nodes at the second level are labelled "Kenney". The terminal nodes of the game tree represent the outcomes that are reached after each player has moved in accordance with the rules of the game. If both choose south, for example, the outcome is three days of bombing as shown at the right-hand terminal node.

The nodes are enclosed in dashed loops to indicate the *information sets* to which they belong. When making a move, a player cannot distinguish between choice points enclosed within a single information set. The initial node in Figure 4.1 is in an information set all on its own, but both of the nodes labelled "Kenney" are enclosed in a single information set. The purpose of this is to show that, at the time of choosing, Kenney does not know whether he has reached the left-hand or the right-hand node; in other words he does not know whether the Japanese commander has chosen to sail north or south. This means that the game is one of imperfect information – the players move simultaneously or in ignorance of any preceding moves – and the game would be strategically equivalent if it were portrayed with the initial node labelled "Kenney" and the succeeding "Imamura" nodes enclosed in a single information set.

If the game were one of perfect information, on the other hand, then every node would be a singleton enclosed in its own information set, like the initial node in Figure 4.1, and the sequence of moves represented in the game tree would assume significance. The extensive form of a perfect-information game such as chess, for example, would have to be represented in that way, although in practice it would be impossible to draw a game tree for chess because the number of branches would run into billions after only a few moves. It is none the less possible to *imagine* a tree representing the extensive form of any finite game, even if it cannot be drawn in practice, and this is all that is required for some purposes. For an introduction to game trees, see Rasmusen (1989, chap. 2) or, for a very detailed discussion with many examples, Singleton and Tyndall (1974, chaps 1 and 2).

A more compact method of representing a finite, strictly competitive game is by means of a rectangular array of numbers, called a *payoff matrix*, which displays the *normal form* of the game. Each row corresponds to one of Player I's strategies, and each column to one of Player II's strategies. Because a strategy is a complete plan of action specifying in advance how a player will move at any choice point that may arise in the course of play (see chapter 1), the normal form allows a game involving a sequence of moves to be depicted statically, with the players simultaneously choosing a single row and column. By convention, the matrix element at the intersection of each row and column represents the payoff to Player I (the row-chooser) and, because the game is zero-sum, Player II's payoffs are simply negatives of those shown in the matrix. Any finite game in extensive form can be represented in normal form without loss of strategically relevant information. Matrix 4.1 shows the normal form of the Battle of Bismarck Sea game.

Matrix 4.1
The Battle of Bismarck Sea

Imamura

N   S

		N	S
Kenney	N	2	2
	S	1	3

The normal form of this game is agreeably simple because each player chooses between only two options under conditions of imperfect information; the players' strategies are therefore simply their options (more complex examples will be discussed later in this chapter).

4.3 Games with saddle points: Nash equilibria

How might General Kenney have analysed the game depicted in Matrix 4.1? Without the benefit of game theory, one might assume that nothing can be said about his optimal strategy without knowing what the enemy intentions are, but it will shortly become apparent, perhaps surprisingly, that this is not so.

If the Japanese decide to sail north of the island, then Kenney's best counter-strategy is to search north and obtain the outcome of two days of bombing. If they sail south, then Kenney does better by searching south and obtaining three days of bombing. But Kenney has no foreknowledge of the Japanese commander's intentions, so at this level of analysis his best counter-strategy remains indeterminate.

The doctrine of decision in the American armed forces was (and is) based on enemy *capabilities* rather than enemy *intentions* (Haywood, 1954, pp. 365–366). In the light of this doctrine, Kenney may therefore have examined each of his available options from the viewpoint of the worst possible outcomes that could follow, given the options available to the Japanese. This pessimistic approach leads to the following conclusions: by searching north, Kenney is assured a minimum of two days of bombing, whereas if he searches south the worst possible outcome is one day of bombing. In other words, Kenney's worst possible payoff if he chooses his northern strategy is two days, and the worst possible payoff if he chooses his southern strategy is one day of bombing. It follows that by choosing his northern strategy

Kenney maximizes his minimum payoff. This choice is therefore called his *maximin* strategy; it has the property of ensuring the best of the worst possible outcomes. By choosing it, Kenney can guarantee that the payoff will not be less than two days of bombing; this figure is the maximin value of the game to him.

The Japanese commander Imamura may have analysed the game in the same way. His objective is to minimize rather than to maximize the number of days of bombing. If he sails north, the worst that can happen from his point of view – the maximum amount of bombing – is two days, and if he sails south, the worst possible outcome is three days of bombing. These numbers represent negative payoffs, in other words losses, to the Japanese. In order to ensure the best of the worst possible outcomes, he must therefore sail north. This choice corresponds to Imamura's *minimax* strategy because it *mini*mizes the *maxi*mum payoff to the enemy (the row-player, whose payoffs are always the ones shown in the matrix). In other words, the minimum that the column player can guarantee (the minimax) is equal to the maximum that the row player can guarantee (the maximin): both are equal to two days of bombing.

According to the minimax principle of game theory, the optimal strategies available to players in zero-sum games are their maximin and minimax strategies. In zero-sum games, both are commonly referred to as minimax strategies for convenience, because a strategy that maximizes the minimum payoff is also the one that minimizes the maximum payoff to the opponent, but in mixed-motive games (which will be introduced in chapter 6) this is not generally true, and maximin and minimax will need to be carefully distinguished. In the Battle of Bismarck Sea game, players who are rational according to the minimax principle will choose their northern strategies, and the value of the game to both of them is two days of bombing, because that is the payoff that results from rational play on both sides. These minimax strategies were in fact the ones chosen by General Kenney and the Japanese commander Imamura in February 1943, and the Japanese suffered the most decisive defeat of the war in the South Pacific up to that time: their convoy of 10 warships and 12 transports carrying about 15 000 men was destroyed. The outcome cannot be attributed to any strategic error on the part of Imamura; it was inherent in the unfair payoff structure of the game, whose value was positive and hence favourable to Kenney. In the event, the outcome would have been no better for the Japanese had Imamura deviated unilaterally from his minimax strategy (they would still have suffered two days of bombing), and if Kenney had deviated unilaterally, he would have obtained a worse outcome (one day of bombing instead of two).

The players' minimax strategies are optimal because they intersect in an *equilibrium point* of the game, nowadays more often called a *Nash equilibrium* after the game theorist John Nash (1950a, 1951) who proved some basic theorems about them. In any game, a Nash equilibrium is a combination of players' strategies that are best against one another. A key property of a Nash equilibrium is that no player has any incentive to deviate unilaterally from it, so that it gives the players no cause to regret their strategy choices when the other players' choices are revealed. In a strictly competitive game a Nash equilibrium represents a rational solution for the following reason: it determines a minimax strategy for each player that yields the best possible payoff – the value of the game – against an opponent who also chooses optimally and a payoff at least as good against one who chooses non-optimally.

It is worth commenting, although this point is often ignored by game theorists, that a minimax or equilibrium strategy does not necessarily take full advantage of irrational play on the part of an opponent. If there is good reason to suspect that an opponent will choose a non-minimax strategy, then a non-minimax choice may be the best counter-strategy. For example, if Kenney had good reason to suspect that the Japanese planned to sail south, then it would be hard to deny that his best counter would have been to search south, although this choice would be irrational according to formal game theory. The minimax principle offers a persuasive definition of rational choice in strictly competitive games, provided that there are no reasons to doubt that one's adversary is rational. Against an irrational adversary, it could be argued that it loses some of its persuasive force, but in games against human opponents the assumption of rationality is usually justified.

The Nash equilibrium of the Battle of Bismarck Sea game is easy to find because the payoff matrix contains a *saddle point*. It is so called because a saddle sits on a horse's back at the lowest point on the animal's head-to-tail axis and highest point on its flank-to-flank axis. Analogously, a saddle point of a payoff matrix is an element that is a minimum in its row and a maximum in its column. The top left element in Matrix 4.1 has this property, and it is therefore the Nash equilibrium of the game. Both of the numbers in row N are row minima, because there is no number in that row less than 2. Only one of them is also a column maximum, and it is the one in column N; therefore the (N, N) cell is the unique saddle point of the matrix.

If the payoff matrix of any strictly competitive game has a saddle point, then it represents a Nash equilibrium, its value is the value of the game, and the players' equilibrium or minimax strategies are simply the row and column that intersect at that point. But not all matrices have saddle points, and if no saddle point exists, then the maximum that Player I can guarantee by choosing one of the rows – the maximin – is bound to be less than the minimum that Player II can guarantee to hold Player I's payoff down to by choosing one of the columns, namely the minimax. If maximin and minimax are equal, then and only then, there must be a saddle point in the payoff matrix where its value occurs. The fact that a saddle point necessarily corresponds to the intersection of the players' equilibrium or minimax strategies is particularly useful for solving games that are more complicated than the Battle of Bismarck Sea game. This is illustrated in the apparently complex Matrix 4.2.

Because there is a saddle point in Matrix 4.2, the Nash equilibrium, minimax strategies, and value of the game can be found almost at a glance. By checking the minimum elements in each row to see whether any of them is also a column maximum, the saddle point is quickly located. It is situated at the intersection of row 2 and column 6. Player I's maximin is therefore equal to Player II's minimax, and each player can guarantee, by choosing the appropriate strategy, that the payoff will be no worse from that player's point of view than zero. The solution to this game is as follows: Player I should choose row 2, Player II should choose column 6, and the value of the game is zero (it is a fair game, unlike the Battle of Bismarck Sea game). Neither player has any incentive to deviate from the Nash equilibrium provided that the other player does not.

If either player deviates from the prescribed minimax strategy while the opponent adheres to it, the non-minimax player will receive a less favourable payoff than the value of the game: Player I will be punished for

Matrix 4.2

II

		1	2	3	4	5	6	7	8
	1	−1	−2	−3	−5	1	−2	2	1
	2	1	3	2	2	1	◆0	2	1
	3	−1	0	−3	−3	3	−4	2	−1
	4	−2	−2	−6	−8	4	−2	4	0
I	5	0	3	−1	−1	4	−5	4	0
	6	−2	2	−1	−2	3	−1	2	−1
	7	−3	0	−4	−7	4	−3	4	0
	8	−1	5	−1	0	4	−1	4	0

unilateral deviation with one of the negative payoffs in column 6, and Player II's payoff following unilateral deviation will be one of the positive elements in row 2 (which represent losses for Player II). In either case, of course, the minimax player will be rewarded with a corresponding gain over and above the value of the game. The minimax strategies are thus in equilibrium in the sense that they are best against each other, and so the players would not regret choosing them when their opponents' choices were revealed.

Regrettably, not all payoff matrices have saddle points. Games whose matrices are without saddle points require more difficult methods of solution that will be discussed later in section 4.4. But a word needs first to be said about the opposite state of affairs, namely games with multiple saddle points. A simple example of this kind is shown in Matrix 4.3.

Matrix 4.3

II

		A	B	C
	A	4	2*	2*
I	B	7	2*	2*
	C	3	0	1

All four of the matrix elements marked with asterisks in Matrix 4.3 are saddle points. Games of this kind present no new problems, however. It is easy to prove (see, for example, Friedman, 1991, pp. 78–80; Luce and Raiffa, 1957, p. 66; Singleton and Tyndall, 1974, pp. 47–51) that *all* of Player I's minimax strategies invariably intersect with *all* of Player II's, and the saddle points are all of equal value. In other words, the saddle points are always *equivalent* and the strategies associated with them are always *interchangeable*. The solutions to the game shown in Matrix 4.3 are as follows: Player I should choose either row *A* or row *B* (both are optimal), Player II should choose either column *B* or column *C*, and the value of the game is 2 units. All of the saddle points are of course Nash equilibria inasmuch as a player who deviates unilaterally from a saddle-point strategy to a non-saddle-point strategy will obtain a worse outcome than the value of the game, and the other player will be rewarded by a corresponding amount.

4.4 Games without saddle points

The ideas discussed in the previous section cannot be applied without modification to all strictly competitive games. The following simple example from Sir Arthur Conan Doyle's story, *The Final Problem*, first subjected to game theory analysis by von Neumann and Morgenstern (1944, pp. 176–178), clarifies the difficulties:

> Sherlock Holmes desires to proceed from London to Dover and hence to the Continent in order to escape from Professor Moriarty who pursues him. Having boarded the train he observes, as the train pulls out, the appearance of Professor Moriarty on the platform. Sherlock Holmes takes it for granted – and in this he is assumed to be fully justified – that his adversary, who has seen him, might secure a special train and overtake him. Sherlock Holmes is faced with the alternative of going to Dover or of leaving the train at Canterbury, the only intermediate station. His adversary – whose intelligence is assumed to be fully adequate to visualize these possibilities – has the same choice. Both opponents must choose the place of their detrainment in ignorance of the other's corresponding decision. If, as a result of these measures, they should find themselves, *in fine*, on the same platform, Sherlock Holmes may with certainty expect to be killed by Moriarty. If Sherlock Holmes reaches Dover unharmed he can make good his escape. (p. 177)

Holmes's chances of escaping with his life are zero if he and Moriarty choose the same railway station. Let us assume further that his chances of survival are 100 per cent if he escapes via Dover, but only 50 per cent if he chooses Canterbury while Moriarty chooses Dover, because in the latter case the pursuit continues. It is reasonable to assume that Holmes's preferences correspond to his chances of survival and that Moriarty's preferences are the negatives of these. If all these facts are *common knowledge* (as defined in section 1.2), then the payoff structure of the game can be represented as in Matrix 4.4.

It is immediately obvious that this matrix has no saddle point, because there is no matrix element that is the minimum in its row and the

Matrix 4.4 *Holmes v. Moriarty*

Moriarty

		Canterbury	Dover
Holmes	Canterbury	0	50
	Dover	100	0

maximum in its column. Payoff matrices without saddle points are by no means uncommon. If a 2 × 2 (two-row, two-column) matrix is constructed at random, the probability that it will have a saddle point is .67; in a 3 × 3 matrix the probability is .33; in a 4 × 4 matrix the probability is only .11; and in larger matrices the probabilities are extremely small. But payoff matrices are not random arrays of numbers, and it is reasonable to enquire whether there is any easily recognizable class of games whose matrices always have saddle points. Almost a century ago, Zermelo (1912) made the first major contribution to the theory of games of strategy by giving an answer to this question. Zermelo proved that the condition of perfect information is sufficient to ensure a saddle point in the payoff matrix of a finite, strictly competitive game. Zermelo's theorem, which is proved by *backward induction*, that is, by reasoning backwards through the game tree, applies to games that are far too complex to depict in extensive or even in normal form, let alone to solve. The payoff matrix of chess, for example, cannot be depicted because it contains billions and billions of rows and columns, and the game tree cannot be drawn for a similar reason. But chess is a finite, strictly competitive game of perfect information, and its payoff matrix is therefore known to possess a saddle point corresponding to optimal strategies for White and Black, although no one knows what these optimal strategies are or even whether the value of the game is a win for White, a draw, or conceivably a win for Black (see von Neumann and Morgenstern, 1944, pp. 124–125). Some intriguing mathematical ideas behind winning strategies for many other interesting games are discussed in Berlekamp, Conway, and Guy (1985) and Conway (1976). An informal and simple proof of Zermelo's theorem can be found in Davis (1970, pp. 16–18).

Holmes v. Moriarty is a game of imperfect information whose payoff matrix is without a saddle point, but it is possible nevertheless to find a rational solution to it. If the players try to outguess each other, the analysis goes round in circles. The principle of choosing the strategy that ensures the best of the worst possible outcomes, which works with saddle-point matrices, also breaks down completely in this case. According to this principle, Holmes may choose either option, ensuring a maximin payoff of zero. Moriarty, who wishes to minimize Holmes's payoff, should choose Dover, thereby holding the payoff down to a minimax of 50. But these machinations do not lead to a satisfactory solution for two reasons. The first is that the value of the game remains indeterminate because maximin is not equal to minimax; the most that can be said is that the value lies somewhere between 0 and 50. Second, if Moriarty's optimal strategy is indeed to choose Dover, then Holmes can anticipate this and counter by choosing Canterbury. At this point in the analysis, Moriarty's argument for choosing Dover collapses. The point is that Moriarty will be able to anticipate Holmes's choice of Canterbury, and will therefore be forced to reconsider the wisdom of choosing Dover. In the light of this, Holmes will also, of course, have to reconsider. This conclusion is crippling to the whole argument, and it arises from the fact that the payoff matrix has no saddle point.

There is no pair of strategies that are in equilibrium, and consequently one of the players will always have cause to regret his choice when his opponent's is revealed. A security problem, unknown in games with saddle-point matrices, therefore exists: it is vitally important for both players to conceal their intentions from their opponents. The surest way of concealing one's intentions is by leaving the decision to chance, and according to game theory that is precisely what a rational player in a game whose matrix has no saddle point ought to do! In order to ensure that a specific choice cannot be anticipated by the opponent, but that each strategy will have a predetermined *probability* of being chosen, a player can choose randomly by tossing a coin, rolling dice, consulting a table of random numbers, or using some other suitable randomizing device. A player who behaves in this way is described in the terminology of game theory as adopting a *mixed strategy*. A strategy corresponding to a single row or column of a payoff matrix is often called a *pure strategy* to distinguish it from a mixed strategy.

It may seem paradoxical that a rational player should ever resort to a mixed strategy. A military commander, business executive, or political leader who made important decisions by turning them into gambles would be considered insane – the diagnosis seems amply justified in some cases; see, for example, Luke Rhinehart's (1972) bizarre novel, *The Dice Man*. But the fact that randomized choice can in some circumstances be perfectly rational becomes clear when transparently simple examples are examined. Consider the well-known children's game referred to as "handy-dandy" by Shakespeare in *King Lear* (I. iv. 94) and others (see Avedon and Sutton–Smith, 1971, p. 36). Player I conceals a small object in one fist and Player II guesses "left" or "right". Player I wins if the guess is wrong, and Player II wins if it is right. Matrix 4.5 shows the payoff structure of this game, assuming a payoff of one unit for a win.

Matrix 4.5

II

		L	R
I	L	–1	1
	R	1	–1

Any player who chooses deliberately, according to any chain of reasoning whatever, risks being outguessed by the opponent. This explains why adults, more often than not, manage to beat children at this game. By choosing a pure strategy, Player I can do no better than ensure a maximin of –1, and Player II do no better than hold the payoff down to a minimax of 1.

Suppose, however, that Player I uses a mixed strategy that assigns equal probabilities to left and right, by secretly tossing a coin. Although the *specific* outcome of the game is unknown, the *expected* value of the game – the average value that would arise from many repetitions of the game – can be calculated easily according to the principles outlined in connection with games of chance in section 2.3. If Player II chooses left, the expected payoff is $(1/2)(-1) + (1/2)(1) = 0$, and if Player II chooses right it is $(1/2)(1) + (1/2)(-1) = 0$. The expected payoff also works out as zero against any mixed strategy that Player II might use. Player I's maximin expected payoff is therefore zero, which is considerably better than the maximin of –1 that Player I can guarantee through the use of a pure strategy. The specific outcome of the game depends, of course, on whether Player I chooses left or right after consulting the randomizing device and whether Player II chooses left or right. But by using the mixed strategy, Player I's chances are exactly even. Similar considerations apply to Player II, who can hold the minimax expected payoff down to zero by using the same mixed strategy. The same expected payoffs apply against a player who uses any mixed strategy.

The maximin and minimax expected payoffs, like the maximin and minimax payoffs in a game whose matrix has a saddle point, are therefore equal. The comparison can be carried further, and the ideas discussed in connection with pure strategies generalize easily to mixed strategies. The mixed strategies constitute a Nash equilibrium: neither player can profit by deviating unilaterally from the prescribed mixed strategy, although in this simple case a player who deviates unilaterally does not actually suffer any loss. These strategies are therefore referred to as *minimax mixed strategies*, they constitute a *mixed-strategy Nash equilibrium* (or a *mixed-strategy saddle point*), and they are considered optimal in formal game theory. Together with the value of the game, which is obviously zero because it is a fair game, they constitute the Nash equilibrium solution.

Mixed strategies are increasingly often interpreted in a slightly different way. John Harsanyi (1973a) showed that Player I's mixed strategy can almost always be interpreted as Player II's uncertainty about which pure strategy Player I will choose, and vice versa. This is achieved by assuming that the figures in the payoff matrix are not exact, but that each player's true utilities are the matrix payoffs plus or minus small random fluctuations whose values are the private information of that player (the basic mathematical ideas are explained in Gibbons, 1992, chap. 3). Aumann (1987) suggested a slightly different way of interpreting Player I's mixed strategy as a subjective belief of Player II about what Player I will choose, and vice versa, but see Sugden (1991, pp. 765–768) for a critique.

Some interesting and important refinements of the Nash equilibrium solution were developed by game theorists in the 1970s and 1980s. The most important of these are the *subgame perfect equilibrium*, and *the trembling-hand equilibrium*. These refinements are of limited significance for strictly competitive games, where the classical Nash equilibrium solution provides a compelling solution, but they are useful in the analysis of certain non-zero-sum games. They will therefore be outlined in section 6.2.

John Von Neumann (1928) was the first to prove the fundamental minimax theorem, which establishes that *every* finite, strictly competitive game has an equilibrium point in mixed strategies. A game whose payoff matrix has a saddle point may be thought of as merely a special case in which each player's mixed strategy assigns a probability of 1 to one pure strategy and probabilities of zero to the others. A simple proof of the minimax theorem is given in the appendix. This theorem is the foundation stone of formal game theory, and any reader with at least school mathematics who wishes to acquire a proper understanding of the theory is strongly urged to study it.

Matrix 4.6 *Holmes v.*
Moriarty: Minimax Solution

Moriarty

		Canterbury	Dover	
	Canterbury	0	50	2/3
Holmes				
	Dover	100	0	1/3
		1/3	2/3	

It is at last possible to provide a solution to the Holmes v. Moriarty game. Its payoff structure is reproduced in Matrix 4.6 with the Nash equilibrium mixed strategies indicated in the right-hand and lower margins. Suppose that Holmes resolves to roll a die in order to choose the station at which he will leave the train. If 1, 2, 3, or 4 comes up (he decides in advance), he will alight at Canterbury, and if 5 or 6 comes up he will continue on to Dover. What are the expected payoffs against each of Moriarty's pure strategies? If Moriarty chooses Canterbury, Holmes's expected payoff is $(2/3)(0) + (1/3)(100) = 33.33$. If Moriarty chooses Dover, it is $(2/3)(50) + (1/3)(0) =$

33.33. Holmes's minimum expected payoff is therefore 33.33, irrespective of Moriarty's choice, which is a substantial improvement on the maximin of zero that results from his use of pure strategies only.

Suppose now that Moriarty uses a similar randomizing device to make his choice, but assigns a probability of 1/3 to Canterbury and 2/3 to Dover. The expected payoff if Holmes chooses Canterbury is (1/3)(0) + (2/3)(50) = 33.33, and the expected payoff against Holmes's choice of Dover is (1/3)(100) + (2/3)(0) = 33.33. The minimax expected payoff is therefore again 33.33, which is considerably better from Moriarty's point of view than the minimax of 50 that he can hold Holmes down to by using a pure strategy.

By using the indicated mixed strategies, Holmes can guarantee that his expected probability of survival will be no less than 33.33, and Moriarty can guarantee that it will be no more than 33.33. The mixed strategies are therefore minimax mixed strategies that constitute a Nash equilibrium: neither player can do better by deviating unilaterally or obtain a better result by using any other (pure or mixed) strategy if his opponent plays minimax. The solution to the game is this: Holmes should choose randomly between Canterbury and Dover with probabilities of 2/3 and 1/3 respectively, Moriarty should randomize between the same options with probabilities of 1/3 and 2/3 respectively, and the value of the game is equivalent to a 33.33 per cent chance of Holmes's survival. In Sir Arthur Conan Doyle's story, Holmes alighted at Canterbury and watched triumphantly as Moriarty sped past on his way to Dover. Those were the strategies most likely to be chosen according to game theory, and from the novelist's point of view they had the added virtue of allowing the harrowing pursuit to continue.

There is an important difference between 2 × 2 mixed-strategy games like the ones so far considered in this section and larger games. In the 2 × 2 case it is sufficient for one of the players to use a minimax mixed strategy to ensure that the expected payoff will be the value of the game, no more and no less. This means that a player is bound to obtain the same expected payoff by using any strategy, pure or mixed, against an opponent who plays a mixed strategy that is optimal according to formal game theory. In larger mixed-strategy games, on the other hand, it is possible for players who deviate unilaterally from minimax strategies to receive expected payoffs *worse* than the value of the game while their opponents benefit correspondingly. This possibility arises if a player uses a pure strategy that is not among the ones included in the minimax mixed strategy.

The well-known Italian game, morra, whose payoff matrix is 9 × 9, illustrates the full force of the minimax principle. The solution to this game, originally calculated by Williams (1966, pp. 163–165), is far from obvious (though it is easy to memorize), and a player who knows it is at an advantage against an opponent who does not. The rules are as follows: each player extends one, two, or three fingers and at the same time calls out a number between one and three. The number called out is a guess regarding the number of fingers extended by the opponent, which is not known in advance because the rules stipulate that the players move simultaneously. If only one player guesses correctly, then the loser pays the winner an amount corresponding to the total number of fingers displayed, otherwise the payoff is zero. If, for example, Player I extends one finger and calls out "one" (this pure strategy may be written 1–1), and Player II extends one finger and calls "three" (1–3), then the outcome is two units of payment to Player I, because only Player I's guess is correct and the total number of fingers extended is two. The complete payoff structure of this game is shown in Matrix 4.7.

Matrix 4.7 has no saddle point, and the game therefore requires a solution in mixed strategies. The Nash equilibrium mixed strategy is the same for both players, as is to be expected in a completely symmetrical game. The solution turns out to be for both players to ignore all options except 1–3, 2–2, and 3–1, and to randomize among these three with probabilities of 5/12,

Matrix 4.7 *Morra*

II

		1–1	1–2	1–3	2–1	2–2	2–3	3–1	3–2	3–3
	1–1	0	2	2	–3	0	0	–4	0	0
	1–2	–2	0	0	0	3	3	–4	0	0
	1–3	–2	0	0	–3	0	0	0	4	4
	2–1	3	0	3	0	–4	0	0	–5	0
I	2–2	0	–3	0	4	0	4	0	–5	0
	2–3	0	–3	0	0	–4	0	5	0	5
	3–1	4	4	0	0	0	–5	0	0	–6
	3–2	0	0	–4	5	5	0	0	0	–6
	3–3	0	0	–4	0	0	–5	6	6	0

4/12, and 3/12 respectively, and the value of the game is zero (it is fair). A rational way of playing the game might be as follows. Keep five red, four green, and three blue marbles in a convenient pocket. Before playing the game, select one of the marbles at random and secretly examine its colour. Depending on whether it is red, green, or blue, extend one finger and guess "three", extend two and guess "two", or extend three and guess "one" respectively. Against an opponent who uses the same mixed strategy, your chances of winning would then be even. Against an opponent who uses any pure or mixed strategy that includes one of the forbidden strategies, you may reasonably expect to win and would certainly come out on top in a sufficiently long series of repetitions.

In simple, naturally occurring strategic interactions, people sometimes use minimax mixed strategies intuitively, without conscious calculation. Davenport (1960), for example, analysed the strictly competitive game between Jamaican fishermen, who have to choose between fishing grounds, and their prey; he showed that not only the fishermen but *both* players stick rather closely to the Nash equilibrium mixed strategies prescribed by the minimax principle! (The Jamaican fishing game has been reinterpreted by Kozelka, 1969, and by Walker, 1977.)

4.5 Dominance and admissibility

If two of a player's pure strategies are compared, one is said to *dominate* the other if it yields an outcome at least as good against any of the pure strategies that the opponent may choose and a better outcome against at least one of them. The dominance is *strict* rather than *weak* if it yields a better outcome against all of the opponent's pure strategies. In either case, a player would clearly be acting irrationally by choosing a dominated strategy, because it cannot produce a better outcome than the strategy that dominates it and may produce a worse one. A pure strategy that is dominated by another is *inadmissible* in the terminology of game theory, and a rational player in the game theory sense will never choose it. (It may seem obvious that a player who was rational in *any* sense would never choose a dominated strategy, but the paradoxes arising from the Prisoner's Dilemma game, to be discussed in section 6.7, and Newcomb's problem, to be discussed in section 12.3, make that conclusion far from obvious.) A strategy that is not dominated by any other is *admissible*. The concepts of dominance and admissibility extend naturally to mixed strategies, but they are especially useful when applied to pure strategies. The game depicted in Matrix 4.8 illustrates the basic ideas.

Row *A* strictly dominates row *B* because it leads to a better outcome for Player I whichever column Player II may choose. If Player II chooses column *A*, then row *A* is better than row *B* because 3 is greater than 1, and if Player

Matrix 4.8

II

		A	B
I	A	3	2
	B	1	0

II chooses column B, then it is better because 2 is greater than 0. Player I therefore has only one admissible strategy, namely row A. Player II, whose payoffs are the negatives of those shown in the matrix, seeks to minimize these losses. Bearing this in mind, column B clearly dominates column A because 2 is less than 3 and 0 is less than 1. Hence column B is Player II's only admissible strategy.

The game is therefore solved and the Nash equilibrium has been found: Player I should choose strategy A, Player II should choose strategy B, and the value of the game is 2 units. Not all strictly competitive games can be solved in this way, of course. The method cannot lead to a determinate solution unless there is a saddle point in the payoff matrix, and even then it is not always applicable. Zermelo's theorem referred to in section 4.3 above established, however, that if the game is one of perfect information – if the players move one at a time in full knowledge of all preceding moves – then not only will its corresponding matrix necessarily have a saddle point, but the game will be soluble by the method of deleting dominated rows and columns.

Matrix 4.9

II

		A	B	C
I	A	3	6	4
	B	0	4	-2
	C	-2	-4	8

This method of solving games is not always quite as straightforward as Matrix 4.8 suggested; the deletion of dominated rows and columns sometimes has to proceed by successive stages. A case in point is shown in Matrix 4.9. Row *B* is dominated by row *A*, but no column appears to be dominated by any other. Because row *B* represents a dominated strategy, however, a rational player will never choose it, so it is reasonable to delete it from the payoff matrix. *After deleting the inadmissible row B,* we are left with a 2 × 3 matrix in which column *C* is dominated by column *A*. On the assumption that Player I will not choose row *B*, therefore, Player II can safely disregard column *C*. This assumption is reasonable because there are no circumstances in which Player I can do as well by choosing row *B* as by choosing another row.

After deleting column *C*, what is left is a 2 × 2 matrix in which row *A* dominates row *C*. The deletion of row *C* results in a 1 × 2 matrix in which column *A* dominates column *B*. Finally deleting column *B*, we are left with a 1 × 1 matrix. Only the first row and the first column of the original matrix have survived the successive deletion of dominated strategies, and they intersect (as they are bound to) in the Nash equilibrium saddle point at row *A* and column *A*. The solution is therefore for both players to choose their first pure strategies, *A* and *A*, and the value of the game is 3 units. Any game of perfect information can, in principle, be solved in this way, and so can some others. The solutions can usually be found more easily by simply locating the saddle points, but the technique of *iterated deletion of dominated strategies* helps to clarify the assumptions and logical reasoning underlying the solution. The technique is discussed in Rasmusen (1989, pp. 30–32). The dominance arguments can be applied to many games that are not strictly competitive, as will be shown in chapters 6 and 9, and their practical usefulness in connection with tactical voting will be discussed in chapter 10.

4.6 Methods for finding solutions

The minimax theorem asserts that every finite, strictly competitive game has a Nash equilibrium in pure or mixed strategies, but it offers no help in discovering it and thereby solving the game. There are, however, efficient methods for solving all such games, although some are quite difficult to apply without the help of a computer.

The simplest case is a game whose payoff matrix has one or more saddle points. When confronted with a strictly competitive game requiring solution, it is always wise to begin by examining its payoff matrix for saddle points which, if they exist, allow a solution to be read off immediately. Happily, this method suffices for solving all finite, strictly competitive games of perfect information.

Games with non-saddle-point matrices are almost as easy to solve, provided that each player has only two pure strategies. In the 2 × 2 case, a player's optimal mixed strategy yields the same expected payoff against each of the opponent's pure strategies, and this fact allows a simple method of solution to be applied. Player I's optimal mixed strategy may be written as a pair of probabilities p and $1-p$ for row 1 and row 2 respectively. The expected payoffs yielded by this mixed strategy against column 1 and column 2 can then be expressed in terms of these probabilities. Because the minimax theorem ensures that the expected payoffs are the same for both players, they can be equated, and the value of p can be found by solving the equation. Player II assigns probabilities of q and $1 - q$ to columns 1 and 2 respectively and obtains the same expected payoff from this mixed strategy against row 1 and row 2, hence the value of q can be found by solving an analogous equation.

In Matrix 4.4, for example, Player I (Sherlock Holmes) assigns a probability of p to row 1 (Canterbury) and $1-p$ to row 2 (Dover). In the light of the minimax theorem, his expected payoffs against column 1 and column 2 may be equated as follows:

$$0p + 100(1 - p) = 50p + 0(1 - p),$$

$$p = 2/3.$$

Thus Holmes should assign a probability of 2/3 to row 1 (Canterbury) and $1 - 2/3 = 1/3$ to row 2 (Dover). From Moriarty's point of view,

$$0q + 50(1 - q) = 100q + 0(1 - q),$$

$$q = 1/3.$$

Column 1 (Canterbury) should therefore occur with a probability of 1/3 in Moriarty's optimal mixed strategy, and column 2 (Dover) with a probability of 2/3.

The value of the game is, by definition, the expected payoff when both players use optimal minimax strategies. In the 2 × 2 case, however, this expected payoff is assured even if only *one* of the two players uses a minimax mixture while the other chooses a pure strategy or any non-minimax mixed strategy. In a 2 × 2 game, the value of the game can therefore be found by substituting for p or q in any of the expressions on the left-hand or right-hand sides of the above equations. Suppose, for example, that Holmes uses his minimax mixed strategy while Moriarty chooses Canterbury. The expected payoff, and therefore the value of the game, is then $(0)(2/3) + (100)(1 - 2/3)$, which is equal to 33.33.

This method is meant for 2 × 2 games, but it can sometimes be used to solve larger games after they have been reduced to 2 × 2 games by (possibly iterated) deletion of dominated strategies. An example is shown in Matrix 4.10. Column *B* is inadmissible; it is dominated by column *A* because Player

Matrix 4.10

II

		A	B	C
	A	-3	5	-2
I	B	1	3	7
	C	4	4	2

II, who wants to minimize the payoff, does at least as well by choosing column *A* as by choosing column *B* against any of Player I's strategies and better in some cases. After deleting column *B*, we are left with a 3 × 2 matrix in which row *A* turns out to be dominated by rows *B* and *C*. Once row *A* has also been deleted, we are left with a 2 × 2 matrix. Further reduction through dominance is impossible and there is no saddle point. But the solution to the 2 × 2 subgame can be found by the methods described above, and the solution lifts back into the original 3 × 3 game. The deleted strategies – row *A* and column *B* – should be assigned zero probabilities, and the optimal mixed strategies in the residual 2 × 2 game should be applied to rows *B* and *C* and columns *A* and *C* of the original game. It turns out that Player I should mix strategies *A*, *B*, and *C* with probabilities of 0, 1/4, and 3/4, and Player II should mix strategies *A*, *B*, and *C* with probabilities of 5/8, 0, and 3/8. The value of the game is 13/4. If either player uses an inadmissible strategy, or any mixed strategy that assigns a non-zero probability to it, the expected payoff will be worse than 13/4 from that player's point of view, provided of course that the other player uses a minimax strategy.

A theorem proved by Shapley and Snow (1950) shows that any game in which one of the players has just two pure strategies, even if the other player has more than two, can be solved by methods applicable to 2 × 2 games. The theorem asserts that one of the 2 × 2 sub-matrices embedded in the 2 × *n* or *m* × 2 payoff matrix has a solution that is also a solution to the larger game. This means that to solve the original game it is necessary only to solve each of its component 2 × 2 subgames and to check each of these solutions in the original game. If the player with only two pure strategies obtains an expected payoff from the minimax mixed strategy against every one of the opponent's deleted pure strategies that is at least as favourable as the value of the 2 × 2 game, then a complete solution has been found. If the wrong 2 × 2 matrix has been used, the solution will not work in the larger game. An example is shown in Matrix 4.11.

Matrix 4.11

II

		A	B	C
I	A	−4	1	6
	B	9	0	−3

There is no saddle point in this payoff matrix, and it cannot be reduced by deleting dominated rows or columns. Nevertheless, in view of the Shapley–Snow theorem, one of the 2×2 sub-matrices formed by arbitrarily deleting a single column *must* have a solution that lifts back into the original game. Let us try deleting column C. We may solve the residual subgame as follows:

$$-4p + 9(1 - p) = p + 0(1 - p),$$

$$p = 9/14.$$

$$-4q + (1 - q) = 9q + 0(1 - q),$$

$$q = 1/14.$$

Player I should therefore use row A with probability 9/14 and row B with probability 5/14, Player II should mix columns A and B with probabilities of 1/14 and 13/14 respectively, and the value of this 2×2 subgame is $-4(9/14) + 9(1 - 9/14) = 9/14$. If this is a valid solution to the original 2×3 game, then Player I's mixed strategy will yield an expected payoff at least as favourable as the value of the game against column C; if it does not, we shall have to try out one of the other 2×2 sub-matrices. In fact, the expected payoff against column C is $6(9/14) - 3(5/14) = 39/14$, which is clearly better for Player I than 9/14, so we need proceed no further; the mixed strategies and value already calculated are optimal in the original 2×3 game, and Player II should neglect strategy C.

If a payoff matrix without a saddle point has two rows and several columns, or if it has several rows and two columns, then the method described above based on the Shapley–Snow theorem will always yield a solution. The amount of labour involved may, however, be considerable if the game contains a large number of embedded 2×2 sub-matrices. A matrix with two rows and eight columns, for example, contains 28 2×2 sub-matrices, all of which may have to be solved before a solution to the 2×8 game is found. In general, if the larger dimension of the matrix is n, the number of 2 × 2 sub-matrices embedded in it is $n(n - 1)/2$. Graphical methods that enable the critical 2 × 2 sub-matrices to be located quickly are, however, available (see, for example, Williams, 1966, pp. 71–81).

The solution of 3 × 3 and larger games, when none of the methods so far described applies, is best done with the help of a computer. The most efficient procedure, which is applicable to all finite, strictly competitive games without exception, is based on the fact that the solution can always be reduced to that of a standard linear programming problem. The details of the *simplex algorithm* for solving these problems are beyond the scope of this chapter. The fundamental ideas are explained with great clarity in Papadimitriou and Steiglitz (1982); a simpler account is given in Singleton and Tyndall (1974, chaps 8, 9, 10, and 11); and the actual step-by-step procedure for working it all out by hand is painstakingly described in Williams (1966, chap. 6). I shall conclude this section by outlining a much simpler procedure, based on fictitious play, that does not produce an exact solution but enables it to be approximated with any desired degree of accuracy.

Imagine two players, both ignorant of game theory, playing the same game over and over again. Both are statistically inclined and keep records of the pure strategies chosen by their opponents. Being quite unable to analyse the matrix, their initial choices are arbitrary, but on every subsequent occasion each chooses the pure strategy that yields the best expected payoff against the opponent's mixed strategy, estimated on the basis of the relative frequency with which the opponent has thus far chosen each pure strategy. Julia Robinson (1951) proved that the players' choices are bound to converge towards optimal mixed strategies in any two-person zero-sum game. Consider the example shown in Matrix 4.12.

Suppose the players arbitrarily choose row *A* and column *A* to start. Player I's second choice will be row *C*, because it is best against column *A*, and Player II's second choice will be column *C*, which minimizes against

Matrix 4.12

II

		A	B	C
	A	5	8	1
I	B	2	5	10
	C	9	0	5

row A. Then Player I will again choose row C, because it maximizes the expected payoff against Player II's 1/2, 1/2 mixture of columns A and C, and Player II will again choose column C because it minimizes against Player I's 1/2, 1/2 mixture of rows A and C. The process can be continued indefinitely with arbitrary choices being made whenever more than one pure strategy is best against the opponent's mixture. The following computational algorithm simplifies the procedure:

(1) Copy row 1 and column 1 on to a sheet of paper. Column 1 may be written horizontally for convenience.
(2) Mark the minimum element in the row and the maximum element in the column with asterisks. Choose any minimum or maximum if there is more than one.
(3) Note the position of the asterisked column element among the row totals and add the corresponding row to the first row. For example, if the second column element is asterisked, add row 2 to row 1, element by element. Note the position of the asterisked row element among the column totals and add the corresponding column to the first column element by element.
(4) Asterisk the minimum element in the new row total and the maximum element in the new column total. If the values of these two elements are sufficiently close to each other, then stop.
(5) Note the position of the column total element asterisked in (4), and add the corresponding row to the row total. Note the position of the row total element asterisked in (4) and add the corresponding column to the column total.
(6) Go to (4).

The algorithm may be applied to Matrix 4.12 as shown in Table 4.1. The game has been played fictitiously 10 times. Each asterisk among the row totals indicates that Player II was about to choose the corresponding column on the following trial, and the asterisks among the column totals show which rows Player I was about to choose on the following trials. Counting the asterisks among the column totals we find that Player I chose rows A, B, and C with relative frequencies of 3/10, 5/10, and 2/10, or 0.3, 0.5 and 0.2, respectively. The asterisks among the row totals show that Player II chose columns A, B, and C with relative frequencies of 0.3, 0.5, and 0.2 respectively.

   The bottom sets of figures show each player's total payoff after 10 trials against each pure strategy that the opponent might choose. Player I's worst possible total payoff, given the mixed strategy effectively used, is 43 units, shown asterisked. This would have been Player I's total if Player II had chosen column A on every trial. The mixture used by Player I therefore yields a minimum possible payoff of 4.3 units per trial. The worst that could

Table 4.1 Fictitious play on Matrix 4.12

Row totals				Column totals		
col. *A*	col. *B*	col. *C*		row *A*	row *B*	row *C*
5	8	1*		5	2	9*
14	8	6*		6	12	14*
23	8*	11		7	22*	19
25	13*	21		15	27*	19
27	18*	31		23	32*	19
29	23*	41		31	37*	19
31	28*	51		39	42*	19
33*	33	61		47*	47	19
38*	41	62		52*	49	28
43*	49	63		57*	51	37

have happened to Player II is a total payoff of 57, which would have been the result if Player I had chosen row *A* on every trial as shown by the position of the last asterisk. Player II's mixture thus holds the maximum possible payoff down to 5.7 per trial.

We know from the minimax theorem that the maximum that Player I can ensure by using an optimal mixed strategy is the same as the minimum that Player II can ensure by doing likewise, because both are equal to the value of the game. The above calculations show that the value of the game lies somewhere between 4.3 and 5.7. The difference between these two estimates is equivalent to 14 per cent of the range of payoffs in the game. It reflects the degree to which the strategy mixtures deviated from optimality, and a higher degree of accuracy can be obtained by repeating the fictitious play over more trials.

When the calculations are extended over 20 repetitions, the range of error decreases to the difference between a minimum of 4.5 and a maximum of 5.5, or 10 per cent of the payoff range. The relative frequencies with which Player I chooses strategies *A*, *B*, and *C* become 0.40, 0.25, and 0.35 respectively, and those of Player II also become 0.40, 0.25, and 0.35. These figures approximate the true solution found through the simplex algorithm, which yields a value for the game of exactly 5.00 and prescribes probabilities of 0.42, 0.33, and 0.25 for both players. This method of fictitious play can be used for finding an approximate solution to any finite, strictly competitive game. The approximation can, of course, be made as close as desired.

4.7 Ordinal payoffs and incomplete information

Throughout this chapter, the assumption has been made that the figures in the payoff matrices represent fully numerical utilities as defined in chapter 1, in other words that the players' preferences are measured on interval scales. The condition of *complete information* has also been assumed throughout. This means that the players are assumed to have full and accurate knowledge of their payoff matrices. In everyday conflicts, however, the protagonists often lack such accurate and complete information about their opponents' or even their own degrees of preference. In this section I shall therefore investigate some of the consequences of relaxing the assumptions of interval-scale payoffs and complete information.

It will be useful to establish first of all in what ways a payoff matrix can be modified without altering the strategic structure of the underlying game. As pointed out in chapter 1, utilities are unique up to a positive linear transformation. This means that the strategic properties of a matrix remain the same if a constant is added to each element or if each element is multiplied by a positive constant. Consider Matrices 4.13.

Matrices 4.13 *Positive Linear Transformations*

	II 1	II 2
I 1	0	2
I 2	3	1

(a)

	II 1	II 2
I 1	0	24
I 2	36	12

(b)

	II 1	II 2
I 1	8	10
I 2	11	9

(c)

	II 1	II 2
I 1	−2	−12/7
I 2	−11/7	−13/7

(d)

The optimal minimax strategies are identical in all four matrices. In each case Player I should mix rows 1 and 2 with equal probabilities, and Player II should mix columns 1 and 2 with probabilities of $1/4$ and $3/4$ respectively. The reason for this coincidence is that Matrices (b), (c), and (d) are positive linear transformations of (a). Matrix (b) is formed from (a) by multiplying each element by 12; (c) is formed by adding 8 to each element; and (d) is formed by multiplying each element by $1/7$ and adding −2 to it. The values of the four games reflect these transformations: the value of (a) is $3/2$, and the values of (b), (c), and (d) are $(3/2)(12) = 18$, $3/2 + 8 = 19/2$, and $(3/2)(1/7) -2 = -25/14$ respectively.

Adding a constant to the payoffs of a game has the effect of altering the zero point of the utility scale on which they are measured, and multiplying by a positive constant merely changes the units of measurement of the utility scale. It is often convenient to transform a matrix in order to eliminate negative elements and fractions prior to solving it by hand. Whenever this is done, however, it is necessary to perform the inverse transformation on the resulting value of the game in order to bring it back into the original scale of measurement, but the prescribed minimax strategies are unaffected.

Some games can be solved on the basis of only fragmentary information about their payoff matrices. This is the case, for example, if the payoffs associated with just one row and one column of a matrix are known and they intersect in a saddle point. An example of this is shown in the degenerate Matrix 4.14. There is a saddle point in this matrix at the

Matrix 4.14 *Incomplete Information*

II

		1	2	3	4
	1	1	2	7	1
	2	0	?	?	?
I	3	−1	?	?	?
	4	0	?	?	?

intersection of row 1 and column 1, and its existence is quite unaffected by the unknown payoffs in the other rows and columns. The players' first pure strategies are therefore optimal, and the value of the game is one unit. (Other solutions might of course emerge if more information about the payoff structure came to light, but in that case the values of the newly discovered saddle points would be one unit as well.) This example shows how games with saddle-point matrices can sometimes be solved by the players themselves or by game theorists in ignorance of many of even most of the possible outcomes.

A rigorous method of dealing with incomplete information was first put forward by John Harsanyi (1967, 1968a, 1968b), who showed that any game of incomplete information can be transformed into a game of complete but imperfect information. Before Harsanyi published his results, classical game theory could not handle games of incomplete information rigorously, except in special cases such as Matrix 4.14, and this was a major limitation of the theory because real-life interactions are often games of incomplete information in which the players have only limited information about the strategy sets, payoff functions, and expectations of the other players.

The Harsanyi transformation involves defining as many *types* of players, each with a different payoff function and set of expectations about the other players' payoff functions, as are necessary to cover the range of possibilities contemplated by the players. For example, in a two-person game, Player I may consider three possible types representing Player II's payoff function and expectations (hence three different payoff matrices that could possibly represent the game), and Player II may consider just two possible types for Player I (and hence two possible payoff matrices). The fictitious player Nature makes the first move of the game by selecting which particular types of players will actually participate in the game and which particular payoff matrix will therefore apply. Each possible combination of a type for Player I and a type for Player II will have a predetermined probability p_{ij} of being selected, depending on the subjective probabilities that the players assigned to each of the types. After the payoff matrix representing the designated pair of types has been chosen by Nature, the players play the game. They are ignorant of which payoff matrix Nature has chosen and therefore of the other player's type, but they know the probability that the other player is of a particular type, because the probabilities p_{ij} are assumed to be common knowledge. This ingenious transformation reduces a game of incomplete information into a game of imperfect information that is fully accessible to the standard methods of game theory analysis.

Many critics of game theory, and some game theorists, have drawn attention to the basic problem of measuring the players' utilities on an interval scale. Shubik (1964), for example, has had this to say:

> The numbers in the payoff matrix have to be obtained in some manner or the other. It is difficult enough to be able to state with certainty that an individual prefers to see Jones as a senator rather than Smith; it is more difficult (and some may say impossible) to state by how much he prefers Jones to Smith. (p. 19)

The truth of the matter is that strictly competitive games can often be solved convincingly without any appeal to such quantitative preferences. Any game in which the players move one at a time in full knowledge of all preceding moves – that is, any game of perfect information, and any other game with a saddle-point matrix for that matter – can be solved on the basis of purely ordinal preference rankings. In order to solve such a game it is not necessary to know the players' degrees of preference; one needs merely to know which outcomes they consider best, second best, and so on. Brams (1980b) has analysed many two-person conflicts from the Old Testament on the basis of ordinal payoffs. The following example, based loosely on one of Brams's models (pp. 132–139), shows how this is done.

Saul, the king of Israel, appointed David, "a mighty valiant man, and a man of war, and prudent in matters, and a comely person" (I Sam. xvi: 18) in command of his soldiers. David set out with the army, slaughtered great numbers of Philistines, and was greeted on his homecoming by women dancing and singing "Saul hath slain his thousands, and David his ten thousands" (I Sam. xviii: 7). Saul became jealous and afraid of David's growing popularity and made a number of attempts on his life. David was eventually persuaded to flee into exile.

At that point in the story, Saul may reasonably be assumed to have had two options: to pursue David (*P*) or not to pursue him (*DP*). David, for his part, had two options: to flee from Saul (*F*) or not to flee (*DF*). While it is impossible to assign accurate numerical utilities to the various possible outcomes of this game more than two millennia after the event, certain reasonable assumptions can be made about the payoffs. To begin with, the conflict is evidently strictly competitive: an outcome that is good from Saul's point of view is correspondingly bad from David's, and vice versa. The game is therefore zero-sum. Second, the outcomes can be arranged in order of preference without too much difficulty. The best possible outcomes for Saul are those in which he pursues David and David does not flee, because in those cases David is killed and the threat is eradicated, which is what Saul evidently wants. Saul's worst possible outcomes are those in which he does not pursue David and David does not flee, because David's popularity is then likely to eclipse Saul's. Other possible outcomes are intermediate from Saul's point of view, because David remains in exile but the problem is unresolved. David's preferences among the various possible outcomes are, of course, simply the reverse of Saul's.

Because David moves after Saul, and in full knowledge of Saul's move, the game is one of perfect information and its matrix must therefore have a saddle point. This means that it will have a Nash equilibrium solution in pure strategies. In the normal form of the game, Saul's pure strategies are simply to pursue (*P*) or not to pursue (*DP*), but David, moving second, has four pure strategies:

F/F: flee if pursued, flee if not pursued;
F/DF: flee if pursued, don't flee if not pursued;
DF/F: don't flee if pursued, flee if not pursued;
DF/DF: don't flee if pursued, don't flee if not pursued.

The normal form of this game is displayed in Matrix 4.15, with the payoffs to Saul labelled *g* (good), *f* (fair), and *b* (bad).

Matrix 4.15 *Saul and David*

David

		F/F	F/DF	DF/F	DF/DF
	P	*f*	*f*	*g*	*g*
Saul					
	DP	*f*	*b*	*f*	*b*

A saddle point is situated at the intersection of the first row and second column of the matrix. It can be identified as a saddle point because "fair" is a minimum payoff in row 1 (it is obviously worse than "good") and a maximum in column 2 (it is better than "bad"). In fact the first row dominates the second because it leads to an equal or preferable payoff to Saul no matter which column is chosen by David, and the second column is dominant because it leads to outcomes equal or worse for Saul (and thus equal or better for David) than any other column irrespective of Saul's choice. There is thus only one admissible strategy available to each player: Saul should pursue David, and David should flee only if he is pursued. The value of the game is "fair". The biblical account of what actually happened confirms that these minimax strategies were in fact chosen.

Games whose matrices have no saddle points cannot be solved without interval-scale measurement of the players' preferences. But even in these games a certain amount of progress towards a solution can sometimes be made on the basis of incomplete information. Let us return for the last time to the example of Holmes v. Moriarty discussed in section 4.4 and assume that information about the players' preferences is incomplete.

Holmes and Moriarty can each choose to alight at either Canterbury or Dover. Holmes wants to maximize his chances of survival and Moriarty to minimize them, but let us assume now that neither player can quantify these chances. Ordinal payoffs can be assigned without fuss. If both players choose the same station, then the outcome is clearly "bad" for Holmes; if Holmes chooses Canterbury and Moriarty Dover, the outcome is "fair" for Holmes; and if Holmes chooses Dover and Moriarty Canterbury, the outcome is "good" for Holmes. Moriarty, of course, ranks the outcomes in the opposite order. The payoff structure is shown in Matrix 4.16.

There is no saddle point in this ordinal payoff matrix; the best payoff that Holmes can guarantee for himself by using a pure strategy is "bad", and the worst that Moriarty can guarantee to hold it down to by doing likewise is "fair". The value of the game therefore lies somewhere between the "bad"

Matrix 4.16 *Holmes v.*
Moriarty: Ordinal Payoffs

Moriarty

Canterbury   Dover

		Canterbury	Dover
	Canterbury	b	f
Holmes			
	Dover	g	b

maximin and the "fair" minimax. To obtain a Nash equilibrium, both players must therefore use mixed strategies.

Holmes's minimax mixed strategy can be worked out in the usual way by assigning a probability of p to Canterbury:

$$bp + g(1 - p) = fp + b(1 - p),$$

which yields

$$p = (b - g)/(2b - g - f).$$

Holmes should assign this probability to Canterbury, and

$$1 - p = 1 - (b - g)/(2b - g - f)$$

to Dover. Simple algebraic manipulation reveals that the ratio of Canterbury to Dover in Holmes's optimal mixed strategy is simply $(g - b):(f - b)$. He should therefore assign a larger probability to Canterbury than to Dover because the difference between "good" and "bad" must be larger than the difference between "fair" and "bad". Similar calculations show that Moriarty's optimal mixed strategy requires that he assign probabilities to Canterbury and Dover in the ratio $(f - b):(g - b)$, which means that he should assign a larger probability to Dover. Holmes's chances of survival if both players are rational according to the dictates of game theory are somewhere between "bad" and "fair" because, as indicated earlier, the value of the game lies in that range. Without exactly solving the game, we have succeeded in revealing a certain amount about its optimal mixed strategies and value.

4.8 Summary

The chapter began with a discussion of zero-sum games and an explanation of why two-person zero-sum games, unlike any others, are strictly competitive. Formal game theory defines a solution – optimal ways of playing and a value that then results – to every conflict of this kind in which both of the players choose from finite strategy sets. In section 4.2 the main methods of representing the abstract structure of strictly competitive games – game trees and payoff matrices – were illustrated with examples. Sections 4.3 and 4.4 were devoted to the fundamental ideas behind the minimax solution and the Nash equilibrium, and in section 4.5 the concepts of dominance and admissibility, which simplify the solutions of many games and clarify the logic behind the solutions, were explained and illustrated. Section 4.6 centred on methods, based on saddle points, dominance, simple probability calculations, and fictitious play, for solving finite, strictly competitive games of all kinds and sizes. In section 4.7, cases in which information about the players' preferences is incomplete or non-numerical were discussed, and it was shown how they can sometimes be solved or partly solved, either in their original form or after converting them via the Harsanyi transformation into games of imperfect rather than incomplete information.

5

Experiments with strictly competitive games

5.1 Ideas behind experimental games

Unlike most conventional theories in other branches of the social and biological sciences, game theory is incapable of being empirically tested and falsified; in this respect it resembles probability theory or statistics rather than, say, psychophysics or relativity theory. The function of game theory is to provide an abstract framework for modelling situations involving interdependent choice. In some cases, including all finite, strictly competitive games, it helps us to discover how rational decision makers *ought* to behave in order to attain certain clearly defined goals; but about how people actually *do* behave it says nothing. The ways in which human beings typically respond to problems of interdependent choice is an essentially empirical question, and it is investigated through experimental games in which decision making is observed under controlled conditions.

In experimental games, groups of subjects are presented with tasks involving interdependent decision making, and their choices are carefully recorded and analysed. A variety of decision tasks have been used in the long tradition of research in this area, but the most popular have undoubtedly been matrix games. In a conventional experimental matrix game, pairs of subjects are presented with a payoff matrix. One member of each pair is assigned the role of row-chooser and the other the role of column-chooser, and they are usually required to make a series of simultaneous choices. After each trial the subjects are awarded points, symbolic tokens, or small amounts of money according to the payoff structure of the matrix.

Various modifications of this basic paradigm are possible. In some investigations of games of incomplete information, the subjects are not fully informed about the payoff structure; in others they are pitted against opponents who respond with programmed sequences of choices; and sometimes the subjects are required to choose sequentially rather than simultaneously. The payoff matrix can even be dispensed with entirely: in negotiation games the subjects may simply engage in verbal bargaining in an attempt to agree, for example, on a price for an imaginary commodity that one must sell and the other must buy, or on how to split a hypothetical cake (see, e.g., Binmore, Swierzbinski, Hsu, and Prolux, 1993). Multi-person experimental games, discussed in chapters 8 and 9, require slightly different techniques of investigation.

It is not difficult to explain the enormous popularity of experimental games in the investigation of interdependent choice. The first and most important reason is the apparent ease and precision with which the experimenter can manipulate the form of the subjects' interdependence. The strategic structure of any two-person interaction that is likely to arise in everyday life can (on the face of it at least) be reproduced without difficulty in an experimental game via an appropriately chosen payoff matrix. Second, experimental games offer a means of studying fierce conflicts and hostile actions, albeit only through symbolic or simulated interactions, without the ethical problems usually associated with the investigation of potentially antisocial forms of behaviour. Third, the extremely abstract nature of the task confronting the subjects in a matrix game appears to enable "pure" strategic behaviour to be investigated in an idealized cognitive environment from which all irrelevant information and extraneous sources of variance have been removed. The last reason is that experimental games are economical and easy to perform, yet they provide objective and quantitative information – that cannot be obtained in any other way – about important aspects of strategic decision making. In spite of this impressive catalogue of virtues, however, the experimental gaming tradition has been subjected to a number of searching criticisms, some of which are discussed later in this chapter.

In every finite, strictly competitive game, an optimal method of play can be prescribed for both players (see chapter 4). Comparatively few experiments have been devoted to games of this type, most researchers preferring to concentrate on mixed-motive games of various kinds. There appear to be two main reasons for this. The first is the belief of many researchers that the existence of rational solutions robs strictly competitive games of psychological interest: because the players' optimal strategies are prescribed by the minimax principle and the Nash equilibrium, experiments can reveal nothing more than the extent to which their choices are rational. Second, the fact that most everyday conflicts are mixed-motive is thought by many to make strictly competitive games less worthy of experimental investigation.

Both of these arguments can be challenged. It should be borne in mind, first of all, that the minimax principle, which leads to the Nash equilibrium in strictly competitive games, is not an entirely persuasive prescription for rational choice against an opponent who is expected to behave irrationally. Even in the simplest saddle-point game a non-minimax strategy may offer the best prospects against an opponent who is expected to deviate from the Nash equilibrium. In everyday life one is often confronted by opponents who behave unpredictably – or predictably but irrationally. Against a rational opponent a minimax strategy is always optimal in a strictly competitive game, but the solution is often far from obvious to someone unfamiliar with game theory, and the equilibrium solution and minimax strategies may be difficult to find. It is clearly of some interest to investigate the factors influencing behaviour in such circumstances in order to discover some of the limits of human rationality. And although most everyday conflicts may indeed be mixed-motive, there is no doubt that many socially significant economic, military, political, and interpersonal conflicts are zero-sum (see chapter 4); the rarity of strictly competitive conflicts has probably been greatly exaggerated (Kahan and Rapoport, 1974a; Webb and Krus, 1993). For all of these reasons, the relative neglect of strictly competitive games by empirical researchers seems somewhat unwarranted.

The literature on strictly competitive experimental games does not appear to have been reviewed in detail elsewhere, and therefore a fairly comprehensive survey is provided in this chapter. The survey is restricted chiefly to experiments on strictly competitive matrix games; the literature on two-person negotiation games has been thoroughly reviewed by Morley and Stephenson (1977), Tysoe (1982), Pruitt (1993), and Druckman (1994), among others.

Section 5.2 will contain a review of experiments based on games without saddle points and section 5.3 a review of experiments on saddle-point games. There will be a certain amount of unavoidable overlap between these two sections, because saddle point and non-saddle-point games have occasionally been included in the same investigation. Section 5.4 will focus on framing effects – effects of varying interpretations of a game on strategy choices within it. Section 5.5 will contain a discussion of some of the major criticisms that have been levelled at experimental games, and in section 5.6 a brief summary of the chapter will be given.

5.2 Empirical research on non-saddle-point games

Several early investigations centred on the behaviour of subjects competing in pairs in zero-sum games without saddle points. Atkinson and Suppes (1958) and Suppes and Atkinson (1960, chap. 3) used three 2 × 2 games. Two were saddle-point games and in one of these both players had dominant strategies (see section 4.5); the third was a non-saddle-point game. Each game was played 200 times in succession under conditions of incomplete information: the subjects were ignorant of the payoff matrices and were not directly informed about their opponents' choices. The results showed that minimax strategies "were not even crudely approximated" (Atkinson and Suppes, 1958, p. 374) in any of the games. In a later experiment by the same investigators (Suppes and Atkinson, 1960, chap. 9) subjects played a 2 × 2 non-saddle-point game 210 times in succession either under conditions of incomplete information or with a conventional payoff matrix. In neither case did the subjects conform at all closely to the minimax principle. Kaufman and Lamb (1967) investigated the behaviour of pairs of subjects over 100 repetitions of four 2 × 2 non-saddle-point games, and found that "under the conditions of the present experiment, players do not learn to play a game theory optimal strategy" (p. 958). The subjects in this experiment were given spinners resembling roulette wheels that could be used as randomizing devices to generate mixed strategies, but they made little use of them: "they [did] not play any mixed strategy in the sense of choosing a given alternative randomly with a fixed probability" (p. 959).

A few investigators have, however, reported a slight tendency for subjects to converge towards minimax strategies over trials when competing in pairs in free-play experiments. Sakaguchi (1960) examined the behaviour of two pairs of subjects in two simple saddle-point games, and found that in both cases one of the subjects approached the minimax strategy after 50 or 60 repetitions while the other did not. Malcolm and Lieberman (1965) reported a slight convergence towards minimax in the course of 200 free-play repetitions of a 2 × 2 non-saddle-point game: on the last 25 trials, 10 of the 18 subjects were conforming very roughly to the minimax prescription. Payne (1965) reported a similar small but significant tendency towards minimax in four 5 × 5 non-saddle-point games played 200 times in succession.

All of the experiments discussed so far involved free play between subjects competing in pairs, and for this reason the results are difficult to interpret. As explained in section 4.4, a Nash equilibrium minimax strategy is not unambiguously "optimal" or "rational" if there is reason to believe that the opponent will deviate from the Nash equilibrium; in that case a non-minimax strategy may exploit the opponent's play to better advantage. Over repeated trials in an experiment, a subject may with good reason come to expect a non-minimax pattern of choices from the opponent, whereupon it is arguably rational for the first player to deviate from minimax also in order to take maximum advantage of the opponent's "non-optimal" play. I shall return to this point later; for the present it is sufficient to point out that the interpretation of non-minimax strategies on the part of subjects in free-play experiments is highly problematical. For this reason a number of investigators have pitted subjects against computers or human opponents programmed to adopt minimax or non-minimax strategies, but unfortunately most have used 2 × 2 matrices, which leads to further problems of interpretation. The relevant findings and the problems with their interpretation are reviewed in the following paragraphs.

Lieberman (1960a, 1962) used a 2 × 2 game and reported a general convergence towards the "optimal" exploiting strategy on the part of subjects pitted against a non-minimax programmed opponent's strategy over 300 trials, but against a minimax program none of the subjects approached minimax at all closely. The failure of the subjects to respond to minimax with minimax has been interpreted, not only by Lieberman but also by subsequent commentators (see for example Rapoport and Orwant, 1962, p. 10) as indicating "irrational" or "non-optimal" play on the part of the subjects. But because a 2 × 2 game was used, this interpretation seems dubious: it was explained in section 4.4 that all 2 × 2 non-saddle-point games have the property that if Player I uses a minimax strategy, then Player II's expected payoff is the same whatever strategy Player II uses. Lieberman's subjects therefore lost nothing by using non-minimax strategies against the minimax program, and it therefore seems unfair to interpret their behaviour in this treatment condition as irrational. In spite of this problem, virtually all subsequent investigations of responses to programmed strategies in non-saddle-point games have used 2 × 2 matrices, and non-minimax responses to minimax programs have almost invariably been interpreted as "non-optimal", "irrational", "incorrect", or as "errors".

The following findings were also derived from investigations of responses to programmed strategies using 2 × 2 non-saddle-point games, and they are difficult to interpret for the reasons outlined above. Lacey and Pate (1960) reported that their subjects closely approximated minimax strategies against minimax programs and tended towards "optimal" exploiting strategies against non-minimax programs, especially when their opponents were nonhuman devices rather than human players. Kaufman and Becker (1961) used five 2 × 2 matrices, one of which had a saddle point, and reported wild deviations from minimax in response to minimax programs in every game, especially in the saddle-point game. Pate (1967) used a 2 × 2 game whose value was negative from the subject's point of view; that is, the subject's expected payoff with optimal play on both sides was –1/8 per trial. No convergence towards minimax was observed over 120 trials, although the subjects who recognized that they were playing a losing game were less likely than the "non-recognizers" to accept the offer to play a further 120 trials.

Pate and Broughton (1970) used a non-minimax program and found a slight tendency towards the "optimal" exploiting strategy over 240 trials. Fox (1972) found that his subjects tended to converge towards "optimal" exploiting strategies against a non-minimax program and towards minimax against a minimax program. The exploitation effect against a non-minimax program was replicated in an experiment by Fox and Guyer (1973). Kahan and Goehring (1973) also reported an exploitation effect against a non-minimax program, and against a minimax program "subjects' performance was not optimal but was sufficiently and consistently close to it that arguments in terms of differences between perceived and objective probabilities provide an attractive explanation for the difference" (p. 27). Finally, Pate, Broughton, Hallman, and Letterman (1974) replicated both the exploitation effect against a non-minimax program and the slight tendency towards minimax against a minimax program. They also reported that both effects were most pronounced in subjects who were relatively low in dogmatism.

The most unusual experiment in this category was reported by Flood, Lendenmann, and Rapoport (1983). The experimental subjects were 12 Blue Spruce hooded male rats at 80–85 per cent normal body weight. Payoffs were manipulated by delaying food reinforcement by 0, 5, 15, or 20 seconds after each lever press in a modified double-lever Skinner box. Pairs of subjects played 1000 repetitions of a 2 × 2 constant-sum non-saddle-point game. The results showed that the subjects' choices did not approximate optimal minimax strategies but appeared to approach maximax pure strategies over trials. This study also included two 2 × 2 saddle-point games and a mixed-motive Prisoner's Dilemma game (see section 6.7), each of which was played by 12 pairs of rats over 1000 repetitions. Although a tendency was observed for choices to fixate on dominant strategies where these were available to subjects, the principal effect appears to have been a propensity on the part of the subjects to choose maximax strategies.

The use of 2 × 2 matrices in all of the above experiments militates against a clear interpretation of the findings. The investigators evidently believe that subjects "ought" to use minimax strategies against minimax programs and use "optimal" exploiting strategies against non-minimax programs if they are rational. But, in the first place, a non-minimax strategy is not unambiguously irrational or non-optimal against a minimax program in a 2 × 2 non-saddle-point game, because *any* pure or mixed strategy yields the same expected payoff in such a game. The fact that subjects tended to converge towards minimax strategies against minimax programs in some experiments is somewhat surprising in view of the fact that they derived no advantage by doing so.

Second, against non-minimax programs, so-called "optimal" exploiting strategies are not *unambiguously* optimal. A deviation from minimax is clearly optimal only if the opponent's choices can be predicted with certainty; in the absence of certainty it could be argued that it is irrational – indeed it *is* irrational according to formal game theory – because it exposes a player to the risk of outcomes worse than the worst that can result from a minimax strategy. In other words, against a non-minimax program a player has a perfectly rational justification, namely ensuring the best of the worst possible outcomes, for using a minimax rather than an "optimal exploiting" strategy.

In an unusually well-designed experiment, Messick (1967) used a 3 × 3 non-saddle-point game. Forty-two subjects played 150 repetitions of this game against a computer programmed to use either a minimax or one of two non-minimax strategies against them. Messick concluded from his results that "the study reported here unambiguously indicates that human Ss do not behave in a manner consistent with the minimax theory" (p. 46). In fact, Messick's sophisticated analysis of his data revealed no significant tendency among the subjects even to move towards minimax over trials in any of the treatment conditions; neither did they succeed in evolving "optimal" exploiting strategies against the non-minimax programs. These findings convincingly refute those of several less well-designed experiments described above.

Before leaving strictly competitive non-saddle-point games, some brief mention is necessary of games of timing in pure conflict, particularly so-called silent duels. Games of timing are a class of two-person zero-sum games in which each player's set of strategies is infinitely large and comprises the set of real numbers between zero and one. Unlike the more conventional matrix games, the problem facing the player is not *what* action to take, but rather *when* to take action. The initial resources of the players are limited by the rules of the game and they are not necessarily equal, but each player can make only a fixed number of decisions to take action within the time interval $0 \leq t \leq 1$. At $t = 0$ every attempt fails, at $t = 1$ every attempt succeeds, and at any other time there is a positive probability of success. The typical Western duel between two gunfighters walking closer and closer towards each other is an example of a game of timing.

Two classes of games of timing have been distinguished (Karlin, 1959). In the first class are so-called noisy duels, which are games of perfect information: when either player acts, this action and its effects are immediately known to the opponent. In the second class are silent duels in which a player does not know when the opponent has fired and missed. In most discussions of games of timing, the players know their own and their opponents' initial resources. Unlike many other infinite games, games of timing have minimax solutions analogous to those of finite games. Noisy duels have solutions in pure strategies – saddle points – and silent duels have mixed-strategy solutions. See Rapoport (1989, pp. 197–203) and Owen (1968, chap. 4) for an outline of the relevant theory.

A detailed review of experiments concerning the behaviour of subjects in noisy and silent duels would be out of place in the present context, but a brief comment is desirable for the sake of completeness. In a review of several independent studies in this area, Rapoport, Kahan, and Stein (1976) report the mean correlation between observed firing times in 34 duels and the 34 prescribed minimax strategies to be .959. The authors interpret these findings to mean that the minimax principle is an extremely good predictor of the behaviour of subjects in games of timing, both in their saddle-point and non-saddle-point forms, although the latter appear to be somewhat more difficult for the subjects.

5.3 Empirical research on saddle-point games

Very few empirical studies of behaviour in saddle-point games have been reported. One reason for this may be that the "correct" or "optimal" or "rational" strategies prescribed by formal game theory seem rather more obvious in these cases than in games requiring mixed strategies. But in spite of this the results do not suggest that subjects invariably succeed in solving saddle-point games.

The experiments by Atkinson and Suppes (1958, Suppes and Atkinson, 1960, chap. 3) and by Flood, Lendenmann, and Rapoport (1983), which incorporated both saddle-point and non-saddle-point games, has been discussed above, as has the mixed study of Kaufman and Becker (1961). Mention has also been made of several investigations of noisy duels, which may be regarded as infinite saddle-point games (Rapoport, Kahan, and Stein, 1976). Only a handful of other experiments on saddle-point games appear to have been published. Lieberman (1959, 1962) used a very simple 2×2 saddle-point game repeated 200 times. The game was presented to the subjects in conventional matrix form. Of the 14 undergraduate subjects who participated in the experiment, 10 came to adopt the minimax pure strategy consistently and 4 exhibited behaviour similar but not identical to the prescribed pure minimax behaviour.

In a methodologically similar experiment with a slightly more compli-cated 3×3 saddle-point game (Lieberman, 1960b), the following results emerged. About half of the 30 undergraduate subjects conformed to the minimax prescription 100 per cent of the time after between 10 and 125 trials, and on the final 20 trials 94 per cent of the subjects were making consistent minimax choices. Many of the non-minimax choices made by the subjects in the later trials of this experiment were, on their own accounts, motivated by a desire to alleviate the boredom of the task.

Morin (1960) presented 28 undergraduate subjects with 28 different 2×3 games, all of which had saddle points. In addition, the minimax strategy could be found in each case by eliminating dominated strategies from both players' repertoires. Each subject, acting as the player with two pure strategies, made one choice on each of the 28 matrices. Out of 784 choices, 140 were "errors" (non-minimax choices). Morin noted that "errors" were made more often in games in which the average expected value (assuming random behaviour on the part of the opponent) of the non-minimax strategy was greater than that of the minimax strategy.

Suppes and Atkinson (1960, chap. 6) reported an experiment involving two 2×4 saddle-point games. The subjects (96 undergraduate subjects) were randomly assigned to one of two treatment conditions in which they competed in pairs; the two conditions involved slightly different payoffs. In each case 200 repetitions of the game were played. The experiment was somewhat unusual (although similar to an experiment by the same investigators on non-saddle-point games described above) in that the subjects were not shown the payoff matrix and had to infer it as the experiment proceeded. They were, however, aware of each other's existence, and of the nature of the task. The results were summarized as follows: "The observed asymptotic response probabilities ... clearly show that the pure game-theory strategies are not even roughly approximated. There is not even any appreciable tendency for the observed probabilities to move away from the learning-theory predictions and toward the optimal game-theory strategies" (p. 151). In interpreting these results it should, however, be borne in mind that, on account of the subjects' ignorance of the payoff matrices, and other peculiarities in the design, this experiment was not concerned with choices under complete information typical of other investigations in this area.

Brayer (1964) presented 100 undergraduate subjects with 90 3 × 3 games, all of which had saddle points. Subjects played three trials on each game against an opponent who either chose randomly or else adhered consistently to the minimax strategy. Against the randomizing opponent, a subject's highest expected value was attainable in each case by consistently choosing one of the non-minimax pure strategies. The results showed that subjects adopted their minimax strategies 0.59 times on average (out of a possible maximum of 3) when playing against a randomizing opponent compared with an average of 2.75 against a minimax opponent. A subsidiary finding of interest was that subjects used the minimax strategy more often when the absolute value of the game, which represented the best payoff they could guarantee themselves on each trial, was high than when it was low, although according to formal game theory the absolute value is irrelevant to the logic of the situation.

Colman (1982c, pp. 85–92) investigated behaviour in a simple 2 × 2 saddle-point game designed to elicit a substantial proportion of non-minimax choices. Following Brayer's (1964) finding, the value of the game was negative from the subject's point of view (it was a "losing game" for the subjects), and in view of Morin's (1960) results, the expected payoff of the subject's non-minimax strategy, assuming 50–50 randomization by the opponent, was higher than that of the minimax strategy. The 84 undergraduate subjects made 30 choices against programmed opponents' strategies that were either consistently minimax, consistently non-minimax, or random with equal probability assigned to each pure strategy. The subjects' choices showed frequent departures from minimax. The frequency of subjects' minimax choices increased over trial blocks in response to the opponent's consistent minimax strategy and decreased in response to the opponent's consistent non-minimax strategy. Some decrease in minimax choices was also found in response to the opponent's random strategy. Averaged over trial blocks, significantly more minimax choices were made in response to the consistent minimax than to the random, and in response to the random than to the consistent non-minimax opponent's strategy.

In a post-experimental interview, many of Colman's (1982c, pp. 85–92) subjects revealed an intuitive appreciation of the rationality of the minimax principle. Almost two-thirds of the subjects exposed to the minimax opponent's strategy described their opponents in terms like "clever", "sensible", "did as I would have done", and the like, but none of the subjects exposed to the consistent non-minimax form of opponent's strategy made comments of this type and only three exposed to the random opponent's strategy did so. This pattern was reversed for comments to the effect that the opponent was "silly", "stupid", "lacking in understanding", and so on; of the 25 subjects who commented in this way, all but two were exposed to one of the non-minimax opponent's strategies.

The findings on strictly competitive saddle-point games are not quite as confusing and confused as those on non-saddle-point games, if only because there are fewer of them. The problems associated with free-play experiments and the interpretation of non-minimax choices in response to non-minimax opponents' strategies bedevil several of the experiments reviewed in this section, and it is unnecessary to reiterate the comments that were made in section 5.2 about these problems. In spite of the problems, certain general conclusions seem warranted.

In most of the studies devoted to saddle-point games, wild departures from minimax were observed in the subjects' strategy choices. In the remaining handful of studies, Lieberman (1959, 1962) found that most subjects managed to converge on the minimax strategy after numerous trials, and Brayer (1964) and Colman (1982c, pp. 85–92) reported a much stronger predilection for minimax among subjects exposed to a minimax opponent's strategy than among those exposed to a non-minimax opponent's strategy. This latter finding highlights the weakness of the minimax principle in circumstances in which an opponent is expected to behave "irrationally", because it is arguably in the subjects' rational self-interest to deviate from the minimax principle in those circumstances, and that is precisely what subjects in Brayer's and Colman's experiments tended to do in response to non-minimax opponents' strategies.

5.4 Framing effects

A person facing a decision problem necessarily interprets it in a particular way. A different interpretation of the same problem may, in some circumstances, lead to a different decision. In one experiment, for example, subjects who ate ground beef described as "75 per cent lean" rated the meal more favourably than subjects who ate the same ground beef described as "25 per cent fat" (Levin and Gaeth, 1988). The effects of varying interpretations or descriptions on decision making are called *framing* effects because they are mediated by the decision maker's interpretive frame of reference (Bell, Raiffa, and Tversky, 1988; Fischhoff, 1983; Kahneman and Tversky, 1982, 1984; Slovic, Fischhoff, and Lichtenstein, 1982; Tversky and Kahneman, 1981, 1982, 1988).

A particularly striking framing effect was reported by McNeil, Pauker, Sox, and Tversky (1982) and McNeil, Pauker, and Tversky (1988). McNeil and her colleagues studied how variations in the way information is presented to hospital patients, doctors, and others affect their choice of therapy. The subjects in the first investigation were 238 hospital patients, 424 physicians, and 491 graduate students; in the second the subjects were 792 medical, radiology, and science students. In both studies, the subjects were asked to imagine that they had lung cancer and had to choose between two therapies on the basis of statistical information. Some were given the relevant statistical information in terms of survival:

> Of 100 people having surgery, 90 will live through the surgery, 68 will be alive at the end of the first year, and 34 will be alive at the end of 5. Of 100 people having radiation therapy, all will live through the treatment, 77 will be alive at the end of the first year, and 22 will be alive at the end of 5 years. (McNeil, Pauker, and Tversky, 1988, pp. 563–564)

In both studies, only 18 per cent of subjects in this "survival frame" favoured radiation therapy. But when the *identical* statistical information was presented to other subjects in a manner designed to induce a "mortality frame" ("of 100 people having the surgery, 10 will die during the treatment, 32 will have died by 1 year", and so on), the percentage who favoured radiation therapy rose to 44 per cent in the first study and to 47 per cent in the second. The relative attractiveness of radiation therapy over surgery evidently increases dramatically when it is interpreted as a reduction of the risk of imminent death from 10 per cent to zero per cent, rather than as an increase in the rate of imminent survival from 90 per cent to 100 per cent, and so on. Numerous other framing effects have been reported, and many of them conform to a pattern of risk aversion for choices involving gains and risk seeking for choices involving losses (Tversky and Kahneman, 1988).

Colman's (1982c pp. 85–92) experiment on choices in a 2 × 2 saddle-point game outlined in section 5.3 included an experimental manipulation specifically designed to examine possible framing effects. A direct comparison was made between behaviour in two structurally equivalent but psychologically different frames: (a) an abstract matrix game similar to those used in other experiments on strictly competitive experimental games, and (b) a simulation of a lifelike strategic interaction having an identical payoff structure to the matrix. Subjects in the abstract frame were shown the payoff matrix and encouraged to try to maximize the number of points they accumulated over the 30 trials of the experimental session. Subjects in the simulation frame were given no payoff matrix but were presented with a hypothetical situation in which they were asked to imagine themselves. The scenario involved a political campaign in which the subject and an opponent from a rival political party can choose either to agree or to refuse to take part in a live debate on a local radio station, and the number of votes gained or lost in each outcome were assumed to be known with accuracy.

The results showed significant framing effects. Subjects in the abstract frame made significantly more minimax choices overall than those in the lifelike political frame, and this difference was due very largely to the fact that they increased the frequency of their minimax choices over trial blocks in response to the consistent minimax opponent's strategy, while subjects in the lifelike frame failed to do so. This implies that only in the abstract frame did the subjects learn the prudence of minimax in response to minimax through experience in the game. The frequency of minimax choices in response to the consistent non-minimax opponent's strategy declined over trial blocks in both the abstract and the lifelike frames as expected, but only in the abstract frame did minimax choices decline in response to an opponent's random strategy.

The results of Colman's (1982c, pp. 85–92) experiment showed that subjects in a conventional matrix version of a simple 2×2 saddle-point game behaved more rationally when confronted with an opponent's strategy that was optimal according to formal game theory than did subjects who were induced to frame the strategically identical problem as a lifelike political conflict. Against an irrationally randomizing opponent's strategy, the subjects in the abstract frame were also more successful in exploiting the situation to their own advantage. The consistent minimax opponent's strategy elicited the most frequent minimax choices from the subjects, and the consistent non-minimax opponent's strategy elicited the fewest, and this difference was more pronounced in the abstract frame than in the lifelike frame. The reasons for the framing effects are not entirely clear, but it is possible that the lifelike frame, which provided a "rich" decision context filled with irrelevant and potentially distracting details, may have interfered with the subjects' strategic thinking. Superfluous information may distract attention from the essential strategic ingredients of the situation, and it may be difficult to make coldly rational choices in a "rich" decision frame filled with irrelevant facts.

The findings are in harmony with some previously reported results (e.g., Brayer, 1964), and they suggest that extrapolations from abstract matrix games to strategic interactions in natural environments may be unwise. The lifelike frame represents a more realistic version of the game than the traditional payoff matrix; it occupies an intermediate position between a meaningless, abstract matrix and a naturally occurring strategic interaction. It is not known whether behaviour in the lifelike frame accurately reflects the way the subjects would have behaved had the imagined situation actually arisen, but it is almost certainly a better reflection of their likely behaviour than the data from the matrix game. What is clear is that the framing of a game can have a significant effect on the way that it is played.

5.5 Critique of experimental gaming

The experiments reviewed in sections 5.2, 5.3, and 5.4 represent only a tiny fraction of the experimental gaming literature, most of which has been devoted to mixed-motive rather than strictly competitive games. In spite of its enormous popularity, especially during the 1960s and 1970s, the whole research tradition has been subjected to a number of criticisms that are worth examining in some detail.

Many commentators (e.g., Argyle, 1991, chap. 2) have expressed misgivings about the external and ecological validity of experimental games. According to one way of classifying validity, the *internal validity* of an experiment is the extent to which its results are true within the limits of the particular subjects and methods used, its *external validity* is the extent to which its conclusions are generalizable beyond the particular experimental subjects and methods used, and its *ecological validity* – which became a fundamental concern of social psychologists during the 1970s – is the extent to which its results can be generalized to non-experimental, naturally occurring situations. Experimental games, because of their abstract and highly artificial nature, seem especially vulnerable to criticisms regarding their external and ecological validity. A typical comment along these lines is the following:

> A price must be paid in moving from complex situations in the world to simple games in the laboratory. When people are put in a simple artificial situation, one might argue, they will behave in ways appropriate to a simple artificial situation, thereby revealing nothing about how they will behave in a complex real situation. (Hamburger, 1979, p. 231)

One of the strongest critics was Charlan Nemeth (1972), who argued that the apparently irrational behaviour of subjects in experimental games "is due primarily to the essential incomprehensibility of the situation in which the subject is placed" (p. 213).

Researchers have responded to this line of criticism in two different ways. Some have claimed that behaviour in abstract laboratory games is sufficiently interesting and important in itself to warrant continued research without making any claims about behaviour in naturalistic interactions. The most influential spokesman for that point of view has been Anatol Rapoport, a uniquely important figure in the experimental gaming field on account of his numerous research reports, books, and review articles. Rapoport has consistently argued against attempts to generalize the findings of experimental games beyond the abstract and idealized laboratory situations on the grounds that the same laws do not govern "both the events in the laboratory and those of the cosmos" (1970, p. 40). Most researchers, on the other hand, are in favour of generalizing from the laboratory to the cosmos in spite of the technical and theoretical problems that this entails. In an influential review article, Pruitt and Kimmel (1977) expressed the view that "there is continuity between the laboratory and the real world"" (p. 367) and that "it is preferable for researchers to try to generalize their findings, because an analysis of limitations to plausible generalization can stimulate hypothesis building and the development of new research tasks" (p. 368).

One cannot help being struck by the paucity of "new research tasks" that have sprung from concern with the ecological validity of experimental games. In particular, few attempts have been made to compare behaviour in abstract experimental games with behaviour in more lifelike strategic interactions. After a comprehensive survey of research on mixed-motive games, Wrightsman, O'Connor, and Baker (1972) had this to say:

> What surprises us most, in our review of research, is that apparently no studies have compared [behavior] in a laboratory ... game with [behavior] in different real-world tasks. While artificiality can also be assessed through laboratory manipulations, comparisons of ... behavior across settings should be undertaken. (p. 277)

Tedeschi, Schlenker, and Bonoma (1973) stated bluntly that "criteria for the assessment of ecological validity are nonexistent for experimental games" (p. 202) and that "no generalizations about social phenomena based exclusively on laboratory experiments could be safely assumed to be applicable in natural social environments without further inquiry" (p. 203). Schlenker and Bonoma (1978) suggested in a later publication that "theoretical considerations determine judgments about generalizability, and boundary experiments can be performed to assess the limits of the hypotheses" (p. 33).

A second major criticism, at least as serious as the challenge regarding ecological validity, though less often voiced, concerns the uncertain payoff structures of experimental games. The experiments purport to investigate behaviour in games with precisely specified strategic properties, and the assumption is always made that the subjects' preferences among the outcomes correspond to the various points, tokens, or small monetary rewards assigned to them by the experimenter. But there is every reason to believe that the subjects' preferences may be influenced by factors outside the explicit payoff structures of the games. It is not difficult to imagine circumstances in which experimental subjects may, for example, prefer to receive the same payoffs as their opponents rather than to maximize their own gain at their opponents' expense. This implies that an investigator's assumptions about the payoff structure of an experimental game may not accurately reflect the subjective utilities governing the subjects' choices.

The problem was expressed most forcefully by Erika Apfelbaum (1974):

> When used in social psychological studies, however, the matrix is a payoff device; it does not refer to utilities or, speaking more loosely, to

the subjective values of the different outcomes. These values are initially unknown. ... There is no reason to assume that they are fixed *a priori*. (p. 108)

This criticism is potentially crippling to the whole experimental gaming tradition, implying as it does that investigators are simply ignorant of the underlying strategic structures of the games that their subjects have played. There is no guarantee that experiments purporting to investigate behaviour in specific games do not reflect behaviour in games with quite different – and unknown – strategic structures.

5.6 Summary

The relationship between game theory and experimental games was discussed in section 5.1. Game theory cannot be empirically tested and falsified on account of its non-predictive character, but experimental games have the potential to reveal how fallible human decision makers behave in strategic interactions whose structural properties are understood in terms of the theory. The experimental literature on strictly competitive games was comprehensively reviewed in sections 5.2 and 5.3, and it was argued that few clear-cut conclusions are justified on the basis of the published research. In section 5.4 research into framing effects on decision making in general and on strictly competitive games in particular was discussed. Section 5.5 was devoted to a critique of experimental gaming, particularly on the grounds of the doubtful external and ecological validity of conventional experiments and the uncertain nature of the subjects' preferences among the outcomes in laboratory games.

—— 6 ——

Two-person mixed-motive games: informal game theory

6.1 Mixed-motive games

Games in which the players' preferences among the outcomes are neither identical, as they are in pure coordination games, nor diametrically opposed, as they are in zero-sum or constant-sum games, are called *mixed-motive* games. This term highlights the complex strategic properties that motivate the players partly to cooperate and partly to compete with one another. A player in a mixed-motive game has to contend with an *intra*personal, psychological conflict arising from this clash of motives in addition to the *inter*personal conflict of the game. At an abstract level, a mixed-motive game can be distinguished from a zero-sum or constant-sum game by the fact that the sum of the payoffs differs from one outcome to another; it is not the case that what one player gains the other(s) must necessarily lose. Mixed-motive games are therefore sometimes called *variable-sum* or *non-zero-sum* games, but this can lead to misunderstandings because coordination games are also generally variable-sum.

Many of the concepts of formal game theory introduced in chapter 4 can be applied to mixed-motive games, but formal solutions of the power and generality of those applicable to strictly competitive games are not available. In particular, mixed-motive games often have multiple Nash equilibria that are *non-equivalent*, each one assigning different payoffs to the players, and equilibrium strategies that are *non-interchangeable*, in the sense that if both players choose strategies associated with Nash equilibria, the outcome is not necessarily a Nash equilibrium. Furthermore, Nash equilibria do not generally correspond to maximin and minimax strategies, which robs them of their normative power. Lastly, in strictly competitive games, the best payoff that the row player can guarantee (the maximin) is equal to the best payoff that the column player can guarantee (the minimax), but in two-person mixed-motive games this is not generally true, so maximin and minimax need to be carefully distinguished.

In practice, it is necessary to resort to informal or – what amounts to the same thing – common-sense analyses of individual cases or classes of games in order to discover rational methods of play or *solution concepts*, as they are often modestly called, although Harsanyi and Selten (1988) have suggested a unified general theory that invariably selects a single equilibrium point. The mathematical inconclusiveness of mixed-motive game theory is, however, balanced by its real-world applicability and the abundance of psychologically interesting phenomena, such as cooperation and competition, risk taking and caution, trust and suspicion, altruism and spite, threats, promises, and commitments, for which it provides strategic models that are often illuminating.

This chapter is concerned with two-person mixed-motive games; multi-person games will be discussed in chapters 8 and 9. The following section will provide an outline of subgame perfect and trembling-hand equilibria. Section 6.3 will outline a framework for classifying the simplest kinds of 2 × 2 mixed-motive games. Sections 6.4, 6.5, 6.6, and 6.7 will discuss the properties of the four most interesting of the archetypal 2 × 2 games, and in section 6.8 their similarities and differences will be discussed. Section 6.9 will be devoted to the theory of metagames. Section 6.10 will contain a detailed discussion of bargaining solutions for two-person cooperative games, and a brief summary of the chapter will be given in section 6.11.

6.2 Subgame perfect and trembling-hand equilibria

Informally, a subgame is any part of a game that remains to be played after a specified move or series of moves, starting at any point in the game at which both players know all the moves that have been made up to that point. A slightly more formal definition of a subgame, based on the extensive form of a game (which was introduced in section 4.2), is any part of a game tree that (a) begins at a decision node that is a singleton in its own information set; (b) includes all nodes that follow this node but not any nodes that do not follow it; and (c) leaves all information sets of the original game intact. The Battle of Bismarck Sea game, which was presented in extensive form in section 4.2, has only one subgame, namely the original game itself, which is therefore not a *proper* subgame. It is true in general that games of imperfect information – that is, games in which the players move simultaneously or in ignorance of one another's moves – lack proper subgames. In such games it is impossible to form any proper subgames out of the original game trees because of requirement (c) above: no part of a game tree can be sectioned off without splitting an information set. A game that *does* have a proper subgame is shown in Figure 6.1.

The game depicted in Figure 6.1 contains two subgames: the entire original game, beginning at Player I's initial decision node, and the proper subgame beginning at Player II's decision node. This tree may be interpreted as the game of Predatory Pricing, which was first analysed by Robert Rosenthal (1981). A multi-person extension of it, called the Chain-store game or Chain-store paradox, will be discussed in section 9.2. Player I is a

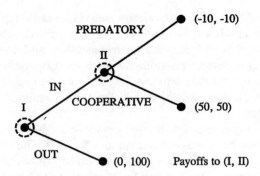

Figure 6.1 *Predatory pricing: Extensive form*

publisher (let us say) who is hoping to launch a new newspaper into a specified market. Player II is another publisher whose newspapers currently dominate the market. Player I chooses whether or not to enter the market by launching the new newspaper: thus Player I has two possible moves, which are labelled IN and OUT in Figure 6.1. If Player I chooses IN, Player II chooses either PREDATORY, a predatory pricing move involving slashing the price of its own product to prevent the competitor from building up a customer base, or COOPERATIVE, a cooperative move. If Player I stays out of the market, let us set Player I's payoff to zero and Player II's payoff to 100 units, indicating maximum profits. If Player I chooses IN and Player II responds with PREDATORY, let us assume that both players suffer small losses, equivalent to 10 per cent of Player II's profits if unchallenged, so that each receives a payoff of –10 units. Finally, if Player I chooses IN and Player II responds with COOPERATIVE, let us assume that they end up with equal market shares and profits, so that each receives a payoff of 50 units. The normal form of this game is shown in Matrix 6.1.

In representing two-person mixed-motive games, it is customary to display both players' payoffs in the matrix, because it cannot be assumed –

Matrix 6.1
Predatory Pricing: Normal Form

		II	
		PREDATORY	COOPERATIVE
I	IN	–10, –10	50, 50
	OUT	0, 100	0, 100

as it can in two-person zero-sum games – that Player II's payoffs are simply the negatives of Player I's. By convention, the left-hand number in each cell represents Player I's payoff and the right-hand number represents Player II's. Notice also that the players' strategies have slightly different inter- pretations. Strategy IN (or OUT) means that Player I chooses to enter the market (or to stay out of the market) at the beginning of the game. The strategies labelled PREDATORY and COOPERATIVE, on the other hand, have a special interpretation: they mean that Player II responds with a predatory pricing or a cooperative move *if Player I chooses IN*; if Player I chooses OUT, then Player II has no move to make; in other words, Player II moves only if Player I chooses IN.

The first thing to notice in Matrix 6.1 is that there are *two* pure-strategy Nash equilibria: if Player I chooses IN and Player II chooses COOPERATIVE, then neither player has any incentive to deviate unilaterally, and the same is true if Player I chooses OUT and Player II chooses PREDATORY: in each case, neither player could receive a better payoff by defecting unilaterally to a different strategy. In strictly competitive games, multiple Nash equilibria always involve identical payoffs to the players, but in this case, and in mixed- motive games in general, the players prefer different Nash equilibria and the solution to the game is therefore obscure at this stage of the analysis.

It is possible, none the less, to analyse this game more deeply. The normal form conceals important information about the dynamics of the game, and in reality one of the Nash equilibria can be discounted: it represents irrational behaviour and irrational expectations by the players about each other's behaviour. This emerges from an examination of the extensive form of the game in Figure 6.1. Player I will choose OUT only on the expectation that Player II will choose PREDATORY, because otherwise IN offers Player I a better payoff. But it is irrational for Player I to expect Player II to choose PREDATORY. The game has perfect information, so Player II, moving second, knows whether Player I has chosen IN or OUT. In the subgame beginning when it is Player II's turn to move, Player II effectively chooses between a payoff of 50 from the move COOPERATIVE and a payoff of –10 from the move PREDATORY. It is thus clear that, in this one-person subgame, the strategy COOPERATIVE dominates the strategy PREDATORY for Player II, and Player II, if rational, will certainly choose COOPERATIVE if this decision node is ever reached. In fact, the outcome if Player II chooses COOPERATIVE is a Nash equilibrium in the subgame, because Player II would have no incentive to deviate from it. Knowing all this, at the beginning of the original game Player I effectively chooses between a payoff of 50 from the move IN and a payoff of zero from the move OUT; so Player I, if rational, will certainly choose IN, and the outcome will be one of the Nash equilibria of the game. But this suggests that the only rational equilibrium is the one resulting from Player I choosing IN and Player II choosing COOPERATIVE.

Something important was lost in condensing the extensive form of the game into the normal form. The above argument shows that Nash equilibria can be spurious in the sense that they would never be chosen by rational players. The concept of a *subgame perfect equilibrium*, which was introduced by Reinhard Selten (1965, 1975; see Gibbons, 1992, pp. 122–129 for a brief introduction), eliminates spurious equilibria such as these by nullifying the effects of non-credible threats and promises. A subgame perfect equilibrium of a game, sometimes called simply a *perfect equilibrium*, is one that corresponds to a Nash equilibrium in every subgame of the original game. To find a subgame perfect equilibrium, first identify the smallest subgames that include terminal nodes in the original game tree, and replace each of these subgames with their Nash equilibrium payoffs. Treating these payoffs as if they were terminal payoffs in a truncated game tree, repeat the procedure, and continue in this way pruning the game tree back to its initial node. This procedure identifies a series of moves that constitute a subgame perfect equilibrium: it guarantees that the players' moves constitute Nash equilibria in every subgame of the original game. It eliminates imperfect equilibria, and with them a great deal of nonsense.

The method of argument underlying subgame perfectness is *backward induction*. A similar application of backward induction leads to a curious paradox that was first discovered by Robert Rosenthal (1981) and came to be called the Centipede game (see Sugden, 1991, for a further discussion of this game). It is a two-person mixed-motive game, one interpretation of which is as follows. Two players alternate in choosing whether to stop the game or to go on with it, and whenever either player decides to go on with it, that player is fined £1 and the other player is rewarded with £10. To begin, therefore, Player I chooses whether to STOP the game, in which case both players receive zero payoffs, or to GO, in which case Player I is fined £1 and Player II receives £10. Then it is Player II's turn to move. Player II can choose to STOP the game, in which case no further payments are made, or to GO, in which case Player II is fined £1 and Player I receives £10, whereupon it is Player I's turn to make another move. Once again, Player I can choose to STOP, with no further payments, or to GO, in which case Player I is fined another £1 and Player II receives another £10. After Player I's second move, whether it is STOP or GO, the game ends. Longer versions of this game are possible, of course. The Centipede game is depicted in extensive form in Figure 6.2, which looks more like a centipede when it includes 100 moves.

Assuming only that both players are rational and that their rationality is common knowledge – that is, each player knows that both are rational and knows that the other knows it, and so on – backward induction leads to the surprising conclusion that Player I should stop the game at the very first move. Suppose the game has reached the third decision node at which Player I is about to make the last move of the game. Player I can choose to STOP or to GO, but the only rational choice is to STOP and pocket the payoff of £9,

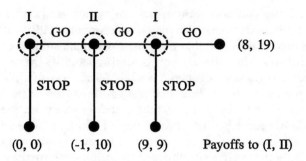

Figure 6.2 *The Centipede game*

rather than to GO and receive a lesser payoff of £8. This means that at the previous decision node, Player II effectively chooses between stopping the game and receiving £10 or continuing it and receiving £9 when Player I, who is assumed to be rational, responds by stopping the game on the following move; Player II will therefore choose STOP at the second decision node. This in turn means that Player I, at the first decision node of the game, effectively chooses between stopping the game immediately and receiving a zero payoff or going on and losing £1 when Player II stops the game at the second node. Player I will therefore choose STOP immediately and will be content with the zero payoff. The outcome with both players receiving zero payoffs is the unique subgame perfect equilibrium point of the game – in fact it is the unique Nash equilibrium of any kind. Even if the Centipede has 100 feet and has enormous payoffs towards its head, the backward induction argument leads inexorably to the same conclusion: Player I, if rational, will stop the game at the very first move, in spite of the fact that vastly better payoffs are guaranteed for both players if they both go on with the game. This conclusion (in common with an analogous conclusion regarding the multi-person Chain-store game to be discussed in chapter 9) is extremely puzzling, as many commentators have pointed out (e.g., Bicchieri, 1993, pp. 91–98; Pettit and Sugden, 1989; Rosenthal, 1981; Sugden, 1991).

One problem with the backward induction argument is that it fails to prescribe rational choices in certain situations that might arise in practice. Suppose that Player I's first move in the Centipede game is GO; what then would be a rational response from Player II? The backward induction argument provides no answer, because it has already proved that Player I will not make this move, and that Player II knows this. In order to decide rationally how to respond, Player II would first have to understand what was going on in the game, and according to the backward induction argument, the situation is unintelligible.

Reinhard Selten (1975) introduced the concept of the *trembling-hand equilibrium* partly to deal with problems of this type. According to this approach, at every decision node in the extensive form of a game there is some small probability e that the player's rationality will break down for some unspecified reason and that the player will make a mistake, that is, an unintended move. After these small error probabilities have been introduced, the resulting game is called a *perturbed game*. When a player's hand "trembles", the move that is then made is assumed to be determined by a random process, and every move that could possibly be made at that decision node has some positive probability of being made. Assuming that the players' trembling hands are common knowledge in a game, Selten proved that only the perfect equilibria of the original game are equilibria in the perturbed game and they remain so as the probabilities of the trembles tend to zero. Thus the standard game theory assumption of fully rational players is reinterpreted as a limiting case of incomplete rationality.

In the Predatory Pricing game of Figure 6.1, if Player I tries to choose the rational move IN, there is a small probability e that a tremble will occur and the move OUT will be chosen. In this perturbed game, Player I's move is perfectly intelligible as a simple lapse of rationality, and it is no longer rational for Player II to respond to OUT with PREDATORY, because there is a positive probability that IN will accidentally be played, and Player II would then have to respond by making the costly move PREDATORY. The implication is that PREDATORY is no longer a purely hypothetical and therefore satisfactory reply to OUT, and (OUT, PREDATORY) is no longer an equilibrium point – this pair of strategies are no longer best against each other. In the perturbed game, bearing in mind the possibility that Player I's hand will tremble, Player II's uniquely best response to OUT is COOPERATIVE. As the probability e of a tremble tends to zero, PREDATORY remains an irrational move at this decision node.

To see how this helps to understand the Centipede game (Figure 6.2), consider again the dilemma facing Player II at the second decision node, after Player I has chosen GO on the very first move. The first point to notice is that, when the players' trembling hands are common knowledge, Player II can understand Player I's move as an unintended random error; the situation is no longer unintelligible and beyond the scope of rational analysis. The probability that Player I will make the same mistake next time – that is, at the third decision node – is small, so Player II's rational move in the perturbed game is still to choose STOP and to take the payoff of £10 rather than to choose GO with a very high probability $(1 - e)$ of a payoff of £9 and a tiny probability e of £19 (in the event of Player I's hand trembling with probability e at the following decision node). This implies that, at this second decision node, Player II's best strategy is STOP irrespective of Player I's intended choice at the first decision node. If Player I intends to choose STOP at the first decision node, Player II's best reply, in case Player I's hand trembles and the game actually continues, is to choose STOP at the second decision node. In the original game, it was costless for Player II to choose

GO in reply to Player I's STOP, because no payoffs were involved. But in the perturbed game, GO is a bad response to STOP because Player I's hand may tremble and payoffs may ensue. As the probabilities of random lapses tend to zero, the only equilibrium in the game is the one in which both players choose STOP regardless of the other player's choices, and this is therefore the unique subgame perfect equilibrium of the Centipede game. Trembling-hand theory allows mistakes to coexist with rationality and provides a rationale for players' responses to seemingly irrational moves. More generally, it refines the concept of the Nash equilibrium and provides a method for determining subgame perfect equilibria.

6.3 Classification of 2 × 2 mixed-motive games

The range of strategic possibilities in mixed-motive interactions is so unimaginably vast that theorists and experimentalists have tended to concentrate mainly on the simplest cases. Because a strategic interaction requires a minimum of two decision makers each faced with a choice between a minimum of two strategies, the simplest conceivable mixed-motive games are 2 × 2.

In formal game theory, the payoffs are assumed to be utilities measured on interval scales (see sections 1.2 and 4.7), and an interval-scale classification scheme for all 2 × 2 games has been devised by Richard Harris (1969a, 1972). For most practical purposes, however, a simpler ordinal-scale scheme proposed by Rapoport and Guyer (1966) is sufficient. This system ignores differences of degree and considers only the order of preference of the outcomes from the point of view of each player. Games in which the ordinal relations among the payoffs are the same are regarded as strategically equivalent in this system of classification. Using ordinal assumptions, Rapoport and Guyer were able to show that there are exactly 78 strategically distinct 2 × 2 games. No one has yet attempted to classify larger games in this way because there are, for example, in excess of 1828 million strategically distinct 3 × 3 games.

Among the 78 2 × 2 games, 12 are symmetric in the sense that the situation is unchanged if the players swap roles. Eight of these symmetric games possess *optimal equilibrium points* corresponding to dominant strategies of both players, and these are considered to be strategically uninteresting. An example of such a game is shown in Matrix 6.2.

The payoffs in Matrix 6.2 have only ordinal significance, as explained above. That is, 3 represents "best", 2 "second best", and 1 "worst". It is clear that both players have dominant strategies and that the corresponding outcome is optimal for both. Row 1 is at least as good from Player I's point of view as row 2 whichever column Player II chooses, and it is better if Player II chooses column 1, and column 1 is at least as good for Player II as

Matrix 6.2
Optimal Equilibrium Point

II

		1	2
	1	3, 3	1, 2
I			
	2	2, 1	1, 1

column 2 whichever row Player I chooses, and it is better if Player I chooses row 1. If both players choose their dominant strategies – which is clearly the only rational way to play this game – then both receive their best possible payoffs. The outcome in the top left-hand cell is a Nash equilibrium because neither player has any incentive to deviate from it unilaterally. Experimental evidence outlined in section 7.2 reveals, however, that subjects do not invariably choose their dominant strategies in games with optimal equilibrium points. This suggests that their subjective preferences do not correspond to the explicit payoff structures of the games they are supposed to be playing. Instead of simply aiming for the best possible payoff, a player may, for example, prefer to spite the "opponent" by maximizing the difference between their respective payoffs. This implies, of course, that the player has changed the payoff structure of the game.

There are only four symmetric 2 × 2 games without optimal equilibria, and they are strategically interesting. Two of them have attracted a great deal of attention from experimental investigators. The four basic structures have been described by Rapoport (1967b) as the archetypes of the 2 × 2 game. The least well known of these archetypes is discussed in the following section.

6.4 Leader

The ordinal payoff structure of the game of Leader is shown in Matrix 6.3. This strategic structure arises in numerous everyday interactions, but the following familiar example will suffice to illustrate its essential properties. Two motorists are waiting to enter a heavy stream of traffic at an intersection, and both are in a hurry to get to their destinations. When a gap in the traffic occurs, each must decide whether to concede the right of way to the other (C) or to drive into the gap (D). If both concede, both will be delayed, which is the second-to-worst outcome for both, with payoffs of (2, 2). If both drive out together, a collision may occur (1, 1). But if one drives

Matrix 6.3 *Leader*

II

		C	D
I	C	2, 2	3, 4
	D	4, 3	1, 1

out while the other concedes the right of way, then the leader will be able to proceed immediately (the best payoff) and the follower will have to wait a few seconds longer (the second best payoff). Depending on who is leader, the payoffs are (4, 3) or (3, 4). The payoffs shown in Matrix 6.3 agree with these common-sense assumptions about the motorists' orders of preference among the possible outcomes.

There are no dominant strategies in the game of Leader; neither player has a strategy that yields a preferable payoff irrespective of the other's choice. According to the maximin principle – the cautious policy of ensuring the best of the worst possible outcomes and hence avoiding the worst possible outcomes – both players should choose C; this ensures that neither can receive a payoff less than 2 (the possibility of a collision is ruled out). But the maximin strategies do not constitute a Nash equilibrium, because each player would have an incentive to deviate unilaterally from that outcome; in other words, each player would have cause to regret this choice when the other's strategy was revealed. This illustrates the complete collapse of the maximin principle as a prescription for rational choice in mixed-motive games.

There are in fact two pure-strategy Nash equilibria in Matrix 6.3, in the top right-hand and bottom left-hand cells respectively. If Player I chooses D, Player II can do no better than to choose C and vice versa; neither can benefit by deviating unilaterally from such an equilibrium outcome. But Player I prefers the (D, C) Nash equilibrium and Player II the (C, D) one. Formal game theory provides no satisfactory way of resolving this difference of opinion. In a lifelike strategic interaction with the structure of Matrix 6.3, however, a sensible way of choosing may emerge from the fact that both participants recognize one of the Nash equilibria to be more *salient* than the other. The concept of salience was discussed at length in chapter 3 in connection with coordination games. In the example above of manoeuvring in traffic, cultural factors outside the abstract structure of the game may guide the motorists towards a practical solution based on salience. They may, for example, tacitly agree on the principle of "first come, first served", or if one is a (chivalrous) man and the other a (non-feminist) woman, on the principle of "ladies first", or if the game is repeated a number of times the players may agree tacitly to alternate in playing the roles of "leader" and "follower". In sharp contrast to strictly competitive games, it can be in the players' interests in a mixed-motive game to communicate with each other; the motorists may smile, glower, gesticulate, or flash their headlamps, for example. Informal considerations like these are often necessary in order to find sensible ways of playing mixed-motive games which, after all, share some of the properties of coordination games. But there is no completely rigorous criterion of rationality in these cases.

6.5 Battle of the Sexes

The ordinal structure of the second of the four archetypal 2 × 2 games is depicted in Matrix 6.4 (which is actually an improved version of Luce and Raiffa's model of the marital problem). The following well-known predicament, christened "Battle of the Sexes" by Luce and Raiffa (1957, p. 91), provides an interpretation of Matrix 6.4. A married couple has to choose between two options for an evening's entertainment. The man prefers one kind of entertainment and the woman the other (a prize fight and a ballet, in Luce and Raiffa's stereotyped version), but both would rather go out together than alone. If both opt for their first choices (C, C), each ends up going out alone, with payoffs (2, 2), and a worse outcome with payoffs of (1, 1) results if both make the heroic sacrifice of going to the entertainments they dislike (D, D). If one chooses his or her preferred option and the other plays the role of hero, however, the payoffs (4, 3) or (3, 4) are better for both, but not quite as good for the hero as for the hero's partner.

Battle of the Sexes resembles Leader in many ways. Neither player has a dominant strategy, the maximin strategies intersect in the non-equilibrium (C, C) outcome, and both (C, D) and (D, C) are in equilibrium. A player who deviates unilaterally from maximin in Battle of the Sexes, however, benefits

Matrix 6.4 *Battle of the Sexes*

II

		C	D
I	C	2, 2	4, 3
	D	3, 4	1, 1

less from doing so than the other player and may therefore be described as a hero (Rapoport, 1967b), whereas a player who deviates unilaterally in Leader benefits more than the other player. In Battle of the Sexes, as in Leader, a player can gain an advantage by communicating with the other player in order to indicate a binding commitment to choose the *D* strategy. The man may, for instance, announce that he is irrevocably committed to his chosen entertainment. If the woman acts in her own best interests, this will work to his advantage, but he has the problem of convincing her that his commitment is really binding. One way of solving this problem would be to produce a pair of tickets that he has already bought although, as Luce and Raiffa (1957) have pointed out, "to some spirited females, such an offhand dictatorial procedure is resented with sufficient ferocity to alter drastically the utilities involved in the payoff matrix" (p. 91). The problem of credible commitment plays a central role in many mixed-motive interactions. As I commented elsewhere:

> The most striking conclusion that has emerged from a theoretical analysis of such situations is somewhat counter-intuitive; it contradicts conventional wisdom and "common sense". It is that bargaining power derives largely from some voluntary and irreversible sacrifice of freedom of choice. "Keeping all options open" is a faulty policy based on incomplete understanding, and one that may significantly weaken one's bargaining position. The practice among invading armies of burning their bridges (or boats) and thereby voluntarily relinquishing the option of withdrawing is strategically analogous to the tactic of the suffragettes of chaining themselves to the railings. By this action they rendered themselves impervious to threats to disperse or be punished. (Colman, 1975, p. 20)

The strategy of commitment arises in an especially ugly form in the following game.

6.6 Chicken

The third of the archetypal 2 × 2 games, whose ordinal structure is shown in Matrix 6.5, is one that has attracted a certain amount of empirical research.

Matrix 6.5 depicts the ordinal structure of Chicken, the prototype of the dangerous game (Swingle, 1970a). Its name derives from various versions of a gruesome pastime that originated among Californian teenagers in the 1930s and became notorious in 1955 through Nicholas Ray's powerful film, *Rebel Without a Cause*, starring James Dean. The game itself is, of course, as old as time. Schelling (1966, p. 117) cites an example from Homer's *Iliad* in which Antilochos won a game of Chicken against Menelaos 3000 years ago. The most familiar version is this: two motorists speed towards each other. Each has the option of swerving to avoid a head-on collision and thereby

Matrix 6.5 *Chicken*

II

		C	D
	C	3, 3	2, 4
I			
	D	4, 2	1, 1

being "chicken" (C) or of resolutely driving straight ahead (D). If both players are "chicken", the outcome is a draw with payoffs of (3, 3), and if both drive straight ahead, they risk death or serious injury (1, 1). But if one chickens out by swerving while the other exploits this cautious choice by driving straight on, the "chicken" loses face (but is not killed), and the "exploiter" wins a prestige victory based on courage or *machismo*, (2, 4) or (4, 2) depending on who is chicken.

Once again, there are no dominant strategies and the maximin strategies intersect in the (C, C) outcome. This outcome is not a Nash equilibrium, so a player can benefit by deviating unilaterally from it. The pure-strategy Nash equilibria in Chicken are the asymmetric (C, D) and (D, C) outcomes. The "exploiter" who deviates unilaterally from maximin gains an advantage and, in contrast to the games examined above, invariably affects the other player adversely by so doing. By trying to get the maximum payoff, the "exploiter" not only harms the other player but also exposes both players to the risk of a disastrous outcome. This is what makes Chicken a dangerous game.

The game of Chicken has some very peculiar properties. The first is its compulsive character: it is impossible to avoid playing with someone who is insistent. A person who has refused a challenge to play Chicken has effectively played and lost. The second peculiarity concerns the effects of commitment. A player who succeeds in making a credible commitment to choose the risky D strategy is bound to win at the expense of the other player, provided the other player is rational. This provides a game theory interpretation of the motto "Who dares wins" of the dreaded British Special Air Service (SAS). A person who enjoys a reputation of recklessness is at a decided advantage in a game of Chicken on account of the fear that this induces in any rational opponent. For this very reason, long-term prisoners often cultivate reputations for recklessness, as the following quotation from a famous ex-convict illustrates:

> A con like "Harry", who had a record of violent assaults on both warders and other prisoners, could come into the T.V. room and virtually dictate what programme would be watched. With no more than a perfunctory

remark such as, "What, we having the film on?" as he switched to the programme of his choice, he could control what thirty other cons were going to watch. On one occasion when I observed him do this, I'd just witnessed a show of hands which had voted for the programme which Harry had turned off. Nobody, however, protested at Harry's action. The next day I casually questioned some of the cons who'd acquiesced to Harry's demands. A few gave an account of what happened which accorded with the reality of the incident. "Well, Harry gets his own way 'cause he can have a right row", one replied. Other cons, though, rationalized explanations for what happened in order to protect their self-image from the implication that they'd backed down. ... Another commented, "I couldn't give a fuck what was on. Like the film or the football, what's the difference?". Yet this con, like the others, had voted for the football which Harry had decided wouldn't be watched. (McVicar, 1981, pp. 225–226)

If a game of Chicken is repeated a number of times, a player who gains an early advantage is likely to maintain and increase it: nothing succeeds like success in the field of brinkmanship. Players who have successfully exploited others gain confidence in their ability to get away with the risky strategy in the future, and this makes their opponents all the more fearful of deviating from the cautious maximin strategy.

A third peculiarity of Chicken revolves around what Daniel Ellsberg (cited in Schelling, 1960, p. 13) called "the political uses of madness". A player who is seen to be irrational, not in control, or frankly "crazy", gains a paradoxical advantage in a game of Chicken: people tend to give a wide berth to a lunatic. The following imaginary example, in which a player of automobile Chicken deliberately acts irrationally in order to create fear in the opponent and thereby gain a strategic advantage, is taken from Herman Kahn's (1965) book *On Escalation*:

The "skilful" player may get into the car quite drunk, throwing whisky bottles out of the window to make it clear to everybody just how drunk he is. He wears very dark glasses so that it is obvious that he cannot see much, if anything. As soon as the car reaches high speed, he takes the steering wheel and throws it out of the window. If his opponent is watching, he has won. If his opponent is not watching, he has a problem; likewise if both players try this strategy. (p. 11)

The American president Richard Nixon reportedly used the same principle during the Vietnam war. He told his aide H. R. Haldeman: "I call it the Madman Theory, Bob. I want the North Vietnamese to believe that I've reached the point where I might do *anything* to stop the war. We'll just slip the word to them that 'for God's sake, you know Nixon is obsessed about Communism. We can't restrain him when he's angry – and he has his hand on the nuclear button' and Ho Chi Minh himself will be in Paris in two days begging for peace" (Haldeman and DiMona, 1978, p. 83).

Small children are remarkably adept at the political uses of madness, and so are some inmates of psychiatric hospitals. Even at the level of international politics, Adolf Hitler won a series of important games of Chicken largely on account of his carefully cultivated reputation for irrationality. It is ironical that game theory, a discipline devoted to the logic of rational decision making, should provide a strategic justification for irrationality.

The game of Chicken has been used to model a variety of incidents involving bilateral threats in national and international politics. One encounter with the strategic structure of Chicken was the Cuban missile crisis of October 1962, involving the United States and the Soviet Union (as it then was), which brought the world to the brink of a nuclear holocaust. The crisis was precipitated by the discovery of Soviet nuclear missile emplacements in Cuba. The two major strategies considered by the United States were (a) to mount a naval blockade of the island, and (b) to launch a "surgical" air strike to knock out the missiles. The Soviet leaders had to choose between (a) withdrawing, and (b) maintaining their missiles. A model of this situation, based on game theory analyses by Howard (1971, pp. 181–184) and Brams (1975, pp. 39–47; 1976, pp. 114–126) is shown in Matrix 6.6.

Matrix 6.6 *Cuban Missile Crisis*

USSR

		Withdraw	Maintain
US	Blockade	3, 3 Compromise	2, 4 Soviet victory
	Air strike	4, 2 US victory	1, 1 Nuclear war

In the event, the United States chose the naval blockade and the Soviet Union (USSR) chose to withdraw its missiles. On 28 October 1962 the crisis ended and the immediate danger of a thermonuclear war was averted. Dean Rusk, the United States Secretary of State, commented revealingly: "We're eyeball to eyeball, and the other fellow just blinked" (quoted in Cohen and Cohen, 1980, p. 289).

It is obvious that the same strategic structure underlies many industrial disputes in which a failure on the part of either management or union to yield leads to an outcome, such as the bankrupting of the firm, that is disastrous for both sides. There is no completely convincing rational solution to such disputes, or to other Chicken-type strategic interactions.

6.7 Prisoner's Dilemma

The ordinal structure of the last and most interesting of the four archetypal 2 × 2 games, and the one that has generated by far the most empirical research, is shown in Matrix 6.7.

Matrix 6.7 *Prisoner's Dilemma*

II

		C	D
I	C	3, 3	1, 4
	D	4, 1	2, 2

Attention was first drawn to this peculiar game by Merrill Flood and Melvin Dresher at the RAND Corporation in 1950 or 1951, and shortly thereafter Albert W. Tucker named it "Prisoner's Dilemma" for a seminar on game theory in the psychology department of Stanford University (Raiffa, 1992; Straffin, 1980). The name derives from the following imaginary strategic interaction. Two people are arrested and charged with involvement in a serious crime. They are held in separate cells and prevented from communicating with each other. The police have insufficient evidence to obtain a conviction unless at least one of the them discloses certain incriminating information. Each prisoner is faced with a choice between concealing information from the police (C) and disclosing it (D). If both conceal, both will be acquitted (3, 3). If both disclose, both will be convicted (2, 2). If only one prisoner discloses the information, that prisoner will not only be acquitted but will receive a reward for giving Queen's evidence, while the "martyr" who conceals the information will receive an especially heavy sentence from the court: (4, 1) or (1, 4) depending on who discloses and who conceals. These payoffs are assumed to take into account the players' moral attitudes towards obstructing the course of justice, betraying a comrade, and so on; for some people in the situation described in the story, the payoffs would not correspond to the Prisoner's Dilemma game. It is customary to interpret the *C* strategies as cooperative and the *D* strategies as defecting choices.

An intuitively more vivid interpretation due to Douglas Hofstadter (1983) is the following. Player I is very keen to buy some item (a diamond, say) from Player II for a price that has been agreed, and Player II is very keen to sell it for that price. For some unspecified reason, the trade must take place in secret. Each player agrees to leave a bag at an agreed place in the woods and to pick up the other's bag at a different agreed place. If they both choose cooperatively to leave full bags, the outcome (*C, C*) is satisfying to them both. Each player fears that the other may choose *D* and leave an empty bag, but *whether the other player leaves a full or an empty bag* each player obtains a better payoff by leaving an empty bag than a full one: Player I gets the diamond for nothing if Player II cooperates and avoids paying out for nothing if Player II defects, and Player II gets paid without giving up the diamond if Player I cooperates and avoids giving it up for nothing if Player I defects. If both players follow this logic, they will both leave empty bags, but they would both have been better off if they had both cooperated.

The Prisoner's Dilemma game presents a genuine paradox. The *D* strategies are dominant for both players, because each receives a larger payoff by choosing *D* than by choosing *C* against either counter-strategy of the other player. The maximin strategies intersect in the (*D, D*) outcome, which is the only Nash equilibrium in the game: neither player has any incentive to deviate from a *D* choice if the other also chooses *D*. In other words, it is in the interest of each player to disclose the incriminating evidence (or to leave an empty bag) *whatever* the other player does. But – and this is the paradox – if both players adopt this individualistic approach, the payoffs (2, 2) are worse for both of them than if they both chose their inadmissible (dominated) *C* strategies, in which case the payoffs are (3, 3). In game theory terminology, the dominant strategies intersect in a *Pareto deficient equilibrium point*.

In the logic of this game there is a curious clash between individual and collective rationality. According to purely individualistic criteria, it is clearly rational for both players to choose their *D* strategies, but if both opt to be martyrs by choosing *C*, then the outcome is preferable for both. What is clearly required in order to ensure a better outcome for both is some principle of choice based on collective interests.

The best-known principle of this type is the Golden Rule of Confucius, which found its way into the New Testament: "Whatsoever ye would that men should do to you, do ye even so to them" (Matt. vii: 12). But the naivety of the Golden Rule is evident; one of George Bernard Shaw's "maxims for revolutionists" was "Do not do unto others as you would that they should do unto you. Their tastes may not be the same." Shaw's point is illustrated by the Battle of the Sexes (Matrix 6.4), for example, in which the players have different tastes regarding evening entertainments. If both players adopt the Golden Rule by playing the "hero", the outcome is the worst possible one for both of them: each spends a lonely evening out attending a disliked entertainment.

A more sophisticated principle of collective rationality is embodied in the categorical imperative of Immanuel Kant (1785): "Act only on such a maxim that you can at the same time will to become a universal law" (p. 52). The categorical imperative (which will be examined more closely in section 12.4) offers no solution to games with asymmetric equilibrium points in which the players need to choose different strategies. But the Prisoner's Dilemma game requires both players to choose cooperatively. None the less, the fact cannot be escaped that this cooperative "solution" is not a Nash equilibrium and is therefore unstable in the sense that both players are tempted to defect from it. From an individual point of view, there is simply no rational justification for being a martyr through making a cooperative choice. A defecting choice not only ensures a better payoff irrespective of what the other player does, but it also has the maximin property of maximizing a player's security level by ruling out the possibility of the worst payoff.

The Prisoner's Dilemma game raises subtle problems of trust and suspicion. A player who trusts the other to behave cooperatively has a plausible justification for doing likewise, but one who suspects that the other may defect has only one reasonable course of action, namely to defect. For this reason there is a tendency for a pair of players to adopt increasingly similar patterns of play when the game is repeated a number of times. Exactly the opposite tendency is built into the dynamic structure of the game of Chicken, as explained earlier, on account of its asymmetric equilibrium points. The payoff matrices of the two games look rather similar, but they could hardly be more dissimilar in their strategic properties.

Although it is customary to interpret a C choice in the Prisoner's Dilemma game as cooperative and a D choice as competitive, it is important to bear in mind that cooperation also necessarily involves an element of risk. Players are likely to be cooperative, if they are rational, only in an atmosphere of mutual trust. Defecting choices are relatively safe and may be motivated by suspicious defensiveness rather than competitiveness. Whether or not it is sensible to trust the other player in a strategic interaction depends ultimately on the circumstances in which people typically behave in trustworthy or untrustworthy ways. This is an empirical question that needs to be investigated by experimental methods. The relevant experimental findings are outlined in chapter 7.

Everyday strategic interactions often turn out, on analysis, to correspond to the Prisoner's Dilemma game. Lumsden (1973) showed empirically that the preferences of Greek and Turkish Cypriots make the Cyprus conflict a Prisoner's Dilemma game. The following example was discovered by Rapoport (1962) in Puccini's opera Tosca. Tosca's lover has been condemned to death, but the police chief, Scarpia, offers to save his life by instructing the firing squad to use blank cartridges in return for Tosca's sexual favours. Both protagonists face a choice between keeping their ends of the bargain or double-crossing the other. The payoff structure of this situation evidently corresponds to Matrix 6.7. Predictably, Tosca and Scarpia both opt for their (dominant) double-crossing strategies: she stabs him as he is about to embrace her and he turns out not to have given the order to the firing squad to use blank cartridges. The tragic outcome could have been avoided, to their mutual benefit, if they had trusted each other.

The Prisoner's Dilemma game is a standard model of any bilateral arms race (see, e.g., Brams, 1975, pp. 30–39; 1976, pp. 81–91; Hamburger, 1979, pp. 76–79, 96–99). During the Cold War, for example, the United States and the Soviet Union each faced a choice between limiting or increasing their production of nuclear arms. A simplified model of this situation is shown in Matrix 6.8. This

Matrix 6.8 *Nuclear Arms Race*

USSR

		Limit production	Increase production
US	Limit production	3, 3 Status quo	1, 4 Advantage to USSR
	Increase production	4, 1 Advantage to US	2, 2 Arms race

example illustrates in the most vivid way imaginable the inadequacy of the dominance principle of rational choice in this game. The superpowers tended to choose their dominant strategies between 1945 and 1990, and the world was set on a course that may yet lead to megadeath. To describe this outcome as "rational" is to do violence to the ordinary meaning of that word. No rational solution based on selfish philosophies is possible, but the theory of *metagames* outlined in section 6.9 offers a possible – though debatable – escape from the terrible paradox of the Prisoner's Dilemma game.

6.8 Comparison of the archetypal 2 × 2 games

A generalized paradigm of symmetric 2 × 2 games is shown in Matrix 6.9. The four interesting symmetric games without optimal equilibrium points can be defined compactly by specifying the ordinal inequalities that they each satisfy:

Leader: $T > S > R > P$;
Battle of the Sexes: $S > T > R > P$;
Chicken: $T > R > S > P$;
Prisoner's Dilemma: $T > R > P > S$.

In this notation, the payoff T represents the temptation to defect from the jointly cooperative (C, C) outcome, R is the reward for joint C choices, P is the punishment for joint D choices, and S is the sucker's payoff (or in the case of Battle of the Sexes the selfish player's payoff) for choosing C while the other player defects to D. (The labels are merely convenient mnemonics and should not be taken too seriously.) This method of defining the games has the advantage of making clear the fact that the criteria of classification depend on the ordinal properties of the payoff structures. When the payoffs are measured on interval scales, an infinite number of instances can be found of each archetypal game. For example, if $T = 10$, $R = 5$, $P = -5$, and $S = -10$, the game is a Prisoner's Dilemma, because $10 > 5 > -5 > -10$.

Matrix 6.9 *Generalized 2 × 2 Matrix*

II

		C	D
	C	R, R	S, T
I			
	D	T, S	P, P

A great deal of confusion exists in the experimental gaming literature about these archetypal structures. Not only are games frequently misidentified, but important strategic differences tend to be glossed over. It is not uncommon, for example, to find D choices being described (and interpreted) as competitive in a game whose underlying structure corresponds to the Battle of the Sexes. This is, of course, nonsensical because a D choice in that game can never benefit a player more than it benefits the other player.

There are, to be sure, certain family resemblances between the four archetypes. Leader, Battle of the Sexes, and Chicken, in particular, share a number of strategic features in common. The first is that in each of these games there is a "natural" outcome that results if both players cautiously opt for their maximin (C) strategies, and in each case this outcome is a non-equilibrium point that is vulnerable in the sense that both players are tempted to deviate from it. Second, each of the three games has two asymmetric pure-strategy Nash equilibria, neither of which is strongly stable because the players disagree about which is preferable. Third, none of the three games has a dominant strategy for either player. Fourth, in all three games the worst outcome for both players results if both choose their non-maximin (D) strategies. The Prisoner's Dilemma game shares none of these characteristics.

Although Leader, Battle of the Sexes, and Chicken share important features in common, they also differ strategically in a number of ways. In Leader, if a player deviates unilaterally from maximin, both players are rewarded, but the player who deviates is rewarded more than the other. It is for this reason that Rapoport (1967b) described a unilateral defector in this game as a "leader". In Battle of the Sexes, a unilateral defector is rewarded *less* than the other player and is therefore described as a "hero". In Chicken, a unilateral defector is rewarded while the other player is punished, so the unilateral defector is called an "exploiter". In all three games, joint defection results in the worst possible outcome for both players, and that is what makes the games strategically problematical. As Rapoport pointed out, there is no room for two leaders, two heroes, or two exploiters. The reason, presumably, is that a leader needs a follower, a hero needs an admirer, and an exploiter needs a victim.

The Prisoner's Dilemma game is quite different from the other three. In this game the maximin (D) strategies intersect in the game's only Nash equilibrium where the payoffs are (P, P), and neither player is motivated to deviate unilaterally, although both would benefit from joint deviation. In contrast to the other three games, both players have dominant strategies that are also maximin strategies. A player who deviates unilaterally from maximin is *punished* while the other player is *rewarded* – a complete inversion of the Chicken case. A unilateral defector may therefore be described as a "martyr". But if both players choose their dominated (C) strategies, the payoffs (R, R) are better for both. The world of the Prisoner's Dilemma game is therefore big enough for two martyrs!

In all four games a maximin choice may be motivated by cautiousness, and a non-maximin choice necessarily entails an element of risk. The cautious strategies in Leader, Battle of the Sexes, and Chicken are C choices, whereas in the Prisoner's Dilemma game caution dictates a D choice. Competitiveness, defined as an attempt to gain at the expense of the other player, leads to D choices in Leader, Chicken, and Prisoner's Dilemma, and to C choices in Battle of the Sexes, and cooperativeness reverses these choices. Cautious and competitive motives therefore conflict in Leader and Chicken, whereas cautious and cooperative motives conflict in Battle of the Sexes and the Prisoner's Dilemma game.

In each game it is in a player's interest to instil a certain attitude in the other player. In Leader and Chicken, a player benefits by instilling *fear* in the other player by appearing irrevocably committed to a D choice. In Battle of the Sexes, a player who appears committed to a C choice is at an advantage and induces in the other player a feeling of *resignation*. In the Prisoner's Dilemma game, it is helpful if a player appears willing to risk a C choice, and this can foster in the other player a feeling of *trust*; furthermore, both players benefit when the feeling of trust is mutual.

6.9 Theory of metagames

The theory of metagames was developed by Nigel Howard (1971, 1974, 1987) and has been discussed by Lyn Carey Thomas (1984, chap. 6), among others. Some game theorists believe that metagame theory provides a rational solution to the Prisoner's Dilemma and to other mixed-motive games, but most remain unconvinced. The fundamental ideas can be explained quite simply.

An embryonic version of the metagame approach can be found in von Neumann and Morgenstern's (1944) classic exposition of game theory (pp. 100–105). The basic idea involves the construction of a model that transcends the strategies of a basic game. In the metagame model, each player is assumed to choose from among a set of *metastrategies* that are conditional on the strategies that the other player might choose. These metastrategies could be given to a referee who, after examining them, would be able to make the necessary moves on behalf of the players in accordance with their wishes.

Taking the Prisoner's Dilemma game (Matrix 6.7) as an illustration, the first-level metagame is constructed as follows. Player I is assumed to have the same pure strategies as in the basic game, that is, C and D. Player II, however, is assumed to choose from among the following four metastrategies:

(1) choose C regardless of what Player I is expected to choose;
(2) choose D regardless of what Player I is expected to choose;
(3) choose the same basic strategy as Player I is expected to choose;
(4) choose the opposite basic strategy to what Player I is expected to choose.

The structure of this preliminary metagame is shown in Matrix 6.10.

In this metagame there is a single Nash equilibrium at the intersection of row D and the column labelled "D Regardless". It corresponds to the familiar deficient equilibrium point (D, D) of the basic game. In order to eliminate the paradox, a more elaborate metagame must be constructed. Suppose now that Player II has the same four metastrategies as in the first-level metagame but

Matrix 6.10 *First-level Metagame of Prisoner's Dilemma*

II

		C Regardless	D Regardless	Same	Opposite
I	C	3, 3	1, 4	3, 3	1, 4
	D	4, 1	2, 2	2, 2	4, 1

that Player I makes a choice conditional on the *metastrategies* that Player II may choose. In this second-level metagame, Player I has 16 metastrategies based on Player II's possible metastrategies. One of Player I's metastrategies, for example, is "Choose C regardless of which of the four metastrategies Player II is expected to choose"; this metastrategy may be denoted by C/C/C/C. Another is "Choose C unless Player II is expected to choose 'Opposite', in which case choose D"; this is denoted by C/C/C/D. The complete second-level metagame of the Prisoner's Dilemma game is displayed in Matrix 6.11.

This second-level metagame turns out, like the first, to have an equilibrium point corresponding to the one in the basic game. It is located at the intersection of row D/D/D/D and column D Regardless. The outcome, with payoffs of (2, 2), shows what happens if Player I chooses the metastrategy "Choose D regardless of what metastrategy Player II is expected to choose" and Player II chooses the metastrategy "Choose D regardless of what strategy Player I is expected to choose"; obviously in this case both players are bound to choose D in the basic game.

The most important features of Matrix 6.11 are two brand new equilibrium points that have sprouted where rows C/D/C/D and D/D/C/D intersect with the column labelled "Same". These two outcomes correspond to joint cooperative (C, C) choices in the basic game. The first is one in which Player I says, in effect, "I'll choose C if I expect you to choose either C regardless of what you expect me to choose or the same basic strategy as you expect me to choose, otherwise I'll choose D", and Player II says, in effect, "I'll choose the same basic strategy as I expect you to choose". In the equilibrium associated with row D/D/C/D, Player I says "I'll choose C if and only if I expect you to choose the same basic strategy as you expect me to choose" and Player II says "I'll choose the same basic strategy as I expect you to choose".

The new equilibrium points represent Nash equilibria in the second-level metagame in the sense that neither player would have any incentive to deviate from them unilaterally and neither would regret the choice of metastrategy if the other player's metastrategy became apparent. If Player I

Matrix 6.11 *Second-level Metagame of Prisoner's Dilemma*

	C Regardless	D Regardless	Same	Opposite
C/C/C/C	3, 3	1, 4	3, 3	1, 4
C/C/C/D	3, 3	1, 4	3, 3	4, 1
C/C/D/C	3, 3	1, 4	2, 2	1, 4
C/D/C/C	3, 3	2, 2	3, 3	1, 4
D/C/C/C	4, 1	1, 4	3, 3	1, 4
C/C/D/D	3, 3	1, 4	2, 2	4, 1
C/D/C/D	3, 3	2, 2	3, 3[e]	4, 1
D/C/C/D	4, 1	1, 4	3, 3	4, 1
C/D/D/C	3, 3	2, 2	2, 2	1, 4
D/C/D/C	4, 1	1, 4	2, 2	1, 4
D/D/C/C	4, 1	2, 2	3, 3	1, 4
C/D/D/D	3, 3	2, 2	2, 2	4, 1
D/C/D/D	4, 1	1, 4	2, 2	4, 1
D/D/C/D	4, 1	2, 2	3, 3[e]	4, 1
D/D/D/C	4, 1	2, 2	2, 2	1, 4
D/D/D/D	4, 1	2, 2[e]	2, 2	4, 1

[e] equilibrium points

chooses *C/D/C/D*, for example, Player II can do no better than choose "Same", and vice versa. Given that Player I has chosen *C/D/C/D*, Player II receives a payoff of 3 from choosing "Same" and cannot improve on this unilaterally but may receive a *less* desirable payoff from choosing a different column such as "*D* Regardless" (which yields a payoff to Player II of only 2). Analogously, Player I cannot do better than choose *C/D/C/D* if Player II chooses "Same" and may receive a payoff of only 2 instead of 3 as a result of choosing, for example, *D/D/D/D*. The Nash equilibrium points in this metagame represent rational metastrategies, according to metagame theory, because neither player can achieve a better payoff – and may do worse – by deviating from an equilibrium point while the other player sticks to it. This is the familiar property of a Nash equilibrium, applied in this case to a metagame rather than a game.

The problem remains of choosing between the three equilibrium points in the second-level metagame. The deficient equilibrium in the bottom row of the matrix can be eliminated from consideration because it yields a worse payoff to each player than the other two. If each player assumes that the other will pursue rational self-interest, then Player II will choose the column labelled "Same" and Player I will be free to choose between rows *C/D/C/D* and *D/D/C/D*. Player I's choice turns out to be straightforward, because the second of these rows dominates the first. That is to say, metastrategy *D/D/C/D* yields a payoff at least as good as metastrategy *C/D/C/D* whatever metastrategy Player II may choose and a better payoff in one contingency (if Player II chooses "*C* Regardless").

The rational choices are thus unambiguously prescribed by metagame theory. Player I should choose *D/D/C/D* and Player II should choose "Same". These choices result in both players making cooperative *C* choices in the basic game. The outcome is a payoff of 3 to each player, which is the maximum possible joint payoff in the game. The paradox of the Prisoner's Dilemma game appears to have been dissolved and individual and collective rationality reconciled.

The second-level metagame could equally well have been constructed the other way around, by assigning four metastrategies to Player I and 16 (meta)metastrategies to Player II. Howard (1971) showed that the end result is the same in both cases. He also managed to prove that the solution remains the same if the matrix is expanded further to take account of Player II's expectations regarding Player I's 16 metastrategies. There is an infinite hierarchy of metagames, each one larger than its predecessor, starting from any basic game; but a two-person game, if it is expanded beyond two levels, does not give birth to any further equilibrium points. In general, all of the meta-equilibria in an *n*-person game emerge in the *n*th metagame.

In the late 1960s and 1970s, some influential game theorists argued that metagame theory provides a solution to the paradox of the Prisoner's Dilemma game. The most influential was Anatol Rapoport (1967a), who described the approach as providing an "escape from paradox". The first to challenge this view was Richard Harris (1969b), and a lengthy debate ensued in the pages of the journal *Psychological Reports* throughout 1969 and 1970, with comments, replies, notes, and rebuttals from the "paradox lost" and "paradox regained" factions. A different challenge to metagame theory was later mounted by Robinson (1975), and the debate shifted to the journal *Behavioral Science*. The root of the problem is that the metagame solution depends on each player being able to predict the other's strategy and metastrategy choices, and in practice a player may not know what to expect from the other. Strictly defined, a metagame is "the game that would exist if one of the players chose his strategy after the others, in knowledge of their choices" (Howard, 1971, p. 23), and a metagame solution is the outcome that results "from each player choosing his strategy on the assumption that the other players will choose the strategies they do choose" (op. cit., pp. 50–51). But players do not normally know what the other players will choose, and consequently metagame theory has an other-worldly quality to it. By the mid-1980s, the initial enthusiasm for metagame theory as a solution to the Prisoner's Dilemma game had faded, and most game theorists had accepted the arguments of the "paradox regained" faction (Poundstone, 1993, pp. 226–228).

Application of the metagame approach to the game of Chicken (Matrix 6.5) reveals a metagame equilibrium point corresponding to joint *C* choices in addition to the two unstable pure-strategy equilibria of the basic game (Howard, 1971, pp. 181–184; Brams, 1976, pp. 114–126). The "compromise" equilibrium corresponds to Player I's choice of *D/D/C/D* and Player II's choice of "Same", exactly as in the Prisoner's Dilemma game. If the Cuban missile crisis is modelled by a game of Chicken, the following startling conclusions emerge from the metagame analysis (Howard, 1971, p. 184):

(1) For the compromise (*C*, *C*) outcome to be stable, both of the superpowers would have to have been willing to risk nuclear war;
(2) If one superpower but not the other had been willing to risk nuclear war, that superpower would have won;
(3) If neither superpower had been willing to risk nuclear war, no stable outcome would have been possible.

These conclusions are surprising in view of the fact that the *C* strategies ("Blockade" and "Withdraw") in the basic Cuban missile crisis game (Matrix 6.6) appear to produce a safe outcome. But this safety is illusory, because the (*C*, *C*) outcome is not a Nash equilibrium in the basic game. The "compromise" metagame equilibrium – which leads to *C* choices in the basic game – is stable only because if one player refuses to give in, then the other will precipitate nuclear war rather than give in. The players choose *C* only if they expect each other to choose the prescribed metastrategies. This metagame analysis reveals an appalling aspect of the nuclear "balance of terror" of the cold war era.

6.10 Two-person cooperative games: bargaining solutions

The discussion up to this point has assumed that players are unable to communicate with each other in order to coordinate their strategies. An important branch of game theory is devoted to *cooperative games* in which they can negotiate binding and enforceable agreements – commitments, promises, and threats – without affecting the payoffs of the game. This form of communication is called *bargaining* or *negotiation*, and when a disinterested party proposes a "fair" or "equitable" solution, it is often called an *arbitration scheme*. The distinction between cooperative and non-cooperative games was introduced by John Nash (1950a, 1951), and the term "cooperative games" is unfortunate and potentially misleading, because it suggests games in which the players are motivated to cooperate with one another – what have come to be called *coordination games* (see chapter 3) – rather than games in which they are motivated to bargain or negotiate with one another. A better term for cooperative games would have been *negotiable games*. Furthermore, Nash defined cooperative games as those in which the players are permitted *both* to communicate *and* to negotiate binding and enforceable agreements but, as Harsanyi and Selten (1988, pp. 1–4) have pointed out, this is logically unsatisfactory and unnecessary because sometimes communication is possible without binding and enforceable agreements and it is such agreements that are crucial.

In strictly competitive (two-person zero-sum) games, negotiation is futile; there is no possibility that both players could simultaneously gain an advantage, because by definition of a strictly competitive game, any gain by one player is exactly matched by the other player's loss. In coordination games, on the other hand, negotiation is not futile but trivial, because the interests of the players coincide exactly; if they can communicate, then they can agree on a mutually optimal solution immediately without any horse-trading. It is only in mixed-motive games that negotiation comes into its own, because the interplay of common interests and conflicting interests provides ample scope for argument, and negotiation is therefore neither futile nor trivial.

The most straightforward and familiar class of cooperative games is the class of *bargaining games*. The process of bargaining involves a seller and a prospective buyer of some commodity or service. If the seller's asking price is no more than the buyer's stated maximum, then bargaining is superfluous and the transaction will take place immediately. If the seller's asking price exceeds the buyer's stated maximum, then bargaining may take place, but it can succeed only if the minimum price that the seller is really (secretly) willing to accept is at least as much as the maximum price that the buyer is really (secretly) willing to pay. Assuming that this is so, the buyer and the seller have a common interest, because both would prefer a completed transaction to no sale. If a sale does take place, the price paid will be in the

Matrix 6.12
A Bargaining Game

II

		A	B
I	A	1, 2	8, 3
	B	4, 4	2, 1

feasible region between the minimum price that the seller is willing to accept and the maximum price that the buyer is willing to pay. In the terminology of bargaining games, the outcome that results from "no sale" is the *status quo* point, and the payoffs associated with it represent the *threats* that the bargainers can use to extract concessions from each other.

These ideas can be extended to cooperative games in general, although the definition of the status quo point loses its natural interpretation. Let us

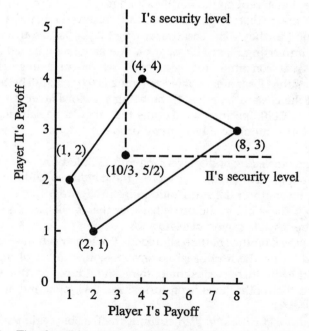

Figure 6.3 *The feasible region and players' security levels in the game specified in Matrix 6.12*

consider a specific example (taken from Thomas, 1984, p. 73). The game, shown in Matrix 6.12 and Figure 6.3, is assumed to have interval-scale payoffs indicating not merely the players' orders of preference among the payoffs but their degrees of preference among the outcomes.

Notice that the game represented in Matrix 6.12 has two pure-strategy Nash equilibria at outcomes (A, B) and (B, A), but Player I prefers the first and Player II the second. Figure 6.3 depicts the feasible region of the game in the manner that is conventional in two-person bargaining games. The horizontal axis represents Player I's payoffs and the vertical axis Player II's. The four basic outcomes of the game are plotted as the vertices of the feasible region, and by using coordinated mixed strategies the players can ensure that the expected payoffs will be anywhere along the edges or in the interior of the feasible region. In particular, they can agree to confine the outcomes to the two Nash equilibria (A, B) and (B, A), mixing only those two in certain proportions. In that case the outcome will always lie somewhere on the north-east edge of the feasible region, represented by the line segment joining the payoffs $(8, 3)$ and $(4, 4)$. They would not have been able to achieve this in a non-cooperative version of the game, because without negotiation there would be no way of preventing the (A, A) and (B, B) outcomes from occurring.

The players will obviously not accept a negotiated settlement anywhere in the feasible region except on the north-east edge, because any other feasible point would mean that both players could receive a better payoff by choosing a point further to the east (improving Player I's payoff) *and* further to the north (improving Player II's payoff). The payoffs on the edge joining $(8, 3)$ and $(4, 4)$ constitute the *negotiation set* or *bargaining set*. In the negotiation set, the closer a negotiated outcome is to $(8, 3)$, the better it is for Player I, and the closer it is to $(4, 4)$ the better it is for Player II.

John Nash (1950b) specified six axioms that should be satisfied by any rational and fair solution to a bargaining problem:

N_1 *Individual rationality*: both players' payoffs should be at least as great as the status quo payoffs; in other words, the payoffs should not lie to the west or the south of the status quo point in Figure 6.3.

N_2 *Feasibility*: the solution should be feasible; that is, the payoffs should lie within the feasible region of Figure 6.3.

N_3 *Pareto optimality*: the solution should be *Pareto optimal*; this means that it should lie on the north-east edge or negotiation set of the feasible region; this in turn means that there should be no other feasible outcomes that both players consider at least as good and at least one player prefers.

N_4 *Independence of irrelevant alternatives*: if the feasible region is extended to include additional points without changing the status quo point, then the solution should either be part of the extension (in which case it is relevant) or else it should not be affected by the extension (because it is irrelevant); similarly, if any irrelevant points are deleted, this should not affect the solution. (A version of this axiom was discussed in section 2.5, and it will reappear in section 10.5 in connection with voting games.)

N_5 *Invariance under positive linear transformations*: the solution should not be affected by multiplying all payoffs by a positive constant and/or adding a constant to them, because they are assumed to be utilities and thus measured on an interval scale (see section 2.4).

N_6 *Symmetry*: the solution should be unaffected by the labelling of the players; that is, the solution should not be affected if the players exchange roles.

Nash proved that there is invariably exactly one solution that satisfies all six axioms. If $y = f(x)$ is the equation of the negotiation set, and (x_0, y_0) is the status quo point, then the solution (x, y) is found by maximizing the product $(x - x_0)(y - y_0)$. A concise proof of Nash's theorem is given in Myerson (1991, pp. 377–379).

Before Nash's solution can be applied to a non-cooperative game such as the one shown in Matrix 6.12 and Figure 6.3, it is first necessary to define the status quo point (x_0, y_0). In the simple bargaining game, the status quo point is defined naturally as the outcome resulting from "no sale", but in other cooperative games the status quo point is often unclear. A number of suggestions have, however, been made.

6.10.1 Maximin bargaining solution

Perhaps the most intuitively obvious choice for a status quo point is the point corresponding to the players' security levels, that is, the payoffs that they can guarantee for themselves by using their maximin strategies. To find Player I's security level, we can ignore Player II's payoffs and treat the left-hand payoffs in Matrix 6.12 as though they represented a two-person zero-sum game. There is no pure-strategy saddle point, so Player I's security level is maximized by using a maximin mixed strategy, and using the methods explained in chapter 4, it is easy to find it. Setting the probability of A in Player I's mixed strategy to p and the probability of B to $1 - p$,

$$p + 4(1 - p) = 8p + 2(1 - p),$$

$$p = 2/9.$$

The value of the game for Player I is realized against any pure or mixed strategy of Player II's. Taking Player II's pure strategy A, the value of the game for Player I is $v_I = p + 4(1 - p) = 2/9 + 28/9 = 10/3$. By ignoring the left-hand payoffs in Matrix 6.12 and treating Player II's payoffs like a two-person zero-sum game, exactly the same reasoning reveals that Player II's security level is $v_{\text{II}} = 5/2$. Thus Player I can guarantee a payoff of 10/3 against any counter-strategy, and Player II can guarantee a payoff of 5/2 against any counter-strategy. The point (10/3, 5/2) can therefore be taken as an intuitively reasonable status quo point (x_0, y_0), and it is shown in Figure 6.3.

This yields the *maximin bargaining solution* first suggested by Lloyd Shapley (1953). Following Nash's theorem, we wish to maximize the product $(x - 10/3)(y - 5/2)$. We first find the equation for the north-east edge of the feasible set. The general equation for a straight line is $y = ax + b$. The points at either end of the negotiation set show that when $y = 3$, $x = 8$, and when $y = 4$, $x = 4$. Therefore $3 = 8a + b$ and $4 = 4a + b$, and we have two equations in two unknowns which can be solved to give $a = -1/4$ (the slope of the edge) and $b = 5$ (the intercept of the edge on the y axis), and we have the equation of the negotiation set, $y = -x/4 + 5$. To find the maximin bargaining solution we can substitute for y, so that instead of maximizing $(x - 10/3)(y - 5/2)$ we can maximize $(x - 10/3)(-x/4 + 5 - 5/2)$. Multiplying out the expression, we get $-x^2/4 + 5x/2 + 5x/6 + 25/3$. Differentiating this expression and setting the derivative equal to zero to find the maximum, we get $-2x + 40/3 = 0$, which simplifies to $x = 20/3$. Substituting for x in the equation for the negotiation set, we find that $y = (-1/4)(20/3) + 5 = 10/3$. The unique maximin bargaining solution is therefore the point (20/3, 10/3). A multi-person generalization of this idea will be discussed in section 8.5.

6.10.2 Nash bargaining solution

A different solution concept, called the *Nash bargaining solution* or *threat bargaining solution*, was suggested by Nash (1953) himself. It differs from the Shapley maximin bargaining solution only in the choice of the status quo point (x_0, y_0). In the maximin bargaining solution, the status quo point is taken to be the players' security levels, that is, the best payoffs that they can obtain without any bargaining. Although this seems intuitively reasonable, Nash felt that it fails to take account of the relative strengths of the players' bargaining positions. Depending on the payoff structure of the game, a player may be able to inflict great damage to the *other* player's payoff if that player fails to make concessions, and Shapley's maximin bargaining solution ignores such latent threats.

The calculations that are used to find the *threat point* (x_0, y_0) for the Nash bargaining solution are very similar to those used to find the maximin point for the maximin bargaining solution. The difference is that instead of finding the points v_{I} and v_{II} that represent the best payoffs that the players can obtain without any bargaining, we find the points w_{I} and w_{II} that represent the *worst* payoffs that they can hold *each other's* payoffs down to. In other words, w_{I} is a point in the feasible region that represents the minimum that Player I can guarantee to hold Player II's payoff down to, and w_{II} is the minimum that Player II can guarantee to hold Player I's payoff down to. Having located the threat point (x_0, y_0), which may be a vertex of the feasible region, representing pure strategies, or a point on one of the edges or in the interior of it, representing mixed strategies, the unique threat bargaining solution to the game is found in exactly the same way as before by maximizing the product $(x - x_0)(y - y_0)$.

6.10.3 Raiffa–Kalai–Smorodinsky bargaining solution

Howard Raiffa (1953) suggested a solution or arbitration scheme based on slightly different principles, and the idea was developed further by Ehud Kalai and Meir Smorodinsky (1975). According to these game theorists, a mixed-motive game should first be broken down into its cooperative and competitive components, and then each component should be dealt with in turn. The players should cooperate in agreeing to choose among the outcomes that yield the maximum *joint payoff* in the negotiation set, and they should then split this joint payoff according to their relative bargaining positions, which are determined by playing a certain zero-sum game.

The player's payoffs are first normalized by setting each player's worst payoff to zero and best payoff to 1, with intermediate payoffs transformed proportionally. This is supposed to ensure, without assuming interpersonal comparability of utilities, that the zero points and units of measurement of the players' payoffs are measured on the same scale, because unlike the Nash and Shapley solutions, the Raiffa solution is not invariant with respect to linear transformations of the payoffs. (But some game theorists believe that Raiffa's method of normalization smuggles interpersonal comparison of utilities in by the back door.) The normalized mixed-motive game is then transformed into a zero-sum game by replacing the pairs of payoffs in each cell by the value of Player I's (normalized) payoff minus Player II's (normalized) payoff. The players then play this zero-sum game to decide on the difference in the payoffs, which of course Player I wants to maximize and Player II wants to minimize, and the solution to this zero-sum game shows the relative sizes of the payoffs that the two players should receive. If the value of the game turns out to be 1, then Player I should receive the whole of the joint payoff; if it is zero, then the two players should share it equally; if it is $-1/3$ (the value of the saddle-point solution to the normalized version of Matrix 6.12), then it is two-thirds of the way from $+1$ to -1 and Player II should receive two-thirds of it; and so on. These proportions are then fed into the equation for the negotiation set line, and the particular point on the line that results is the bargaining solution or arbitration scheme.

Various other bargaining solutions have been suggested (see Binmore and Dasgupta, 1987, and the brief summary in Friedman, 1991, chap. 6). One of the most prominent is an idea suggested by Braithwaite (1955), which is basically similar to Raiffa's inasmuch as the players decide on the division of a maximized joint payoff by playing a zero-sum game constructed from the differences in their normalized payoffs, but which uses a different method of normalization. The existence of multiple solutions (or solution concepts) to two-person mixed-motive cooperative games is in sharp contrast to the unique and persuasive solution to two-person zero-sum non-cooperative games. The various solutions that have been suggested for mixed-motive cooperative games have been defended on the basis of a number of different assumptions, about which there is no general agreement, and none of them is wholly persuasive.

Surprisingly little empirical research into behaviour in bargaining games has been reported. Rapoport (1989, pp. 302–310) described an experiment by Rapoport and J. Perner, the results of which suggested that (a) threat outcomes were infrequent, indicating that players generally succeeded in arriving at mutually advantageous negotiated outcomes; (b) threats played a significant role, with the "underdog" usually getting considerably smaller average payoffs than the "top dog"; (c) discrepancies between observed and predicted outcomes appeared to be due to players paying attention to the absolute sizes of the payoffs rather than their interval values, which tends to disconfirm Nash's axiom relating to invariance under positive linear transformations. D. Gordon (cited by Rapoport) also found that the absolute sizes of the payoffs influenced the bargainers and reported a tendency for negotiated outcomes to be more egalitarian than the distribution proposed by Nash's solution. Schellenberg (1988) reported three experiments designed to test predictions based on various bargaining solutions, including the Nash and Raiffa–Kalai–Smorodinsky solutions. Each of the solutions turned out to be consistent with some of the results, but none of the solutions was consistent with all of the results. Similarly inconclusive results have been reported by Hamermesh (1973), Bartos (1974), Nydegger (1977), and Heckathorn (1978).

6.11 Summary

The chapter opened with a discussion of the mixed-motive character of variable-sum games which, in contrast to zero-sum games, generate intrapersonal as well as interpersonal conflicts. Section 6.2 introduced the concepts of subgame perfect and trembling-hand equilibrium points, which refine the basic Nash equilibrium concept, and illustrated them with the Predatory Pricing game and the backward induction paradox. Section 6.3 outlined a classification, based on ordinal preference rankings, of all symmetric, two-person two-choice games. Sections 6.4, 6.5, 6.6, and 6.7 discussed the formal and informal properties of the four archetypal 2 × 2 mixed-motive games, namely Leader, Battle of the Sexes, Chicken, and the Prisoner's Dilemma games respectively. Several real-world examples, from manoeuvring in traffic to the Cuban missile crisis and the arms race between the superpowers, were used to illustrate the fundamental ideas. In section 6.8 some of the major similarities and differences between the four archetypal games were commented on. Section 6.9 was devoted to an outline of metagame theory, the debatable solution that it provides to the paradox of the Prisoner's Dilemma game, and the surprising conclusions about the game of Chicken to which it leads. Finally, section 6.10 outlined the formal theory and related empirical evidence on bargaining solutions to cooperative games, which might less misleadingly have been called negotiable games, in which the players can negotiate binding agreements. Among the proposals discussed were the maximin, Nash, and Raiffa–Kalai–Smorodinsky bargaining solutions.

___ 7 ___

Experiments with Prisoner's Dilemma and related games

7.1 The experimental gaming literature

Throughout the period from the early 1950s to the middle 1970s, experimental gaming research centred chiefly on two-person mixed-motive games, especially the Prisoner's Dilemma game. It is not difficult to account for the attraction of experimental researchers to these games. Apart from the factors underlying the appeal of experimental games in general (see section 5.1), Prisoner's Dilemma and related games provide simple methods for investigating interesting and important aspects of strategic interaction, such as cooperation and competition, trust and suspicion, and individualism and collectivism, that are difficult or impossible to study by other means.

A necessary assumption, of course, is that behaviour in complex strategic interactions in everyday life depends, to some significant degree at least, on the principles governing behaviour in idealized and artificial laboratory games. The same kind of assumption underlies the idealized and artificial experiments through which physicists investigate the gas laws, for example, or the deliberately idealized and artificial experimental conditions created by engineers to study the behaviour of materials, but its validity in the study of social interaction has not gone unchallenged. From the mid-1970s onwards, the external and ecological validity of simple experimental games were increasingly called into question, and the balance of research activity began to shift towards multi-person social dilemmas that seemed to model a wider range of naturally occurring strategic interactions (see chapter 9).

Well over 1000 experiments based on the Prisoner's Dilemma and related games have appeared in print, and it would be futile to try to review them comprehensively in this chapter. A number of surveys have been published elsewhere, and a reader who wishes to gain a thorough grasp of the literature may find the following review of reviews helpful. The first published review of experimental games, which discussed eight early experiments with the Prisoner's Dilemma and related games, was that of Rapoport and Orwant (1962). Gallo and McClintock's (1965) review was the first to focus specifically on two-person mixed-motive experimental games, of which about 30 had been published by then. Both of these early reviews provide clear and informative summaries of the early findings. A number of other review articles appeared during the 1960s, and a short while later the first books devoted exclusively to mixed-motive experimental games were published; they were by Swingle (1970b), Wrightsman, O'Connor, and Baker (1972), and Tedeschi, Schlenker, and Bonoma (1973). The second of these covered the widest area and contained a virtually comprehensive bibliography of approximately 1100 items on "cooperation, competition, and exploitation in mixed-motive games and coalition-formation situations".

Sixteen of the items in the Wrightsman, O'Connor, and Baker bibliography were reviews of the literature in the conventional sense (as opposed to the liberal sense in which the bibliography was classified). A large number of reviews, both general and specialized, have appeared since then, and most have adopted a more critical tone than the earlier ones. Among the most relevant to the issues discussed in this chapter are the reviews by Nemeth (1972), Apfelbaum (1974), Davis, Laughlin, and Komorita (1976), Pruitt and Kimmel (1977), Schlenker and Bonoma (1978), Eiser (1980, chap. 7), Colman (1982b), Grzelak (1988), Rapoport (1989, chap. 12), Argyle (1991, chap. 2), Good (1991), and Rabbie (1991, pp. 244–252). Several more specialized reviews will be referred to in the following pages.

The rest of this chapter contains an introductory review of some of the more interesting and important findings on the Prisoner's Dilemma and other two-person mixed-motive games. The findings will be discussed under the following broad headings: strategic structure (section 7.2); payoffs and incentives (section 7.3); communication effects (section 7.4); responses to programmed strategies (section 7.5); Axelrod's computer tournaments (section 7.6); sex differences and cross-cultural studies (section 7.7); attribution effects (section 7.8); and framing effects (section 7.9). Section 7.10 is devoted to a brief summary of the chapter.

7.2 Strategic structure

Two-person mixed-motive experimental gaming has focused mainly on symmetric 2 × 2 games. Apart from the Prisoner's Dilemma game, most attention has been paid to Chicken and to the theoretically trivial Maximizing Difference game. The theoretical properties of these games, and the others discussed below, were outlined in chapter 6.

The experimental evidence concerning behaviour in Leader, Battle of the Sexes, and various asymmetric 2 × 2 games is scanty but interesting. Guyer and Rapoport (1972) investigated one-off choices in a variety of these relatively neglected games and found that the majority of subjects tended to choose their maximin strategies: the percentage of maximin choices ranged from 74 to 92. Differences across games were largely explicable on common-sense grounds. For example, subjects chose maximin more often in games in which maximin strategies were also dominant, which is entirely consistent with common sense.

In Leader, defined according to the inequalities $T > S > R > P$ (see Matrix 7.1), 78 per cent of choices were maximin (C), that is, the majority of subjects cautiously avoided the worst possible payoff that might arise from a D choice. In Battle of the Sexes (which the authors call "Hero"), defined by $S > T > R > P$, 82 per cent of choices were maximin (C) choices, in other words more than four out of five subjects followed the maximin principle rather than the Golden Rule. One of the games included in this investigation was a version of the Maximizing Difference game ($R > T > S > P$) in which neither player could benefit by deviating from maximin (C) whatever the other player chose. In this game, 90 per cent of subjects chose the maximin strategy, and the investigators attributed the choices of the remaining 10 per cent to simple errors.

Matrix 7.1
Generalized 2 × 2
Payoff Matrix

II

		C	D
I	C	R, R	S, T
	D	T, S	P, P

Experimental subjects' choices are less predictable when games are played more than once, that is, when they are *iterated* over a series of trials. Turning first to the iterated Prisoner's Dilemma game (PDG), the most striking general finding is undoubtedly the (D, D) lock-in effect. In addition to the defining inequalities $T > R > P > S$, most PDG experiments have used matrices in which $2R > S + T$, so that coordinated alternations between (C, D) and (D, C) outcomes are less profitable to the players than repeated (C, C) outcomes. When the game is iterated many times there is a tendency for long runs of D choices by both players to occur. Although the D strategy is dominant and corresponds to maximin in this game, both players are better off if both choose C. Luce and Raiffa (1957) therefore predicted that iterations of the PDG would lead to (C, C) joint cooperative outcomes: "We feel that in most cases an unarticulated collusion between the players will develop. ... This arises from the knowledge that the situation will be repeated and that reprisals are possible" (p. 101).

A year after the publication of Luce and Raiffa's book, however, Flood (1958) reported that a (D, D) lock-in is the usual outcome. This finding was replicated by Scodel, Minas, Ratoosh, and Lipetz (1959) and has since then been confirmed literally hundreds of times. It has even been found in pairs of albino rats that were rewarded with different numbers of food pellets, matching the strategic structure of the PDG, according to which goal box they ran to; (D, D) lock-ins were most common and joint cooperative (C, C) outcomes least common, especially when visual communication between the rats was removed (Gardner, Corbin, Beltramo, and Nickell, 1984).

Some illumination of the (D, D) lock-in has been provided by studies in which the game was iterated literally hundreds of times. The most detailed and thorough study of this kind was undoubtedly the work of Rapoport and Chammah (1965), who were the first to map the long-term time course of PDG choice behaviour. Their results, which have been confirmed by many subsequent investigators, showed that three phases typically occur in a long series of iterations. On the first trial, the proportion of cooperative (C) choices is typically slightly greater than $1/2$, but this is followed by a rapid decline in cooperation, which they called the *sobering period*. After approximately 30 iterations, cooperative choices begin to increase slowly in frequency (the *recovery period*), usually reaching more than 60 per cent by trial 300.

The moderately high proportion of initial C choices has been interpreted variously as indicating an initial reservoir of goodwill or simply a naive lack of comprehension on the part of the subjects of the strategic structure of the game. The sobering period may consequently reflect a decline in trust and trustworthiness, an increase in competitiveness, or merely a dawning understanding of the payoff matrix. The recovery period can be interpreted relatively unambiguously: it probably reflects the slow and imperfect growth of the "unarticulated collusion" between the players that was predicted by Luce and Raiffa (1957). The following remark from a mathematical textbook of game theory is to the point in spite of the fact that the author was evidently oblivious of relevant empirical evidence: "If ... the game is played *many* times then it is arguable that collective rationality is more likely to come into play. For although the prisoners cannot communicate directly, they can signal their willingness to cooperate with each other by playing cooperative strategies" (Jones, 1980, p. 78).

Other interpretations of C and D choices in the PDG are of course possible. Deutsch (1982) distinguished between various psychological orientations that are elicited in different kinds of social interactions and tend to favour cooperation or competition; he labelled these psychological orientations cognitive, emotional, motivational, and normative. In this area of research, most attention has been devoted to the ideas of McClintock (e.g., 1972), who distinguished between social value orientations on the part of the players to *maximize joint payoffs* (leading obviously to C choices), to *maximize individual payoffs* (for which the appropriate choices if the game is iterated depend on the choices of the co-player), and to *maximize relative payoffs*, that is, to "beat the opponent" (leading to D choices). McClintock pointed out that, because of the motivational ambiguity regarding the appropriate strategy for individual payoff maximization, the interpretation of behaviour in the PDG is inherently problematical. To be specific, C choices may reflect attempts to maximize either joint payoffs or individual payoffs on the basis of trust, and D choices may reflect attempts to maximize either individual payoffs on the basis of mistrust or relative payoffs.

When other factors are held constant, the game of Chicken (with $T > R > S > P$, and $2R > S + T$ to make coordinated alternation less profitable than joint C choices) tends to elicit a higher proportion of C choices than the PDG. This is in line with common sense, because in the PDG the D strategy is both dominant and relatively safe (maximin) whereas in Chicken neither strategy is dominant and C is the safer strategy. The most thorough investigation of behaviour in Chicken was reported by Rapoport and Chammah (1969). They found that the frequency of C choices on early trials was about 65 per cent on average, and this was followed by a shallower dip than in the PDG over approximately the next 30 trials and a steady increase from that point onwards, reaching more than 70 per cent after 300 iterations.

The problem referred to earlier of distinguishing between motives of joint, individual, and relative payoff maximization apply equally to the game of Chicken as to the PDG. This problem does not arise, however, in the Maximizing Difference game (MDG) in which the only justification for a D choice – in so far as it can be justified at all – is relative payoff maximization. Because both players in the MDG receive their highest possible payoffs if both choose C, a D choice must presumably be motivated by a desire to "beat the opponent" in spite of the personal sacrifice that the D-chooser must make to achive that end. The version of the MDG used in most experiments has the following parameters: $T = 5$, $R = 6$, $P = 0$, $S = 0$ (see Matrix 7.1). A number of investigations of behaviour in this game (reviewed by McClintock, 1972) revealed surprisingly high frequencies of D choices, which were usually interpreted as attempts at relative payoff maximization. For example, McClintock and McNeel (1967) found that pairs of Belgian students who were given the opportunity to win substantial sums of money over 100 trials in the MDG chose C only about 50 per cent of the time, and subjects who were offered smaller monetary rewards chose C even less frequently. McClintock (1972) interpreted the results as follows:

> In effect, the high reward subjects were still willing to forego [sic] considerable material gain that would have obtained if they had maximized joint gains to ensure that they would have more points than the other, or at least, not fall appreciably behind the other in score. (p. 291)

This interpretation is fine as far as it goes; the only other explanation for D choices is a failure on the part of the subjects to understand the payoff matrix, and evidence from other types of games makes this seem unlikely.

But neither McClintock nor subsequent commentators have drawn the disturbing conclusion from this interpretation that many if not most of the subjects must have been playing the game according to a utility structure different from the payoff matrix. Their preferences among the possible outcomes of the game evidently did not correspond to the MDG payoff structure. For if, as McClintock implies, a subject prefers the (D, C) to the (C, C) outcome, then, in terms of what economists call *revealed preferences*, R is not greater than T and the (subjective) game is not MDG. The findings of research with the MDG therefore demonstrate beyond reasonable doubt that subjects in experimental games do not invariably play according to the explicit payoff structures presented to them. This problem strikes at the heart of experimental gaming and has never been adequately addressed.

7.3 Payoffs and incentives

Numerous experiments have centred on the effects of varying the relative magnitudes of the payoffs within a specified strategic structure. In the PDG or Chicken, for example – and the majority of experiments have been based on these two games – it is possible to vary the relative magnitudes of the four parameters in Matrix 7.1 above, namely T (the temptation for unilateral defection), R (the reward for joint cooperation), S (the sucker's payoff for unilateral cooperation), and P (the punishment for joint defection), while preserving their ordinal ranking. Some research has also been devoted to the effects of varying the monetary incentives associated with the payoffs.

In the PDG, the results of payoff variations have usually been in line with common-sense predictions. As might be expected, when R is increased relative to P, the proportion of C choices tends to increase, and when T is increased relative to S, the proportion of C choices decreases. Rapoport and Chammah (1965) found that a *cooperation index* given by the ratio $r = (R - P)/(T - S)$ is a fairly reliable indicator of the proportions of C choices generated by different PDG matrices. The correlation between the (log transformed) cooperation index r and the proportion of C choices across matrices was found to be .641.

With regard to the Chicken game, Rapoport and Chammah (1969) investigated five matrices in which $T = 2$, $R = 1$, and $S = -2$, while P varied from –3 to –40. A strong relationship emerged, as expected, between the degree of dangerousness of the game, as indexed by the value of P, and the proportion of C choices. Subjects tended to behave more cautiously, that is, to choose C more frequently, the worse the punishment for joint defection. The authors appended the following comment:

> Penologists sometimes argue that certainty of conviction is a more powerful deterrent of crime than severity of punishment. Something of this sort may also be at the basis of the various theories of measured

response that have supplanted the short-lived doctrine of massive retaliation in the thinking of American strategists. Our results with Chicken seem to show the opposite: More severe punishment seems to be a more effective deterrent than more certain punishment. (Rapoport and Chammah, 1969, p. 169)

Two decades later, Rapoport (1989) commented that "the effect illustrates the fallacy of brinkmanship and of excessive deterrence" (p. 251).

In the PDG, Chicken, and other mixed-motive games, subjects generally respond in understandable ways to payoff manipulations (Grzelak, 1988). These findings, incidentally, seem to contradict the belief of some critics of experimental gaming that the behaviour of subjects "is primarily due to the essential incomprehensibility of the situation in which the subject is placed" (Nemeth, 1972, p. 213). If the situation were essentially incomprehensible, then behaviour would presumably not conform to common-sense notions of rational choice, which it evidently does.

The problem of incentives has bedevilled experimental gaming ever since the 1960s when it was first suggested that experimental subjects might not be taking their tasks seriously. Limited research funds and ethical considerations make it impossible in most experiments to attach anything more than small monetary rewards to the payoffs. In their early review, Gallo and McClintock (1965) suggested that the surprisingly low levels of cooperation generally found in PDG experiments might be attributable to the absence of substantial monetary incentives. Gallo's own doctoral dissertation (Gallo, 1966) addressed this question, and his findings supported the view that large monetary incentives might generate higher levels of cooperation. But the evidence was only indirect, because Gallo used a "trucking" game (see section 7.9) whose payoff structure is quite different from the PDG. Later research involving high and low incentives (reviewed by Oskamp and Kleinke, 1970) has generated equivocal results. Some experiments on the PDG (e.g., Wrightsman, 1966) and Chicken (e.g., Sermat, 1967a, 1967b) found no incentive effects, whereas others (e.g., Stahelski and Kelley, 1969) found significantly *more* C choices in high-incentive conditions, and still others (e.g., Gumpert, Deutsch, and Epstein, 1969) found *fewer* C choices in high-incentive conditions.

The only reasonable conclusions seem to be (a) that monetary incentives do not affect behaviour in the PDG or Chicken in any pronounced or consistent manner, and (b) that incentives probably interact with other unknown variables in determining choices in these games. In the Maximizing Difference game (MDG) with $T = 5$, $R = 6$, $P = 0$, and $S = 0$ (see Matrix 7.1), on the other hand, incentives do seem to be positively related to the frequency of C choices (e.g., McClintock and McNeel, 1967). This is hardly surprising in view of the fact that C choices are clearly the only rational strategies in the MDG (see section 6.3): subjects are more likely to pursue their own interests rationally by choosing C when the incentive for doing so is large.

7.4 Communication effects

In most traditional experimental games, the participant subjects have been forbidden to communicate verbally with each other; in other words, bargaining and negotiation have been disallowed. But it is perhaps more usual in naturally occurring mixed-motive interactions for the participants to be able to issue threats, promises, and commitments – in other words, to negotiate. A number of commentators have suggested that the strikingly uncooperative behaviour observed in many mixed-motive gaming experiments "stems mainly from the subjects' inability to communicate their goals or preferences" (Nemeth, 1972, p. 213). Common sense certainly suggests that communication should facilitate mutually beneficial collaboration. A number of researchers have examined this hypothesis experimentally, and the results have been reasonably described by one reviewer as "highly consistent" (Grzelak, 1988, p. 296).

One of the classic experiments in this area is that of Evans (1964). This study investigated PDG behaviour under three conditions: enforceable promises with stiff penalties for breaking them, unenforceable promises, and no communication. As expected, the highest level of C choices was found in the enforceable-promises condition and the lowest in the no-communication condition. The nature of the communication was strictly controlled in the Evans experiment, but when subjects are permitted to promise, threaten, lie, and deceive without restriction, the effects are more difficult to predict. Deutsch (1958) was the first to discover that unrestricted communication leads to increases in the frequency of C choices only when the subjects have a particular motivational set. Deutsch's subjects received instructions calculated to encourage either a competitive, a cooperative, or an individualistic set. Opportunities for communication made little difference in the competitive and cooperative conditions; it was only when the subjects were instructed to think solely of their own interests that communication led to increased levels of C choices. This finding, which has been replicated a number of times, makes sense in the light of McClintock's (1972) theoretical analysis of the motivational bases of C and D choices in the PDG. The optimal strategies for relative payoff maximization, which is equivalent to Deutsch's competitive set, and joint payoff maximization, which is equivalent to Deutsch's cooperative set, are obviously C and D respectively, but the optimal strategy for individual payoff maximization is by no means obvious. There is thus more scope for interpersonal influence in individualistically motivated pairs.

Wichman (1972) reported an elaborate study of communication in the PDG. Visual and auditory communication were manipulated separately in this experiment. Individualistically motivated subjects were assigned to four treatment conditions in which they could either (a) see their co-players but not to hear them; (b) hear their co-players but not to see them; (c) both see and hear their co-players, or (d) neither see nor hear their co-players. The results indicated that subjects chose C most frequently in the see-and-hear condition (c), less frequently in the hear-only condition (b), less frequently still in the see-only condition (a), and least frequently of all in the no-communication condition (d). It was only in the see-and-hear condition (c) that subjects succeeded in establishing and maintaining high levels of joint C choices over the series of 70 trials. The results of this investigation show that both verbal and non-verbal communication can facilitate the development of cooperation and trust and that the effects of communication are rather more subtle than was previously assumed. Presumably threats, promises, and commitments can be communicated not only verbally but also to some extent by posture, gesture, and facial expression (see Bull and Frederikson, 1994, for a review of relevant research into non-verbal communication).

Lindskold, Betz, and Walters (1986) reported the results of two experiments designed to investigate the effects of certain types of verbal (written) and non-verbal messages on cooperation in a PDG. In the first experiment, subjects were pitted against a co-player who began by intensifying the conflict through unresponsive and uncooperative behaviour (responding more quickly to D than to C choices, and coercing cooperative choices with verbal threats in order to exploit them), but after a number of trials began to communicate conciliation through analogous verbal and non-verbal messages. The results showed significant increases in cooperation by the subjects following the co-player's switch of behaviour. In the second experiment, the co-player began with verbal threats, insults, or challenges, then became conciliatory, and finally became uncommunicative. In this experiment, the subjects' behaviour changed from uncooperative in the first phase to cooperative in the second and back to uncooperative in the third. Taken together, these experiments show a remarkable willingness on the part of subjects to respond to a co-player's attempt to transform the climate of a relationship from competitive to cooperative, even when threats and insults have been issued. In this connection, see also Deutsch (1982).

7.5 Programmed strategies

A useful review of the evidence concerning the effects on behaviour of the co-player's strategy in two-person mixed-motive games was provided by Oskamp (1971). Experiments in this area involve pitting subjects against a simulated co-player in the form of a computer, or an accomplice of the experimenter's, programmed in advance to make predetermined sequences of choices. In most (though not all) of these experiments the subjects were led to believe that they were playing against ordinary co-players. The experiments by Lindskold, Betz, and Walters (1986), which manipulated programmed strategies as well as communication effects, have already been discussed in the previous paragraph.

The two simplest programmed strategies are those in which the co-player chooses either C on every trial (ALL C) or D on every trial (ALL D). These extreme programmed strategies elicit quite different responses in the PDG and Chicken (e.g., Sermat, 1967b). In the PDG, ALL C, often called *unconditional cooperation*, elicits much higher frequencies of C choices from subjects than ALL D (*unconditional defection*). That is, of course, in line with expectations, because considerations of self-defence force a subject to choose D against the ALL D program in order to avoid the worst possible payoff (the sucker's payoff). Many subjects reciprocate the cooperation of the ALL C programmed strategy, but what is surprising is that approximately half of the subjects seize the opportunity of exploiting the unconditionally cooperative program to the hilt by choosing D. The tendency for many subjects to exploit analogous *pacifist strategies* in games other than the PDG was confirmed by Shure, Meeker, and Hansford (1965), although the level of exploitation depends on a number of circumstantial factors (Reychler, 1979).

Grzelak (1988) has pointed out that "social life brings us the same experience: being an obliging person is often interpreted as weakness" (p. 296). Experimental evidence has shown that highly competitive individuals tend to judge cooperative behaviour of co-players on a potency (strong–weak) dimension as "weak", "naive", and "purposeless", whereas highly cooperative individuals tend to judge the same cooperative behaviour on an evaluative (good–bad) dimension as "sincere", "fair", and "honest" (Beggan and Messick, 1988; Liebrand, Jansen, Rijken, and Shure, 1986). Beggan and Messick drew attention to an implication of this, namely the possibilities for misunderstanding that would exist in negotiations involving both cooperators and competitors: "Although cooperators would have a tendency to focus on the rights and wrongs of the problem, competitors would be expected to be concerned with strength versus weakness. Efforts to reach consensus could be impeded by the lack of a common dimension of evaluation" (p. 611).

Exploitation of the ALL C programmed strategy is even more common in the game of Chicken, but in comparison with ALL D, the pattern of results is exactly the reverse of that in the PDG (Sermat, 1967b). In Chicken, ALL C elicits significantly *fewer* C choices from subjects than ALL D. This difference is perfectly intelligible, because Chicken differs from the PDG in that the only way to avoid the worst possible payoff against the ALL D program is to choose C. The experimental evidence on the extreme programmed strategies harmonizes well with the theoretical analyses of the PDG and Chicken outlined in sections 6.6 and 6.7.

A conditional programmed strategy in the PDG that has attracted a great deal of interest is the "tit for tat" (TFT) strategy in which the computer or accomplice chooses a cooperative C strategy on the first trial and then, on each subsequent trial, chooses the strategy chosen by the subject on the previous trial. This may be interpreted as a way of signalling to the subject: "I'll cooperate if and only if you cooperate". Possibly because it seems such an eminently sensible way of playing the PDG, most reviewers (including Davis, Laughlin, and Komorita, 1976, p. 518; Pruitt and Kimmel, 1977, p. 380) claim that it elicits more frequent C choices from subjects than other programmed strategies including ALL C, but a careful reading of the evidence does not support this interpretation unequivocally. There is evidence to show that whereas TFT is relatively effective in eliciting cooperation from individualistically oriented subjects, the ALL C programmed strategy is more effective with cooperative individuals (Kuhlman and Marshello, 1975; Schulz, 1986). The TFT strategy does, however, elicit more C choices than a randomly mixed strategy containing an equivalent number of C choices (Chammah, 1969; Crumbaugh and Evans, 1967), which proves that the *pattern* of C choices has an effect over and above the mere *frequency* of C choices in a programmed strategy.

A number of experiments have been devoted to the effects of programmed strategies involving changing frequencies of C choices over trials. Harford and Solomon (1967) were the first to examine *reformed sinner* and *lapsed saint* strategies. The reformed sinner initially chooses ALL D, then switches to ALL C, then uses TFT in the final phase. The lapsed saint begins with ALL C and then switches to TFT. During the final TFT phase, both programs are the same, but their histories differ, and this affects the responses of subjects exposed to them. In the PDG, Harford and Solomon found that the reformed sinner program elicits much higher levels of C choices than the lapsed saint program, and this effect has been replicated several times.

7.6 Axelrod's computer tournaments

New life was breathed into experimental PDGs in the 1980s by the computer tournaments organized by Robert Axelrod (1980a, 1980b, 1984) and discussed in an article by Axelrod and Hamilton (1981) that won the Newcomb Cleveland Prize of the American Association for the Advancement of Science for that year. Thoughtful summaries and discussions of this research have also been provided by Douglas Hofstadter (1983) and William Poundstone (1993, chap. 12), and the ideas have been developed further by Maynard Smith (1984), Rapoport (1984), Selten and Hammerstein (1984), Molander (1985), Bartholdi, Butler, and Trick (1986), Beer (1986), Donninger (1986), Swistak (1989), Bendor, Kramer, and Stout (1991), Bendor (1993), and Nowak and Sigmund (1993), among others.

Axelrod's work was motivated by a desire to find an answer to a question that he believed had been neglected by previous researchers: what is the most effective strategy in practice of playing the iterated PDG? For the conduct of everyday life, this amounts to asking: "When should a person cooperate, and when should a person be selfish, in an ongoing interaction with another person? Should a friend keep providing favors to another friend who never reciprocates? Should a business provide prompt service to another business that is about to be bankrupt?" (Axelrod, 1984, p. vii). Because the *D* strategy dominates the *C* strategy, game theory clearly specifies *D* as the only rational choice if the game is played only once, although it leads to the paradoxical outcome of (*D*, *D*) in spite of the fact that both players would prefer (*C*, *C*) (see section 6.7). But in a PDG that is iterated many times, the best strategy is perhaps not quite so clear, especially if neither player knows which iteration or trial is to be the last, thus evading a simple but logically compelling backward induction argument, based on the method of reasoning explained in section 6.2, for playing *D* every time.

In 1979 Axelrod invited game theorists to enter a round-robin Prisoner's Dilemma game tournament to see which strategies performed best in practice. The strategies were to be submitted as computer programs for playing PDG, and the winner was to be the program that ended up amassing the most points after each program had been pitted against each of the others in a gigantic tournament. The parameters of the PDG that was used were $T = 5$, $R = 3$, $P = 1$, $S = 0$ (see Matrix 7.1). Programs were submitted by 14 psychologists, economists, political scientists, mathematicians, and sociologists, and as a baseline for comparison Axelrod added a 15th one called RANDOM that alternated randomly between *C* and *D*, as though the strategy were chosen on the basis of a coin toss each time. Some of the entries were long, complicated, and subtle, running in one case to 77 lines of the programming language Basic, and the shortest and simplest was just four lines long. Each program played 200 iterations (trials) of the game against each of the others and against its own twin, and the tournament was repeated five times to smooth out the results.

The results were surprising. The program called RANDOM came last (which was no great surprise), but the unexpected winner was a program submitted by the psychologist Anatol Rapoport called TIT FOR TAT, which was the shortest and simplest of all the programs entered. In line with the tit for tat programmed strategy discussed in section 7.5, TIT FOR TAT cooperates on the first trial and then on every subsequent trial simply copies the other player's previous choice. TIT FOR TAT beat all the other programs including the sneaky program JOSS, submitted by the Swiss mathematician Johann Joss, which played mainly TFT but threw in a random *D* in response to the co-player's *C* choice 10 per cent of the time. When JOSS is pitted against TIT FOR TAT, JOSS's first random *D* causes TIT FOR TAT to respond with *D* on the following trial while JOSS "innocently" goes back to *C*, which leads to a (*D*, *C*) outcome. This causes JOSS to retaliate with *D* on the following trial, leading to a (*C*, *D*) outcome, and these (*D*, *C*) and (*C*, *D*) outcomes then alternate until JOSS throws in another one of its random D responses to TIT FOR TAT's C, which leads to a (D, D) lock-in that lasts for all remaining trials.

The reverberations of JOSS's attempts at exploitation, together with TIT FOR TAT's single retaliatory act, lead ultimately to a simulation of a complete breakdown of trust and lack of cooperation, and it is the original exploiter JOSS that suffers the most. The double-cross turns out to be ultimately self-defeating, and Axelrod believes that people who behave in this way in everyday life have usually not thought deeply enough about the consequences of their actions *for themselves*. This shows, incidentally, that if both players choose TFT in the iterated Prisoner's Dilemma game, if either player has a trembling hand (see section 6.2) and defects by mistake, then the consequence is an endless sequence of alternations with one player cooperating and the other defecting (Selten and Hammerstein, 1984).

After studying the tournament results, Axelrod (1980a, 1984) drew the general conclusion that, "surprisingly, there is a single property which distinguishes the relatively high-scoring entries from the relatively low-scoring entries. This is the property of being *nice*, which is to say never being the first to defect. ... Each of the top-ranking entries (or rules) is nice. None of the other entries is" (Axelrod, 1984, p. 33). The trouble with JOSS is that it is not entirely *nice*. TIT FOR TAT, on the other hand, has the property of niceness, although it always defects if provoked. There was also a second property that distinguished the high-scoring entries. Of all the nice programs, the one that scored lowest was the one that was least *forgiving*. A forgiving program is one that is still willing to cooperate at some point after the other player has defected. TIT FOR TAT, for example, is not only nice but also forgiving, inasmuch as it defects only once in retaliation for a defection from the other player, and after that has a propensity to let bygones be bygones. A totally unforgiving massive retaliation program called FRIED-MAN, which responds to defection with unrelenting defection, was the one that scored worst of the nice programs. There are big gains to be made from being forgiving and not bearing grudges indefinitely, and even the expert strategists who entered the tournament did not give sufficient weight to this quality. In general "the entries were too competitive for their own good" (Axelrod, 1984, p. 40).

The nice, forgiving programs scored well in the tournament largely because they scored well against one another, and because there were enough of them to raise one another's score substantially. In a more hostile social environment might they perhaps have scored less well? In order to find out, Axelrod (1980b, 1984) organized a second round of the tournament. He sent the results of the first round, together with his summary and analysis of the findings, to everyone who had entered the first round and invited them to submit entries to the second round. Many other game theorists were also invited to join the tournament at this stage. The rules were similar to those of the first round although this time the entrants did not know the exact number of iterations that would be played. Entrants from the United States, including a 10-year-old American computer hacker, and from Canada, the United Kingdom, Norway, Switzerland, and New Zealand submitted a total of 62 entries to the second round, and on the whole the software tended to be more sophisticated than the entries in the first round.

The results of the second round were even more surprising than those of the first. TIT FOR TAT, the simplest program that had won the first round and had been resubmitted without alteration by Anatol Rapoport, won again. RANDOM came second from bottom. Among the top 15 entries in terms of final scores, there was only one that was not nice (and it came eighth), and among the bottom 15, there was only one that *was* nice. Once again, forgiving programs generally performed better than unforgiving ones, and programs like FRIEDMAN that resorted to unrelenting massive retaliation (what might be called *mafia strategies*) tended to perform especially badly.

Two further qualities of the most successful programs, in addition to being nice and forgiving, emerged from the results of the second round. The first is the propensity to be *provocable* (or *retaliatory*, as Axelrod called it): a provocable program is one that retaliates in response to defection of the other player, and the most successful programs tended to be provocable. TIT FOR TAT is highly provocable; in fact it invariably retaliates immediately in response to a defection by the other player. But TIT FOR TWO TATS, an entry from the British biologist and game theorist John Maynard Smith that defects only after the other player has defected twice in a row, came 24th, probably because, although it is nice and very forgiving, it is insufficiently provocable. The other quality of successful programs that became apparent in the second round was *clarity*. A program is clear if it is easy to recognize and its non-exploitability is easy to appreciate. Once encountered, TIT FOR TAT is very easy to recognize, and its non-exploitability is transparently obvious. Complicated or devious programs are never clear.

According to the results of Axelrod's two computer tournaments, therefore, it appears that in order to be successful, one should be nice and forgiving, but also provocable and clear. And one very simple way to implement that policy is by adopting a tit for tat strategy in social interactions. Axelrod (1984, chap. 6) suggested the following four maxims for "how to choose effectively":

(a) don't be envious (a curious property of TFT is that it scores well in spite of never outscoring any of its co-players in head-to-head meetings);
(b) don't be the first to defect (in other words, be nice);
(c) reciprocate both cooperation and defection (be forgiving and provocable);
(d) don't be too clever (or, to put it more clearly, be clear).

Finally, Axelrod carried out an ingenious "ecological tournament" in order to study the evolution of cooperation. Each program's score was taken as a measure of its (Darwinian or evolutionary) fitness, and fitness was defined as the number of copies of the program (representing offspring) that would survive into the next generation. Survival and evolution were simulated by running successive rounds of the tournament to represent successive generations, with the numbers of copies of the various programs in each round altered in line with their relative fitness in the previous round, so that successful programs would become more numerous from one round to the next and unsuccessful ones less numerous. The results of this "ecological tournament", which simulates survival of the fittest, were that across 1000 generations TIT FOR TAT thrived spectacularly, increasing its relative numbers from generation to generation to emerge the clear evolutionary winner. It grew from 1.6 per cent of the population (one program among the 63 entries) at the start to more than 14 per cent of the population by the 1000th generation. This is especially striking in the light of the fact that TIT FOR TAT was quite incapable of defeating any of the other programs, or in fact any conceivable program, in a head-to-head contest; at best it can only draw. TIT FOR TAT won the ecological tournament, not by beating any other program with which it was paired, but by behaving in a way that elicited mutually profitable cooperative behaviour from its co-players. The weakest programs were all virtually extinct after about 50 generations. Some of the most exploitative or "predatory" programs thrived for a while but eventually declined as the weak "sucker" programs on which they had successfully preyed declined; both types ended up as endangered species after 1000 generations.

Axelrod (1984) summarized the results of his computer tournaments as follows:

> What accounts for TIT FOR TAT's robust success is its combination of being nice, retaliatory [i.e., provocable], forgiving, and clear. Its niceness prevents it from getting into trouble. Its retaliation discourages the other side from persisting whenever defection is tried. Its forgiveness helps restore mutual cooperation. And its clarity makes it intelligible to the other player, thereby eliciting long-term cooperation. (p. 54)

Hofstadter (1983) entered a note of caution by pointing out that there is no evidence that TIT FOR TAT is the ultimate strategy that would outperform all other programs in any conceivable social environment. I would add that no one has proved a theorem to show that TIT FOR TAT is necessarily best. It has been proved, on the contrary, that TIT FOR TAT would not necessarily outperform every other program in terms of evolutionary fitness (Selten and Hammerstein, 1984; Swistak, 1989). Furthermore, some further computer tournaments were run since Hofstadter made his comment, and TIT FOR TAT has not invariably won them (e.g., Bendor, Kramer, and Stout, 1991;

Donninger, 1986; Lorberbaum, 1994; Nowak and Sigmund, 1993). Nowak and Sigmund's research showed that a version of the strategy WIN-STAY, LOSE-CHANGE, which was discussed in a different context in sections 3.3 and 3.4 and which has been called PAVLOV because of its almost reflex-like properties (Kraines and Kraines, 1989), clearly outperforms TIT FOR TAT and many other strategies in the long run (e.g., 10 million generations), although unlike TIT FOR TAT, PAVLOV cannot invade a population of unconditional *D* players. The evolutionary stability of TIT FOR TAT will be discussed in section 11.5.

7.7 Sex differences and cross-cultural studies

A striking and unexpected finding of early mixed-motive gaming experiments was the apparent tendency for females to exhibit much lower levels of cooperation than males in both the PDG and Chicken. Considering traditional gender roles, one might expect females to behave more *cooperatively* than males. However, in their extensive investigation of PDG behaviour, Rapoport and Chammah (1965) found an average of 59 per cent *C* choices in male pairs and only 34 per cent *C* choices in female pairs; in mixed pairs the average was about 50 per cent *C* choices. The sex difference was not detectable in mixed pairs, presumably because the strategic structure of the PDG strongly encourages players to choose the same strategies as their co-players (see section 6.7). Rapoport and Chammah's evidence suggests that, in mixed pairs, females converged towards their male co-players' more cooperative play to a greater extent than the males converged towards the females. The marked difference between same-sex pairs, which was found in all of the seven matrices used in the investigation, was due largely to a steeper and longer-lasting sobering period (initial decline in *C* choices) among the females than the males. In a later investigation, Rapoport and Chammah (1969) found a similar sex difference in the game of Chicken, with females once again exhibiting fewer *C* choices than males. In both games, the *initial* frequencies of *C* choices were broadly the same among males and females.

More than 100 experiments containing data on this sex difference have been published, but the effect is still imperfectly understood. Many researchers replicated the original findings in the United States (e.g., Hottes and Kahn, 1974), Britain (Mack, 1975) and elsewhere, but some found no significant sex difference (e.g., Kanouse and Wiest, 1967), and a (very) few found *greater* frequencies of *C* choices among females than males (e.g., Tedeschi, Bonoma, and Novinson, 1970). It has been claimed by some that the sex difference, at least in the PDG, is an artifact, and some evidence has been produced to show that it decreases or disappears entirely when the experimenter is female (e.g., Skotko, Langmeyer, and Lundgren, 1974), but other researchers have found a clear sex difference in experiments controlled by female experimenters (e.g., Gibbs, 1982). Gibbs's results suggest that the sex difference may be more pronounced with a male experimenter, but experimenters of either sex were shown to differ markedly from one another in the degree to which they elicited the sex difference. Both male and female experimenters evidently differ widely in the extent to which they create an atmosphere encouraging gender-related behaviour. The presence of a male experimenter often enhances the salience of gender roles, but some female experimenters have the same effect.

Why do females generally behave more competitively than males in mixed-motive games when gender roles are salient? Stated in this way, the phenomenon seems rather counter-intuitive. But it was pointed out in sections 6.7 and 6.8 that D choices invite a variety of alternative interpretations apart from competitiveness. It is tempting to explain the generally lower frequency of C choices among females in the PDG by the fact that D is the relatively *safe* strategy in this game, thus females may have a tendency to behave more *cautiously* (rather than more competitively) than males. It is not unreasonable to assume that, in western industrial cultures, males are brought up to behave with more boldness, daring, and risk taking than females, and this would account for their greater willingness to choose non-maximin C choices in the PDG in spite of the danger of receiving sucker's payoffs. But this plausible theory collapses in the light of the evidence showing the same tendency in Chicken, because the cautious policy in Chicken is to choose C, and this choice is more characteristic of males than of females. Hottes and Kahn (1974) argued that females respond more *defensively* to the demand characteristics of a PDG experiment than males, but why do they not manifest this greater defensiveness by choosing C more frequently in Chicken experiments?

A D choice in the PDG shares one property in common with a D choice in Chicken, and this suggests a possible clue to the sex difference mystery. In both games a D choice insures a subject against the possibility of receiving a worse payoff than the other player. The following hypothesis is consistent with nearly all of the evidence. Perhaps some experimenters, including probably the majority of male experimenters, induce a stronger feeling of *evaluation apprehension* in female than in male subjects. If the subjects then construe the gaming experiment as a competition in which their intelligence or skill is being judged in relation to that of their co-players, then females may choose D more frequently than males in order to rule out the possibility of ending up at a *relative* social disadvantage by "losing" what they see as a competition. The motive to avoid appearing more foolish than the other player may in these circumstances override the explicit payoffs in the matrix; the subjective utility of the sucker's payoff may be worse in the minds of anxious subjects than in the matrix. If this hypothesis is correct, then it is misleading to suggest that "women have a greater tendency to respond suspiciously, resentfully, conservatively, and thus competitively more than do men" (Bixenstine and O'Reilly, 1966, p. 263). One might rather say that in certain circumstances women are more anxious than men to avoid relative social disadvantage *vis-à-vis* their co-players. This is nothing more than a reasonable conjecture, but it has the virtues of being empirically testable and consistent with both the PDG and the Chicken findings.

Some interesting research has been devoted to cross-cultural investigations of cooperation and competition, and useful critical reviews have been provided by Smith and Bond (1993, chap. 7), Argyle (1991, chap. 4), and Bethlehem (1982). Some of the data come from experiments with the PDG and other two-person mixed-motive experimental games. For example, less western-educated Kpelle people in Liberia were found to be more cooperative in an experimental PDG than more western-educated people (Meeker, 1970). Rural Tonga people in the Gwembe valley in Zambia were found to be more cooperative in an experimental PDG than westernized Tongas or Asian students at the University of Zambia (Bethlehem, 1975). In a study based on the PDG within the United States, Cox, Lobel, and McLeod (1991) found white students to be less cooperative than Hispanic, Black, and Asian Americans. The following groups of children were found to differ in cooperativeness in an experimental Maximizing Difference game (MDG), with the most cooperative groups mentioned first and the least cooperative last: French-speaking Belgian boys, Mexican-American children, white American children, Greek children, and Japanese children (McClintock and Nuttin, 1969; Toda, Shinotsuka, McClintock, and Stech, 1978).

McClintock and McNeel (1966) and McNeel, McClintock, and Nuttin (1972) found Flemish-speaking Belgian students to be significantly *less* cooperative than American students in a Maximizing Difference game, but Faucheux (1976) criticized this research and pointed out that the Belgians had been competitive only when they were losing, and may have been trying to maintain equity, whereas the Americans had been competitive when winning. Indian university students in Delhi were found to be less cooperative in experimental MDG and Chicken games than Canadian students (Carment, 1974), but Alcock (1974, 1975) showed that Canadians were more competitive than Indians when time pressure was added, and that only the Indians became more competitive when they were winning. Finally, Carment and Alcock (1984) found Indians once again to be less cooperative than Canadians in a Maximizing Difference game, but when the matrix was modified to make much larger winnings available to one player, Canadians became more competitive when they held the advantage, whereas Indians became less competitive.

These findings have been supplemented by many others derived from different methods of measuring cooperativeness (see Argyle, 1991, chap. 4; Bethlehem, 1982; Smith and Bond, 1993, chap. 7). It appears superficially that cultures differ markedly as regards the cooperativeness or competitiveness of their members. By and large, cultures that place a value on cooperation, especially rural societies, produce cooperative citizens, and those that encourage competitiveness produce competitive citizens. There is evidence to suggest that industrialization and the division of labour tend to transform a culture, in the terminology of the nineteenth-century German sociologist Ferdinand Tönnies, from *Gemeinschaft* (community) to *Gesellschaft* (society), which implies a decline in cooperative or collectivistic behaviour and an increase in individualistic behaviour. But Smith and Bond (1993), after reviewing the experimental gaming evidence, suggest sensibly that "rather than labelling this or that nation as more or less competitive, it is better to look at what situations evoke competitive behaviour from each national sample" (p. 126).

7.8 Attribution effects

A series of interrelated studies by Kelley and Stahelski (1970a, 1970b, 1970c) focused on the effects of people's beliefs about their co-players' intentions on behaviour in the PDG. In the course of iterated plays of the game, a person can hardly avoid attributing intentions to the other player on the evidence of the latter's behaviour. There is plenty of scope for attributional errors, however: a *C* choice can be misinterpreted as indicating a cooperative overture when in fact it is calculated to lure the other player into making a *C* choice with a view to exploitation, or vice versa; and a *D* choice can be misinterpreted as a competitive act when in fact it is motivated by self-protective considerations based on an expectation that the other player will choose *D*, or vice versa. In the PDG there are numerous other plausible motives and attributions, and it is of some importance to know how accurately people are able to infer each other's intentions and what effects these inferences have.

Kelley and Stahelski (1970a) invited a group of subjects to express their own cooperative or competitive intentions to the experimenter before playing 40 trials of a PDG in pairs. After each block of 10 trials they were questioned about their inferences regarding their co-players' intentions. Attributional errors were found to relate to competitiveness in an interesting way. Subjects whose own intentions were cooperative were generally able to infer their co-players' intentions – whether cooperative or competitive – beyond the level of chance after only 10 trials. Subjects whose own intentions were competitive, on the other hand, were generally unable to infer the intentions of cooperative co-players even after 40 trials. Kelley and Stahelski put forward an intriguing theory to account for these findings. Consider the implications of *projective attributional errors* that arise from the false but common assumption that other people are similar to oneself. Cooperative people may tend to assume, in the absence of any evidence to the contrary, that others are generally cooperative, and competitive people may tend to assume that others are generally competitive. But cooperative people are likely to discover through bitter experience in everyday mixed-motive interactions that people vary in their cooperativeness, and the projective attributional error is therefore likely to be corrected. Competitive people, in contrast, are less likely to have their projective attributional errors refuted by experience. The reason for this is that competitive behaviour forces other people to respond competitively; in the PDG, a player who expects a *D* choice from the other player has to choose *D* to avoid the worst possible payoff even if that player would prefer to cooperate, given half a chance. The Germans have a saying: "Wie man hineinruft, so schallt es heraus" (the way you shout determines the sound of the echo).

The implication of the above line of argument is this: people who behave competitively and predict that others will behave similarly tend to elicit competitive behaviour from those with whom they interact. A classic self-fulfilling prophecy is at work, and the projective attributional errors of competitive people, far from being corrected, are likely to be confirmed and reinforced by experience.

A crucial empirical assumption built into this theory is that cooperative and competitive people hold widely differing world views. Kelley and Stahelski (1970c) produced some impressive empirical evidence in support of this assumption. Subjects who favoured competitive solutions to a wide range of problems – the PDG, bargaining conflicts, and even socio-political disagreements – were found to believe, in general, that others are uniformly competitive, whereas cooperative subjects tended to believe that some people are cooperative and others competitive. This relationship between cooperative or competitive intentions and attributions of intent towards others is referred to by the authors as the *triangle hypothesis* because of its visual appearance when depicted as in Table 7.1. The table shows that very cooperative people, represented in the top row, attribute the full range of intentions to others, whereas very competitive people, represented in the

Table 7.1 The triangle hypothesis

		Attributions of intent to others		
		Cooperative	Neutral	Competitive
	Cooperative	X	X	X
Own intentions	Neutral		X	X
	Competitive			X

bottom row, tend to attribute only competitive intentions to others. According to Kelley and Stahelski, competitive people have a cynical and authoritarian outlook on life; they believe in *and create* a social environment of competitive and untrustworthy adversaries against whom they feel impelled to defend themselves by behaving competitively. Cooperative people, on the other hand, are less pessimistic in outlook and have a more realistic appreciation of the diversity of human nature.

Eiser and Tajfel (1972), using a non-PDG mixed-motive game, showed that cooperative subjects are usually more eager than competitive subjects to obtain information that might reveal the motives governing each other's behaviour. This provides indirect support to the triangle hypothesis, according to which only cooperative subjects would need to know the predispositions of others in order to formulate their own strategies; competitive subjects presumably think they know that all people are motivated like themselves. Other researchers have argued against over-extending the triangle hypothesis and have shown that there are many situational factors that need to be taken into account. Miller and Holmes (1975) and Kuhlman and Wimberley (1976), for example, have confirmed the triangle hypothesis in the PDG but found it inadequate to account for behaviour in certain other games. This is in line with common sense because it is in the PDG that choices are most open to misinterpretation.

7.9 Framing effects

The basic ideas and empirical findings related to framing effects were introduced in section 5.4. It was pointed out there that people facing decision problems necessarily interpret them in particular ways, and that different interpretations of the same problem may sometimes lead to different decisions. This section is devoted to framing effects in two-person mixed-motive experimental games including the PDG and Chicken.

It is possible to frame a game in a variety of apparently different but logically equivalent ways, and there is some evidence that framing can powerfully influence choice behaviour. An interesting line of research has focused on *decomposed* or *separated* PDGs. A conventional PDG and two of its derivative decompositions are displayed in Matrices 7.2. The particular decompositions shown (Matrices 7.2b and c) are merely illustrative: if a PDG can be decomposed at all, and this is possible only if $T - R = P - S$, then there are always infinitely many ways to do so. (Chicken and other games without dominant strategies cannot be decomposed.)

A decomposed matrix such as 7.2b (or 7.2c) is read as follows. A player's strategies are labelled as usual C and D. The choice of either strategy yields a payoff to the player who chooses it and, simultaneously, a payoff to the other player. To play the game, each player chooses a row from the same

Matrices 7.2 *PDG and Two Derivative Decompositions*

		II: *C*	II: *D*
I	*C*	3, 3	1, 4
	D	4, 1	2, 2

(a)

	Own Payoff	Other's Payoff
C	0	3
D	1	1

(b)

	Own Payoff	Other's Payoff
C	1	2
D	2	0

(c)

decomposed matrix, and to determine a player's total payoff we add together that player's "own payoff" and the co-player's "other's payoff". To clarify how this works, let us examine the first decomposed PDG (Matrix 7.2b). If an experimental subject is presented with this matrix and told that the other member of the pair has an identical copy, then it is possible to work out the consequences of any joint decision. Choosing *C*, for example, means awarding oneself no points and awarding the other player three points. Thus if both players choose *C*, each ends up with three points, all of which come from the other player's choice. These payoffs (3, 3) correspond to those in the (*C*, *C*) outcome in the conventional matrix (Matrix 7.2a). If both choose *D*, then both receive one point from their own choices and one point from each other's choices, so each ends up with two points, which again corresponds to the payoffs in Matrix 7.2b. The consequences of other combinations of choices can be worked out in the same way. The important point is that this decomposition (b) is mathematically equivalent to the conventional payoff matrix (a), and it is easily verified that the other decomposition (c) is likewise equivalent to (a). Each version conveys exactly the same information framed in a different way.

A decomposition of the kind shown in Matrix 7.2c invites players to frame the PDG in terms of generosity versus stinginess, as Pruitt and Kimmel (1977, p. 373) pointed out. For example, people who are next-door neighbours often have to choose between lending (*C*) and refusing to lend (*D*) each other eggs, milk, garden tools, baby-sitting services, the use of their telephones, and the like. Matrix 7.2c reflects these choices if we assume (reasonably) that lending yields little direct benefit to the lender, but considerably more to the recipient, and that refusing to lend may save the lender a certain amount of trouble but may cause the recipient much more. Both neighbours are clearly better off in the long run if both consistently agree to lend than if both consistently refuse. At the individual level, most of the benefit goes to the other person, but at the level of collective rationality, virtue is its own reward.

A number of investigators (e.g., Evans and Crumbaugh, 1966; Pruitt, 1967) reported higher levels of cooperation in decomposed PDGs than in conventional PDGs with equivalent payoffs. Cooperative behaviour is most common in decompositions such as Matrix 7.2b which encourages the players to frame the dilemma in a way in which they seem to depend entirely on each other for payoffs. Decompositions of this type provide a frame that makes plain the players' dependence on each other's goodwill and generosity, and this evidently facilitates the development of mutual trust and trustworthiness. A similar conclusion has emerged from research in the field of social identity theory (Rabbie, Schot, and Visser, 1989) and other areas of social psychology (Argyle, 1991, chap. 11). Experiments have shown that, in a decomposed PDG that elicits high levels of cooperation, subjects are especially quick to reciprocate C choices and especially slow to defect to D in response to the other players' defecting choices (Pruitt, 1970; Tognoli, 1975).

Various non-numerical methods of framing mixed-motive games have been tried by researchers. The purpose is usually to create a laboratory mixed-motive interaction that is less abstract and meaningless than the conventional payoff matrix or, for that matter, than a decomposed matrix. One of the more extensively researched of these non-numerical games is Deutsch and Krauss's (1960) *trucking game*. Useful discussions of the trucking game have been provided by Grzelak (1988) and Harvey and Smith (1977, pp. 311–323). The essential features of the game are as follows. The two subjects play the roles of truck drivers for the Acme and Bolt companies respectively trying to deliver a load to a certain destination as quickly as possible. Each has a choice between two possible routes, one considerably shorter than the other. The short route, however, includes a stretch of single-track road that the trucks have to traverse in opposite directions; thus if both subjects choose the shorter route simultaneously, a head-on blockage occurs and both lose valuable time until one decides to back away and switch to the longer route. In some conditions, one or both of the subjects controls a "gate" that can be used to prevent the other from passing beyond the single-track stretch of the road.

Playing iterated trials of the trucking game without gates, Deutsch and Krauss's (1960, 1962) subjects quickly learned to cooperate by alternating on the shorter route. But when both subjects controlled gates – the *bilateral threat* condition – frequent blockages were typical and, somewhat surprisingly, no improvement took place over trials. The *unilateral threat* condition, in which only one member of the pair controlled a gate, produced intermediate levels of cooperation and efficiency. Deutsch interpreted these results as showing that the availability of potential threats encourages people to behave competitively, and he has argued (Deutsch, 1969) that this conclusion has vital implications for international relations, disarmament, and military deterrence. There is some evidence in support of Deutsch's interpretation (e.g., Smith and Anderson, 1975), but Kelley (1965) pointed out that the control of gates may increase the level of competition simply because it permits a player to maximize relative gain by blocking the other player in the single-track stretch and taking the longer route. When neither player controls a gate, of course, neither can do anything to gain at the other's expense because blockages are always mutual. Although the results of research with the trucking game are often compared with – or even assimilated to – the results of matrix gaming experiments, they ought really to be treated as coming from an independent line of enquiry of particular relevance to the study of threats. The trucking game is a two-person mixed-motive game, but its strategic structure is extremely complex in the threat conditions, and it does not correspond to the game of Chicken (as many believe) or to any other well-known matrix game.

A few studies of framing effects have compared choices in abstract, matrix games with choices framed in relatively lifelike ways. Orwant and Orwant (1970) compared the choices of 165 students of journalism in 10 conventional PDG payoff matrices with their choices in 10 "interpreted" versions of these matrices. The major finding was that "the interpreted version[s] elicited significantly more cooperation than the abstract version[s]" (p. 95). But there are several peculiarities about this experiment that make it unsafe to draw any firm conclusions from the results. Most importantly, the strategic structures of the "interpreted" versions did not correspond to those of the matrix games, and this lack of correspondence may, in part at least, explain the observed differences in choice behaviour. Even the rank order of outcome preferences was not the same in the "interpreted" and matrix versions, and some of the "interpreted" versions were not even PDGs.

Young (1977) investigated behaviour in an abstract and a "structurally equivalent" lifelike version of a mixed-motive game. He hypothesized that the realism of the lifelike version would engage norms of reciprocity and social responsibility and thus elicit more cooperative choices than the abstract version, but his results revealed exactly the reverse. Unfortunately, the "abstract" version was not entirely abstract: in *both* treatment conditions the subjects were told that the decisions involved a situation in which a football team captain, played by the subject, comments to a team coach in one of two alternative ways about a problem of team morale, and the coach responds in one of two alternative ways. Secondly, the strategic structures of the abstract and lifelike versions were quite different from each other: the former was an ill-defined asymmetric game and the latter was a PDG. These and other flaws in the design and statistical analysis of this experiment make it hazardous to draw any conclusions from the results.

Sermat (1970) reported four experiments in which the behaviour of subjects who had previously displayed either highly cooperative or highly competitive behaviour in the PDG or Chicken was examined in a specially constructed Paddle game or in a picture-interpretation task. The comparison was not, however, made within the same experiment with irrelevant variables held constant. The results showed that, in contrast to their behaviour in the matrix games, nearly all of the subjects were highly cooperative in the Paddle game. There was very little relationship between behaviour in the matrix games and behaviour in the Paddle game, and no relationship was found between game behaviour and picture interpretations. The Paddle game, which involved manoeuvring a stick backwards and forwards in a slot, "was assumed to be relatively similar to conventional mixed-motive games like the Game of Chicken" (p. 94). In reality, however, the strategic structures of the two games were quite different: the Paddle game turns out, on analysis, to correspond to a sequence of 3 × 3 zero-sum games, whereas Chicken is a 2 × 2 mixed-motive game. Sermat was aware of the shortcomings of his investigation, but he argued that, if evidence for a relationship between laboratory game behaviour and behaviour in other situations is not forthcoming, then "the theoretical contribution of game research may have to be stated in terms other than its relevance to interpersonal behavior in real-life situations" (p. 108).

Eiser and Bhavnani (1974) investigated the behaviour of 80 subjects over 10 trials in a PDG against a programmed TFT strategy from the co-player. The subjects made their choices on the basis of an identical payoff matrix, but the instructional set was varied in a way calculated to influence their framing of the problem. Some of the subjects were given no contextual frame, some were told merely that it was a simulation of economic bargaining, some thought it had to do with international negotiations, and some were led to believe that it concerned friendly or unfriendly interactions between pairs of individuals. The investigators hypothesized that the framing of the game situation in terms of economic bargaining would tend to engage competitive motives and lead to more *D* choices than the "international" and "interpersonal" frames, because economic bargaining "provides an excuse for exploitative self-interest" while in the other two frames "cooperation is more highly valued" (Eiser and Bhavnani, 1974, p. 94). The hypothesis was confirmed: the frequencies of *C* choices in the abstract and economic frames were fairly typical of frequencies reported in the literature on the PDG, but the frequencies of *C* choices in the "international" and "interpersonal" frames were significantly higher. The authors concluded that "extrapolations from the results of PDG experiments to particular kinds of real-life situations must depend for their validity at least partly on whether the subjects themselves interpret the game as symbolic of the situations in question" (p. 97).

A framing experiment reported by Colman (1982c, pp. 131–136) was based on four structurally equivalent versions of the PDG, including a conventional payoff matrix and a simulation of a lifelike strategic inter-action. In the matrix version, 80 undergraduate and postgraduate subjects played 30 trials for points, and in the lifelike version, which involved two restaurateurs competing for the same clientele who have to decide whether or not to provide expensive floor shows in their respective establishments, they played for imaginary financial profits. An interval-scale equivalence was preserved between the payoff structures in the two versions. Because the two versions of the game were structurally equivalent, all significant differences can be attributed to strategically irrelevant decision frames in which the subjects found themselves. The major hypothesis was that the lifelike simulation, because of its commercial frame, would elicit fewer C choices than the abstract versions of the game, and this hypothesis was confirmed. This result corroborates and extends Eiser and Bhavnani's (1974) finding that an economic decision frame tends to enhance competitive behaviour in the PDG, presumably because of the cultural value associated with competitiveness in business dealings. It suggests, furthermore, that the external and ecological validity of abstract gaming experiments depends, in part at least, on psychological features of the naturally occurring interactions to which they are generalized. The results suggest that they cannot be generalized straightforwardly in all circumstances.

Colman (1982c, pp. 136–140) also reported a framing experiment based on the game of Chicken. A conventional matrix version of Chicken and a lifelike simulation of a structurally equivalent strategic interaction were used, and the experimental design and procedure were similar to the experiment with abstract and lifelike versions of the PDG described above. In the Chicken experiment, the lifelike frame, which involved a simulation of an economic conflict between two firms exporting fresh vegetables to an island by sea or air freight, was expected to engage cultural values associated with competitiveness and risk taking and to lead to fewer C choices than the abstract, matrix frame. The subjects were 80 undergraduate and postgraduate students. An interval-scale equivalence was preserved between the payoff structures of the matrix and lifelike versions. A significant difference was once again found between frequencies of C choices in the two versions of the game. As hypothesized, significantly fewer C choices were made in the lifelike simulation, presumably because it involved an economic conflict between imaginary firms that was calculated to engage cultural values associated with competitiveness and risk taking. The results of this experiment cast further doubt on the view that the findings of conventional experiments with matrix games can be generalized straightforwardly to more lifelike strategic interactions with this payoff structure.

Furnham and Quilley (1989) presented the PDG to 109 subjects framed in two different ways – either as a conventional matrix or as a simulation of a series of business decisions modelled on the Colman (1982c, pp. 131–136) experiment with the PDG. The results replicated those of Colman: significantly fewer cooperative choices were made by subjects who had been induced to frame the situation as a series of business decisions. The subjects were paired with co-players who had scored similarly to themselves on a scale designed to measure a personality trait associated with the Protestant work ethic – independent-mindedness, competitiveness, perseverance, and so on. The results showed that, as predicted, high scorers made significantly fewer cooperative C choices than low scorers in both frame conditions.

The results of experiments designed to investigate framing effects in two-person mixed-motive games have shown unequivocally that frames make a difference – that the interpretations that experimental subjects are induced to make of the decision problems of the games have large and predictable effects on the choices that they make. This general conclusion casts a shadow of doubt over the external and ecological validity of the large body of research findings based on matrix games. On the other hand, it suggests that there is still a rich seam of information about framing effects in experimental games waiting to be mined by future researchers.

7.10 Summary

This chapter opened with some general comments on two-person mixed-motive experimental games and a "review of reviews" of the literature in this area. In section 7.2, the effects of strategic structure on choice behaviour were discussed, and it was concluded that experimental subjects generally choose in a manner that seems rational on the basis of informal game theory or common sense. In the PDG, however, there is a tendency for subjects to become "locked in" to the unsatisfactory (D, D) outcome when the game is iterated many times, and in the Maximizing Difference game apparently irrational choices are common, indicating that the explicit payoff structure does not accurately reflect the subjects' subjective preferences. Section 7.3 focused on the effects of payoff variations and monetary incentives within particular strategic game structures, and in section 7.4 on the effects of opportunities for communication in experimental games. In section 7.5, the responses of experimental subjects to programmed strategies, including unconditional cooperation (ALL C), unconditional non-cooperation (ALL D), TIT FOR TAT, "reformed sinner", and "lapsed saint" programmed strategies was reviewed, and in section 7.6 a summary and discussion were provided of Axelrod's software tournament of Prisoner's-Dilemma-playing computer programs and the research that it inspired. Section 7.7 focused on the puzzling sex differences that has been found in experimental games, with females generally choosing more "competitively" than males, and on the findings of cross-cultural research into cooperation and competition, and in section 7.8 the interesting theoretical and experimental work that has been devoted to the effects on experimental subjects' game-playing behaviour of their attributions of intent to their co-players were reviewed. Finally, in section 7.9 a detailed review was provided of the effects of the framing of two-person mixed-motive experimental games on cooperation.

8

Multi-person cooperative games: coalition formation

8.1 *N*-person cooperative games

From a theoretical point of view, the simplest decision problems are one-person games in which a solitary player tries to obtain as high a payoff as possible or, if the game involves an element of risk, as high an *expected* (statistically average) payoff as possible. The involvement of a second player whose choices also affect the outcome leads to new and qualitatively different problems. In a two-person game, strategic problems that cannot be reduced to simple payoff maximization arise and, depending on the payoff structure, the players may be motivated to coordinate, to compete, or to strike a suitable balance between coordination and competition. A further quantum leap in strategic complexity arises in games involving three or more players, which are called *multi-person* or *n-person* games. Georg Simmel, the turn-of-the-century German sociologist and philosopher, was apparently the first to point out an important phenomenon that emerges when the transition is made from two-person groups (dyads) to three-person or larger groups: "The essential point is that within a dyad, there can be no majority that could outvote the individual. This majority, however, is made possible by the mere addition of a third member" (quoted in Luce and Raiffa, 1957, p. 155).

In the terminology of game theory, the strategic implications of *coalition formation* have to be taken into account in *n*-person cooperative games (which, as was argued in section 6.10, might less confusingly have been called *n*-person *negotiable* games). This branch of game theory relates to games in which there are three or more players who are free to negotiate binding and enforceable agreements about the formation of coalitions and the division of the payoffs that result from their coordinated actions. A clear and comprehensive review of the relevant literature has been provided by James Kahan and Amnon Rapoport (1984), and briefer summaries are available in Murnighan (1978), Komorita and Kravitz (1983), Komorita (1984), and Anatol Rapoport (1989, chap. 16).

N-person cooperative games in which the decision makers' interests coincide exactly are simply pure coordination games. In these rather special cases, the distinction between two-person and *n*-person games is relatively unimportant, and examples of both kinds were included in chapter 3. In pure coordination games the players have identical preferences, so they have no incentive to split into competing coalitions, because the only profitable coalition is the one containing all the players. For example, the strategic problem of deciding whether to dress formally or informally for a social gathering, if one's sole objective is to match the choice(s) of the other guest(s), is the same whether the occasion is an intimate two-person tête-à-tête or a large party. Coordination may be achieved by advance communication between the guests or, if communication is not feasible, by the discovery of socially or culturally *salient* features of the situation that can serve as focal points for coordination (see section 3.2).

Regarding zero-sum and mixed-motive games, on the other hand, there are qualitative differences between two-person and *n*-person cases, because only in *n*-person games may the players be motivated to split into alliances, blocs, cliques, factions, teams, gangs, caucuses, unions, syndicates, or cartels whose collective interests diverge. This possibility can radically alter the character of a game. For example, although every two-person zero-sum or constant-sum game is strictly competitive (see section 4.1), it would make no sense to describe an *n*-person zero-sum or constant-sum game as strictly competitive, because if two of the players have interests that are diametrically opposed, then a third player cannot have interests that are diametrically opposed to both of the others. In a cooperative *n*-person zero-sum game some of the players may stand to benefit by forming a cooperative coalition against the others.

N-person game theory falls into two categories. The theory of *n*-person non-cooperative games is based on an extension of the Nash equilibrium concept discussed at length in previous chapters. In this context, the adjective *non-cooperative* refers to the rules of the game, which forbid the negotiation of binding and enforceable agreements, rather than to its payoff structure. In these games, the players choose their strategies independently without such negotiation, and coalition formation is therefore impossible. Non-cooperative solutions to *n*-person games are open to all of the objections raised against equilibrium solutions to two-person mixed-motive games (see section 6.1), but they can sometimes be extremely illuminating none the less. They are discussed in more detail in chapter 9. The theory of *n*-person cooperative games, on the other hand, is based on models in which the rules allow binding and enforceable agreements regarding coalition formation and the division of payoffs, which is how many everyday multi-person interactions are conducted. Von Neumann and Morgenstern (1944) laid the foundations of this branch of game theory in their classic *Theory of Games and Economic Behavior*, and numerous theoretical and empirical contributions have since been added to this field of research. As with two-person cooperative games, theorists have suggested several different solutions – or solution concepts, as they are sometimes more modestly called. This led one commentator to remark: "The diversity of theories ... proves that if the players wish to arrive at a tacit agreement, even or perhaps especially if they are mathematicians, there is a good chance that they will not settle on the same point" (Jean-Pierre Séris, 1974, p. 91, my translation).

In section 8.2 the characteristic function form of a game will be introduced, initially with reference to the familiar two-person Prisoner's Dilemma game and then with larger games, and the concept of an imputation will be explained. In section 8.3 the solution concepts of the core and the stable set will be discussed, and in section 8.4 these fundamental ideas will be illustrated with reference to Harold Pinter's play, *The Caretaker*. Section 8.5 will be devoted to a solution concept called the Shapley value, and section 8.6 to the kernel, the nucleolus, and the least core. Section 8.7 will introduce theories that predict not merely how the payoffs will be divided, but also which particular coalitions will form, and section 8.8 will review experimental studies of coalition formation. In section 8.9 the chapter will be briefly summarized.

8.2 Characteristic function and imputation

Von Neumann and Morgenstern (1944) approached the analysis of n-person cooperative games by introducing the concept of the *characteristic function* denoted by the symbol v. The characteristic function of any game is a rule that assigns a maximin payoff, called the *value* of the game to every logically possible coalition of players that might form (hence the use of the letter v to symbolize it). The coalition's value is the best payoff that the coalition can achieve irrespective of the strategy choices of the remaining players. It represents the coalition's security level in exactly the same way that the value of a two-person game to an individual player represents that player's security level. From a mathematical point of view, the phrase "every logically possible coalition of players" is taken to mean every subset of the set of players. This includes not only the sets that one would normally think of as potential coalitions, but also the empty set containing none of the players, symbolized by $\emptyset$, all one-element sets containing individual players, and the set representing the *grand coalition* of all the players, symbolized by N.

A restriction on the nature of the characteristic function is the natural requirement that the value of the game to the empty coalition is zero, that is, $v(\emptyset) = 0$. A further requirement that is generally (though not invariably) made relates to collective rationality and is called *superadditivity*. A game is superadditive if any two coalitions S and T with no members in common can achieve at least as high a payoff by joint effort as they can obtain separately. Mathematically, superadditivity is expressed as follows:

$$v(S \cup T) \geq v(S) + v(T) \quad \text{for all } S,\, T \subseteq N \text{ such that } S \cap T = \varnothing.$$

This means that two subsets of players can always do at least as well in terms of total payoffs by joining together and coordinating their strategies in a larger coalition as they can do independently. It also implies that the grand coalition of all the players is always collectively rational, because the total payoff to the players is always at least as much if they act together as a single coalition as it would be if the players acted as members of smaller coalitions or as individuals.

The superadditivity requirement states that larger coalitions can guarantee for themselves *at least as much*, in terms of total payoffs, as smaller coalitions can guarantee, but not that they can necessarily guarantee *more*. Games in which at least one possible coalition can increase the total payoff of its members are called *essential*, and those in which there is no coalition that improves the total payoff are called *inessential*. Mathematically, an essential game is one in which at least one of the superadditivity inequalities is strict (so that $\geq$ means $>$ rather than $=$). Every two-person zero-sum or constant-sum game is inessential, because the payoff that each player can guarantee through unilateral action (the maximin or minimax) is determined by the value of the game and cannot be improved on through collaboration; but zero-sum games involving more than two players are often essential, which is a consequence of the fact already mentioned that they are not strictly competitive. Non-zero-sum games are generally essential. For example, a cooperative version of the mixed-motive Prisoner's Dilemma game, which was discussed in section 6.7 and is displayed once again in Matrix 8.1 for convenience, is essential, because both players can benefit by establishing a two-person coalition.

Let us assume that the game is played cooperatively and that the payoffs represent units of utility to the players (and not just rank-order preferences). The characteristic function assigns a value $v(S)$ to each and every possible coalition. As already explained, it is assumed that the value of the game to

Matrix 8.1
Prisoner's Dilemma game

II

		C	D
	C	3, 3	1, 4
I	D	4, 1	2, 2

the empty coalition $\emptyset$ is always zero, so the first value of the characteristic function is $v(\emptyset) = 0$. Player I, acting alone, can be sure of a payoff of at least 2 units of utility, because that is Player I's maximin security level guaranteed by choosing the D strategy. In some games, of course, a player can achieve a better security level by using a mixed strategy, but that is not the case in the Prisoner's Dilemma game. Player II's maximin is also 2 units, because the game is perfectly symmetrical, so two further values of the characteristic function have thus been found: $v(I) = 2$ and $v(II) = 2$. Finally, because the game is cooperative, Players I and II can negotiate a grand coalition acting as a single player, agreeing to choose row C and column C respectively, therefore the two-person coalition is guaranteed a total payoff of 6 units, and that is the best that the grand coalition can guarantee by concerted action, because (C, D), (D, C), and (D, D) all pay less to the coalition as a whole. It is clear, therefore, that the final value is $v(N) = v(I, II) = 6$. The complete characteristic function of the game is therefore

$$v(\emptyset) = 0, v(I) = 2, v(II) = 2, v(I, II) = 6.$$

It satisfies the superadditivity requirement because each coalition earns at least as much as the sum of the payoffs to the smaller coalitions (including one-member and zero-member coalitions) of which it is composed.

This method of specifying a game in *characteristic function form* (rather than extensive or normal form) can be extended without difficulty to n-person games. Consider the following three-person game, which I shall call the Shareholders' game. A bequest of 24 gold watches has been made by a benefactor to a corporation consisting of three shareholders. The shareholders have to reach a collective decision about how to divide the watches among themselves. The decision is made by majority voting, but the weight of each vote is proportional to the percentage of shares that the shareholder owns. This type of arrangement is called a *weighted majority game*. It is common not only in business corporations but also in legislatures and trade unions, where votes are often weighted in proportion to the number of members they represent.

It is conventional in this branch of game theory to label the Players A, B, C, and so on, so let us suppose that Players A, B, and C own 50, 40, and 10 per cent of the shares respectively and that their votes are weighted accordingly. Each player can vote in favour of any feasible division of the 24 watches among the three players, and if an absolute majority in favour of some particular division does not emerge from the voting – if there is a tie – then none of the players receives anything (the watches are donated to charity). In the characteristic function form of the game we do not have to list the numerous strategies from which each player must choose, but we assume as usual that each player is individually rational and thus seeks to maximize individual gain. It is clear that none of the players acting alone can be sure of receiving any of the watches, because no single shareholder has an absolute majority of the votes. Hence $v(A) = v(B) = v(C) = 0$. Players A and B jointly command a majority (they control $50 + 40 = 90$ per cent of the votes), and they can therefore form a coalition taking all of the watches for themselves: $v(A, B) = 24$. Players A and C also have a majority, but Players B and C do not, because their coalition cannot outvote player A and could lead to a deadlock with all the watches being forfeited. The value of the game to the grand coalition of all three players is obviously 24. The characteristic function of this weighted majority game is therefore:

$$v(\varnothing) = 0;$$

$$v(A) = 0, \, v(B) = 0, \, v(C) = 0;$$

$$v(A, B) = 24, \, v(A, C) = 24, \, v(B, C) = 0;$$

$$v(A, B, C) = 24.$$

The characteristic function of the Shareholders' game is clearly super-additive, because the value of each coalition is at least as great as the value of the smaller units that compose it.

  The players can do at least as well for themselves collectively by forming the grand coalition as by doing anything else, so the grand coalition is collectively rational as it is in every superadditive game. But some smaller coalitions can do better *for their members*. Which coalitions will form in practice is a question that has been approached with specialized descriptive theories and experimental techniques to be discussed later in this chapter in sections 8.7 and 8.8.

  Assuming that collective rationality prevails and the grand coalition forms, how will the players divide the joint payoff among its members? The division of the joint payoff $v(N)$ among the n players may be represented by the payoff vector $(x) = (x_1, x_2, \ldots, x_n)$, where x_i is the payoff to player i in the grand coalition N. If the division is to be optimal in terms of both individual and collective rationality, then two requirements need to be satisfied. The first relates to individual rationality: the payoff to each player in the grand coalition must be at least as much as that player can obtain by acting as an individual (a one-member coalition). This is expressed mathematically as follows:

$$x_i \geq v(i), \, i = 1, 2, \ldots, n.$$

The second requirement relates to collective rationality. It states that the sum of the payoffs to be divided among the players in the grand coalition should equal the value of the grand coalition, so that nothing is wasted. Mathematically,

$$\Sigma x_i = v(N).$$

An apportionment of payoffs $(x) = (x_1, x_2, \ldots, x_n)$ satisfying the above pair of assumptions relating to individual and collective rationality is called an *imputation*. An imputation is a rational division of the payoff in which the players each receive at least as much as they would by acting independently, and they receive jointly as much as they would by acting as a grand coalition (nothing is wasted).

8.3 Core and stable set

The notion of collective rationality that lies behind the concept of an imputation can be generalized to include not just the grand coalition but all other possible coalitions of players as well. In other words, we can complete the picture by adding to the requirements of individual rationality and collective rationality of the grand coalition, which are already present in the definition of an imputation, a further requirement of the same type applicable to every subset of players, so that

$$\Sigma x_i \geq v(S) \text{ for all } i \in S, \text{ for all } S \subset N.$$

This further requirement states that, for every subset of players S that might form a coalition, the sum of the payoffs to those players from the division of the joint payoff should be at least as much as the value of the coalition S or, in other words, at least as much as the payoff that the coalition S could guarantee for itself irrespective of the strategies of the remaining players. If this requirement were not satisfied, then the members of the subset S would have an incentive to defect from the grand coalition and form the coalition S in order to ensure for themselves a higher joint payoff $v(S)$ than they receive in the grand coalition.

The set of imputations satisfying this further requirement constitutes the *core* of a game. The core, which satisfies individual, collective, and coalition rationality, was introduced by Gillies (1953) and has remained popular ever since, because it is the simplest and most intuitively persuasive of all solution concepts. It seems reasonable to stipulate that a rational solution to any game should be an imputation in the core. This would ensure that the division of the joint payoff would reflect the rationality of every player and every subset of players in the game. The problem is that there are many games in which no imputation satisfies the last requirement, in other words, there are many games with empty cores. Included among these are all essential zero-sum and constant-sum games.

To see this clearly, consider a simplified version of the Shareholders' game discussed in section 8.2. Three players try to agree by majority vote how to divide 24 gold watches among themselves, and if agreement cannot be reached, then all the watches are forfeited, but in this version the players' votes are weighted equally. The grand coalition, with an equal division of the payoff among the three players, would be equitable, but that solution is unstable. Suppose that Players A and B agree to form a coalition excluding Player C and to split the watches equally between themselves, taking 12 watches each instead of the eight that they would receive in an equitable division in the grand coalition. Player C could then approach Player B with an offer to form a different coalition, excluding player A, and agree to a division of the payoff that would be better for both of them, namely 13 watches for Player B (instead of 12) and 11 for Player C (instead of none). But it would be dangerous for Player B to agree to this division of the payoff, because it gives Players A and C an incentive to form a coalition excluding Player B altogether and agreeing to divide the watches equally between themselves. Player A then gets 12 watches instead of none and Player C gets 12 instead of 11. And so it goes on indefinitely, like a dog chasing its own tail, if the shareholders are rational in the game theory sense. There is no obvious stable solution to this game, because it is essential and constant-sum and therefore has an empty core.

Imputations in the core, where they exist, have a certain stability, because no player or subset of players has any incentive to defect from the grand coalition. But in view of the fact that many games have empty cores, the core fails to provide a *general* solution for *n*-person games in characteristic function form. Von Neumann and Morgenstern (1944) proposed a different solution concept, which also relies on the notion of stability but is more generally applicable than the core. That proposal is called the *von Neumann-Morgenstern solution* or the *stable set*.

The stable set is based on the concept of *dominance*, which needs to be explained first. One imputation is said to dominate another if there is a subset of players who all prefer the first to the second and can enforce it by forming a coalition; they have both the will and the power to impose the dominant imputation. Mathematically imputation $(y) = (y_1, y_2, \ldots, y_n)$ is said to *dominate* imputation $(x) = (x_1, x_2, \ldots, x_n)$ if there exists some subset S of players for which the following two inequalities are satisfied:

$$y_i > x_i \text{ for every } i \in S;$$

$$\Sigma x_i \leq v(S) \text{ for } i \in S.$$

The first inequality states that every player belonging to the subset S stands to receives a higher payoff from the imputation (y) than (x) and is therefore motivated to form the coalition S. The second inequality states that members of the subset S have the power to form the coalition, because the value of the game to the coalition is at least as much as the sum of the payoffs to the players in the imputation (x).

In the simplified Shareholders' game, any payoff vector $(x) = (x_A, x_B, x_C)$ in which the x_i are positive integers and $\Sigma x_i = 24$ is an imputation. The imputation $(y) = (12, 12, 0)$ dominates $(x) = (8, 8, 8)$, because there is a subset S of players, namely Players A and B, with each member of the subset standing to receive a higher payoff – 12 watches rather than 8 – in (y) than in (x), and they have the power to form this coalition because the value of the game to the coalition $v(S)$ is 24, which is greater than the sum of the payoffs to Players A and B in imputation (x), which is $8 + 8 = 16$. But if we consider the imputations $(x) = (12, 12, 0)$ and $(y) = (0, 12, 12)$, neither imputation dominates the other because there is no subset of players for which both of the inequalities that define dominance are satisfied. It follows that the dominance relation does not necessarily exist between a pair of imputations. Furthermore, where it does exist, it is strangely not necessarily transitive, as the following three hypothetical imputations from the simplified Shareholders' game show: $(x) = (10, 1, 13)$, $(y) = (5, 7, 12)$, $(z) = (2, 5, 17)$. It is easily verified that (x) dominates (y) through the subset of Players A and C, (y) dominates (z) through the subset of Players A and B, and (z) dominates (x) through the subset of Players B and C.

Von Neumann and Morgenstern's stable set is the set of imputations with the following properties: (a) no imputation in the set dominates any other in the set; and (b) every imputation outside the set is dominated by at least one imputation in the set. The stable set of imputations, considered in its totality, has a certain inner robustness, because no rational player or subset of players has both the will and the power to form a coalition that lies outside it. The core, if it exists, is always in the stable set.

There are two serious drawbacks to the stable set as a solution concept, one relating to uniqueness and the other to existence. In the first place, the stable set typically contains a plethora and often an infinity of imputations. Von Neumann and Morgenstern interpreted them as different "standards of behaviour" governed by social and moral conventions, but there are no rational criteria for choosing among them. This is the case, for example, in the simplified Shareholders' game. One of its stable sets is $\{(12, 12, 0),$ $(12, 0, 12), (0, 12, 12)\}$, and it is the most intuitively appealing, because it means that two of the three players will divide the 24 watches between them, but it is rather feeble as a solution to the game, as the earlier discussion of it showed. Concerning the more serious issue of the existence of stable sets, von Neumann and Morgenstern (1944) had this to say:

> There can be, of course, no concessions as regards existence. If it should turn out that our requirements concerning a solution S are, in any special case, unfulfillable, – this would certainly necessitate a fundamental change in the theory. (p. 42)

Twenty-four years later, William F. Lucas (1968) came up with a 10-person game that has no stable set. Meanwhile, game theorists had been seeking other solution concepts, to which I shall turn after a brief digression.

8.4 Harold Pinter's *The Caretaker*

Harold Pinter's (1960) play *The Caretaker* provides a dramatic illustration of some of the principles outlined in the previous section. There are just three characters in the play, namely Davies, a bigoted old tramp, Aston, a young man suffering from the after-effects of electric shock treatment, and Mick, Aston's younger brother. The action takes place in a room in a dilapidated house in London that is owned by Mick but occupied by Aston.

In Act I Aston invites the tramp Davies, who needs to get himself "sorted out" in some unspecified way, to stay with him on a temporary basis. In Act II Mick visits the house while Aston is out and bullies Davies, who he says is "stinking the place out". When he discovers that his brother Aston invited Davies to stay, he abruptly changes his tune and ingratiates himself with Davies. He tells Davies that he (Mick) is the legal landlord, and he agrees to allow Davies to stay on as caretaker.

In Act III Davies's attitude towards Aston cools dramatically. When Aston buys him a new pair of shoes, he complains that "they don't fit" although "they can do, anyway, until I get another pair". He suggests darkly that Aston should go back to where he came from (presumably the mental hospital) because he is "queer in the head", and he even menaces Aston with a knife. Aston eventually says "I think it's about time you found somewhere else. I don't think we're hitting it off". When Mick hears about these developments he shouts at Davies: "You're violent, you're erratic, you're just completely unpredictable. You're nothing but a wild animal, when you come down to it. ... It's all most regrettable but it looks as though I'm compelled to pay you off for your caretaking work." Mick and Aston look at each other, smiling faintly.

After Mick has left the room, Davies makes an attempt to regain Aston's favour. He tries to convey his willingness to switch his allegiance back from Mick to Aston: "I'd look after the place for you, for you, like, not for the other ... not for ... for your brother, you see, not for him, for you, I'll be your man." When Aston reiterates his request for Davies to leave, Davies says, "But you don't understand my meaning!" and the play ends with this attempted negotiation unresolved.

Three two-person coalitions are possible between the three protagonists in this play. Each one forms, achieves its ends, and dissolves in one of the acts. In Act I the (Aston, Davies) coalition forms. It is beneficial to both, because Aston gains a room-mate who treats him as "normal" and Davies gains a place to live while he sorts himself out. But this coalition is unstable, because both Davies and Mick prefer the (Davies, Mick) coalition, and they have the power to impose it. The (Davies, Mick) coalition, which forms in Act II, seems better for Davies because Mick is the legal landlord, and is better for Mick because Davies's allegiance is transferred to him.

From a strategic point of view, Davies ought to allow the grand coalition (Aston, Davies, Mick) to form: that is the collectively rational solution to the game. But in Act III he commits the blunder of opting for a smaller coalition (Davies, Mick) that has the power to freeze Aston out. He therefore turns on

Aston. But the (Davies, Mick) coalition is also unstable. Both Mick and Aston can improve their payoffs by forming a coalition against Davies. Both brothers now prefer Davies to leave; they form the (Mick, Aston) coalition and Davies is out in the cold, where he was before the action of the play began.

Davies is quick to realize that the (Mick, Aston) coalition is also unstable in the sense that both he and Aston would benefit by re-establishing the original (Aston, Davies) coalition, and they have the power to impose it. Possibly because he feels wounded by Davies's past behaviour, Aston is unwilling to join this coalition. It is Davies who is coldly logical about the strategic structure of the situation, and he seems to think that Aston is not pursuing his own strategic self-interest, because he keeps saying: "But you don't understand my meaning!" The curtain goes down with the possibility of the whole cycle of coalition formation repeating itself from the beginning.

The instability of the situation arises from the fact that every coalition is dominated by another, so the core of the game is empty; in other words, for every coalition that might form there is a subset of players who have the incentive and the power to subvert it. The intuitively "natural" von Neumann-Morgenstern stable set is {(Aston, Davies), (Davies, Mick), (Mick, Aston)}, but this game illustrates the inadequacy of the stable set as a solution concept, because the game goes round in circles and nothing is resolved. The *set* of coalitions in the stable set may indeed deserve the adjective "stable" inasmuch as none of the three coalitions within it dominates any of the others and no coalition outside it dominates any within it, but that does not produce any *particular* coalition that is stable.

Harold Pinter (1972) described his literary style as follows: "For me everything has to do with shape, structure, and overall unity" (p. 33). In *The Caretaker* he depicted, with astonishing simplicity and clarity, the shifting pattern of coalitions in a three-person cooperative game with an empty core and an unsatisfactory stable set. Three coalition patterns among three players are represented in three acts. There is, of course, much more to the play than the strategic instability that it illustrates, but it is easy to miss the wood for the trees. Trussler (1973) pointed out that on seeing a Pinter play for the first time, "one can be merely baffled at a relatively simple but promising piece of work ... or one can be deceived by the apparent profundity" (p. 182). From the point of view of game theory, *The Caretaker* is both simple and rather profound.

The Caretaker has been subjected to metagame analysis by Howard (1971, pp. 140–146). A number of other works of literature, ranging from the Bible and Shakespeare's plays to short stories by Edgar Allan Poe, have been analysed from the perspective of game theory. See Brams (1994) for a useful survey of these contributions.

8.5 Shapley value

Lloyd Shapley's bargaining solution for two-person cooperative games, which was discussed in section 6.10.1, can be extended to n-person cooperative games in characteristic function form. First, the two-person case may be reinterpreted as follows. Player A begins by joining the empty coalition $\emptyset$, thereby forming a one-member coalition and contributing to it a guaranteed payoff equal to the maximin or security level that is the value of the game to Player A. Then Player B joins the coalition, turning it into a two-person grand coalition, and by joining it generally increases the coalition's value. Alternatively, Player B joins first, contributing a payoff equal to the value of the game to that player, and Player A joins second, contributing an increase in the value of the coalition. Assuming that the two orders of joining are equally probable, each player's share of the payoff is the average of that player's two contributions to the total payoff of the coalition.

The *Shapley value* (Shapley, 1953) is a generalization of these ideas to n-person cooperative games (see Roth, 1988, for an extensive collection of articles on it). One interpretation of it is that the Shapley value is the *a priori* value to each player of playing a game with a particular characteristic function and coalition structure. More intuitively, it is the *a priori* value that each player contributes to the grand coalition in a game with a particular characteristic function. On either interpretation, it suggests a rational way of dividing a payoff among the players according to these *a priori* values. Following the second, more intuitive interpretation, all possible permutations of joining the grand coalition must be considered, and in an n-person game, there are $n! = n(n-1)(n-2) \ldots (2)(1)$ permutations of the players (for example, in a 3-person game, the number of permutations is $3! = 3 \times 2 \times 1 = 6$).

To each coalition that might form in a cooperative game there is a value $v(S)$ defined by the characteristic function. The value to the empty coalition is zero by definition, so $v(\emptyset) = 0$. If we imagine the players joining this initially empty coalition one by one until the grand coalition has formed, it is possible to determine how much value each player adds to the coalition by joining it. The Shapley value assigns to each player a share in the joint payoff proportional to the amount that the player adds to the coalition's value. Because the amount that each player adds may depend on the order in which the coalition builds up, all possible permutations are examined, and it is the average amounts of value that the players bring to the coalition, taking all possible orders into account, that determine their relative shares of the joint payoff.

The Shapley value is the best-known and most widely used solution concept for n-person cooperative games (Chun, 1989), so for the benefit of mathematically minded readers it is worth defining it formally. If $N = \{1, 2, \ldots, n\}$ is the set of players, $S \subseteq N$ is a coalition of size (that is, number of members) $|S|$, and $v(S)$ is the value of the coalition, the function $\phi(v)$ assigns a payoff $\phi_i(v)$ to each player i in the game, and the Shapley value is defined by

$$\phi_i(v) = \sum_{S:i \in S} \frac{(|S| - 1)! \, |N - S|!}{|N|!} \, [v(S) - v(S - i)].$$

The Shapley value may be illustrated with the weighted majority voting version of the Shareholders' game introduced in section 8.2. Three shareholders have to reach a majority decision about how to divide 24 gold watches among themselves, and the voting strengths of Players A, B, and C are 50 per cent, 40 per cent, and 10 per cent respectively. Now imagine a grand coalition building up from scratch. Because this is a so-called *simple* game in which every coalition that might form is either winning or losing, and in this case the value of a coalition is either 24 or zero, each of the players stands a chance of being the pivotal voter who changes an impotent coalition with a security level of zero into a winning one with a guaranteed minimum payoff of 24 gold watches. We must consider all possible orders of coalition formation.

The first player to join the coalition is never pivotal in this game, because no single shareholder commands a majority (more than 50 per cent) of the votes. If Player A, with a 50 per cent vote, joins first, then the second player to join is bound to be pivotal. On the other hand, if Player B, with a 40 per cent vote, joins first and is subsequently joined by Player C, with a 10 per cent vote, then an absolute majority is still lacking, and it is Player A who is pivotal in making the coalition winning by joining last. Continuing in this vein for all six permutations of the three players, we arrive at the results shown in Table 8.1.

In four cases out of six, Player A is pivotal in transforming a coalition into a winning majority. Players B and C are each pivotal in one of the six cases. It follows that if the six orders of coalition formation are equiprobable, then the probability that Player A would be pivotal is 2/3, the probability that Player B would be pivotal is 1/6, and the probability that Player C would be pivotal is 1/6. If the payoff is distributed according to the Shapley value, then Player A, who adds 2/3 of the total payoff of 24 watches to the grand coalition's value, receives 16 of the 24 gold watches, and Players B and C, each of whom adds 1/6, receive 4 watches each.

Table 8.1 Coalitions and pivots in the Shareholders' game

Order	A-B-C	A-C-B	B-A-C	B-C-A	C-A-B	C-B-A
Pivot	B	C	A	A	A	A

This result is rather unexpected, and it illustrates how the players' voting strengths can be a misleading index of their real *a priori* power in a weighted majority game. Player *A*, who commands only 50 per cent of the vote, commands a relative power of 67 per cent. The reason for this is that no winning coalition can form without Player *A*'s cooperation. Even more surprising is the fact that Players *B* and *C* have equal *a priori* power. Although Player B commands 40 per cent of the vote and Player C only 10 per cent, the power index of each is approximately 17 per cent. This is because they are equally likely to be pivotal, and from Player *A*'s point of view Player *C* is just as good a coalition partner as Player *B* in spite of the difference in their voting strengths.

Unlike the core and the stable set, the Shapley value exists for every *n*-person cooperative game in characteristic function form. Unfortunately, in a game that does have a core, the Shapley value may be an imputation outside the core. This highlights the contrasting virtues of the core and the Shapley value, namely stability and equity respectively. An imputation in the core has the virtue of stability that no player or subset of players has any incentive to defect from the grand coalition, whereas the Shapley value has the virtue of equity that the players' relative shares of the joint payoff are proportional to the average contributions that they provide in the process of coalition formation (or, in another interpretation, to the value to each player of playing the game).

Applications of the Shapley value to measure the distribution of power in real-world decision-making bodies have produced interesting results. Shapley and Shubik (1954) performed an analysis, essentially similar to the one described above, on the United Nations Security Council. They showed that in the 1950s the permanent members of the Security Council with the power to veto resolutions, namely the United States, the Soviet Union, China, the United Kingdom, and France, controlled 98.7 per cent of the power, while the six non-permanent members controlled only 1.3 per cent. In 1965 four new non-permanent members were added to the Security Council with the express purpose of reducing the relative power of the permanent members, but the effect of this was only marginal (Brams, 1975, p. 187; Riker and Ordeshook, 1973, p. 172). Shapley and Shubik also calculated that, in the United States legislature, the power indices for a single congressman, a single senator, and the president are in the proportions 2:9:350. The president thus has 175 times as much *a priori* power as a representative and almost 40 times as much as a senator.

8.6 Kernel, nucleolus, and least core

The solution concept called the *kernel*, introduced by Davis and Maschler (1965), is based on pairwise comparisons of all players in a game in terms of the "excess" payoff that one of the players could potentially gain by forming a coalition that excludes the other. The kernel of a game is the set of all payoff vectors and coalitions such that every pair of players within the same coalition are in equilibrium in the sense that neither player outweighs the other when this comparison is made.

In any specified coalition, it is possible to compare every pair of players i and j with regard to all the potential coalitions to which each of them could belong. Player i's *maximum excess* over Player j is the largest increase in payoff that Player i could achieve by defecting to some other coalition that excluded Player j. It may be interpreted as Player i's hope of the best that might be possible in an ideal world without j. The assumption is that by defecting from the current coalition and forming the new coalition S that excludes Player j, Player i would receive all the excess payoffs that the coalition S can earn over and above what the members of S receive in the current coalition, because that would leave the other members of S no worse off than they are in the current coalition. Mathematically, all of the excess represented by $v(S) - \Sigma x_i$ for $i \in S$ is assumed to be available to Player i in the hypothetical alternative coalition S. Conversely, Player j's maximum excess over Player i is the largest increase in payoff that Player j could achieve by defecting to a coalition that excluded Player i.

Comparing any two players in a specified coalition, the player with the larger maximum excess is clearly the stronger, in the sense of being able to gain more by excluding the other player than the other player could gain by excluding the first. But if Player i has a larger maximum excess than Player j, Player i can *outweigh* Player j only if Player j's payoff in the current coalition is more than Player j could obtain alone, that is, if $x_j > v(j)$, because otherwise Player j has no positive incentive to remain in the current coalition and is therefore invulnerable to Player i's blandishments despite Player i's greater strength. But if (a) Player i's maximum excess exceeds Player j's, and (b) Player j's payoff in the current coalition is greater than the value of the game to Player j operating alone, then Player i outweighs Player j. If neither player outweighs the other, then the pair is said to be in equilibrium within that coalition. The kernel of the game is then simply the set of all payoff vectors and coalitions such that every pair of players within the same coalition are in equilibrium.

As an example, consider the following game:

$$v(\emptyset) = 0;$$

$$v(A) = 0, v(B) = 0, v(C) = 0;$$

$$v(A, B) = 18, v(A, C) = 16, v(B, C) = 14;$$

$$v(A, B, C) = 21.$$

Suppose Players A and C are considering forming a coalition and dividing the joint payoff of 16 so that Player A receives 9 and Player C receives 7, so that the payoff vector would be $(x) = (9, 0, 7)$. There are two possible coalitions that include Player A but exclude Player C, namely the "coalition" containing Player A alone and the coalition containing Players A and B. In the first of these, Player A would be worse off by 9 units, because the current payoff vector offers 9 units and $v(A) = 0$. But in the second potential coalition Player A, by taking all the excess payoffs, would be better off by 9 units, because $v(A, B) = 18$ and $18 - 9 - 0 = 9$. The maximum excess of Player A over Player C in the coalition (A, C) is therefore the greater of the two numbers -9 and 9, so it is 9. It is easily verified that Player C's maximum excess over Player A is 7. Furthermore, Player C's payoff in the current coalition is more than Player C could obtain alone, that is $x_C > v(C)$, so Player C has an incentive to remain in the coalition with Player A. The pair is therefore not in equilibrium, because Player A outweighs Player C, and the coalition of Players A and C with the proposed payoff vector is not in the kernel of the game.

Consider now the grand coalition of Players A, B, and C and the payoff vector $(x) = (9, 7, 5)$. In this case the maximum excess of every player over every other player in pairwise comparisons is 2 units, and therefore all pairs are in equilibrium and the coalition and payoff vector is in the kernel of the game. Davis and Maschler (1965) proved that for every coalition structure of every game in characteristic function form there exists at least one payoff vector in the kernel, and that for every three-person game there is exactly one payoff vector in the kernel for any coalition structure.

The *nucleolus* is a solution concept that was introduced by Schmeidler (1969). It is closely related to the kernel because it relies on the idea of an "excess" that can be gained by defecting from the current coalition structure, but the kernel compares players to players, whereas the nucleolus compares coalitions to coalitions. The nucleolus combines the core's virtue of stability with the Shapley value's virtue of equity. Every game has one and only one nucleolus, and unless the game's core is empty, the nucleolus is part of the core. Furthermore, the nucleolus is always part of the kernel.

The basic idea behind the nucleolus is to find an imputation that makes the unhappiest potential coalition happier than the unhappiest potential coalition under any other imputation. Assuming that the grand coalition has formed, consider the imputation $(x) = (x_1, x_2, \ldots, x_n)$, and assume that S is a subset of the set of players who have an incentive to defect from the grand coalition and form a smaller coalition. If that is the case, then the sum of their payoffs in the grand coalition is less than the payoff that they could guarantee in some coalition outside the grand coalition, or mathematically, $\Sigma x_i < v(S)$ for $i \in S$. A measure of how unhappy the members of S are when they contemplate defecting and forming this coalition is the quantity e by which they could increase their joint payoff by forming the coalition S. If the value of the coalition were reduced by the amount e, then it would be no greater than the sum of its members' payoffs in the grand coalition, or

$\Sigma x_i \geq v(S) - e$, and the unhappiness of the members of S would therefore be eliminated.

To construct the nucleolus, we therefore find the smallest e for which $\Sigma x_i \geq v(S) - e$ for all $i \in S$, for all $S \subset N$. In addition, we ensure that the x_i satisfy the collective rationality requirement of an imputation that the sum of the payoffs to the players in the grand coalition should equal the joint payoff to the grand coalition, so that nothing is wasted, or mathematically, $\Sigma x_i = v(N)$. The set of imputations $(x) = (x_1, x_2, \ldots, x_n)$ satisfying these conditions is called the *least core* of the game. The least core is closely related to the core, because the core (which was defined in section 8.3 as the imputation satisfying $\Sigma x_i \geq v(S)$ for all $i \in S$, for all $S \subset N$) is merely a special case of the least core when $e = 0$. There may be more than one imputation in the least core, and to select the one that is the nucleolus we choose the one that minimizes the unhappiness e of the unhappiest potential coalition under it (see Thomas, 1984, pp. 99–101 for a succinct exposition of the mathematical computations involved in finding the nucleolus).

8.7 Coalition-predicting theories

The theories that have been discussed so far address the question of how the members of a coalition are likely to divide the joint payoff in an n-person cooperative game. But equally important, from the practical point of view, is the question of which particular coalitions are likely to form. The classical theories of coalition formation tend to ignore this second question, because from a normative point of view the grand coalition is always as good as any other coalition structure. This is a consequence of the usual requirement mentioned in section 8.2 that the characteristic function should be superadditive, which was expressed mathematically as

$$v(S \cup T) \geq v(S) + v(T) \quad \text{for all } S, T \subseteq N, \text{ such that } S \cap T = \varnothing.$$

This implies that the grand coalition of all the players is always collectively rational, because the total guaranteed payoff to the players is always at least as high if they act together as a single coalition as it is if the players act as members of smaller coalitions or as individuals. But the grand coalition does not always or even generally form in practical situations, and some theories have been devised specifically to address the question of which particular coalitions will form.

8.7.1 Equal excess theory

Equal excess theory (Komorita, 1979) is one of the very few theories designed to deal with both coalition formation and payoff division. This theory conceptualizes the bargaining process as a series of discrete rounds of negotiation in which each player has *a priori* expectations of payoff from each potential coalition that could include that player. At the beginning of the negotiation process, according to equal excess theory, all players expect equal shares in any coalitions in which they are included, and they try to form the coalitions that maximize those expectations. On subsequent rounds, the theory predicts that each player expects a share equal to the payoff available in the best alternative coalition that the player could potentially join. As the negotiation proceeds, the players' expectations and claims change because of the different coalitions to which they might belong.

As far as the formation of coalitions is concerned, equal excess theory predicts that the most likely coalitions are the ones that jointly maximize the expectations of their members. At the end of the negotiation process, the expectations of the players in each coalition are summed and the total is compared to the value $v(S)$ of the agreed coalition. Any excess payoff that is left over after the players have all received what they expected is divided equally between them, or alternatively, if the sum of the expectations exceeds the value $v(S)$ of the coalition, the difference is subtracted equally from each of their claims, so that they all make equal sacrifices.

The following example is taken from Kahan and Rapoport (1984, pp. 150–151):

$$v(\varnothing) = 0;$$

$$v(A) = 0, \; v(B) = 0, \; v(C) = 0;$$

$$v(A, B) = 90, \; v(A, C) = 80, \; v(B, C) = 70;$$

$$v(A, B, C) = 0.$$

At the start of the negotiation process, the players have expectations of equal division of payoffs, so for the coalition (A, B) each player expects 45, for the coalition (A, C) they each expect 40, and for the coalition (B, C) they each expect 35. If the game terminates immediately, the most likely coalition is (A, B) with the payoff vector $(x) = (45, 45, 0)$. If negotiations continue to the next round, then for coalition (A, B), Player A's best alternative is coalition (A, C) with a payoff of 40, and Player B's best alternative is coalition (B, C) with a payoff of 35. In the light of this, Player A's expectation in the coalition (A, B) rises to the value of the best alternative plus an equal share of the excess, or $40 + (90 - 40 - 35)/2 = 47\frac{1}{2}$, and Player B's expectation in the same coalition falls to $35 + (90 - 40 - 35)/2 = 42\frac{1}{2}$. It can be shown similarly that Player A's expectation in the coalition (A, C) becomes 45, Player C's expectation in (A, C) becomes 35, Player B's expectation in (B, C) becomes $37\frac{1}{2}$, and Player C's expectation in (B, C) becomes $32\frac{1}{2}$. If the game ends there, then the most likely coalition is (A, B) with the payoff vector $(x) =$

$(47\frac{1}{2}, 42\frac{1}{2}, 0)$. The negotiations are repeated in the same way for an indefinite number of rounds, and it can be shown that the payoff vector converges to the limiting values $(x) = (50, 40, 0)$.

8.7.2 Caplow's theory

Caplow's (1956, 1959) theory of coalitions in the triad had a strong influence on social psychological research in the 1960s but was less often referred to in the succeeding decades. It is a sociological theory based on social psychological assumptions and restricted to three-person games that are simple (in which a coalition is either winning or losing) rather than multi-valued. The four assumptions on which it rests are: (a) members of a triad may differ in strength, and a stronger member who can control a weaker one will do so; (b) control over two others is preferred to control over one, which is preferred to control over none; (c) the strength of a coalition is equal to the additive strength of its members; and (d) any attempt by a stronger member to coerce a weaker member into joining a non-advantageous coalition will provoke the formation of an advantageous coalition to oppose the coercion. These assumptions are treated like axioms, although they lack the usual property of axioms of being transparently obvious, and Caplow provided no evidence to demonstrate their truth. On the basis of the assumptions, the theory predicts which coalitions are most likely to form. For example, if Player A is stronger than Player B, Player B is stronger than Player C, and Players B and C together are stronger than Player A, then "A seeks to join both B and C, and C seeks to join both A and B, but B has no incentive to enter a coalition with A and has a very strong incentive to enter a coalition with C" (Caplow, 1959, p. 490). The prediction is therefore that either Players A and C or Players B and C will form a coalition.

8.7.3 Minimal winning coalition theory

Riker's (1962) minimal winning coalition theory is based on the idea that if a coalition is large enough to win, then it should avoid taking in any superfluous members, because the new members will demand a share in the payoff. If the players seek to maximize their individual payoffs, therefore, one of the smallest (minimal) winning coalitions should form. The ejection of superfluous members allows the payoff to be divided among fewer players, and this is bound to be to the advantage of the remaining coalition members (see also Riker, 1967b, pp. 167–174; Riker and Ordeshook, 1973, pp. 179–180). For example, consider the weighted majority version of the Shareholders' game introduced in section 8.2, in which Players A, B, and C with relative voting strengths 50, 40, and 10 respectively have to agree by majority vote how to divide 24 gold watches among themselves, with a deadlock resulting in a zero payoff to everyone. Minimal winning coalition theory does not predict which of the two minimal winning coalitions (A, B) or (A, C), should form, but it rules out the non-winning coalition (B, C) and the non-minimal winning coalition (A, B, C).

8.7.4 Minimum resource theory

Gamson's (1961) minimum resource theory is more specific. It assumes that each member of a winning coalition should demand a share in the payoff corresponding to that member's relative voting strength in the coalition. According to this principle, in the Shareholders' game Player A can expect a larger individual share in the (A, C) coalition, where Player A has a 50 per cent vote compared with the other coalition member's 10 per cent, than in the (A, B) and (A, B, C) coalitions where Player A's relative voting strength is less. Minimum resource theory therefore predicts that Player A should prefer to form a coalition with Player C, and the winning coalition (A, C) should thus emerge. This coalition has the property of commanding the minimum resource – in this case the minimum total percentage vote – of any winning coalition. It commands a total of 60 per cent (Player A's 50 per cent plus Player C's 10 per cent), whereas the other winning coalitions command 90 and 100 per cent respectively.

8.8 Experiments on coalition formation

The earliest experimental investigation of coalition formation was the study by Kalisch, Milnor, Nash, and Nering (1954). It was followed by Vinacke and Arkoff's (1957) more influential research into coalitions in the triad. Since then, more than two dozen experiments on coalition formation have been published. Critical reviews of the experimental literature have been provided by Gamson (1964); Vinacke (1969); Chertkoff (1970); Stryker (1972); Tedeschi, Schlenker, and Bonoma (1973, chap. 6); Burhans (1973); Miller and Crandall (1980); Komorita (1984); Kahan and Rapoport (1984, chaps. 11, 12, 13); and Rapoport (1987).

Following the lead of Vinacke and Arkoff (1957), most early experimenters used a research methodology based on the Pachisi board game or a variation of it. Pachisi is an ancient Indian board game similar to backgammon. Each player places a counter on the START square of the board, and then rolls a die and moves the counter a certain number of squares towards the HOME square depending on what number came up on the die. In coalition experiments, relative weights are assigned to each player to model voting strengths in a shareholder's meeting or a political assembly, for example.

Thus if the three players are weighted 4, 3, and 2 and the die shows 6, then the first player moves $4 \times 6 = 24$ squares, the second moves $3 \times 6 = 18$ squares, and the third moves $2 \times 6 = 12$ squares towards HOME. The object of the game is to get to HOME before the other players.

In coalition experiments, communication and negotiation between players is allowed, so that pairs or larger groups can form coalitions at any time. A coalition receives a new counter and moves as a single player with a weight equal to the sum of its constituent members' weights, so that if the coalition members are weighted 4 and 3, for example, then their combined weight is 7. A pair or a larger group wishing to form a coalition has to commit itself in advance to a binding agreement regarding the division of the payoff among its members should the coalition win. The first player or coalition to reach HOME receives a payoff (in points or money) and the others receive nothing.

The research methodology based on the Pachisi board game and its variations (Kahan and Rapoport, 1984, pp. 254–259) was later largely supplanted by simulations of weighted majority games involving delegation votes at political conventions or similar scenarios. Gamson (1961a) was the first to use a simulated political convention game in which subjects played the roles of delegates, each controlling a fixed number of votes in the manner of bloc delegations at political party conventions in the United States or representatives at the Council of Ministers of the European Union. Both weighted majority games and the Pachisi game are constant-sum unless complicated modifications are introduced, and they both model simple games in which a coalition either wins or loses. Later researchers who were anxious to model coalition formation in variable-sum and multi-valued games therefore tended to use a methodology based on negotiations in abstract games presented in characteristic function form.

Kahan and Rapoport (1984, chap. 12) provided a critical review of ten experimental studies of three-person cooperative games played in characteristic function form (Kahan and Rapoport, 1974b, 1977; Kaufman and Tack, 1975; Levinsohn and Rapoport, 1978; Lichtenberger, 1975; Maschler, 1978; Medlin, 1976; Rapoport and Kahan, 1976; Riker, 1967a, 1971). Kahan and Rapoport attempted to gauge the degree to which the results of the ten experiments conformed to various theories, including some that were discussed earlier in this chapter, namely the core, the least core, the kernel, and the Shapley value.

On the whole, the theories performed reasonably well, suggesting that experimental subjects do indeed follow game theory prescriptions of rationality to some extent at least. The kernel provided the best overall fit to the experimental data, performing slightly better than the Shapley value, but the evidence suggests that powerful players do not universally extract the full reward that the kernel would allot to them. A critical review of nine experimental studies of n-person cooperative games with $n > 3$ (Kahan and

Rapoport, 1984, chap. 13) led to similar conclusions, although the theories did not perform as well in these experiments.

Komorita (1984) compared the Shapley value, minimum resource theory, equal excess theory, and a few others by examining how well the data from a number of published experiments based on simple and multi-valued experimental games conformed to their prescriptions. Equal excess theory performed better than the others at predicting both which coalitions would form and how the payoffs would be divided among the players, but the Shapley value performed quite well in predicting payoff division in superadditive multi-valued games. In subsequent experiments, equal excess theory received only weak support (Komorita and Ellis, 1988; Komorita and Miller, 1986; Miller and Komorita, 1986).

Earlier experimental research tended to focus on constant-sum simple games (e.g., Chertkoff, 1966, 1971; Kelley and Arrowood, 1960; Psathas and Stryker, 1965; Stryker and Psathas, 1960; Vinacke and Arkoff, 1957). The results showed that winning coalitions formed much more often than losing coalitions, as might be expected. According to minimal winning coalition theory, no incentives exist for coalitions larger than the minimal winning size to form, and in the empirical literature this is often referred to as the *size principle*. For example, in a three-person weighted majority game, if the players' weights are 4, 3, and 2, the theory predicts that (any) two-way coalition will form, whereas in the 4, 2, 1 case no coalitions should form because Player A can win the whole payoff alone and has no incentive to take on any coalition partner. Stringent tests of minimal winning coalition theory require the use of groups containing four or more players, and the evidence from such experiments tends to corroborate the theory. One of the most ambitious and carefully controlled studies was conducted by Michener, Fleishman, Vaske, and Statza (1975), who reported that coalitions without superfluous members formed in 88 per cent of cases out of a total of 288 plays with various weight distributions in four-person groups. The grand coalition of all players accounted for most of the remaining outcomes reflecting, perhaps, anti-competitive attitudes among some subjects.

Riker (1962) and Brams (1975, pp. 220–232) summarized empirical evidence from the field of national and international politics bearing on minimal winning coalition theory. In the international arena the historical record shows that overwhelming and therefore obviously non-minimal coalitions, such as the Allied powers after World Wars I and II, were invariably plagued by internal strife. According to Brams (1975), "the hopes for permanent peace enshrined first in the League of Nations and now in the United Nations founder on the size principle precisely because of the undiscriminating inclusiveness of these international organizations" (p. 223). Further anecdotal evidence comes from the disintegration of superfluous majorities in American politics, and examples have been adduced from French, Danish, Italian, Dutch, West German, Israeli, Japanese, and even tribal African politics (for references, see Brams, 1975, p. 227). Most of this evidence seems to be consistent with Riker's minimal winning coalition theory, but more recently Steunenberg (1992) reported a detailed analysis of coalition formation in Dutch municipalities that provided mixed results: minimal winning coalition theory yielded accurate predictions for the period of coalition bargaining after the elections of 1982 and 1986 but was wildly inaccurate for the negotiations after the election of 1978.

The empirical predictions of minimum resource theory do not contradict those of minimal winning coalition theory, but minimum resource theory is more specific in certain cases and therefore potentially more powerful (and more easily refuted by empirical evidence). Consider once again the case of a triad in which Players A, B, and C are weighted 4, 3, and 2 respectively. Minimal winning coalition theory predicts that one of the smallest winning coalitions (A, B), (A, C), or (B, C) will form, whereas minimum resource theory singles out the cheapest winning coalition (B, C) as the likely outcome. This coalition is the one "in which the total resources are as small as possible while still being sufficient" and it arises, according to the theory, from a "parity norm", that is, a belief likely to be shared by the players "that a person ought to get from an agreement an amount proportional to what he brings into it" (Gamson, 1964, pp. 86, 88). If the players are guided by the parity norm, they are inevitably led to the winning coalition that controls the minimum resources. In the 4, 3, 2 case, Player A will prefer to join with Player C rather than with Player B, because then Player A will be entitled to a larger share of the payoff in a coalition with Player C than in a coalition with Player B where the disparity in the coalition partners' weights would be smaller. For the same reason, Player B will prefer to join with player C, and Player C will prefer to join with Player B. The only one of these choices of partner that is reciprocated is the one between Players B and C who will therefore, according to the theory, form what (inevitably) turns out to be the winning coalition that controls the minimum resources.

Early experimental investigations (e.g., Chaney and Vinacke, 1960; Chertkoff, 1966, 1971; Chertkoff and Braden, 1974; Crosbie and Kullberg, 1973; Kelley and Arrowood, 1960; Vinacke and Arkoff, 1957) tended to confirm the predictions of minimum resource theory about which coalitions are most likely to form. These results were particularly impressive in view of the fact that they were often counterintuitive: in the example above, the player who seems to be most powerful (Player A) tends to be excluded from coalitions precisely as a consequence of having "excessive" power and is actually at a disadvantage compared to the weaker players. In more recent experiments minimum resource theory fared less well (Komorita, 1984). Furthermore, it is not applicable to multi-valued games, and in simple games in which resource weights are not assigned it makes no predictions.

The exclusion of the apparently strongest player from coalitions in games with certain weight distributions is called the *power inversion paradox*. It makes intelligible certain otherwise puzzling political and economic phenomena and provides a strategic interpretation of the way in which people tend to gang up against one who seems too powerful (see sections 10.8 and 11.2 for discussions of closely related phenomena in the context of strategic voting and coalition formation). But it is important to realize that the power inversion paradox arises from an illusion; it has no rational basis. In the 4, 3, 2 example, the players actually have equal power in spite of their disparate weights: any two-person coalition wins, and the weights are only window-dressing. A Shapley value analysis (see section 8.5) confirms that the players' *a priori* power is equal. Several researchers have found that the power inversion effect declines when a simple coalition game of this type is iterated many times with the same group of subjects. Presumably the subjects gradually come to realize that the weights do not reflect real power differences (Kelley and Arrowood, 1960; Psathas and Stryker, 1965; Stryker and Psathas, 1960). Gamson (1962) tested his minimum resource theory on historical data from real presidential nominating conventions over a 53-year period. These data support the theory to a degree, but the fit was far from perfect. Gamson commented that the "modest success here in situations characterized by so many unique historical features is more satisfying than the neater but more easily obtained experimental results" (p. 171).

The predictions of minimum resource theory about the distributions of payoffs to which coalition members will agree are not well supported by experimental evidence either. According to the theory, the players should split the payoffs by applying the parity norm, that is, in proportion to their relative weights. In the 4, 3, 2 example, if Players B and C form a coalition – as they usually do – Player B should get 3/5 and Player C 2/5 of the payoff by mutual agreement. But the evidence consistently shows that subjects tend to reach agreements somewhere between this parity split and an equal division of the payoff (e.g., Chertkoff, 1971; Kelley and Arrowood, 1960). Opinions differ regarding how damaging these findings are to the theory (see, e.g., Crosbie and Kullberg, 1973; Nail and Cole, 1985; Wilke and Mulder, 1971).

Research reported by Samuelson and Allison (1994) may help to explain this particular failure of minimum resource theory. These researchers showed that experimental subjects tend to use *equal* division of payoffs (an equality norm) as a general rule of thumb, or a *social decision heuristic* as the authors call it, to the extent that environmental cues pushing them towards other ways of dividing the payoffs are weak or absent. The results of two experiments showed that the types of environmental cues that encourage unequal division of payoffs include quite subtle aspects of role assignments that evoke feelings of privileged status in the stronger players.

Gamson (1964) suggested that accidental and irrelevant factors like the relative loudness of the players' voices and the seating pattern will determine coalition choices in "difficult" circumstances, that is, when time pressure is severe, there are numerous players, the players are strangers and are unsophisticated, the rules of the game are complicated, communication difficulties exist, the payoff is barely worth striving for, and so forth. The evidence tends to confirm the obvious prediction of what has been called *utter confusion theory* that coalitions will form more or less at random in such circumstances (e.g., Kalisch, Milnor, Nash, and Nering, 1954; Willis, 1962). At the opposite end of the spectrum, when conditions are favourable and the players are strongly motivated, the behaviour of the subjects is more likely to correspond to the prescriptions and predictions of the various theories (Kahan and Rapoport, 1984, chap. 14).

8.9 Summary

Section 8.1 outlined the differences between cooperative (negotiable) and non-cooperative (non-negotiable) n-person games. The basic tools of n-person cooperative game theory, namely the characteristic function and imputation, were explained in section 8.2. The most important of the solution concepts for n-person cooperative games were discussed in the following sections. Section 8.3 dealt with the core and the stable set, and in section 8.4 these concepts were illustrated with reference to Harold Pinter's play, *The Caretaker*, in which a shifting pattern of coalitions occurs in a three-person game with an empty core, so that a potential coalition exists with both the will and the power to subvert any existing coalition. Section 8.5 dealt with the Shapley value, section 8.6 with the kernel, nucleolus, and least core, and section 8.7 with theories that predict which particular coalitions will form: Komorita's equal excess theory, Caplow's theory of coalitions in the triad, Riker's minimal winning coalition theory, and Gamson's minimum resource theory. Section 8.8 reviewed experimental studies of coalition formation designed to evaluate the predictive power of the various theories discussed earlier.

___ 9 ___

Multi-person non-cooperative games and social dilemmas

9.1 *N*-Person non-cooperative games: Nash equilibria

An *n*-person game is an abstract model of a social interaction in which there are three or more decision makers, each with a choice of two or more ways of acting and well-defined preferences among the possible outcomes, which depend on the strategy choices of all the players. If the decision makers are not able to negotiate binding and enforceable agreements regarding their actions and the apportionment of any resulting payoffs, then the appropriate abstract model is an *n*-person *non-cooperative* game. This type of model is used to analyse multi-person interdependent decision making where binding and enforceable agreements are impossible and there are therefore no prospects of coalition formation. In everyday strategic interactions, negotiation and coalition formation are often impossible, and they are sometimes explicitly forbidden where they might otherwise be possible. For example, the antitrust laws in the United States and the Monopolies and Restrictive Practices Act in Britain are expressly designed to ensure that certain economic games are played non-cooperatively.

Formal solutions to non-cooperative games are based on Nash equilibria, which were explained in section 4.3, sometimes with the refinements of subgame perfectness, which was outlined in section 6.2. A Nash equilibrium is a combination of strategies that are best against one another and that therefore gives the players no cause to regret their strategy choices when the choices of the others are revealed. In other words, no player can obtain a better payoff by deviating unilaterally from a Nash equilibrium. John Nash (1950a, 1951) proved that every finite game has at least one equilibrium point in pure or mixed strategies, and John Harsanyi (1973b) later proved that "almost all" finite games have an odd number of equilibrium points. The problem, which was commented on in section 6.1 in relation to two-person games, is that in games that are not finite and zero-sum, and in which the minimax theorem therefore does not apply, there are often several Nash equilibria that are *non-equivalent*, each one assigning different payoffs to the players, and that these equilibria are often associated with strategies that are *non-interchangeable*, so that if each of the players chooses a strategy associated with one of the equilibria, the outcome is not necessarily an equilibrium. In other words, equilibrium points do not provide adequate solutions even to two-person games unless the games are zero-sum. The problems are compounded in *n*-person games, which generally have a large number of non-equivalent equilibria with non-interchangeable equilibrium strategies. Fortunately, in certain specific cases, some of which will be discussed in the pages that follow, it is none the less possible to determine how rational players will behave.

This chapter is devoted to a detailed examination of theoretical and empirical research into a small number of important and interesting multi-person non-cooperative games. In section 9.2 the paradoxical Chain-store game, which is closely related to the game of Predatory Pricing discussed in connection with backward induction and subgame perfectness in section 6.2, will be discussed. Section 9.3 will focus on auction games – the diabolical Dollar Auction game – together with other psychological traps and the empirical evidence related to them. Sections 9.4, 9.5, and 9.6 will deal with discursive and theoretical aspects of social dilemmas and compound games in general, and section 9.7 will review the experimental evidence related to them, especially as regards group size effects, communication effects, individual differences and attribution effects, payoff and incentive effects, and framing effects. The chapter will be summarized in section 9.8.

9.2 The Chain-store paradox and backward induction

The paradoxical Chain-store game was discovered by Reinhard Selten (1978), and it has been discussed by a number of commentators, including Rosenthal (1981), Kreps and Wilson (1982), Milgrom and Roberts (1982), Ordeshook (1986, pp. 451–462), Friedman (1991, pp. 190–193), and Bicchieri (1993, pp. 192–194). It is essentially an *n*-person extension of the game of Predatory Pricing discussed in section 6.2, and it shares a certain family resemblance with the Centipede game that was also discussed in that section.

A chain store has branches in 20 cities and faces one potential competitor in each. The potential competitors decide one by one in order, A, B, ..., T, whether to enter the market, and whenever one of them decides to do so the chain store responds either aggressively with predatory pricing or cooperatively with normal pricing.

Challenger A chooses whether or not to enter the market by opening a competing store in the first city, so challenger A's two possible moves are labelled IN and OUT. If challenger A chooses IN, then Chain store responds with either PREDATORY, a predatory pricing move involving slashing the prices of its products to prevent challenger A from building up a customer base, or COOPERATIVE, a cooperative move. If challenger A stays out of the market, challenger A's payoff is zero and Chain store's is 100 units,

Matrix 9.1 *Single-challenger*
Chain-store Game: Normal Form

Chain store

		Predatory	Cooperative
Challenger	IN	–10, –10	50, 50
	OUT	0, 100	0, 100

representing maximum profits in that city. If challenger A chooses IN and Chain store responds with PREDATORY, both players suffer small losses, equivalent to 10 per cent of the profits that Chain store could have expected in that city if unchallenged, so that each player receives a payoff of –10 units. Finally, if challenger A chooses IN and Chain store responds with COOPERATIVE, they end up with equal market shares and profits, so that each receives a payoff of 50. The normal form of this initial round of the game is shown in Matrix 9.1, and the extensive form is shown in Figure 9.1.

Remember that the players' strategies have slightly different inter-pretations. The rows labelled IN and OUT in Matrix 9.1 represent challenger A's options to enter the market or to stay out of the market at the beginning of the game, but the columns labelled PREDATORY and COOPERATIVE mean that Chain store responds with a predatory pricing or a cooperative move if challenger A chooses IN; Chain store has no move to make if challenger A chooses OUT. After challenger A has made a move and Chain store has responded (if necessary), it is challenger B's turn to choose IN or OUT, and Chain store responds according to the same payoff matrix or game

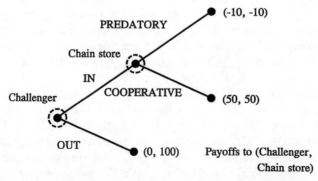

Figure 9.1 *Single-challenger Chain-store game: Extensive form*

tree, and so the game continues until the twentieth potential competitor has had a turn and Chain store has responded if necessary. On every round the payoffs are as shown in Matrix 9.1 or Figure 9.1, and the game is one of perfect information, with every move being made in the full knowledge of all moves that have preceded it.

Although it was shown in section 6.2 that the threat of predatory pricing would fail to deter a solitary potential competitor from entering the market, it seems intuitively obvious that the Chain-store game should be different, because the chain store faces far greater losses and has a much stronger motive to respond aggressively to the early potential competitors in order to deter the later ones. But backward induction shows that this is not the case under the standard assumption of *common knowledge of rationality* (each player is rational and knows that each of the others is rational, that each of the others knows that each of the others knows this, and so on). That is what makes the Chain-store game a paradox.

The backward induction argument begins with the situation after 19 of the 20 potential competitors have made their moves, and the last one, challenger *T*, is ready to move. This subgame of the original Chain-store game is identical to the game of Predatory Pricing discussed in section 6.2, where it was shown that although both (IN, COOPERATIVE) and (OUT, PREDA-TORY) are Nash equilibria, the second of these equilibria is not subgame perfect. It represents irrational behaviour and expectations, and it cannot arise from rational play. Under the assumption of common knowledge of rationality, challenger *T* knows that Chain store will not respond to IN with PREDATORY, because COOPERATIVE gives Chain store a much better payoff, so challenger *T* will choose IN, because IN followed by COOPER-ATIVE from Chain store gives challenger *T* a much better payoff than OUT. Backward induction thus shows that challenger *T* will enter the market and that Chain store will respond with COOPERATIVE in this terminal subgame. This conclusion is not affected by what challengers *A*, *B*, ..., *S* may have done at earlier stages of the Chain-store game, nor by how Chain store may have responded to those earlier moves.

Now consider the stage at which the 19th potential competitor, challenger *S*, is about to make a move. Once again, if challenger *S* chooses IN, Chain store's best response is COOPERATIVE, because we have already seen that predatory pricing will not deter the potential competitor who is to follow, so challenger *S* will choose IN and Chain store will respond with COOPER-ATIVE. It follows that the 18th potential competitor, challenger *R*, will also choose IN, and in that case Chain store will also respond with COOPER-ATIVE, and by backward induction this applies to every potential competitor including the first, challenger *A*. There is only one subgame-perfect equilibrium in the Chain-store game, and that is the outcome in which challengers *A*, *B*, ..., *T* all choose IN and in each case Chain store responds with COOPERATIVE. The inescapable conclusion from backward induction is that every rational competitor will choose IN and Chain store will always respond with cooperative rather than predatory pricing. Selten points out that this conclusion is hard to swallow:

> If I had to play the game in the role of [the chain store], I would follow deterrence theory. I would be very surprised if it failed to work. From my discussions with friends and colleagues, I get the impression that most people share this inclination. In fact, up to now I met nobody who said that he would behave according to induction theory. My experience suggests that mathematically trained persons recognize the logical validity of the induction argument, but they refuse to accept it as a guide to practical behavior. (Selten, 1978, pp. 132–133)

There is no easy escape from this paradox. Pettit and Sugden (1989) examined the paradox in relation to a different game (the finitely iterated Prisoner's Dilemma game) and concluded that, under an assumption of common *belief* (rather than knowledge) of rationality, the players are not in a position to run the backward induction argument. In other words, if the players' beliefs in their own and one another's rationality is contingent on rational choices being made in the game and are liable to break down if irrational choices are made, Pettit and Sugden show that the backward induction argument collapses and the paradox evaporates. Pettit and Sugden admit that their solution to the backward induction paradox does not work under the standard assumption of common *knowledge* of rationality, that is, where the players' rationality is not something about which they can be mistaken.

Rosenthal (1981) suggested a different way out of the paradox by assuming that the players do not assume that one another will *certainly* act rationally but merely that they will *probably* do so. A related approach was taken by Kreps and Wilson (1982) and Milgrom and Roberts (1982) who showed that the paradox can be made to disappear by changing the rules of the game slightly so that there is a small element of incomplete information. For example, if the potential competitors are not sure about Chain store's payoff function, then these authors show that there are circumstances in which it is rational for a potential competitor to choose OUT. But, as Rosenthal (1981) himself pointed out, incomplete information is a debilitating assumption in the Chain-store game, and there are certainly everyday interactions with the same basic strategic structure in which information is probably complete enough. Examples that spring to mind include numerous economic situations in which successions of aspirant competitors consider challenging monopolists, political conflicts in which underground political groups consider trying to wrest concessions from governments by taking hostages, and criminal intrigues in which potential blackmailers consider trying to extort money from wealthy individuals or companies. In such cases the payoff structure of the game is usually sufficiently clear for the backward induction argument to run and therefore for the paradox to remain.

Bacharach (1992) argued that backward induction arguments rely on players' beliefs about what they will later believe, about what they will later believe that they will later believe, and so on, and that there are psychological limits to the depths of these recursive chains of beliefs. Game solutions based on backward induction depend on knowledge that exceeds these depth limits, and according to Bacharach this implies that they cannot be regarded as rational.

9.3 Auction games and psychological traps

During the 1960s the United States became embroiled in an escalating military conflict in Vietnam. When the early victory promised by the president did not materialize, one of the arguments against disengagement was that the United States had "too much invested to quit". To withdraw before defeating the National Liberation Front (Viet Cong) and the North Vietnamese forces would mean wasting all the money and lives that had already been invested. Successive administrations therefore intensified the conflict, only to find themselves increasingly overcommitted, but the argument for escalation in order to justify past investment, for what it was worth, grew increasingly plausible. When it became apparent that victory was beyond its grasp, the United States was eventually forced to withdraw without having achieved any of its objectives.

On a smaller scale and with less devastating consequences, the following European experience illustrates some of the same strategic properties of entrapment and escalation. The cost of the Anglo-French supersonic airliner, the Concorde, rose steeply during its development phase, and it soon became apparent that the project was uneconomical. But British and French governments committed themselves to it increasingly strongly as its cost continued to rise. Continuing to invest in a project simply because so much has already been spent on it, instead of cutting one's losses by withdrawing, has been called the *Concorde fallacy* (Dawkins and Carlisle, 1976).

The dynamic properties of escalation and the Concorde fallacy are present in many areas of behaviour. Gamblers often feel impelled to throw good money after bad in an attempt to rid themselves of escalating debts, and marriage partners often find themselves trapped in escalating spirals of hostility and counter-hostility from which they feel increasingly incapable of extricating themselves on account of past emotional investments. But it was the Vietnam war that was largely responsible for drawing the attention of game theorists to the strategic character of escalation. In particular, Martin Shubik (1971) devised a simple multi-person game, the Dollar Auction game, that brings some of the features of strategic escalation and the Concorde fallacy into sharp focus. It has been discussed by Costanza (1984), O'Neill (1986), Leininger (1989), and Mitchell (1991), among others.

The rules of the Dollar Auction game are as follows. An auctioneer auctions a dollar bill to the highest bidder. (Other currencies can be used, of course, and a less parochial name for this game would have been preferable.) With one crucial modification, the rules resemble those of the *second-price auctions* that are used in London stamp auctions and some fish markets, in which the highest bidder receives the goods for the price of the second-highest bid, and the second-highest bidder pays and receives nothing. In the Dollar Auction game, the highest bidder gets the dollar bill and the second-highest bidder receives nothing, but *both* bidders must pay the auctioneer amounts corresponding to their last bids. Suppose the bidding stops at 40 cents and the second-highest bid, just before the end, was 35 cents. In this case the dollar goes to the person who bid 40 cents, and the auctioneer collects 40 cents from that person and 35 cents from the second-highest bidder (who receives nothing in return). An upper limit on bidding is usually set to ensure that the game does not continue forever, and another useful rule to make the game finite is that bids must be made in whole numbers of cents. Although the rules may initially seem strange, there are many everyday interactions in which competitive bidding has the same basic strategic structure, including arms races in which governments commit non-returnable resources in the hope of gaining supremacy and patent races in which corporations commit research and development costs in the hope of being the first to put a new product or process on the market (Leininger, 1989).

There are three important "moments of truth" in the Dollar Auction game. The first occurs after at least two bids have been made. Suppose bidder *A* bids 10 cents and bidder *B* bids 20 cents. If no other player seems willing to raise the bidding, bidder *A* faces the following dilemma: standing pat is certain to lead to a loss of 10 cents, but bidding 30 cents, say, gives bidder *A* a chance of winning 70 cents provided that no further bids are made. That is the first "moment of truth", and essentially the same dilemma faces the second-highest bidder at every stage in the game.

The second "moment of truth" occurs if the bidding reaches 50 cents. The second-highest bidder must then decide whether to raise the bidding to 51 cents or more. This threshold is critical especially from the auctioneer's point of view, because the sum of the two top bids exceeds one dollar and the auctioneer is bound to make a profit if the threshold is crossed.

The third and most frightening "moment of truth" occurs if the bidding reaches the one-dollar mark. The second-highest bidder must then decide whether or not to bid more than a dollar for the one-dollar payoff. If the second-highest bidder's last bid was 95 cents, and if no one else is willing to bid, then this second-highest bidder is bound to lose 95 cents by standing pat. But by bidding 105 cents, say, this bidder will lose only 5 cents, provided that the bidding stops there. The danger exists, however, that the other bidder will go even higher for exactly the same reason, and the problem will present itself in an even more unattractive form later on. Once the bidding passes the one-dollar threshold, the bidders are motivated to minimize their losses rather than to maximize their gains.

A player who has made a single bid in the Dollar Auction game can avoid loss only by dropping out before the number of active bidders reduces to two or by being the highest bidder if the bidding stops before exceeding one dollar. Once two or more players have entered the bidding, it is certain that at least one of them will lose money. When the bidding passes the one-dollar mark, two players are bound to lose, but each is still motivated to be the highest bidder in order to minimize the loss. If negotiation among the bidders and coalition formation are forbidden (as they are in all reputable auctions), the game must be analysed as a multi-person non-cooperative game. The non-cooperative solution based on Nash equilibria is highly instructive.

One possible strategy for a player may be expressed simply as: "Do not bid". Ignoring certain inessential complications, other strategies take the form: "Enter the bidding and continue (if necessary) until the highest bid is k cents" where k is a number between 1 and the upper limit (if any). A plausible strategy, for example, is to set $k = 100$, in other words to be willing to continue bidding until the highest bid reaches 100 cents. If there is an upper limit of 5 dollars, say, then each player has 501 pure strategies in the normal form of the game. If there is no limit, the game is infinite. In this simplified model, the pure-strategy Nash equilibria, which were first worked out by Colman (1982c, pp. 154–156), can be characterized quite straightforwardly. They are the outcomes in which exactly one player selects some $k \geq 99$, that is, chooses to bid as far as 99 cents or more, and every other player chooses "Do not bid". Using a different argument from the one outlined in the following paragraphs, O'Neill (1986) and Leininger (1989) later derived essentially the same solution. Leininger also showed by representing the game in extensive form and pruning the game tree backwards in the manner described in sections 6.2 and 9.2 that the specified equilibrium points are subgame perfect.

With an upper limit of 5 dollars, there are $402n$ pure-strategy Nash equilibria, where n is the number of players, because each of the n players has 501 minus 99 strategies meeting the requirement $k \geq 99$, and each leads to an equilibrium outcome when all of the others choose "Do not bid". If there is no limit, there is an infinite number of Nash equilibria of the same type. If the outcome is a Nash equilibrium, the bidder will receive the dollar for the price of a first bid (which could be 1 cent, say) and will be more than satisfied with the outcome. The other players, once they are told what the bidder's strategy was, will have no cause for regret, because they could not have won any money by entering the bidding given the existence of a player willing to bid as far as 99 cents or more. In other words, the combination of strategies are best against one another, and no one can benefit by deviating unilaterally from this equilibrium outcome.

All other combinations of strategies lead to non-equilibrium outcomes. To see why this is so, it is necessary to consider three general cases. First, suppose two or more players choose to enter the bidding. One of them is bound to end up as the second-highest bidder, and second-highest bidders invariably lose money, so this player will have cause for regret because the loss could have been avoided by not bidding at all, and the outcome is therefore not a Nash equilibrium. Second, imagine that exactly one player chooses to bid, but only as far as $k = 98$ cents or less. In these outcomes each of the other players, if all of the players' strategies were revealed, would regret not having chosen to bid as far as 99 cents with a gain of at least 1 cent. Finally, suppose every player chooses "Do not bid". In that case every player will regret not having been the sole player to bid 1 cent, thereby gaining 99 cents. It is clear that none of these outcomes is a Nash equilibrium, because they represent combinations of strategies that are not best against one another.

The maximin strategy for every player is "Do not bid"; it is the only way of guaranteeing the avoidance of loss. But if every player chooses maximin, each will have cause to regret not having been more enterprising. The maximin strategies, in other words, do not intersect in a Nash equilibrium. The game possesses numerous Nash equilibria, but they are all non-symmetric and there are no obvious criteria for choosing among them. These non-cooperative "solutions" are characteristically unconvincing, but they do suggest profitable ways of bending the rules of the game by issuing threats.

Suppose that, before the game is played, Player A announces a binding commitment to bid beyond 99 cents if necessary, and to prove it shows the other bidders an affidavit to this effect and a document instructing a lawyer to dispose of a large proportion of Player A's life's savings if the commitment is not honoured. If the others are rational, Player A is bound to be the only bidder and can win 99 cents by bidding 1 cent. But if two or more players establish similar commitments, at least one of them must lose. Something of the sort happens in many political, economic, and domestic conflicts.

Let us now examine the Dollar Auction game as a cooperative multi-person game in which communication and coalition formation are permitted by the rules. Shubik (1971) analysed the characteristic function of the game under the assumption that the auctioneer is one of the players and the payoff structure is zero-sum. In view of the fact that the auctioneer makes no choices that affect the outcomes, however, it seems more accurate to model it as a mixed-motive game in which the only players are the potential bidders. If there are exactly three players, A, B, and C, the characteristic function is as follows:

$$v(\varnothing) = 0;$$

$$v(A) = 0, \ v(B) = 0, \ v(C) = 0;$$

$$v(A, B) = 0, \ v(A, C) = 0, \ v(B, C) = 0;$$

$$v(A, B, C) = 99 \text{ cents.}$$

The general principle is the same with any number of players. The grand coalition of all players acting in concert can always gain 99 cents, so that $v(N) = 99$ cents, and no other coalition can guarantee to win anything. The grand coalition can gain 99 cents by agreeing that one of them, nominated in advance, will bid one cent and no other bids will be made. This guarantees a gain to the coalition of 1 dollar for the price of one cent, and they can then divide the payoff of 99 cents among themselves. How they divide the 99 cents is another question, but it is easy to solve; the Shapley value, for example, assigns each player an equal share in the payoff because they have equal *a priori* power in the game (see section 8.5).

The use of the Dollar Auction as an experimental game presents a number of methodological problems. If real money is used, then the payoff structure of the game is likely to be ambiguous because the subjects may not believe that they are liable to be fleeced by the experimenter. The experimenter could take pains to convince the subjects that they stand to lose money, but an experiment that produces a financial profit at the expense of volunteer subjects would violate ethical codes governing research with human subjects (see Gale, 1994). On the other hand, if the subjects play for points or valueless tokens rather than real money, then an essential psychological ingredient of the game is missing: subjects are less likely to continue bidding merely in order to justify past investments if these investments are trivial or meaningless to them.

Allan Teger (1980) and his colleagues got round these problems in a number of ways, and subsequent experimenters have used similar methods. In Teger's informal field experiments, conducted in the form of classroom demonstrations with post-experimental interviews, the subjects were invited to bid with their own money and were told that credit would be extended to anyone who had insufficient ready cash to pay outstanding debts at the end of the auctions. The experimenters did not, in fact, accept any payments from the subjects after the auctions, although the post-experimental interviews showed that the subjects believed that they would have to pay up.

In Teger's (1980) experiments with signed-up volunteers it was necessary to give each subject an initial monetary stake with which to bid. Subjects normally expect to be paid for participating in experiments and they would probably not have believed that they could lose their own money. The technique of providing subjects with initial stakes with which to bid was pioneered by Tropper (1972), who was the first to report an experiment using an auction game (although Teger and his colleagues did not cite Tropper's work and were probably unaware of it). It is not an entirely happy solution because the money that the subjects stand to lose is, in a sense, not really their own: they did not have it before entering the laboratory, and losing it may not have the same psychological significance as losing money that is unambiguously theirs. The amount given to the subjects turned out, in fact, to be a powerful determinant of bidding behaviour in Teger's experiments.

A third approach adopted by Teger (1980) and his colleagues in some of their laboratory experiments was as follows. Each subject was given 975 points with which to bid for a prize of 500 points, and was told that each point was worth an unspecified amount of money to be cashed at the end of the auction. The subjects did not know that their bidding partners had also been assigned an initial stake of 975 points. The idea behind this arrangement was "that the subjects would not feel that the money we gave them was inconsequential (and thus that they had nothing to lose), or that it was a considerable sum (and thus that they had best quit immediately and take the money without bidding)" (p. 20). The argument is not entirely clear, but the procedure worked in practice.

The results of auction game experiments are surprising and edifying. Shubik (1971) was the first to report that the game "is usually highly profitable to its promoter" (p. 109). Tropper (1972) conducted the first controlled experiment in this area, in which the items auctioned were a dollar bill, a felt-tipped pen worth 49 cents, and a pocket flashlight worth 99 cents. Each subject was given 250 cents with which to bid, and in 16 out of 30 auctions, apparently conducted with pairs of subjects, one or both of the bidders paid more than the (subjectively rated) value of the prize. In approximately 40 informal field experiments with groups of under-graduates, graduates, and faculty members as subjects, Teger (1980, chap. 2) found that the bidding for a dollar bill always exceeded one dollar and sometimes went as high as 20 dollars. Subjects who were caught in the spiral of escalation often became extremely emotional, crying, sweating, and glancing anxiously around for reassurance. One student began bidding to rescue his girlfriend who had bid over a dollar and had told him that she was scared: "He entered the bidding, figuring that their combined resources would enable them to outlast the other bidder" (p. 16). Many subjects interpreted what had happened in a remarkably egocentric way, describing their co-bidders in post-experimental interviews as "crazy" for bidding more than the prize was worth in spite of having done so themselves. Some subjects made bids in spite of having seen the auction being conducted in previous experiments! They claimed that it had not occurred to them that they could be caught in the same trap as the others.

The laboratory experiments reported by Teger (1980, chaps 2, 3, 4, 5) and his colleagues were conducted with pairs of bidders rather than larger groups. Even under these conditions the bidding exceeded the value of the prize in a substantial proportion (40 to 50 per cent) of cases, which replicates Tropper's (1972) findings mentioned earlier. Perhaps the most striking discovery was that in those pairs in which the 1-dollar threshold was crossed the bidding usually continued to escalate until the subjects' resources were entirely depleted. This suggests that the value of the prize serves as a psychological point of no return for most bidders, beyond which they are unable or unwilling to extricate themselves from the game until they are forced to do so. This phenomenon was observed time and time again, whether the subjects were playing with real money or points to be converted into money at an unknown exchange rate after the auction. It is sufficiently striking to deserve a dramatic label; perhaps the *Macbeth effect* is appropriate: "I am in blood / Stepped in so far that, should I wade no more, / Returning were as tedious as go o'er" (*Macbeth*, III. iv).

Subjects given the opportunity to take part in two successive laboratory auctions showed remarkably little evidence of learning from experience: the distributions of bids were similar to those of inexperienced pairs of subjects and the Macbeth effect was not suppressed. This finding is important, because it shows that the phenomenon of escalation is not due merely to a failure on the part of the subjects to appreciate the danger inherent in the situation or the possibility that the bidding may exceed the value of the prize. More interesting psychological processes are evidently at work.

Teger and Carey (1980) investigated the thought processes of subjects during auction games and discovered that an important motivational change takes place in most cases. When making a bid at any stage in the experiment the subjects were requested to indicate on a set of seven-point rating scales the importance of various motives underlying their decisions to bid: "in order to make money"; "in order to show that I am better at the task than the other person"; "in order to regain some of the money that I have lost"; and so on. The results showed that

> the initial bidding appears to be motivated by economic concerns, but the tendency to bid until you are broke is due to a new motivation that develops during the course of the auction – a motivation toward competition that makes the economic considerations less important. (Teger and Carey, p. 60)

The (interpersonal) competitive motive, which appears to stem from face-saving considerations, tends to supplant the (purely individual) economic motive when the bidding exceeds the value of the prize; it is at this point that interpersonal considerations tend to assume major significance.

Teger, Carey, Hillis, and Katcher (1980) monitored a number of physiological stress indicators in subjects taking part in auction games. The results of this experiment confirmed the finding of previous investigations that the most significant "moment of truth" for the subjects occurred when the bidding first passed the value of the prize. In particular, a sharp decrease in heart rate was usually recorded at this point. The physiological pattern observed in subjects at this point of no return is similar to the pattern observed in parachutists just before jumping from an aircraft. It may be due, at least in part, to the subjects' sudden realization that it is possible for the bidding to continue beyond the one-dollar point; a controlled experiment with experienced or pre-educated subjects is necessary to discover to what extent this factor is important (see below).

Because the auction game is, in a sense, a product of the Vietnam war, it is not unreasonable to ask what light it throws on that devastating example of escalation. A content analysis of the speeches of President Johnson on Vietnam from 1964 to 1968 (Sullivan and Thomas, 1972) invites some tentative conclusions. In the early stages of military escalation, the symbolic words used by Johnson were mainly "positive" (democracy, freedom, liberty, justice), but later phases of escalation were associated with the use of "status" words (honour, will, status). It is conceivable that this change may reflect a motivational change in the U.S. administration's approach to the conflict, and it may parallel the motivational change in subjects in auction game experiments, from gaining financially to saving face by beating the other bidder even if it entails enormous loss to both. The "moment of truth" in the Vietnam war may have been reached when the original "positive" goal of a "clean" victory was abandoned in favour of saving face in spite of the massive costs involved.

Carey (1980) argued that auction games are applicable to many naturally occurring strategic interactions, and he cited a number of examples based on industrial relations, divorces, and fights. The Macbeth effect, for example, is clearly discernible in the records of some industrial strikes. Carey's claim that "nearly every interpersonal situation can be seen to have the basic features of the dollar auction game" (p. 129) is perhaps an escalated overstatement, but the relevance of the game to *some* political, economic, military, and interpersonal interactions is striking. The most horrifying examples are surely nuclear arms races, which seem to have many of the formal properties of the Dollar Auction game (Rapoport, 1971).

Gareth Jones (1986) carried out a series of experiments in England, with one pound sterling as the usual prize, to clarify some of the factors affecting escalation in auction games. In the first experiment, undergraduate subjects participated in three successive auction games in three-person groups. The majority of the subjects (76 per cent) bid over the value of the prize, and a learning effect was demonstrated, with higher terminal bids in the first auction than the last. In Jones's second experiment, subjects participated in groups of either two or three and bid either face-to-face or via computer terminals, but there was only one real subject in each auction and the bids of the other supposed participants were programmed in advance. In this experiment 80 per cent of subjects bid over the value of the prize, and a significant statistical interaction emerged, with computer bidding leading to higher escalation than face-to-face bidding in the two-person groups only, perhaps because subjects felt less inhibited in the relative anonymity of larger groups and during computer bidding in both smaller and larger groups.

Jones (1986) conducted three experiments to investigate the effects of collective bidding decisions made by groups rather than individuals. In other words, the bidders in these experiments were not necessarily individuals; in some treatment conditions they were groups of people who had to discuss and agree on their bidding strategies, like a board of directors deciding on a company's financial strategy. In one experiment in this series, 60 undergraduate subjects participated via computer terminals in a single auction game in which they were pitted against a programmed strategy from a single competing bidder. The subjects participated as individual bidders, pair bidders, or triad bidders, and in each case they thought that the opposing bidder was an individual or group of the same size. No significant effect of the number of individuals in bidding groups was found, but 76 per cent of bidders (whether individuals, dyads, or triads) bid over the prize value. In a second experiment on collective bidding using a similar design and methodology, 64 subjects bid as individuals or triads against programmed opponents, and once again the results were non-significant, although 81 per cent of bidders exceeded the prize value. In the final experiment on collective bidding, 61 subjects participated as collective bidders in groups of two, three, or five. In this experiment 55 per cent of bidders exceeded the prize value, and the results showed that both of the larger-sized collective bidding groups escalated significantly further than dyads. The group size effect is probably due to the relative anonymity in the larger groups, or perhaps to the well-established *group polarization phenomenon*, which tends to cause larger decision making groups to make more risky and generally more extreme decisions (Isenberg, 1986).

An experiment reported by Charles Plott (1986) was based on a game with significantly different rules, although he described it as the Dollar Auction game. Its rules were roughly those of a conventional second-price auction: the highest bidder received the prize and had to pay the value of the second-highest bid, but the second-highest bidder paid and received nothing. In five experimental auction games played under these rules, with the number of participants varying from 14 in the first, second, and fourth auctions down to five in the third auction, the dollar was sold for second-price values of $20.00, $1.51, $5.63, $15.00, and $11.20 respectively.

Robert Costanza and Wesley Shrum (1988) reported an experiment in which 92 undergraduate subjects played the standard Dollar Auction game against a programmed opponent under conditions in which some bidders were taxed for bidding above a certain level. The tax had the effect of damping escalation, but the results showed nevertheless that in 53 per cent of auctions the bidding exceeded the prize value of one dollar, and the size of the tax on bidding had much less effect on the level of escalation than did the point at which the tax was implemented, with early implementation curtailing escalation more than later implementation even when the size of the tax was small.

A series of experiments on psychological traps that are closely related to auction games have been described by Jeffrey Rubin and Joel Brockner (1985). In these experiments subjects were invited to invest escalating amounts of time and money in the hope of obtaining valuable prizes. They were free to cut their losses and withdraw at any point, but by doing so they had to forgo the chance of winning prizes. Situations of this sort arise naturally when, for example, one has spent a long time waiting for a bus: the longer one has waited, the less one is inclined to leave the bus stop. This phenomenon can be explained by cognitive dissonance theory (Festinger, 1957). There is an uncomfortable inconsistency between the knowledge that one has invested heavily in something and the belief that it is not worth the time, effort, or money. One way of reducing the psychological inconsistency – and hence the uncomfortable cognitive dissonance – is by developing a more favourable attitude towards the prize. As the investment escalates, one's subjective evaluation of the prize may become unrealistically inflated.

The first experiment in the series (Rubin and Brockner, 1975) provided strong evidence of the entrapment phenomenon. The subjects were each given an amount of money before the experiment began and were promised an additional (much larger) amount if they succeeded in solving a crossword puzzle. But the subjects had to invest money in order to try for the prize: after working on the puzzle for a few minutes they were fined 25 cents for every subsequent minute that elapsed. They were permitted to abandon the puzzle at any point and to retire with what was left of their initial payments. Those who failed to do so found that their initial payments were soon depleted, and they were effectively paying out of their own pockets for remaining in the experiment. The puzzle was too difficult to solve without a dictionary, which the subjects were told was available on a "first come, first served" basis, but circumstances were arranged so that no subject ever got to the front of the queue. While queuing for the dictionary they were not allowed to continue working on the puzzle.

Approximately 20 per cent of Rubin and Brockner's (1975) subjects remained in the queue beyond the point at which their initial payments were depleted and they went into debt. They waited longer, on average, when the fines mounted rapidly rather than slowly, when they were not required to keep careful records of how much money they had lost, and when they thought they were near the front of the queue. The experiment provides a vivid illustration of psychological entrapment. It brings to mind W. C. Fields's famous motto: "If at first you don't succeed, try again. Then quit. No use being a damn fool about it" (quoted in Cohen and Cohen, 1980, p. 114). Later experiments confirmed and extended the earlier findings. Brockner, Shaw, and Rubin (1979) investigated limit-setting and active versus passive decisions to continue investing in an entrapment game. Some of the subjects were required to inform the experimenter in advance of their provisional (non-binding) limits, indicating how much they were prepared to invest; another group had to set private limits; and a third group were not required to set any limits. In each group, half of the subjects had to make repeated active decisions to remain in the experiment while the others remained unless they made active decisions to quit. This latter condition is reminiscent of inertia selling, in which a customer is deemed to have agreed to buy a product unless some positive action is taken. The results showed that subjects became most severely entrapped when they were not required to set prior limits on investment and when they had to make active decisions to quit.

Rubin, Brockner, Small-Weil, and Nathanson (1980) reported further evidence indicating that entrapment tends to be greater under passive inertia-selling conditions than when active decisions have to be made to continue investing, although this effect failed to emerge from one of the two experiments reported in this paper. The other experiment yielded evidence suggesting that male subjects are more vulnerable to entrapment than females. Brockner, Rubin, and Lang (1981) reported two further experiments linking entrapment with face-saving. The results of both experiments revealed that "individuals will become more or less entrapped to the extent that doing so will portray them in a favorable light" (p. 78). The finding is consistent with the results of experimental auction games mentioned earlier. The experiments also revealed that entrapment tends to be reduced if the subjects' attention is directed to the costs of investing rather than the value of the prize. This was achieved by reminding some of the subjects of the advantages of saving money and requiring them to keep charts of their investments continuously up to date. Finally, Strube and Lott (1984) showed that Type A personalities (ambitious, competitive people with an exaggerated sense of time urgency) are more vulnerable than other people to entrapment when they have to estimate the passage of time during which investments have been mounting. For an overall review of Brockner and Rubin's research into psychological traps, see Brockner and Rubin (1985).

9.4 Social dilemmas: intuitive background

Social dilemmas are multi-person decision-making problems in which individual interests are at odds with collective interests. Their defining strategic property is thus essentially that of the Prisoner's Dilemma game, which was discussed in section 6.7. An abstract model of a social dilemma, which is called the N-person Prisoner's Dilemma (NPD), was developed simultaneously and independently by Dawes (1973), Hamburger (1973), and Schelling (1973). Although others had hinted at its existence, these game theorists were the first to provide rigorous definitions and theoretical analyses of the NPD, and their work stimulated the rapid growth of a new field of experimental gaming.

The abrupt emergence of social dilemmas as a field of theoretical and empirical research in the early 1970s is strongly suggestive of an idea whose time had come. Without delving too deeply into the history of ideas, it is possible to pinpoint some of the major reasons for the sudden interest in social dilemmas at that time. The first reason is that a vacuum had been left in the field of experimental gaming by the decline of the (two-person) Prisoner's Dilemma game (PDG) as an empirical research tool. After 20 years of intensive experimental investigation, the empirical properties of behaviour in the Prisoner's Dilemma game had been thoroughly investigated, and experimental researchers were beginning to look for something new. The second reason is that a number of social and economic problems involving the clash of individual and collective interests began to fill newspapers and television screens in the United States and Europe in the early 1970s. The most prominent of these were the problems of inflation and voluntary wage restraint, the "energy crisis" and various problems related to the conservation of other scarce natural resources, and a range of problems arising from environmental pollution. In addition, an increase in international tension following the Soviet invasion of Czechoslovakia, coupled with a proliferation of nuclear weapons, raised the problem of multilateral disarmament with renewed urgency. All of these problems – and many others besides – are essentially social dilemmas. It is reasonable to say that social dilemmas permeate a truly remarkable range of real-world social problems, but a few simple examples will suffice.

9.4.1 The "invisible hand" and voluntary wage restraint

In one of the most influential books in the history of economics, *The Wealth of Nations*, Adam Smith (1776) introduced the theory of the "invisible hand" as follows:

> It is not from the benevolence of the butcher, the brewer, or the baker, that we expect our dinner, but from their regard to their own self-interest. We address ourselves, not to their humanity but to their self-love, and never talk to them of our own necessities but of their advantages (p. 16). ... It is his own advantage, indeed, and not that of society, which he has in view. But the study of his own advantage naturally, or rather necessarily leads him to prefer that employment which is most advantageous to the society (p. 419). ... He generally, indeed, neither intends to promote the public interest, nor knows how

much he is promoting it. ... He intends only his own gain, and he is in this, as in many other cases, led by an invisible hand to promote an end which was no part of his intention. ... By pursuing his own interest he frequently promotes that of the society more effectually than when he really intends to promote it. (p. 421)

The theory of the "invisible hand" has been a cornerstone of conservative economic thinking for more than two centuries, and in Britain during the premiership of Margaret Thatcher in the 1980s it assumed the status of an ideological dogma. Let us examine it in the context of collective wage bargaining.

It is in the narrow self-interest of every trade union or group of workers to negotiate wage settlements that exceed the rate of inflation in the economy as a whole. This remains true irrespective of whether other unions do the same or exercise restraint in their wage demands. But if all groups of workers pursue their narrow self-interest in this way, then the prices of goods and services go up and everyone is worse off than if all exercise restraint. If each worker "intends only his own gain" he is not led by an "invisible hand" that promotes the interest of society as a whole, as Adam Smith argued, but kicked up the backside by an invisible foot that undermines society's interest in the long run.

In October 1974 the Manifesto of the British Labour Party contained an outline of a "social contract" that was supposed to encourage trade unions to exercise voluntary wage restraint in order to reduce the rate of inflation. The social contract was designed to encourage collective rationality in wage bargaining in place of individual rationality:

> Naturally the trade unions see their clearest loyalty to their own members. But the social contract is their free acknowledgement that they have other loyalties – to the members of other unions too ... to the community as a whole. (quoted in Collard, 1978, p. 73)

In the event, the social contract was not a success. No doubt the major reason for its failure was that it left the strategic structure of the wage bargaining game intact.

9.4.2 Conservation of natural resources

There was a severe drought in Britain in the summer of 1976, and water became a scarce resource in most parts of the country. The mass media exhorted people to exercise restraint in their consumption of water – to place bricks in their lavatory cisterns, to avoid washing their cars and watering their gardens, and even to try showering with a friend! Government propaganda was based on a slogan "Save it!" that had first been used to encourage people to save energy when the price of oil doubled two years earlier.

The strategic dilemma confronting an individual citizen during the drought or the earlier "energy crisis" may be crystallized as follows. An individual benefits from restraint only if many thousands of others also exercise restraint. But, in that case, restraint on the part of any single individual is clearly unnecessary: the benefit will be reaped with or without that individual's cooperation, and the individual will share the reward in any case. On the other hand, if most of the others ignore the call for restraint, then restraint on the part of the individual is futile, because the benefit will not be reaped whatever that individual does. It follows that from a single individual's point of view, saving it – water or energy – is therefore either pointless or futile. It is evidently in each individual's rational self-interest to ignore the call for restraint, irrespective of the choices of the others. But the dilemma arises from the fact that if everyone pursues individual rationality in this way, then they all end up worse off than if everyone had pursued a collective form of rationality and had exercised restraint. If everyone tries to be a "free rider", then the danger is that no one gets a ride at all.

In practice, individual rationality usually prevails. During the summer of 1976, only a small minority of British citizens heeded the call for water conservation (Hollis, 1979, p. 2). About 40 per cent of households made only token economies, and 50 per cent made none at all. Edgeworth's (1881) dictum that "the first principle of economics is that every agent is actuated only by self-interest" (p. 16) proved roughly correct in this case as a *descriptive* principle, but as a *prescription* for rational action or a *normative* principle it is clearly deficient, as the conservation problem shows.

9.4.3 The tragedy of the commons

This example is based on a phenomenon commented upon by Lloyd (1833) in a famous lecture on "the checks to population" and later discussed in an influential article by Garrett Hardin (1968).

Expressed as simply as possible, the problem is this. There are six farmers who have access to a common pasture on which to graze their cows. Each farmer owns a single cow weighing 1000 lb. The common can sustain a maximum of six cows without deterioration through overgrazing, and for every additional cow that is added to it, the weight of every animal on the common decreases by 100 lb. This is important to the farmers because the weight of a cow is proportional to its value. Suppose that each farmer has the opportunity to acquire another cow, which will have to graze on the common. If one farmer decides to acquire an additional cow, that farmer's personal wealth in livestock will increase from one 1000-lb cow to two 900-lb cows. The same general principle applies irrespective of how many of the other farmers decide to acquire a second cow. It is always in a farmer's individual self-interest to acquire an additional cow, but if all of them do so, then each farmer ends up poorer (with two 400-lb cows) than if they all stick to the status quo (with one 1000-lb cow each).

The overgrazing of the commons in fourteenth century England, which led to the enclosures and eventual disappearance of most of the commons, is a clear example of this social dilemma. A contemporary parallel is overexploitation of fisheries. According to the United Nations Food and Agricultural Organization (FAO), more than half the world's 17 main commercial fishing grounds are overfished and falling in productivity – for example, herring were long ago fished to near extinction off the coast of England – and the rest are fully exploited (*The Guardian*, 5 August 1994, p. 2). Another sombre example is the slaughter of whales, tigers, and other large mammals for individual gain.

9.5 Formalization of social dilemmas

The three social dilemmas outlined above share a common underlying strategic structure. They can each be modelled by a multi-person non-cooperative game defined by the following properties:

(1) Each player faces a choice between two options that may be labelled C (cooperate) and D (defect).
(2) The D option is dominant for each player, that is, each player obtains a better payoff by choosing D than C no matter how many of the other players choose C.
(3) The dominant D strategies intersect in a Pareto-deficient Nash equilibrium. In particular, the outcome if all players choose their dominated C strategies is preferable from every player's point of view to the outcome if everyone chooses D, but the dominant D strategies are best against one another, and if they are chosen no player is motivated to deviate unilaterally from D.

A game that satisfies these three conditions is by definition an NPD. It is immediately obvious that the (two-person) Prisoner's Dilemma game (PDG) defined in section 6.7 is a special case of the NPD defined above, for it satisfies all three conditions.

In its *n*-person form, this type of social dilemma is ubiquitous. The D strategy corresponds to negotiating for a wage settlement in excess of the rate of inflation in Example 9.4.1 above, disregarding the call for water or energy conservation in 9.4.2, and overgrazing a common in 9.4.3. Here are a few more examples of D choices in everyday social dilemmas: ordering an expensive meal in a restaurant when dining with a group of people after agreeing to split the bill equally (Glance and Huberman, 1994); carrying a concealed weapon (at an individual level) or manufacturing nuclear weapons (at a national level) (Schelling, 1973); refusing to join a trade union while benefiting from its activities (Messick, 1973); rushing for an exit during an escape panic (Dawes, 1975); standing on tiptoe to watch a parade (Caldwell, 1976); neglecting to contribute towards the cost of a neighbour-hood playground (Hamburger, 1979, chap. 7); and increasing the size of one's family in India (Dawes, 1988, chap. 9). In each case – and in numerous others that have been discovered – it is in an individual's self-interest to choose the D option regardless of the choices of the others, but everyone is better off if they all choose the alternative C option. Adam Smith's theory of the "invisible hand", in its broadest interpretation, is refuted in each case. Contrary to *laissez-faire* politico-economic dogma, unchecked market forces can have socially pernicious effects. What is clearly needed is some form of collective rather than individual rationality, such as the principle embodied in Kant's categorical imperative discussed in section 6.7. There is room for n martyrs in a society of n individuals, and virtue would be its own reward in such a utopia.

Let us now examine the formal structure of the NPD in more detail. The simplest instance of it involves three players and integral payoffs of 1, 2, 3, and 4 units of utility. Two assumptions that simplify the analysis further are that the game is symmetric, that is to say that it is the same from every player's point of view, and that each player's payoff function is linear with respect to the number of players choosing C, that is, a player's payoff is directly proportional to the number of players choosing C. If the payoff from a D choice exceeds the payoff from a C choice by a fixed amount of one unit, then the payoff structure is as shown in Matrix 9.2.

Matrix 9.2 *Three-person Prisoner's Dilemma Payoff Matrix*

Number Choosing C	Number Choosing D	Payoff to Each C Chooser	Payoff to Each D Chooser
3	0	3	–
2	1	2	4
1	2	1	3
0	3	–	2

As shown in the first row of the matrix, the payoff to each C chooser is three units if all three players choose C, and in this case the payoff to the (non-existent) D chooser is undefined, which is why there is a dash in the last column. The second row shows what happens if two players choose C and the remaining player chooses D; in that case the payoff to each C chooser is two units and the payoff to the solitary D chooser is four units, and so on. The game is an NPD because it satisfies the three defining conditions mentioned earlier:

(1) each player chooses between two options;
(2) a *D* choice pays better than a *C* choice no matter how many of the other players choose *C*, so that the *D* choice is dominant; and
(3) each player receives a better payoff if everyone chooses *C* than if everyone chooses *D*, but the *D* strategies are best against one another and no one is motivated to deviate unilaterally from *D*, in other words the dominant strategies intersect in a Nash equilibrium that is not Pareto optimal (*everyone's* payoff could be better).

The identical game can be represented in graphical form without loss of information (see Figure 9.2). Note that the payoff functions are those of a single player depending on whether that player chooses *C* or *D*, and the horizontal axis indicates the number of *other* players (excluding that individual) choosing *C*. This is the clearest way of graphing the payoffs, although other methods have been used; it shows what an individual player will get by choosing *C* or *D* for any specified number of *C* choices on the part of the *other* players. The fact that the payoff functions are parallel indicates that the *D* strategy dominates the *C* strategy by a constant amount in this case: a *D* choice yields exactly one unit of payoff more than a *C* choice irrespective of the number of others choosing *C*. The left-hand extremity of the *D* chooser's function is clearly the only Nash equilibrium, because *D* choices are best against one another and a player will always have cause to

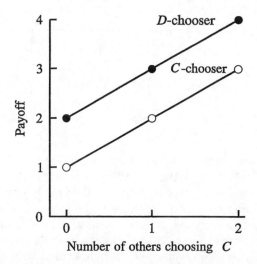

Figure 9.2 *Graphical representation of the uniform NPD shown in Matrix 9.2*

regret a C choice. But the right-hand extremity of the C chooser's function, which represents the payoff to a C chooser when everyone else chooses C, is higher than the Nash equilibrium, indicating that the equilibrium is deficient (not Pareto optimal). The example in Figure 9.2 and Matrix 9.2 is the simplest possible NPD structure, and it can easily be extended for larger numbers of players: the overall form is preserved but the payoff functions are lengthened. For NPDs with non-parallel and non-linear (curved) payoff functions, see Schelling (1973).

The formal relationship between the NPD and the PDG is evident from a careful examination of Matrix 9.3. The game represented in the matrix is a conventional two-person Prisoner's Dilemma game. Suppose that each of three players plays this game with each of the other two players. The resultant compound game then turns out to be the NPD depicted in Matrix 9.2 and Figure 9.2. If all three players choose C, for example, each receives a payoff of 3/2 in each of the games against the co-players, so each player's total payoff is therefore $3/2 + 3/2 = 3$ units, which agrees with the corresponding NPD outcome. If two players choose C, then each C chooser gets 3/2 against the other C chooser and 1/2 against the D chooser, making a total of 2 units, which also agrees with the NPD outcome, and so on. The three-person game may be thought of as a compound game based on the two-person PDG shown in Matrix 9.3. A compound game involving any

Matrix 9.3 *Decomposable PDG*

II

		C	D
I	C	3/2, 3/2	1/2, 2
	D	2, 1/2	1, 1

number of players can be constructed on the basis of the PDG, and it always turns out to be an NPD with the overall form shown in Figure 9.2. But if the PDG is non-decomposable (see section 7.9), then the payoff functions of the corresponding NPD will not be parallel.

A simple algebraic model can be used to represent a decomposable Prisoner's Dilemma (PDG or NPD). Let each of the n players ($n = 2$ in the case of the PDG) receive an amount c for choosing C and an amount d for choosing D. In addition, each player is fined an amount e for every player in the game who chooses D. In the game shown in Matrix 9.2 and Figure 9.2,

$c = 3$, $d = 5$, and $e = 1$. In the two-person case shown in Matrix 9.3, $c = 3/2$, $d = 3$, and $e = 1$. The defining properties of the generalized decomposable Prisoner's Dilemma game are the inequalities

$$d - e > c > d - ne > c - (n - 1)e,$$

which are simply the familiar inequalities $T > R > P > S$ used to define the PDG in section 6.7. Simplifying these inequalities, we find that $n > 1$, which means simply that the number of players must be two or more, and combining them, we arrive at

$$ne > d - c > e,$$

which may be regarded as a generating formula for decomposable Prisoner's Dilemma games of any size.

9.6 Theory of compound games

The NPD is a special case of a compound game based on a 2 × 2 (two-person, two-choice) game. In this section I shall briefly examine some other compound games and derive some general results. This theory of compound games was first put forward in Colman (1982c, pp. 160–166). A method of applying the theory to the study of the evolution of behaviour will be discussed in section 11.4. The theory applies to multi-person games in which the underlying two-person games are symmetric in the sense of being the same from every player's viewpoint, and the payoff resulting from a C or a D choice is a linear function of the number of other players choosing C.

The generalized form of a symmetric 2 × 2 game, which was introduced in chapter 6, is reproduced in Matrix 9.4. The players in the multi-person game each play a 2 × 2 game of this type with each of the others. Considering the multi-person game from a single player's viewpoint, let the number of other players be denoted by n – strictly speaking, we are dealing

Matrix 9.4
Generalized 2 × 2 Matrix

II

		C	D
I	C	R, R	S, T
	D	T, S	P, P

with an $(n + 1)$-person game. Let each player choose C or D, and let the number of other players choosing C be c. The total payoff to a player choosing C, denoted by $P(C)$, and the total payoff to a player choosing D, denoted by $P(D)$, are then defined by the following payoff functions:

$$P(C) = Rc + S(n - c),$$

$$P(D) = Tc + P(n - c).$$

The values of the $P(C)$ and $P(D)$ payoff functions at their end-points are found by setting $c = 0$ and $c = n$. Thus if none of the other players chooses C, that is, if $c = 0$, the payoff to a solitary C chooser is Sn and the payoff to a D chooser is Pn. If all of the other players choose C, that is, if $c = n$, then a C chooser gets Rn and a solitary D chooser gets Tn. It is clear that, in the case of the NPD, Tn can be interpreted as the temptation to be the sole D

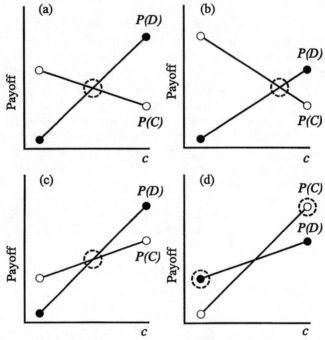

Figure 9.3 *Multi-person compound games based on 2 × 2 matrices. Panel (a) is multi-person Leader; (b) is multi-person Battle of the Sexes; (c) is multi-person Chicken; and (d) is a multi-person Maximizing Difference game. The P(C) and P(D) functions indicate the payoffs to a player choosing C or D when c of the other players choose C. Dashed circles indicate stable Nash equilibria.*

chooser, Rn the reward for joint C choices, Pn the punishment for joint D choices, and Sn the sucker's payoff for being the sole C chooser.

Four multi-person compound games are depicted graphically in Figure 9.3. Figure 9.3(a) shows a multi-person game based on a 2×2 matrix with $T > S > R > P$, referred to as Leader in section 6.4; (b) is a multi-person Battle of the Sexes with $S > T > R > P$; (c) is a multi-person Chicken game with $T > R > S > P$; and (d) is a multi-person Maximizing Difference game with $R > T > P > S$. Nash equilibria are indicated by dashed circles.

In cases (a), (b), and (c), the Nash equilibria are at the intersections of the payoff functions. To see why this is so, consider first the points to the left of the intersection in any of these graphs; this region represents the choice facing a player when relatively few of the others choose C (c is small). In each case the individual player would regret a D choice and would switch to a C choice if the game were repeated, because the C function is above the D function in this region. Thus D choosers will tend to become C choosers and the outcome will move to the right as c increases. To the right of the intersection, exactly the reverse holds: C choosers will switch to D and the outcome will move to the left as c decreases. At the intersection, and only there, no player will have cause for regret and none will be motivated to switch, because the strategies are best against one another given the indicated number of C choosers (the value of c at that point). The intersection is therefore a Nash equilibrium, and any deviation from it will tend to be self-correcting.

In each of the games shown in Figure 9.3, the payoff at the Nash equilibrium is the same whether the individual player chooses C or D. The two payoff functions can therefore be equated at that point:

$$Rc + S(n - c) = Tc + P(n - c).$$

For example, in a 101-person Chicken game (where the number of other players is 100), suppose that $T = 4$, $R = 3$, $S = 2$, and $P = 1$. Then

$$3c + 2(100 - c) = 4c + (100 - c),$$

$$c = 50,$$

and substituting this value of c in either payoff function, the payoff turns out to be 250. This means that with these parameters, if the game is repeated, there will be a tendency towards a stable equilibrium with 50 players choosing C and all players receiving payoffs of 250 units. More generally, it means that a society will tend to evolve towards a state of affairs in which some fixed proportion of individuals adopt threatening types of behaviour towards others in Chicken-type encounters. If all these individuals are locked away, then others are bound to take their places. As in the NPD, the equilibrium is deficient because everyone would be better off if all chose cooperative C strategies, but that outcome would be unstable. Multi-person

Chicken is unlike the NPD in so far as the D function does not dominate the C function across its entire length.

In Figure 9.3(d) we have a different case. This is a multi-person Maximizing Difference game called Backpatting by Hamburger (1979, pp. 167–168), and it has two stable Nash equilibria. It is better to resist than not to resist an invading army if everyone else resists, but it is better not to resist if no one else resists, and the first of these scenarios is better for everyone than the second. If everyone chooses D or if everyone chooses C, then no one is motivated to switch. If only a few choose C, that is, when c is small, they will all switch to D if they are rational, and if most choose C the few who choose D will switch to C. The tendency is always away from the intersection point. In a society in which most people are competitive in encounters with this strategic structure, it is better to compete than to cooperate, whereas if most other people are cooperative it is better to cooperate. But the equilibria are not equivalent: everyone is better off in a society in which all choose C than in one in which all choose D. The direction in which a society will evolve depends on the initial proportion of C choosers; an initial bias in either direction will tend to be self-reinforcing.

9.7 Empirical research on social dilemmas

Social dilemmas began to attract active empirical investigation in the mid-1970s, and the first major review of the experimental evidence was provided by Dawes (1980). Experimental evidence continued to accumulate, and later reviews include those by Dawes and Orbell (1981), Colman (1982c, chap. 9), Messick and Brewer (1983), van Lange, Liebrand, Messick, and Wilke (1992), and Schroeder (1995), among others. The review that follows in this section is not intended to duplicate the earlier ones but rather to provide a general introduction to some of the key empirical issues.

The earliest experimental investigation of behaviour in a social dilemma predated the theoretical development of the n-person Prisoner's Dilemma game by more than two decades and was really a precursor of modern social dilemma research. It was a classic experiment by Mintz (1951) on "non-adaptive group behaviour", which was designed as a laboratory analogue of an escape panic. The basic methodology was simple and ingenious. Groups of subjects were given the task of removing aluminium cones from a narrow-necked bottle as quickly as possible by pulling strings attached to the cones. Each subject held one end of a string, the other end of which was attached to one of the cones. In some treatment conditions the bottle was slowly filled with water from below and the subjects were offered substantial monetary rewards for removing their cones before they became wet. There was enough time for all subjects to get their cones out in an orderly fashion, but the cones were so designed that if two or more of them arrived at the neck of the bottle together a blockage was bound to occur.

In the treatment conditions involving water and monetary incentives, the task is strategically equivalent to the situation that occurs in a crowded theatre or similar building when a fire breaks out and members of the audience are strongly motivated to escape quickly via a narrow exit. Mintz's (1951) water represents the fire, the neck of the bottle represents the theatre exit, and the cones represent the members of the audience. It is not unreasonable to make the simplifying assumption that each individual faces a choice between filing out in an orderly fashion and rushing for the exit. Under this assumption the strategic structure of a Mintz escape panic is an NPD, because from a selfish point of view an individual's chances of survival are better – irrespective of the choices of the others – if that individual rushes (D), but everyone's chances are better if everyone files out in an orderly fashion (C).

The invariable outcome in Mintz's (1951) experiment was a traffic jam at the neck of the bottle, preventing all or some of the cones from being removed. When subjects were allowed to discuss the task and plan their behaviour in advance there was some improvement, although traffic jams still usually resulted. But when the water and the financial incentives were removed and the subjects were instructed merely to withdraw their cones as quickly as possible, serious blockages never occurred. The results are perfectly in accordance with the theory of the NPD. In the water and incentive conditions the rushing strategy is dominant and remains so even if (as a result of prior communication without binding and enforceable commitments to cooperate) the other players' intentions are known in advance. Removal of the water and the incentives, on the other hand, amounts to altering the strategic structure of the underlying game so that rushing for the exit is no longer the dominant strategy; the task becomes a coordination game (see section 3.2) in which the only problem is to agree on an order in which to file out, and there are ample opportunities for tacit communication to achieve this end (first come, first served is a salient solution). Muir and Marrison (1989) replicated Mintz's experiment in a realistic simulation of escape from a crashed aircraft (see Argyle, 1991, p. 33 for a brief summary). Once again, when subjects were given substantial monetary rewards for being among the first to escape, violent competition ensued and the exits often became jammed.

In the majority of experiments that have been conducted since the early 1970s, social dilemmas have been presented to subjects in one of three forms. The first method of presentation is through *NPD games*. This method corresponds closely to the way in which social dilemmas were explained in section 9.5 above. When this method is used, groups of subjects are presented with NPD payoff matrices in which the available strategies are unambiguously identified and the payoff functions are presented numerically, usually in the form of tables of outcomes and corresponding payoffs similar to Matrix 9.2 above. The subjects then make decisions, or sequences of decisions in iterated social dilemmas, usually without communicating with the other group members, and at the end of the session they are usually rewarded with cash according to the number of points that they have accumulated.

A second method of presenting experimental social dilemmas, developed by Jerdee and Rosen (1974) among others, is through the class of games called *commons dilemmas, resource management dilemmas, resource conservation dilemmas*, or simply *resource dilemmas*, which are designed to simulate the shared use of replenishable resources and were inspired by Hardin's (1968) "tragedy of the commons" mentioned earlier. In resource dilemmas, subjects harvest resources (usually tokens or units representing money) from a common resource pool of known size, and after each trial the pool is replenished at a predetermined rate. Subjects can choose, within limits, how much to take from the pool, and the strategic structure of a resource dilemma is crudely similar to an NPD because it is in each person's individual self-interest to take as much as possible from the pool (this corresponds to a D choice in the NPD), but if everyone behaves in this way the pool is exhausted and every player suffers. The resource dilemma research paradigm provides a useful model of everyday social dilemmas involving conservation of natural resources, and the corresponding experimental games are sometimes called *take-some* games.

The third major method of presenting experimental social dilemmas is through the class of games called *public goods dilemmas* or *free-rider problems*, which were inspired by the writings of Mancur Olson (1965, 1982) and developed by Marwell and Ames (1979), among others. For example (Caporael, Dawes, Orbell, and van de Kragt, 1989, p. 687), a group of nine subjects may be given $5 each, and the rules may specify that if five or more of them contribute their money to a central fund, all nine will receive a $10 bonus whether or not they contributed. In this game, if enough players contribute, the net payoff to a contributor is $10 and to a non-contributor it is $15, but if too few contribute, the payoff to a contributor is zero and to a non-contributor it is $5. Public goods games are designed to simulate interactions in which members of a group benefit from actions that are costly to the individual group members who make them. In these games, refusing to perform the act that benefits the group corresponds to a D choice in the NPD, and the underlying strategic structure is again similar to that of a resource dilemma. The public goods research paradigm models everyday social dilemmas in which members of a group reap the benefits of something that is provided publicly regardless of whether they contribute to it, and the corresponding experimental games are sometimes called *give-some* games.

The three most popular methods of presenting experimental social dilemmas amount to different ways of *framing* the dilemmas. It is worth commenting that although the external and ecological validity of the findings can be debated, the games are all capable of eliciting strong emotional involvement among experimental subjects. It is not uncommon for subjects to become angry, upset, and even tearful, and for interpersonal relationships among them to be strongly affected by their joint involvement in an experimental game (e.g., Colman, 1982c, pp. 184–190; Dawes, 1980; van Lange, Liebrand, Messick, and Wilke, 1992).

The major dependent variable in experimental studies has usually been the proportion of cooperative (C) choices, and attention has been devoted to the effects on cooperation of group size, communication between players, individual differences, attribution of intent to other players, payoff and incentive variations, and the framing of the dilemmas. Other independent variables have generated less interesting results; for example, the mysterious sex difference that emerges so robustly in the two-person PDG does not appear with any consistency in multi-person social dilemmas (e.g., Caldwell, 1976; Dawes, McTavish, and Shaklee, 1977; Goehring and Kahan, 1976; McClintock and Liebrand, 1988).

9.7.1 Group size effects

Research into the effects of group size on cooperation in social dilemmas presents methodological problems that have not been satisfactorily solved by all investigators. The problems arise from the fact that it is impossible to hold all aspects of a social dilemma constant while varying the number of players. In an NPD, for example, if the payoff to a C chooser when all other players choose C, the payoff to a D chooser when all other players choose D, and the individual advantage of choosing D rather than C are equated in groups of different sizes, then the extent to which a C choice benefits each of the other players will not be the same.

Different parameters have been held constant by different investigators and, with the exception of one of the three games used by Bonacich, Shure, Kahan, and Meeker (1976), less cooperation has generally been found in larger than smaller groups. Marwell and Schmitt (1972), for example, compared two-person and three-person groups: "The basic data clearly support the hypothesis that rates of cooperation are inversely related to the number of people involved in the interaction" (p. 379). Hamburger, Guyer, and Fox (1975) similarly found significantly more cooperation in three-person than seven-person groups, Fox and Guyer (1977) found significantly more cooperation in three-person than in seven-person or 12-person groups, and Komorita and Lapworth (1982) found significantly more cooperation in two-person than three-person groups and in three-person than six-person groups. Hamburger (1977) attempted to control all factors apart from group size by introducing probabilistic payoffs and using accomplices to fill out the larger groups: pairs of genuine subjects played either a two-person PDG or what appeared to be a three-person NPD including the third player who was an accomplice of the experimenter's using a programmed strategy. The accomplice played in such a manner that the parameters of the two-person and three-person games were identical from the point of view of the genuine subjects. Despite the objective equivalence of the two games, the subjects who thought they were playing the three-person game cooperated significantly less frequently than those in the two-person game.

There is some evidence to suggest that size differences between relatively small groups may be more important than proportionally similar size differences between larger groups. Fox and Guyer (1977) found more cooperation in three-person than seven-person or 12-person groups but failed to find a similar difference between the seven-person and 12-person groups, and Liebrand (1984) found no significant difference in cooperation between seven-person and 20-person groups. Presumably, beyond about seven or eight co-players, psychological factors inhibiting cooperation cease increasing due to some kind of ceiling effect (van Lange et al., 1992, p. 18). But the group size effect is none the less strong and robust for smaller groups.

How can the lower levels of cooperation in larger groups be accounted for? One of the most plausible explanations is the *bad apple* theory. This theory rests on the assumption that it takes only one or a few non-cooperators in a social dilemma to induce the other players to switch to non-cooperation when the dilemma is repeated. There is little or no incentive to cooperate if the goal of collective cooperation cannot be realized: when one sees (or hears) one's neighbours watering their garden during a drought, one may be tempted to follow suit. Now if a fixed proportion of the population has a propensity to behave non-cooperatively, then the probability of one or more of these "bad apples" turning up in a social dilemma increases with the size of the group: it is least likely in a small group and most likely in a large group. As group size increases, so does the probability that one or more "bad apples" will turn up and spoil things for everyone by frustrating the goal of collective cooperation, therefore the less likely it is that anyone in the group will cooperate. In spite of its superficial plausibility, this theory is undermined by the findings of Hamburger (1977) mentioned earlier and by other experiments in which subjects have been pitted against programmed co-players. In these experiments the number of genuine subjects and therefore the number of "bad apples" is the same in the small and the large groups, yet the larger groups still elicit less cooperation from the genuine subjects. But the bad apple theory is not decisively refuted by these findings. It is possible to argue that subjects act on the *assumption* that there are more likely to be "bad apples" in larger groups, and this assumption might function as a self-fulfilling prophecy.

A second explanation for the decline in cooperation with increasing group size centres on the relatively limited degree of *interpersonal control* that is possible in larger groups (Hamburger, 1979, p. 243). Consider the tit for tat (TFT) strategy, for example: this is a fairly effective method of eliciting cooperation from a co-player in a two-person PDG (see section 7.5). But in large NPDs such a strategy cannot generally be put into effect, because it is impossible to reciprocate the other players' previous choices when some have chosen C and others D. If we assume that one of the reasons why players choose C in repeated two-person PDGs is to exercise interpersonal control, then the relatively smaller proportion of C choices in multi-person groups immediately becomes intelligible. Komorita, Parks, and Hulbert (1992) have provided experimental evidence that reciprocity encourages cooperation in small public goods social dilemmas. The interpersonal control theory accounts satisfactorily for the relatively smaller proportion of C choices in multi-person as compared to two-person games. But it does not convincingly explain the differences found in multi-person groups of different sizes: a player has scarcely any more scope for interpersonal control in a three-person than a seven-person NPD, for example.

A closely related but potentially more powerful explanation focuses on *personal efficacy*: people may be less willing to cooperate in larger groups because of a belief that their cooperation will have less effect on the group as a whole. A number of studies using resource management dilemmas have shown that cooperative choices are maximized when subjects believe that their cooperation is essential or crucial to the maintenance of the shared resource pool (e.g., Jorgenson and Papciak, 1981; Samuelson, Messick, Rutte, and Wilke, 1984). In other words, subjects are more willing to make the individual sacrifices involved in cooperating if they believe that their cooperation is likely to have a large effect on the outcome than if they believe that their individual actions are likely to be relatively inconsequential. The notion that perceived personal efficacy is causally related to cooperation in social dilemmas is called the *efficacy-cooperation* hypothesis (Kerr, 1992). Three experiments by Kerr (1989) and two by Rapoport, Bornstein, and Erev (1989) have produced evidence that perceived efficacy in social dilemmas declines as group size increases, even when objective efficacy does not. This suggests that the perceived efficacy of a cooperative choice is likely to be an important factor determining whether that choice is made, and there is direct evidence to show that this happens (e.g., Kerr, 1992; Kerr and Kaufman-Gilliland, 1994). In view of the fact that efficacy tends to decline as group size increases, and that it continues to decline even in large groups, this might explain the group size effect.

The fourth explanation is the *deindividuation* theory originally proposed by Hamburger, Guyer, and Fox (1975). Deindividuation occurs when personal identity and accountability are submerged in a group; in these circumstances individuals become less inhibited about behaving in selfish or antisocial ways. The standard examples of deindividuation in social psychology are taken from mob behaviour and bystander apathy. Hamburger, Guyer, and Fox "make the simple assumption that deindividuation in a group increases as the size of the group increases because, everything else being equal, an individual appears more anonymous in a larger group than in a smaller one" (p. 524). Identity and accountability are unavoidable in a two-person social dilemma because in that limiting case the knowledge that someone has defected necessarily implies knowledge of who it was. Fox and Guyer (1978) tested the deindividuation theory directly in a four-person NPD experiment in which varying degrees of anonymity were allowed to the players. Some groups of subjects exchanged names and background information while others did not, and the subjects' choices were either public or anonymous. The results revealed significantly lower levels of cooperation in the anonymous conditions as predicted by the dein-dividuation theory. Similar findings were reported by Jerdee and Rosen (1974). In an earlier three-person NPD experiment in which the subjects' choices were always anonymous, Kahan (1973) found extremely low levels of cooperation: "The choices made by the individual players were shown to have been made with apparently no regard for the choices of the other two players in the game" (p. 124). All of these findings appear to corroborate the theory of deindividuation.

9.7.2 Communication effects

The effects of communication (without binding and enforceable agreements) among players in social dilemmas have been examined by several investigators and, as in the PDG, communication has usually been found to increase cooperation significantly. The findings of Mintz (1951) on the effects of communication were outlined above. Two other early investigations in this area were those of Caldwell (1976) and Dawes, McTavish, and Shaklee (1977). Caldwell's (1976) experiment was based on a five-person NPD in which the subjects were either allowed to communicate with one another and, in some cases, to penalize defectors, or were forbidden to communicate. The effect of mere communication was statistically non-significant, but when the subjects were permitted not only to communicate but also to penalize defectors by deducting points from their payoffs, a significant increase in cooperation was observed. Caldwell describes this as a "communication effect", but it amounts, in fact, to an effect of altering the strategic structure of the game by decreasing the payoffs for non-cooperation. Caldwell admits that "sanctions may have, in effect, changed the nature of the payoff matrix" (p. 278), but he should have said that they *did* change the matrix. No clear conclusion about the effect of communication is therefore possible on the basis of this study.

The carefully controlled NPD study by Dawes, McTavish, and Shaklee (1977) produced clearer results concerning communication effects. Subjects were assigned to groups varying in size from five to eight, and the effects of four levels of communication were examined: no communication; communication only about matters irrelevant to the game; relevant communication; and relevant communication plus non-binding public announcements of intended choices before each trial. The first two conditions yielded cooperation rates of 30 per cent and 32 per cent respectively, while the last two yielded rates of 72 per cent and 71 per cent. The effect of relevant communication was highly significant, and it is clear from these results that it is discussion of the dilemma rather than merely getting to know the other players that enhances cooperation in the NPD.

Numerous subsequent experiments have confirmed that relevant communication among players promotes cooperation (e.g., Bornstein, 1992; Bornstein, Rapoport, Kerpel, and Katz, 1989; Caldwell, 1976; Caporael, Dawes, Orbell, and van de Kragt, 1989; Dawes, McTavish, and Shaklee, 1977; Jerdee and Rosen, 1974; Jorgenson and Papciak, 1981; Kerr and Kaufman-Gilliland, 1994; Liebrand, 1984; Orbell, van de Kragt, and Dawes, 1988). The communication effect is one of the most robust and interesting findings to emerge from research into behaviour in social dilemmas. Some commentators have expressed surprise that communication does not generate even higher levels of cooperation than it does, but in view of the fact that an individual benefits by non-cooperation in spite of any (non-binding) agreement that might have been reached, the problem is really to explain why it leads to *any* increase in cooperation.

Why does communication among players in the absence of binding and enforceable agreements lead to an increase in cooperation? Various suggestions have been put forward: communication may help to foster interpersonal trust and to allay the cooperatively intentioned players' fears that "bad apples" may be present in the group; communication is bound to enhance personal identity and accountability and therefore to reduce deindividuation; communication may facilitate players' understanding of the dilemmas; communication may humanize fellow group members. In fact, research has failed to corroborate any of these suggestions as an explanation for the communication effect. For example, the suggestion that communication enhances cooperation through humanizing fellow group members is clearly not supported by the findings of Dawes, McTavish, and Shaklee (1977) outlined in the previous paragraph – communication about matters unrelated to the dilemma did *not* enhance cooperation, although it should have had a humanizing effect at least as strong as relevant communication.

A general consensus has emerged among researchers in this area (e.g., Kerr and Kaufman-Gilliland, 1994; Messick and Brewer, 1983; van Lange et al., 1992) that only two explanations of the effects of communication are viable in the light of research findings. First, communication can potentially provide a means of *commitment* whereby players can undertake publicly to cooperate. This could encourage everyone to cooperate if they believe that others will keep their words, and the effect could be almost as though a binding and enforceable agreement were in place. Second, communication can enhance feelings of *group identity or solidarity* and thereby cause individuals to place a greater relative weight on collective rather than individual welfare, which should also encourage cooperation. As Turner, Hogg, Oakes, Reicher, and Wetherall (1987) explain it, "to the degree that the self is depersonalized, so too is self-interest ... cooperation will follow from the shared and mutual perception by ingroup members of their interests as interchangeable" (p. 65).

Regarding the commitment effect, there is empirical evidence that group discussions in experimental social dilemmas consist largely of soliciting and making promises and commitments, and that there are strong psychological pressures on people to honour them once they have been made (e.g., Kerr and Kaufman-Gilliland, 1994; Orbell, van de Kragt, and Dawes, 1988). Nevertheless, some researchers (e.g., Caporael, Dawes, Orbell, and van de Kragt, 1989; Orbell, van de Kragt, and Dawes, 1988) believe that the group identity effect is more important. Several social dilemma experiments by Brewer and Kramer on social categorization (Brewer and Kramer, 1986; Kramer and Brewer, 1984, 1986) have shown that cooperation increases when the social identity of the entire group is made more salient and subgroups within it less salient. The evidence appears to show that the stronger one's sense of group identity, the less sharply one distinguishes between self-interest and collective interest and therefore the more willing one is to promote the common good by cooperating. According to Brewer and Schneider (1990), "social identity may exacerbate social dilemmas by promoting competition at the expense of the collective, or may mitigate selfish behaviour by encouraging healthy competition to provide for the collective welfare. Which effect is realized depends on how subgroups differentiate themselves from each other" (p. 184).

Kerr and Kaufman-Gilliland's (1994) experiment, which used a public goods dilemma, was designed to test the commitment and group identity explanations against each other. In this experiment individual efficacy was varied independently of group size by altering the relative weight that each subject's choice had on the outcomes. The results showed that group discussion enhanced group identity and led to increased cooperation across treatment conditions in which individual efficacy varied. Even when cooperation had practically no impact on the provision of the public good, cooperation was still about 30 per cent higher among groups that discussed the dilemma than among those that did not. Content analysis of group discussions revealed a high rate of commitment to cooperate, and these commitments were closely associated with subsequent cooperative choices and expectations of cooperation from other group members. These findings tend to disconfirm the notion that the effect of communication on cooperation can be explained solely in terms of enhanced group identity. They suggest that the opportunities for commitment that communication affords are probably the most important explanation of the communication effect.

9.7.3 Individual differences and attribution effects

A number of researchers have examined the effects of individual differences on cooperation in social dilemmas. This line of research arises from the obvious fact that people differ from one another, and that some people are generally more cooperative than others.

Evidence has emerged that people vary in their *social value orientations*, and that these orientations affect their propensities to cooperate in social dilemmas. According to McClintock's (1972) taxonomy of social value orientations outlined in section 7.2, people may be motivated to maximize collective payoffs (leading obviously to cooperative choices), to maximize individual payoffs (for which the appropriate strategy, if the dilemma is iterated, depends on the choices of the others), and to *maximize relative payoffs*, that is, to "beat the opponent" (leading to non-cooperative choices). A number of investigators have found that people with cooperative social value orientations choose more cooperatively than individualists or competitively motivated people (e.g., Kramer, McClintock, and Messick, 1986; Kuhlman and Marshello, 1975; Liebrand and van Run, 1985; McClintock and Liebrand, 1988), and also that they expect more cooperation from others (van Lange 1992). There is some equivocal evidence (reviewed in Liebrand and van Run, 1985) that American university students are generally less cooperative in social dilemmas than European university students.

Concerning attribution effects, several studies of the influence of the perceived intentions of others on a player's choices are worth discussing briefly. The findings in this area bear on Kelley and Stahelski's (1970c) triangle hypothesis discussed in section 7.8. Briefly, there are hypothesized to be two classes of people: those who are habitually cooperative and who learn through experience that others vary in cooperativeness, and those who are habitually competitive and whose erroneous attributions of competitive intentions to others are unlikely to be corrected through experience because their competitive behaviour tends to elicit competitive responses from others.

Tyszka and Grzelak (1976), Alcock and Mansell (1977), Dawes, McTavish, and Shaklee (1977), and Marwell and Ames (1979) all reported a strong, positive relationship between propensity to cooperate and attribution of cooperative intentions to others. In the second of these studies, for example, defectors predicted 24 per cent cooperation from the other players while cooperators predicted 68 per cent cooperation, and this difference was highly significant. In the Dawes, McTavish, and Shaklee experiment defectors predicted four times as much defection from other players as was predicted by cooperators, and the correlation between cooperative choices and attributions of cooperative intentions to others was about .60. These findings offer some indirect support for the triangle hypothesis, although they can be explained quite easily without it. The triangle hypothesis was conceived in the context of two-person interactions and cannot be generalized without a certain awkwardness to the multi-person context. A direct test in groups varying in size from 10 to 15 (Kelley and Grzelak, 1972) produced ambiguous results but led to the interesting incidental discovery that cooperators usually have a better understanding of the strategic structure of the game than defectors.

Messick and Rutte (1992) reported the results of an experiment carried out at the Third International Conference on Social Dilemmas in Groningen. A public goods dilemma was created at one of the conference sessions by offering the 43 participants, all of whom were leading authorities on social dilemmas, 10 Dutch guilders each if the total amount of money collected from them was 250 guilders or more, and the participants were also invited to guess how much money would be contributed. In the event, Dfl 245.59 was collected, so all the contributions were sacrificed, but what is most interesting in the present context was that those who predicted that the critical amount would not be reached contributed an average of Dfl 1.83 each, whereas those who predicted success contributed an average of Dfl 7.24 each – nearly four times as much. Thus even among experts on social dilemmas there appears to be a strong relationship between cooperation and expectation of cooperation from others.

Further indirect support for the triangle hypothesis comes from a study by van Lange, Liebrand, and Kuhlman (1990), who compared cooperators and defectors in terms of the trait adjectives that they used to describe cooperative and defecting choices from their co-players in three-person NPD social dilemmas. They found that cooperators tended to attribute defection partly to ignorance (thoughtlessness, lack of intelligence, clumsiness, and so on), whereas defectors tended to attribute cooperation to ignorance. Perhaps cooperators consider defectors to be ignorant because they seem incapable of cooperating, and defectors consider cooperators to be ignorant because they seem not to realize that everyone defects. A few studies, however, have failed to find evidence for the triangle effect in social dilemmas (e.g, Kuhlman and Wimberley, 1976; Liebrand, Wilke, Vogel, and Wolters, 1986), and some authorities believe that it is more applicable to dyadic interaction.

A related interpersonal attitude that has received attention from researchers is trust. People differ in how trusting they are of others (Yamagishi, 1988), and those who are most trusting have been found to be the most cooperative in general. This finding corroborates a line of research going back to Deutsch

(1958) on cooperation and competition in dyads, and it relates to the findings on attribution effects. Also relevant in this connection is a study by van Lange and Liebrand (1989) into the effects of people's perceptions of others' morality on cooperation in a public goods dilemma. The results showed that people were much more willing to cooperate with others whom they believed were moral than with others whom they believed to be immoral, and this was true of people with all social value orientations.

9.7.4 Payoff and incentive effects

A great deal of research (reviewed in section 7.3) into payoff and incentive effects in two-person social dilemmas has suggested that subjects tend to respond in intelligible and more or less rational ways to variations in the payoff structure of games. A number of studies of behaviour in social dilemmas have confirmed that variations in payoffs have predictable effects. Cooperation tends to increase as the relative payoff for cooperative behaviour increases and as the relative payoff for defecting or non-cooperative behaviour decreases (e.g., Bonacich, Shure, Kahan, and Meeker, 1976; Komorita, Sweeny, and Kravitz, 1980). There is also evidence to show that people's cooperation increases significantly as the benefit of their cooperation to others increases (e.g., Caldwell, 1976; Komorita, Sweeny, and Kravitz, 1980). Messick and Brewer (1983) have interpreted these findings as suggesting that cooperation is governed by at least two independent motives, one selfish and the other altruistic. Komorita and Barth (1985) and Komorita (1987) have also found that cooperation increases when subjects believe that their co-players are to able to reward cooperative choices and, perhaps to a lesser extent, when they believe that their co-players are able to punish non-cooperative choices. Mention has already been made of studies using resource management dilemmas that have shown that people are more inclined to cooperate when they believe that their cooperation is efficacious or essential or crucial to the maintenance of the shared resource pool (e.g., Jorgenson and Papciak, 1981; Kerr, 1989, 1992; Kerr and Kaufman-Gilliland, 1994; Samuelson, Messick, Rutte and Wilke, 1984).

Research with two-person social dilemmas (reviewed in section 7.3) suggests that the effects of variations in the monetary incentives associated with the payoffs are neither large nor consistent, but there is evidence to suggest that incentive effects may be stronger in multi-person social dilemmas. Large variations in monetary incentives are difficult to arrange in laboratory experiments, and much of the evidence is derived from naturalistic field studies. A number of studies, summarized by van Lange et al. (1992, pp. 14–15) have found that variations in monetary reward have a strong effect on cooperative behaviour in resource dilemmas involving conservation.

9.7.5 Framing effects

People facing decision problems necessarily interpret them in particular ways, and different interpretations of the same problem may sometimes lead to different decisions. The effects of different interpretations of equivalent problems are called *framing effects*. The basic ideas and empirical findings related to framing effects were introduced in section 5.4, and their relevance to two-person mixed-motive games was discussed in section 7.9. In the paragraphs that follow, their possible relevance to social dilemmas will be examined.

McDaniel and Sistrunk (1991) reported the results of an experiment in which a social dilemma was framed as both a resource dilemma (take-some) and a public goods dilemma (give-some) with equivalent gains and losses in both frames. The subjects (280 graduate business studies students) played the role of Chief Executive Officer of an agricultural firm and had to choose between increasing (*D*) or not increasing (*C*) milk production, in the knowledge that increased production would lead to falling prices (resource dilemma), and between contributing or not contributing to an agricultural cooperative (public goods dilemma). The subjects were given hypothetical information about the level of cooperation anticipated from the other agricultural firms involved. As expected, the subjects cooperated significantly more when they were led to anticipate more cooperation from the other participants, but contrary to expectations, they cooperated significantly more in the public goods dilemma frame than in the resource dilemma frame, especially when they expected high levels of cooperation from the other hypothetical players. This latter finding cannot be considered robust, however, because Brewer and Kramer (1986) found that subjects cooperated more in a social dilemma when it was framed as a resource dilemma than when it was framed as a public goods dilemma; Komorita and Carnevale (1992) found differences in both directions in three experiments; and Fleishman (1988) found no significant differences in cooperation between the two frames. But these findings show that the framing of social dilemmas may have significant (albeit poorly understood) effects on cooperation.

Two experiments reported by Komorita and Barth (1985) used decomposed social dilemmas in which subjects were told either that "for each person who makes the *C* choice a bonus of one point will be awarded to all persons in the group" or that "for each person who makes a *D* choice, a penalty of one point will be subtracted from all persons in the group". The two versions were payoff equivalent, but the first version, in which the dilemma was framed so that a cooperative choice was seen to reward the group members (the bonus frame), elicited greater cooperation than the second version, which was the same social dilemma framed so that a non-cooperative choice was seen to punish the group members (the penalty frame). This is analogous to the difference that shoppers perceive between a cash discount and a credit card surcharge, even if they are simply two ways of framing exactly the same thing. The use of decomposed games was discussed in relation to the two-person PDG in section 7.9. As in the two-person case, when a social dilemma is decomposed it tends to elicit different motives in the players. Komorita and Barth's bonus frame tended to elicit cooperative motives because cooperative choices seemed to benefit the group, whereas in the penalty frame a cooperative choice did not seem to benefit anybody.

A small number of experiments have investigated cooperation and competition in social dilemmas that have been presented in various lifelike frames. Alcock and Mansell (1977) reported three experiments in which a conventional NPD payoff matrix was used, but the subjects were told, in addition, that the game was "a simulation of animal population growth under conditions of scarce resources" (p. 447). They were given a verbal account of the "tragedy of the commons" and were assigned the roles of cattle farmers. Their choices were labelled "Add" (an animal to the pasture) and "Not Add". In free-play conditions the level of cooperation was about 30 per cent, which is certainly no higher than might have been expected in a conventional abstract version of the same game. When subjects were provided with false feedback about the choices of the other players on previous trials, irrespective of how the others had actually chosen, little effect was observed on the subjects' own choices.

Colman (1982c, pp. 184–190) reported an experiment designed to compare behaviour in a conventional abstract NPD with behaviour in the identical game framed as a lifelike social dilemma. In the abstract frame, 120 undergraduate subjects played a conventional three-person NPD for points on the basis of a purely numerical payoff matrix. In the lifelike frame, the subjects played the roles of three finance ministers of rival oil-producing nations deciding between restricted production and full production of oil. The payoffs in this condition were imaginary profits, and they bore an interval-scale correspondence to the payoffs in the abstract frame. The major hypothesis that, over 30 iterations of the dilemma, the lifelike frame would elicit fewer cooperative choices from the subjects than the abstract frame was strongly confirmed. This was probably due to the fact that the lifelike frame involved decision making in a hypothetical business context in which prevailing cultural values encourage competitive behaviour, and it is possible that with a different lifelike frame the effect might be reversed. The experiment shows that the results of social dilemma experiments based on abstract decision tasks cannot be generalized straightforwardly to lifelike situations in which cultural factors play an important part. This is the same conclusion that emerged from the results of experiments on two-person Prisoner's Dilemma and Chicken games described in section 7.9.

9.8 Summary

The chapter opened with some general comments on n-person non-cooperative games and the comparative unhelpfulness of solutions to them based on Nash equilibria. Section 9.2 was devoted to a discussion of the Chain-store game in which logic, in the form of backward induction, and common sense seem to be at loggerheads. Section 9.3 was devoted to the unhappily named Dollar Auction game, the Concorde fallacy, and other psychological traps where people (and sometimes governments) have difficulty extricating themselves from predicaments in which they feel they have "too much invested to quit". Empirical evidence has shown that people often become highly emotional as the process of escalation spirals out of control. Section 9.4 supplied the intuitive background and informal theory of social dilemmas, which underlie a vast range of familiar social problems, from energy and natural resource conservation to inflation and voluntary wage restraint, environmental pollution, overpopulation, multilateral disarmament, and many others besides. The most important property of a social dilemma is that players who all pursue their individual self-interests rationally end up worse off than if they had all acted for the common good instead. Sections 9.5 and 9.6 were devoted to the formal, mathematical definition and properties of social dilemmas and compound games in general, and section 9.7 provided a selective critical review of experimental research in this field. Experiments have been based on N-person Prisoner's Dilemma games, resource dilemmas, and public goods dilemmas, and interesting findings have been reported in relation to the effects on cooperation of group size, opportunities for communication between group members, individual differences, group members' attributions of intent to one another, variations in payoffs and incentives, and the framing of strategically equivalent social dilemmas.

— Part III —

Applications

—— 10 ——

Social choice and strategic voting

10.1 Background

In contemporary societies, multi-person games are often governed by formal rules designed to ensure that the outcomes are fair and democratic. Within this broad category is an important class of games that serve the purpose of aggregating individual preferences into collective choices. For example, committees often have to choose a single course of action from among several proposals favoured by different members. A method of resolving differences of opinion into a specific choice from a set of alternatives or candidates is called a *social choice function* (or a *social choice rule*), and those that have a claim to being fair and democratic are generally voting procedures of one kind or another. Voting procedures are used by electorates for choosing political representatives, by legislatures for choosing laws, by colleges of cardinals for choosing popes, and by juries, boards of directors in industry, groups of shareholders, trade unions, and many other kinds of committees and decision-making bodies.

A number of paradoxes associated with apparently reasonable voting procedures were discovered by mathematicians and physicists of the French Enlightenment. The first major contribution was made by Jean-Charles de Borda (1781), who was followed by the Marquis de Condorcet (1785). During the nineteenth century, the Reverend C. L. Dodgson (1876) (Lewis Carroll) independently rediscovered some of these paradoxes. The subsequent historical development of social choice theory (or collective choice theory) has been traced by Black (1958) and Riker (1961). More recent surveys of the literature include those of Sen (1970); Fishburn (1973a); Kelly (1978); Nurmi (1983); Riker (1982); Ordeshook (1986, chaps 1, 2); Elster and Hylland (1986); and Rapoport (1989, chap. 7).

A tacit assumption underlying classical social choice theory is that voting is *sincere*. This is an assumption about the strategies that the players – in this case the voters – adopt in every voting game. In any genuine ballot, a voter has at least two pure strategies, otherwise there would be no real element of choice. Roughly speaking, voting is said to be sincere if the voters always vote in favour of the alternatives they consider best. More specifically, a voter who prefers an alternative x to another y, and prefers y to a third z, votes sincerely by voting for x whenever it is available in a ballot, and if the choice is between y and z, votes for y. Some voting procedures allow voters to vote for more than one alternative, in which case voting is sincere if a voter who prefers x to y never votes for y but not x. Sincere voting amounts to choosing the maximax strategy (see section 2.5.2). A sincere voter in effect selects the strategy that might produce the best of the best possible outcomes given some conceivable combination of strategy choices by the other voters. Many authors define sincere voting loosely as voting strictly according to one's preferences, but this is misleading because it does not necessarily serve one's interests best. A maximax strategy is not necessarily the most sensible choice in a multi-person game, whether it is a voting game or not. The implications of insincere strategic voting will be spelt out later in this chapter.

Social choice theory, together with the assumption of sincere voting, is logically a branch of one-person game theory (see chapter 2), because the problems with which it deals are formally equivalent to those in which a single decision maker faces a multi-attribute decision task (Rapoport, 1989, p. 143). In a particular case, if the voters all vote sincerely, then they are not really choosing strategically but are merely revealing their preferences, and a referee who knew their individual preference orders could, in principle, combine them into a collective preference order on their behalf. Classical social choice theory is thus formally equivalent to multi-attribute decision making; but as soon as a strategic voting is taken into account, voting must be interpreted as a branch of n-person game theory.

In the following section, the elements of social choice theory will be explained. Some common voting procedures will be outlined in section 10.3. Section 10.4 will be devoted to Condorcet's paradox and other voting paradoxes, and section 10.5 to Arrow's impossibility theorem, which arises from Condorcet's paradox. Section 10.6 will concentrate on proportional representation voting in general and the single transferable vote in particular. Section 10.7 will introduce the fundamental ideas behind strategic or tactical voting, and section 10.8 will deal in detail with Farquharson's concept of sophisticated voting, and section 10.9 will discuss the empirical evidence for sophisticated voting. Section 10.10 will contain a brief summary of the chapter.

10.2 Alternatives, voters, preferences

The following hypothetical example will help to introduce the primitive terms and assumptions of social choice theory. A committee is faced with the problem of choosing one of three candidates to fill a political post. One of the candidates, Leftwich, is known to hold left-wing views; another, Middleton, is politically moderate; and the third, Rightsman, is right-wing. There are three opinion blocs among the committee members. The left-wing committee members (obviously) prefer Leftwich to Middleton and Mid-dleton to Rightsman: their preference order may be written compactly as *LMR*. The moderate committee members prefer Leftwich to Rightsman, so their preference order is *MLR*, and the right-wing committee members' preference order is obviously *RML*. These three opinion blocs are the only ones represented on the committee, and they are of approximately equal voting strength; none commands more than half the total number of votes, so a combination of any two blocs can outvote the third.

In this idealized example, there are three *alternatives* (or *candidates*) from among which a social choice has to be made: L (Leftwich), M (Middleton), and R (Rightsman). The set of *voters* can be defined in two different ways: either as the members of the committee, or as the distinct opinion blocs. In the latter case we need consider only three effectively distinguishable voters, namely left-wing, moderate, and right-wing, and this would be possible even if the choice were being made by an entire electorate with just three opinion blocs, each commanding less than half of the votes. Finally, each voter has *preferences* among the alternatives that we can represent by means of an ordered triple of initials. The assumption here is that each voter is capable, if requested to do so, of ranking the alternatives in order of preference from "best" to "worst".

The primitive terms outlined in the previous paragraphs can be formalized by means of a mathematically defined family of strong ordering relations between pairs of alternatives. It is assumed that there is a finite set *I* of voters or individuals, $I = \{1, 2, \ldots, m\}$, $m \geq 3$, who seek to choose through some voting procedure an element or elements from a non-empty finite set *X* of available alternatives. For technical reasons, and also to take account of certain basic assumptions about human rationality, it is assumed that each voter $i \in I$ has a linear preference ordering P_i on *X*. This means that for every pair of alternatives *x*, *y*, each voter either prefers *x* to *y* or *y* to *x* but not both, no voter prefers any alternative *x* to itself, and if *x*, *y*, and *z* are any three available alternatives, any voter who prefers *x* to *y* and *y* to *z* must also prefer *x* to *z*. (The preference relation is often modified to allow a voter to express indifference between a pair of alternatives, but this leads to complications that are not needed here.) Thus the strong ordering relation *P* ("is preferred to") is defined for each voter and for each pair of alternatives by incorporating these assumptions into the model as axioms:

(A_1) *Completeness*: for all $x, y \in X$, $x \neq y$, for all $i \in I$, either xP_iy or yP_ix.

(A_2) *Irreflexivity*: for all $x \in X$, for all $i \in I$, not xP_ix.

(A_3) *Transitivity*: for all $x, y, z \in X$, for all $i \in I$, if xP_iy and yP_iz, then xP_iz.

If the indexed set of voters' preference orderings on *X* is $D = \{P_1, P_2, \ldots, P_m\}$, then a voting procedure, or more generally a social choice function, is a function whose domain is the set of ordered pairs (X, D) and which assigns to each such pair a non-empty subset $F(X, D)$ of X. In the context of voting, $F(X, D)$ may be interpreted as the set (often a singleton) of winners. The form of the function varies from one voting procedure to another.

Axioms A_1 and A_2 are relatively innocuous; they simply ensure that the preference relation is properly defined for all voters over all pairs of alternatives. But Axiom A_3 implies an important assumption about human rationality that is not as innocent as it seems. Do rational human beings ever prefer x to y, y to z, and z to x? Empirical evidence suggests that individual intransitivities usually arise only from carelessness when people are required to make trivial comparisons, and when the intransitivities are pointed out to them, they usually proceed to eliminate them (Niemi and Riker, 1976).

But there are circumstances in which people express intransitive preferences for deeper reasons (Slovic and Lichtenstein, 1983; Tversky, 1969). In practice, this is most likely to happen when alternatives differing on multiple attributes are ranked. Consider a situation in which you are trying to choose between three similarly priced cars, x, y, and z, that you have rated as follows on three attributes that you consider equally important.

Table 10.1

	Speed	*Comfort*	*Fuel economy*
x	excellent	satisfactory	good
y	good	excellent	satisfactory
z	satisfactory	good	excellent

If the preferences are merely ordinal, it is clear that you prefer x to y, because it is better on two of the three attributes, but you prefer y to z and z to x for the same reason. Thus your preference order is intransitive and in fact cyclic, with xPy, yPz, and zPx. Any such preference order may appear foolish, especially when one realizes that it represents a so-called *Dutch book* that turns the person who holds it into a potential *money pump* (this was first pointed out by Ramsey, 1931; it has been discussed more recently by Border and Segal, 1994; McClennen and Found, 1995; and Schick, 1986).

To see how this can happen suppose in the above example that you decided to cut the Gordian knot and to buy car x. An enterprising salesman could then offer to replace it with z in return for a small sum of money. In view of the fact that you prefer z to x, there must be *some* amount of money that you would be happy to pay to have x replaced by z; but then, having taken possession of z, you will happily pay the same salesman to exchange it for y; and you will then pay something more to have y replaced by x. You will then have returned, poorer but no happier, to where you began when you bought car x, and there is no reason why the salesman should not return to begin the whole cycle over again. The cyclic order of preferences has turned you into a money pump that will stop working only when the well runs dry, that is, when your funds are exhausted. Thus intransitive preferences may appear foolish, but not all social choice theorists regard them as inherently and necessarily irrational. Fishburn (1988), for example, wrote: "I do regard willing participation as a money pump as irrational, or at least naive, but I see this as no reason against the admissibility of cyclic preferences in certain situations as reasonable patterns of judgment" (p. 84). But classical social choice theory usually assumes transitivity of individual preference orders.

Table 10.2 Voters' preferences

	Voters (voting blocs)		
	Left-wing	Moderate	Right-wing
First preference	L	M	R
Second preference	M	L	M
Third preference	R	R	L

The ingredients or primitive terms and axioms of the simple model of social choice involving Leftwich, Middleton, and Rightsman are now assembled. The profile or configuration of voters' preferences can be summarized as shown in Table 10.2.

10.3 Voting procedures

A fairly common voting procedure that is used in the legislatures of West Germany, Denmark, and Norway, and in the Council of Europe (Bjurulf and Niemi, 1981) is the *successive procedure*. A ballot is held on each alternative in turn; the voters vote in favour or against it in each case until a majority votes in favour of one of the alternatives. If none attracts a majority of votes before just two remain, then a final ballot between these two decides the issue. In the example of the committee, the voters might first vote for or against *L* (Leftwich); if a majority votes for *L* then a collective decision has been reached and further balloting is unnecessary, but if a majority votes against *L* (that is, for "*M* or *R*", which means the same as "not *L*") then a second and final ballot is held between *M* and *R*. The successive voting procedure can begin with a ballot on any one of the alternatives and, as we shall see, different orders of voting can lead to different social choices.

If *L* is presented first, then the sincere outcome is as follows:

First ballot: In favour of *L* (Leftwich), left-wingers;
                Against *L*, moderates and right-wingers.
                Result: *M* or *R*. Therefore
Second ballot: In favour of *M* (Middleton), left-wingers and moderates;
                In favour of *R* (Rightsman), right-wingers.
                Final result: *M*.

The social choice is Middleton, the alternative that the moderate voters consider best and the left-wingers and right-wingers consider second best. But if *M* is presented first, then the outcome is:

First ballot: In favour of *M*, moderates;
                Against *M*, left-wingers and right-wingers.
                Result: *L* or *R*. Therefore
Second ballot: In favour of *L*, left-wingers and moderates;
                In favour of *R*, right-wingers.
                Final result: *L*.

With this order of voting, Leftwich wins! It is easily verified that if Rightsman had been presented first, Middleton would have won. An alternative presented in an early ballot under the successive procedure is at a relative disadvantage if voting is sincere. This is called the *agenda paradox* (e.g., Ordershook, 1986, pp. 65–66). An interesting consequence of the agenda paradox is this: if the voters know the preferences of the others, that is to say, if the voting game is one of complete information, and if they are permitted to choose the order in which the votes should be taken, then the left-wingers will favour presenting Middleton first, thus ensuring that Leftwich would be the final choice, and the moderates and right-wingers will favour presenting Leftwich or Rightsman first, because they prefer the final choice to be Middleton rather than Leftwich. There are only two effectively distinct voting orders: "*M* first" and "*L* or *R* first". A single ballot would decide this procedural issue in favour of "*L* or *R* first" because only the left-wingers would favour the other order. The final result of balloting in the order favoured by the majority would be the choice of Middleton.

Procedural votes of this kind are permitted in some decision-making bodies, for example in parliaments such as the Norwegian *Storting* (Rasch, 1987) and the Swedish *Riksdag* (Rustow, 1955), but not in others. They are permitted in British Labour Party conferences, as the following quotation from *The Times* (24 January 1981) shows:

> A procedural strategy adopted by the moderate leaders of the Amalgamated Union of Engineering Workers (AUEW) could threaten the precariously balanced centre-left coalition supporting the com-promise formula [for electing the party leader] favoured by Mr Michael Foot ... by getting delegates to reject the standing orders committee recommendation for debating procedure. (p. 2)

In the event, the order of voting led to the "compromise formula" being eliminated as expected before the final ballot. But the AUEW was hoist with its own petard, because a left-wing motion, granting trade unions the largest say in the election of the party leader, defeated a right-wing motion on the final ballot (*The Times*, 26 January 1981).

Another sequential voting procedure that is often used in legislative bodies is the *amendment procedure*. It is common in Great Britain and all of her former colonies including the United States, and also in Switzerland, Sweden and Finland (Bjurulf and Niemi, 1981; Rasch, 1987). A substantive motion is tabled and an amendment (or a number of amendments) proposed. The first ballot decides for or against amending the motion, and the final ballot then determines whether the (possibly amended) motion is passed or rejected. Rejecting the motion on the final ballot is equivalent to choosing a third (default) alternative. Different orders of voting are possible with this procedure as well, because any of the alternatives might be treated as the substantive motion and any other(s) as the amendment(s). In the committee example, the substantive motion might be "That Rightsman be appointed to the post" and the amendment might be "That the word 'Rightsman' be replaced by 'Middleton'". Leftwich is then the default alternative, assuming that one of the three has to be appointed. The first ballot is then on whether to amend the motion:

First ballot: In favour of M (the Middleton amendment), left-wingers
                 and moderates;
                 In favour of R (Rightsman, the substantive motion),
                 right-wingers.
                 Result: M.
Second ballot: In favour of M, moderates and right-wingers;
                 Against M (that is, in favour of L), left-wingers.
                 Final result: M.

It can easily be checked that with the postulated preferences the same final result emerges from any order of voting under the amendment procedure. But this is not always the case. Had the preference orders of the voters been LMR, MRL, and RLM, then any of the alternatives could emerge as the final choice depending on voting order. This is an example of Condorcet's paradox, to which I shall return in section 10.4. Riker and Ordeshook (1973), Miller (1977), and Bjurulf and Niemi (1981) discussed the conditions under which voting orders influence final choices in various sequential procedures including successive and amendment voting. They also outlined the strategies that voters might be expected to adopt in voting on procedural issues in these circumstances.

The most common voting procedure in committees and elections is undoubtedly the *plurality* (first-past-the-post) procedure, in which all of the alternatives are pitted against one another in a single ballot, and the one that receives the largest number of votes is declared the winner. It is also used in national or municipal elections in countries where more than one candidate must be elected, in Finland, Japan, Jordan, South Korea, and Spain, for example (Felsenthal and Maoz, 1992). In order to determine which alternative would be chosen by plurality voting in the committee example, it is necessary to make additional assumptions about the voting strengths of the opinion blocs.

Most voting procedures include special rules to resolve ties and to ensure that a decisive result is always reached. In committees, for example, the chairman may have a casting vote in addition to an ordinary deliberative vote, to be used in the event of a tie on any ballot. (This is common in most English-speaking countries, though not in the United States.) In the committee example, we may arbitrarily assume either that the left-wingers are the largest of the three voting blocs, or that the voting blocs are of exactly equal size but that the additional casting vote belongs to one of the left-wingers. With these assumptions it is obvious that the result of sincere voting is the choice of Leftwich.

Three common voting procedures have been examined in this section. With the postulated preferences and voting strengths, and assuming that all voters are sincere, the successive procedure results in the choice of Leftwich or Middleton depending on the order of voting, the amendment procedure to the choice of Middleton, and the plurality procedure to the choice of Leftwich. Given a choice of voting procedures, the left-wingers would favour the successive procedure with Middleton presented first, or the plurality procedure, because these procedures ensure the choice of their favourite candidate. Both the moderates and the right-wingers, on the other hand, would favour the successive procedure with Leftwich or Rightsman presented first, or the amendment procedure, because Middleton is then bound to be the final choice and they prefer Middleton to Leftwich. Choosing one of the voting procedures presents problems because a voting procedure of some kind would have to be used in order to make this choice democratically, and opinions might differ on the procedure to be used for choosing a procedure. One is confronted with the prospect of a committee bogged down by an infinite regress of points of order, unable to take any votes at all. Such is the price of sincerity, for it will be shown in section 10.8

that this problem is largely solved, in a manner consistent with the will of the majority, by insincere voting.

10.4 Voting paradoxes

The agenda paradox has already been discussed in section 10.3. The Marquis de Condorcet (1785) seems to have been the first to discover a more profound voting paradox that lies at the centre of modern social choice theory. Its simplest manifestation is in a group of three voters choosing among three alternatives *A*, *B*, and *C*. Assuming as before that the voters' preference orders are complete, irreflexive, and transitive, consider the profile or configuration of preferences shown in Table 10.3. This pattern is called a *Latin square*; it has the property that each symbol appears exactly once in each row and in each column. In other words, each alternative appears exactly once in each position – first, second, third – in the three individual preference orders. This means that no two voters agree about which alternative is best, which is second best, or which is worst. The only other Latin square that can be formed from three alternatives *A*, *B*, and *C* is the profile *ACB*, *BAC*, *CBA*, and this profile also generates Condorcet's paradox.

Table 10.3 Condorcet's paradox

	Voters		
	1	2	3
First preference	*A*	*B*	*C*
Second preference	*B*	*C*	*A*
Third preference	*C*	*A*	*B*

The paradox emerges if we assume that the voters are sincere and then try to determine the social choice according to majority rule. Two of the three voters (1 and 3) prefer *A* to *B*, two (1 and 2) prefer *B* to *C*, and two (2 and 3) prefer *C* to *A*. Thus a majority of the voters prefers *A* to *B*, *B* to *C*, and *C* to *A*. The collective preference order of the group cannot be written down in the normal way. A set of transitive individual preferences has generated an intransitive collective preference order that is called a *cyclic majority*. The "group mind" can therefore violate a basic axiom of rationality (Axiom A_3 in section 10.3 above) even if all of its members are perfectly rational. Condorcet's paradox has disturbing implications for democratic theory and practice, as we shall see.

Some kind of social choice function is needed in order to make a collective decision on the basis of a profile or configuration of individual preferences. Some decision rules are obviously undemocratic. For example "Write each alternative on a separate slip of paper and draw one of them out of a hat at random" is clearly a feasible decision rule, but it is undemocratic because, in the terminology of social choice theory, it is *imposed*: the social choice does not depend in any way on the preferences of the individuals. Another workable decision rule might be: "Choose the alternative that the president considers best". But this rule is *dictatorial*: the choice is determined entirely by the preference of one individual. A rule that seems on the face of it entirely unexceptional is the method of majority decision: "Choose an alternative that is preferred to each of the others by a majority of the voters". This is a rule that has much to recommend it, but unfortunately it is not always feasible. For example, it is impossible to use the method of majority decision to choose an alternative from the cyclic profile of preferences shown in Table 10.3, because there is no alternative that is preferred to each of the others by a majority; in the terminology of social choice theory, there is no *Condorcet winner*.

Condorcet's paradox leads immediately to an elementary impossibility theorem (Colman and Pountney, 1975b): no social choice function could satisfy the following two conditions of workableness and fairness: (a) a single alternative must always be chosen from any profile of individual preferences, that is, $F(X, D) = \{x\}$, $x \in X$; (b) none of the rejected alternatives must ever be preferred to the chosen alternative by a majority of the voters, that is, if $F(X, D) = \{x\}$, then not yMx, where yMx means that a majority of individuals $i \in I$ prefer y to x. The proof is easy: if a social choice function satisfies (a) it must choose an alternative from the profile of preferences shown in Table 10.3. In that case A or B or C would have to be chosen. But A cannot be chosen without violating (b) because a majority of the voters prefers C to A; B cannot be chosen because a majority prefers A to B; and C cannot be chosen because a majority prefers B to C. No social choice function could satisfy both (a) and (b) with the postulated profile of preferences, therefore none could do so in all cases, *QED*. This impossibility theorem is trivial compared to Arrow's (1951, 1963) famous theorem discussed below in section 10.5, but unlike Arrow's, it is transparent, and its proof makes no assumption about the sincerity of the voters.

Condorcet's paradox has often been called the *paradox of voting* since Nanson (1882) so named it. But this phrase is misleading, because a large number of voting paradoxes have now been discovered – see, for example, Fishburn (1974a), Brams (1976), Fishburn and Brams (1983), May (1983), Nurmi (1983), Ordeshook (1986, chap. 2), and Felsenthal and Maoz (1992).

But Condorcet's paradox is uniquely important, and it is therefore worth demonstrating how it might plausibly occur in an election. The following example will also show that the paradox is not restricted to the simple case of three alternatives and three voters.

Imagine a large group of voters – a constituency in an election, say, containing 30 000 members. Roughly one-third are poor, one-third are in the middle-income bracket, and one-third are rich. The main election issue is taxation: some candidates have promised, if they are elected, to impose new taxes on the poor or the rich or both. All voters are in favour of any new tax that does not apply to their own group, because they believe that they might benefit indirectly from the increased government revenue. But all voters strongly object to a new tax on their own group. Four candidates, *A*, *B*, *C*, and *D* contest the election on the following platforms:

A: New taxes on rich and poor.
B: New taxes on poor only.
C: New taxes on rich only.
D: No new taxes.

The preference order of the 10 000 poor voters is (obviously) *CDAB*. The preferences of the 10 000 middle-income earners depend on whether they prefer the rich or the poor to suffer new taxes. Assuming the latter, their preference order is *ABCD*. The preference order of the 10 000 rich voters is clearly *BDAC*.

There is something distinctly peculiar about this profile of preferences. Two out of three voters (the middle-income and rich voters) favour new taxes on the poor, and a similar majority (the middle-income and poor voters) favour new taxes on the rich. None the less, if voting is sincere, Candidate *A*, who promises both of these popular taxes, could be defeated by Candidate *D*, who promises neither, if the other two candidates withdrew before the election took place. This is so because two out of three voters (the poor and the rich) prefer *D* to *A*. On the other hand, if *B* and *C* did not withdraw, *D* would not receive a single vote, because *D* is not the favourite candidate of any voter. The trouble arises from the existence of a cyclic majority: a majority prefers *A* to *B*, *B* to *C*, *C* to *D*, and *D* to *A*. Although this example is slightly artificial, it shows how a cyclic majority might arise in a complex situation with plausible individual preferences. For detailed discussions of Condorcet's paradox arising from the combination of issues and platforms, see Downs (1957) and Hillinger (1971).

Whenever there are at least three alternatives and at least three voters, cyclic majorities are always possible. It seems reasonable to ask how *likely* they are, but this is in fact a very difficult question to answer. It is really an empirical question that needs to be tackled through systematic observations under controlled conditions, and the necessary research has not been done, but some theoretical probabilities of cyclic majorities have been calculated by making certain assumptions. The most elementary assumption about the voters' preferences, which has been used in most of these calculations, is that of an *equiprobable culture*. This is a profile of preferences that arises if each of the logically possible preference orders has an equal probability of being adopted by every voter. In the three-alternative case, for example, an equiprobable culture is one in which each voter adopts one of the six possible preference orders *ABC, ACB, BCA, BAC, CAB,* or *CBA* strictly at random; the probability of a particular preference order being chosen by a particular voter is 1/6.

With three voters, the probability of a cyclic majority can be worked out quite simply by combinatorial analysis. We begin by calculating the number of possible profiles of preferences among the voters. The first voter can choose any one of six preference orders, and for each choice there remain six for the second voter and six for the third. There are thus 6 × 6 × 6 = 216 possible profiles of preferences. For a cyclic majority to exist, the preference orders chosen by the three voters must either be the first, third, and fifth in the set listed in the previous paragraph, or the second, fourth, and sixth. The first voter can choose any one of the six preference orders, but for each choice there remain only two for the second voter and one for the third. There are thus 6 × 2 × 1 = 12 ways in which three voters can choose a set of preferences generating a cyclic majority. Of the 216 possible profiles, 12 are cyclic; therefore if all preference orders are equally likely to be chosen, the probability of a cyclic majority is 12/216 = .056. In other words it may be expected to occur between five and six times in a hundred.

The first to report the above result were Guilbaud (1952) and Black (1958). Similar methods were later used by Garman and Kamien (1968), Niemi and Weisberg (1968), Gleser (1969), DeMeyer and Plott (1970), May (1971), Blin (1973), Kelly (1974) and others (see also Fishburn, 1973a, p. 95; Ordeshook, 1986, p. 58) to calculate the probabilities of cyclic majorities in equiprobable cultures with more than three alternatives and/or voters. Some of the results are summarized in Table 10.4.

Two things are particularly noteworthy about these results. First, the probabilities are relatively insensitive to increases in the number of voters. With three alternatives, the probability is never less than .056, or about 1 in 18, and it is never more than .088, which is still less than 1 in 11. But second, the probabilities are more sensitive to increases in the number of alternatives: as the number of alternatives increases the probability of a cyclic majority rises rapidly towards certainty.

It must be borne in mind when examining the probabilities displayed in Table 10.4 that they are applicable only to equiprobable cultures in which every voter is assumed to be indifferent to the alternatives to the point of choosing a preference order completely at random. In reality this assumption is seldom justified; objective interests and social pressures of various kinds almost always make some alternatives appear preferable to others, at

Table 10.4 Probabilities of cyclic majorities in equiprobable cultures

Number of alternatives	Number of voters				
	3	5	7	. . .	∞
3	.056	.069	.075	. . .	.088
4	.111	.139	.150	. . .	.176
5	.160	.200	.215	. . .	.251
6	.202	.255	.258	. . .	.315
7	.239	.299	.305	. . .	.369
8	.271	.334	.359	. . .	.415
. . .	. . .	. . .	. . .	. . .	. . .
∞	1.000	1.000	1.000	1.000	1.000

least in the opinions of some voters. An equiprobable culture is prima facie highly improbable.

A more promising theoretical approach is the attempt to discover the conditions that a profile of preferences must satisfy in order to guarantee either the existence or the non-existence of a cyclic majority. There is one well-known condition that rules out the possibility altogether. This condition, which is called *single-peakedness*, was discovered by Black (1948a, 1948b). It is satisfied if all of the voters evaluate the alternatives according to the same single criterion. In a political context, for example, a profile of preferences will be single-peaked if all the voters evaluate the candidates solely according to how left-wing they are, as in the example of Leftwich, Middleton, and Rightsman discussed earlier. A profile of preferences is single-peaked if it is possible to arrange the alternatives in some order along a horizontal axis so that the graph of each voter's preference order, with ordinal degrees of preference represented on the vertical axis, has just one peak corresponding to that voter's most preferred alternative.

If Leftwich, Middleton, and Rightsman are arranged in that order along the horizontal axis, for example, then any voter who evaluates the candidates solely according to the left-right dimension of political views will necessarily have a single-peaked preference curve. A left-wing voter's peak will be at the left-hand side of the graph, a moderate's peak will be in the middle, and a right-winger's peak will be on the right. If the voters evaluate the candidates according to multiple attributes, on the other hand, the profile of preferences might not be single-peaked. In that case the voters' preference orders might be *LMR*, *MRL*, and *RLM*, for example; there is then no way of arranging the alternatives so that all three curves are single-peaked. The multi-attribute example discussed earlier in this section in which the voters evaluated the candidates *A*, *B*, *C*, and *D* according to two independent attributes (their policies on taxing the poor and the rich) was specifically designed to violate the single-peakedness condition. In that case, it will be recalled, a cyclic majority emerged. What Black (1948a, 1948b) managed to prove was that, provided the number of voters is odd, the condition of single-peakedness is sufficient to rule out the possibility of a cyclic majority. A more elegant mathematical interpretation of single-peakedness was later given by Coombs (1964, chaps 9, 19) in terms of his unfolding theory.

A number of plausible empirical examples of cyclic majorities have been reported. In most cases, of course, the complete preference orders of the voters are not known; in elections, for example, voters are normally required to indicate their top-ranked alternative only, and even this can be misleading if voting is not sincere. The examples that have been reported in the literature are therefore based on more or less reasonable conjectures about the voters' preference orders. Riker (1965) provided detailed evidence suggesting that Condorcet's paradox has occurred on more than one occasion in the United States Congress; Bowen (1972) showed that it has probably occurred quite frequently in Senate roll call votes; Niemi (1970) gave examples from faculty elections in universities; Brams (1976, chap. 2) summarized a number of empirical examples from the field of politics; and Gardner (1980, 1988) discussed examples from various other spheres of life.

Condorcet's paradox of cyclic majorities cannot occur if the profile of individual preferences is single-peaked, which is bound to be the case if the voters evaluate the alternatives according to the same single criterion. Unfortunately, however, single-peakedness is no guarantee of freedom from paradox; a paradox originally discovered by Borda (1781) can arise even in a perfectly single-peaked profile of preferences. I have called this paradox the *Borda effect* (Colman, 1979, 1980, 1984, 1986; Colman and Pountney, 1978). The simplest manifestation of it can be illustrated most easily by extending the example of Leftwich, Middleton, and Rightsman used earlier in this chapter. If the committee that has to reach a collective decision contains seven members, and if two of them are left-wingers, two are moderates, and three are right-wingers, then the profile of individual preferences will be as shown in Table 10.5.

The profile of individual preferences shown in Table 10.5 is perfectly single-peaked because the committee members all evaluate the candidates according to the same single criterion of their position on the left-right political dimension. But which candidate ought to be chosen by a fair and democratic social choice function? In a simple plurality vote, Rightsman would be chosen (if voting is sincere) because Rightsman is considered best by three voters (5, 6, and 7), whereas Leftwich and Middleton are each considered best by only two voters. But according to a majority rule, that is,

Table 10.5 Seven committee members' preference orders of Leftwich (*L*), Middleton (*M*), and Rightsman (*R*)

	Committee members						
	Left-wing		Moderate		Right-wing		
	1	2	3	4	5	6	7
First preference	L	L	M	M	R	R	R
Second preference	M	M	L	L	M	M	M
Third preference	R	R	R	R	L	L	L

if the committee members voted on each pair of candidates in turn, Middleton would be chosen, because a majority of the committee members (3, 4, 5, 6, and 7) prefer Middleton to Leftwich, a majority (1, 2, 3, and 4) prefer Middleton to Rightsman, and a majority (1, 2, 3, and 4) prefer Leftwich to Rightsman. The collective preference order is complete and transitive, *MLR*, and Middleton is the Condorcet winner. The paradoxical character of the Borda effect is reinforced by the following additional facts: (a) Rightsman is the *Condorcet loser* in the sense that a majority of the voters (the left-wingers and moderates) prefer both of the others to Rightsman; and (b) the plurality winner is the least preferred alternative in another plausible sense: a majority of the voters consider this alternative to be the worst of the three.

The Borda effect always occurs if there is a plurality winner in a cyclic majority (Gillett, 1984), but as the above example shows it can occur even when there is a clear Condorcet winner, in which case it represents *plurality-majority disagreement*. In these cases the plurality voting procedure is shown to violate the *Condorcet condition* that should be fulfilled by any fair voting procedure. Monte Carlo simulations were used by Fishburn (1974a) and Fishburn and Gehrlein (1976) to estimate the effect on the probability of plurality-majority disagreement of variations in the number of alternatives. Their results show that the probability tends to rise quite rapidly as the number of alternatives increases. They also estimated probabilities under various other voting procedures (apart from plurality voting) of failing to choose a Condorcet winner when it exists. Empirical evidence has also been presented by Colman and Pountney (1978) to show that the Borda effect probably occurred in 15 of the 261 constituencies contested by the three main parties only in the 1966 British general election, and in all but one case it was a Conservative Party candidate who was elected in spite of one of the others apparently being preferred to the Conservative by a majority of the voters.

10.5 Arrow's impossibility theorem

Kenneth Arrow (1951) was the first to use Condorcet's paradox to prove that no social choice function can satisfy certain minimal conditions of fairness and workableness. It probably came as a relief to many people when Blau (1957) found an error in Arrow's proof and even produced a counter-example, in the form of a social choice function that satisfied all of Arrow's conditions. But the relief was short-lived, because Arrow (1963) managed to modify his theorem in a way that not only removed the error but also strengthened the conclusion.

Arrow's theorem requires a social choice function to be a *social welfare function*. This is a method of choosing, on the basis of a set of individual preference orders, not merely a single "best" alternative, but a complete and transitive collective preference order of all alternatives (with ties allowed). The simple plurality voting procedure, for example, is a social welfare function because it allows the alternatives to be ranked in order of collective preference. For the case of two alternatives and two individuals, some typical social welfare functions are shown in Table 10.6. The table shows three possible social welfare functions from a much larger set ($2 \times 2 \times 2 \times 2 = 16$) that can be constructed in this simple two-person two-alternative situation. For each possible profile of individual preferences, listed on the left, functions I, II, and III generate different collective preference orders. For example as shown in the first row of the table, if individual 1's preference order is *AB*, and individual 2's is also *AB*, then functions I, II, and III generate the collective preference orders *AB*, *BA*, and *AB* respectively. Function I is evidently *dictatorial*, because the collective order always reflects the preferences of individual 1. Function II is *imposed*, because it is completely unresponsive to the preferences of the individuals. Function III is not obviously unfair; at least it reflects the individual preference orders

Table 10.6 Individual preference orders and social welfare functions: two individuals and two alternatives

Individuals		Social welfare functions		
1	2	I	II	III
AB	AB	AB	BA	AB
AB	BA	AB	BA	AB
BA	AB	BA	BA	AB
BA	BA	BA	BA	BA

when they are unanimous. In other words, function III, unlike function II, satisfies the *weak Pareto* condition (see below). Arrow (1963) assumed that any acceptable social welfare function would have to satisfy the following four apparently mild and seemingly uncontroversial conditions:

U: *Unrestricted domain*. The social welfare function must be wide enough in scope to generate a collective preference order from any logically possible set of individual preference orders. Mathematically, $F(X, D) \neq \emptyset$ for all X for all D.

P: *Pareto condition* (weak form). Whenever all of the individuals prefer an alternative x to another y, x must be preferred to y in the collective preference order. Mathematically, if $x, y \in X$ and xP_iy for all $i \in I$, then xP_Fy, where xP_Fy, denotes that x is preferred to y in the collective preference order determined by the social welfare function F.

I: *Independence of irrelevant alternatives*. The collective preference order of any pair of alternatives x and y must depend solely on the individuals' preferences between these alternatives and not on their preferences for irrelevant alternatives. Mathematically, $F(X, D) = F(X, D')$ whenever D and D' are identical on X, although they may differ in the way they order other alternatives that are not in X.

D: *Non-dictatorship*. The collective preference order must not be dictated by the preferences of any single individual; it must not be the case that whenever a specified individual prefers one alternative x to another y, x is necessarily preferred to y in the collective preference order regardless of the preferences of the other individuals. Mathematically, there is no $i \in I$ such that $F(X, D) = D_i$, where D_i is i's preference order.

The only condition that requires any elaboration is *I*, one version of which was introduced in the context of individual decision making in section 2.5 and another discussed in relation to bargaining solutions to two-person cooperative games in section 6.10. If the social welfare function determines that Leftwich is collectively preferred to Middleton, this must be based solely on the voters' preferences of Leftwich *vis-à-vis* Middleton, and not on irrelevant pairs such as Leftwich *vis-à-vis* Hitler. In other words, the collective preference order of Leftwich and Middleton must remain the same if one or more of the voters change their minds about the relative merits of pairs of irrelevant alternatives, provided that their ordering of Leftwich and Middleton remains fixed.

Arrow's (1963) astonishing theorem asserts that no social welfare function can satisfy all four of the conditions *U*, *P*, *I*, and *D*. The proof proceeds as follows. Condition *U* allows any profile of individual preferences to be postulated, so Arrow postulated a cyclic majority profile like the one in Table 10.3. He then proved that in this case any social welfare function that satisfies *P* and *I* necessarily violates *D*, that is to say it is dictatorial.

A variety of alternative proofs of Arrow's theorem have been devised, and literally scores of related impossibility theorems have been proved. Kelly (1978) has provided a useful "field guide" to this difficult body of literature. When the theorem was first proved, many people believed that its significance could be undermined by criticizing the intuitive plausibility of one of its conditions, most often *I*. But Kelly pointed out that "*for each of Arrow's conditions, there is now an impossibility theorem not employing that condition*" (p. 3, Kelly's italics). The general conclusion is not even restricted to social welfare functions; impossibility theorems have been proved for all types of social choice functions including voting procedures that are designed merely to choose a single "best" alternative (Blair, Bordes, Kelly, and Suzumura, 1976). The conclusion is inescapable: no social choice function or voting procedure can satisfy minimal conditions of fairness and reasonableness.

10.6 Proportional representation: single transferable vote

Elections under the plurality (first-past-the-post) voting procedure produce outcomes that do not always accurately reflect the opinions of the electorate. A notorious example of this was the 1983 British general election, in which the Liberal/SDP Alliance received 25.4 per cent of the votes cast, only slightly fewer than the Labour Party which received 27.6 per cent, but won only 23 seats in the House of Commons compared to the Labour Party's 209. That election illustrated rather dramatically the tendency of the plurality system to overrepresent the largest parties and to underrepresent smaller parties.

Various voting procedures have been devised to achieve better proportionality between the numbers of votes cast and seats won in elections (see, e.g., Bogdanor, 1984, 1992; Guinier, 1994; Reeve and Ware, 1992). The system that is favoured by the Electoral Reform Society and the Liberal Democrat Party in Britain is the *single transferable vote* (STV), which is sometimes called the Hare system after Thomas Hare, a mid-nineteenth-century English lawyer who promoted it. It is "by far the most popular with advocates of proportional representation who do not like systems involving lists drawn up by political parties" (Dummett, 1984, p. 268), and is already used in the Republic of Ireland, Malta, Tasmania, Australia (for elections to the upper house), South Africa, and Northern Ireland (for local elections). In the United Kingdom, trade unions such as the National Union of Teachers, professional bodies such as the British Psychological Society, and various clubs and societies use STV for internal elections.

To achieve a degree of proportionality, STV requires more than one candidate to be elected in each ballot, and in a general election this would require multi-member constituencies. To see how it works, consider a hypothetical three-member constituency with ten candidates standing for election. With three seats to be filled, each of the major parties may well field more than one candidate. The ballot paper would list the ten candidates' names and would invite voters to write the number 1 opposite their first choice and the numbers 2, 3, and so on up to 10 opposite the other names in order of preference. The first step in counting the votes is to calculate the *electoral quota* or *Droop quota*, named after Henry Droop, another nineteenth-century English advocate of STV. This quota is simply the minimum number of votes that a candidate needs in order to be certain of being elected. In a three-member constituency, a candidate who received one-quarter of the votes would be almost certain to win one of the three seats, because however the remaining votes were split they could not give three other candidates more votes than one-quarter each, but it would be mathematically possible for four candidates to receive *exactly* one-quarter of the votes each, in which case there would be a four-way tie. To be absolutely certain of election, a candidate in a three-member constituency must therefore win one-quarter of the votes *plus one*. Suppose 100 000 votes were cast in a three-member constituency. The electoral quota would then be one-quarter of 100 000 plus 1, which is 25 001. By the same logic, the electoral quota that ensures victory in a four-member constituency is one-fifth of the votes plus one; in a five-member constituency it is one-sixth of the votes plus one, and so on. In general, if v votes are cast and there are m positions to fill, the electoral quota is $v/(m + 1) + 1$.

Once the electoral quota has been calculated, the first count is carried out to see whether any of the candidates has reached it. If the electoral quota is 25 001, as in the example, then any candidate who has 25 001 or more first-preference votes is immediately elected. Next, the candidate with the smallest number of first-preference votes is eliminated from the race, and that candidate's votes are transferred to the other candidates' totals in accordance with the second preferences shown on the ballot papers. The excess votes over the electoral quota of any candidates elected on the first count are also transferred to the second-preference candidates for the second count, so wastage of votes is minimized. The second count then takes place, and any candidate who reaches 25 001 or more votes is elected. Once again, the candidate with the smallest total number of first votes is eliminated and the votes transferred, together with excess votes of newly elected candidates, to the second-preference candidates, or to third-preference candidates in cases of votes already transferred to second-preference candidates, and the third count proceeds. The process of eliminating the trailing candidates and transferring their votes to the other candidates, together with the excess votes of elected candidates, continues until the required number of candidates (three in the example given) are elected. That is the gist of the STV voting procedure, although there are complications that have been glossed over.

When used for nation-wide elections, STV ensures that votes even for losing candidates are not wasted as they are in plurality voting and other voting procedures, but STV offers no guarantee of strictly proportional representation across the whole electorate. What it achieves is something more modest, namely very rough proportionality in each individual constituency election. It can produce disturbing anomalies even at that level. Consider a two-member constituency with three candidates running for election – one Conservative, one Labour, and one Liberal Democrat. Let us assume, not unreasonably, that the Labour voters consider Liberal Democrat second best and Conservative worst; that Conservative voters consider Liberal Democrat second best and Labour worst; and that Liberal Democrat voters are split, with four-fifths preferring Labour to Conservative and one-fifth preferring Conservative to Labour. Suppose that 10 000 voters turn out and mark their ballot papers according to these preferences as follows:

Table 10.7

First preference	Lab	Con	Lib	Lib
Second preference	Lib	Lib	Lab	Con
Third preference	Con	Lab	Con	Lab
Number of voters	4000	3500	2000	500

The electoral quota is $10\,000/(2+1)+1 = 3334$. On the very first count, therefore, the Labour and Conservative candidates, who both have more votes than that, are elected. The Liberal Democrat, with a total of 2500 votes, falls by the wayside, and no votes need to be transferred for a second count because there are only two seats to be filled, so that is the end of the matter. It is worth pointing out that the same two candidates would have been elected under the plurality system. But is the outcome fair? Hardly, because the Liberal Democrat who failed to get elected was in fact preferred to each of the other candidates by a clear majority of the voters, in other words the Liberal Democrat candidate was the Condorcet winner. The preference rankings in the table show that 65 per cent of the voters – all voters except those whose first preference was Conservative – preferred the Liberal Democrat to the Conservative, and 60 per cent preferred the Liberal Democrat to the Labour candidate. A clear majority of the voters therefore preferred the Liberal Democrat to each of the other candidates, but the Liberal Democrat lost the election none the less. The example is not based on an unusual or unrealistic profile of preferences; on the contrary, the profile is single-peaked. It is clear that, like the plurality voting procedure, STV fails to satisfy the Condorcet condition of fairness, which is perhaps the most fundamental of all conditions for a democratic social choice function. This problem with STV was discussed by Ordeshook and Zeng (1994).

Another reasonable requirement of any fair voting procedure is that it should not be possible for a candidate who would otherwise win to lose purely as a result of gaining additional support. This condition (with minor variations) is called *monotonicity* (e.g., Fishburn, 1973, pp. 20–25; Richelson, 1981), *non-negative association* (e.g., Doron and Kornick, 1977), or *non-perversity* (e.g., Ordeshook, 1986, p. 61). Formally, if D and D' are two profiles of preferences and $x, y \in X$ are alternatives, and if D and D' differ only in that the number of individuals who prefer x to y is greater in D' than in D, then if $F(X, D)$ includes x, $F(X, D')$ should also include x. Any social choice function that allows an increase in support for a candidate to damage that candidate's chances of election is obviously unfair. Now consider the following profile of preferences that I have devised for a group of 27 voters (trade union members, say, or constituency voters in an election if the numbers are multiplied by 1000). Two representatives are to be elected from among four candidates, A, B, C, and D:

Table 10.8

First preference	A	B	D	C	C
Second preference	D	C	B	D	B
Third preference	B	D	C	B	D
Fourth preference	C	A	A	A	A
Number of voters	10	5	6	4	2

The electoral quota is $27/(2 + 1) + 1 = 10$. On the first count, A achieves the quota and is therefore elected as one of the two representatives. The candidate with the smallest number of first-preference votes is D, so D is eliminated, and because the six voters who placed D first had B as their second preference, six votes are transferred to B, who then has 11 votes and is therefore elected as the second representative.

Suppose now that the two voters in the right-hand column who prefer C to B change their minds so that they prefer B to C: their preference order changes from *CBDA* to *BCDA*. Then on the first count A receives 10 first-preference votes and is elected as before. But now it is C who has the fewest first-preference votes and is eliminated, and C's four second-preference votes are transferred to D, who then has 10 votes and is elected as the second representative. This is a clear violation of the monotonicity condition, because an increase in support for B damaged B's chances of election.

Despite its virtues (avoidance of vote wastage and rough proportionality), STV thus has two very serious defects as a fair voting procedure. It suffers from other problems as well (Colman, 1992; Doron, 1979; Doron and Kornick, 1977; Dummett, 1984, chap. 16; Fishburn and Brams, 1983). As Fishburn and Brams pointed out, STV is a shining example of what can go wrong when an elaborate voting procedure is designed to remedy the problems of a simpler one. In some ways STV represents a step backwards in terms of fairness and reasonableness, yet it remains the most popular proportional voting procedure among electoral reformers (Dummett, 1984). On this point, Iain McLean (1988) has commented aptly that electoral reform and social choice theory are like ships that pass in the night. I would say, adapting a powerful simile, that electoral reform and social choice theory are like the Rhine and the Danube, rising from independent sources, flowing alongside each other for a short while, but then diverging and meandering in different directions before ultimately emptying into widely separated seas.

Arrow's (1963) impossibility theorem established that no voting procedure will ever be able to satisfy certain mild and apparently uncontroversial conditions of fairness and workableness. The problems arise largely from the existence of cyclic majorities and intransitive social preference orders, but unfortunately there is evidence (reviewed by McLean, 1989) confirming the impression of Table 10.4 that cyclic majorities are almost universal in large electorates. Various other proportional voting procedures apart from STV have been proposed (see, e.g., Bogdanor, 1984, 1992; Dummett, 1984; Guinier, 1994; Reeve and Ware, 1992), but they all exhibit properties at least at problematic as those of STV and can, in fact, be self-defeating (Galeotti, 1994). There is a growing consensus among social choice theorists that the best choice procedure when only a single winner is to be chosen is first to search for a Condorcet winner and then, if there is a cyclic majority, to break it by one of a number of methods, but no clear consensus has emerged regarding the fairest procedure of breaking the cycles.

10.7 Strategic (tactical) voting

The discussion so far has been premised on the assumption that voters choose sincere strategies, that is to say that they always vote *myopically* (e.g., Krehbiel, 1986) for the alternatives that they most prefer, although sincere voting does not, of course, ensure that one's favourite alternatives are chosen. Sincere voting is myopic inasmuch as it involves no attempt to consider the consequences of any actions, and it amounts to choosing maximax strategies (see section 2.5.2) which are generally irrational; it is hardly surprising that voters sometimes behave insincerely and strategically by choosing strategies that offer them better prospects.

Strategic voting was apparently quite common in ancient Greece and Rome (Stavely, 1972) and is probably as old as democracy itself. But no serious attempt was made to study its implications until the mid-1950s when Robin Farquharson analysed the problem of voting within the framework of game theory. Farquharson was an eccentric genius who suffered from a manic-depressive mental disorder; he described in an autobiographical book how this led to his arrest for giving away £5 notes in a public house in Thame and for stripping naked on the platform of the St John's Wood underground station in London (Farquharson, 1968, pp. 11, 67–68), and by the time his extremely influential *Theory of Voting* finally appeared (Farquharson, 1969) he was living as a tramp in London (shortly thereafter he met a tragic and violent death). Although Farquharson's slim volume on voting is written in deceptively simple language, it is extraordinarily difficult to understand and is marred by numerous typographical errors – Niemi's (1983) exegesis corrects 37 errors and makes the book easier to understand. The remainder of this chapter is devoted to a clarification of the fundamental ideas behind strategic voting and a summary of the relevant empirical evidence.

For the sake of continuity, I shall return to the example of Leftwich, Middleton, and Rightsman outlined in section 10.2 and summarized in Table 10.2. The political views of these three candidates, it will be remembered, are left-wing, moderate, and right-wing respectively, and a committee or electorate has to choose one of them to fill a political office. There are three distinguishable voters or voting blocs: the left-wing voters' preference order is *LMR*, the moderates' is *MLR*, and the right-wingers' is *RML*. None of these blocs contains more than half the voters, so any two blocs combined can always outvote the third. The left-wing bloc is assumed to be the largest of the three, or if the largest blocs are of equal size, one of the left-wingers has an additional casting vote.

Three common voting procedures – successive, amendment, and plurality voting – were examined in section 10.3. It was shown that, if voting is sincere, the amendment procedure chooses Middleton, the plurality procedure Leftwich, and the successive procedure either Leftwich or Middleton depending on the order of voting. Because the right-wingers fail to obtain the outcome they consider best under any of the voting procedures, the question naturally arises as to whether they can obtain a preferable result by voting insincerely, that is, by choosing some non-maximax voting strategy. The same question may be asked about the left-wingers and moderates when sincere voting yields outcomes that are non-optimal from their points of view. If there are players who can obtain preferable outcomes by unilaterally switching to insincere strategies, then by definition the sincere outcomes are not Nash equilibria.

Let us first examine successive voting to determine whether the sincere outcome is a Nash equilibrium. If Middleton is presented first, the sincere outcome is then:

First ballot: In favour of M, moderates;
Against M, left-wingers and right-wingers.
Result: L or R. Therefore

Second ballot: In favour of L, left-wingers and moderates;
In favour of R, right-wingers.
Final result: L.

This outcome is the one that the right-wingers consider worst. Furthermore, it is obvious that if the right-wingers had voted for rather than against Middleton on the first ballot while the others voted sincerely, the winner would have been Middleton after just one ballot, and this would have been preferable from their point of view. This shows that the sincere outcome L is not a Nash equilibrium: at least one of the players – the right-wingers considered as a single voting bloc – has an incentive to deviate unilaterally from it and would have cause to regret its choice of a sincere strategy once the choices of the others were revealed. It is easy to see that the sincere outcome is not vulnerable to either the left-wingers or the moderates, and that if the right-wingers were to vote strategically in the way indicated, the new outcome would not be vulnerable to any of the players. This means that if the right-wingers voted insincerely for Middleton on the first ballot, and if the others voted sincerely, then the outcome would be a Nash equilibrium that has a claim to being the rational outcome of successive voting.

Let us now examine the amendment procedure. Suppose the substantive motion is "That Rightsman be appointed" and the amendment "That the word 'Rightsman' be replaced by 'Middleton'". Assuming that one of the three candidates must be appointed, the default alternative is Leftwich. The sincere outcome is:

First ballot: In favour of M (the Middleton amendment), left-wingers and moderates;
In favour of R (Rightsman, the substantive motion), right-wingers.
Result: M.

Second ballot: In favour of M, moderates and right-wingers;
Against M (that is, in favour of L), left-wingers.
Final result: M.

Is this sincere result a Nash equilibrium? No; because the left-wingers have an incentive to deviate unilaterally from their sincere strategy and would have cause to regret the outcome otherwise. Acting as a bloc, they can obtain a preferable outcome by switching unilaterally to an insincere strategy. In the first ballot they are required to vote either for their second choice (*M*) or for the their third (*R*). Suppose they voted for *R* instead of *M* in the first ballot while the others stuck to their sincere strategies. In that case *R* would win the first ballot – so the amendment would be defeated – and if all voters were sincere on the second ballot between *R* and *L*, then *L* would win. This outcome is preferred by the left-wingers to the sincere outcome, and the sincere outcome is therefore vulnerable to the left-wingers. But in this case the new outcome when only the left-wingers vote strategically is not a Nash equilibrium either, because the right-wingers would then have cause to regret not voting for *M* rather than *R* on the first ballot, in which case the final result would be *M* rather than *L*, which they prefer. The outcome with both the left-wingers and the right-wingers voting strategically in the prescribed way is a Nash equilibrium.

Under the plurality procedure, the sincere outcome is obviously Leftwich, because we have assumed that the left-wingers constitute the largest voting bloc. But it is equally obvious that this outcome is vulnerable to the right-wingers and is therefore not a Nash equilibrium. The right-wingers can vote in favour of Middleton instead of Rightsman, and if the others vote sincerely the winner is Middleton (the right-wingers' second preference) rather than Leftwich (their least favourite candidate). This strategic outcome is clearly a Nash equilibrium, because no player can gain an advantage by deviating unilaterally from it.

I have shown informally how Nash equilibria can be found in voting games by assuming that voting always occurs in blocs. Two comments need to be made about Nash equilibria, however. The first concerns voting games that satisfy the condition of complete information. If all of the voters are fully aware of the preferences of the others, then a non-equilibrium outcome can never occur – provided that the voters choose their strategies rationally, because a non-equilibrium outcome is vulnerable to one or more players, and these players, if they are rational, will always take advantage of the opportunities for improvement that it presents. Second, all voting games possess Nash equilibria in pure strategies. It is clear, for example, that if all voters choose the same alternative on each ballot – for example, if all vote for *L* under the plurality procedure – then the result must be a Nash equilibrium, because no voting bloc would then have the power to change the result by changing its strategy unilaterally.

Unfortunately, the usual problems with Nash equilibria as solutions to *n*-person games apply to the special case of voting games, in spite of the fact that pure-strategy equilibria are known to exist. One difficulty arises from the fact that there are no simple algorithms for finding all Nash equilibria in an efficient way, apart from listing the entire set of outcomes and examining each one for stability. Another is that voting games, like other *n*-person games, often possess multiple equilibria, some of which seem more rational than others. The only ones that are truly rational are subgame perfect equilibria (see section 6.2). Brigitte Sloth (1993) has proved that at least for sequential voting procedures such as the successive and amendment procedures, the solutions discussed below are subgame perfect equilibria.

Before returning to sequential procedures, let us consider once again the relatively simple example of three alternatives and three voting blocs choosing via plurality voting. Each player has three pure strategies: L (vote for Leftwich), M (vote for Middleton), and R (vote for Rightsman). Even assuming that there are only three players, in other words that the voters choose their strategies *en bloc*, there are no fewer than 27 profiles in which the pure strategies of the three players (left-wingers, moderates, right-wingers) may be combined: (L, L, L), (L, L, M), (L, M, L) and so on down to (R, R, R). Some of these combinations result in equilibrium outcomes, and others do not. We have already seen that the sincere outcome (L, M, R) is not a Nash equilibrium. If the right-wingers vote insincerely for M, on the other hand, the outcome (L, M, M) is a Nash equilibrium. But this property alone is not a compelling criterion for a rational solution, because there are other equilibria in the game. For example, (L, L, L), (M, M, M), and (R, R, R) are also Nash equilibria, because no single voting bloc can outvote the other two combined, and so none would have any incentive to deviate unilaterally from these outcomes. Some of the equilibria are obviously not subgame perfect – they are absurd. The combination (R, R, R), for example, could never occur if the voters were all rational: the left-wingers would never vote for Rightsman, because voting for Leftwich or Middleton produces an outcome that in every possible contingency is at least as good for them and sometimes better than the outcome produced by voting for Rightsman. A rational solution to a voting game must clearly be a Nash equilibrium, but we need some rational criteria for eliminating undesirable Nash equilibria and arriving (if possible) at determinate solutions. In other words we need a method of finding subgame perfect Nash equilibria.

Returning to the example of successive voting discussed above, it is clear that the players must choose from the following set of pure strategies:

(S_1) Vote for M on the first ballot; if M loses vote for R on the second ballot.

(S_2) Vote for M on the first ballot; if M loses vote for L on the second ballot.

(S_3) Vote against M on the first ballot; if M loses vote for R on the second ballot.

(S_4) Vote against M on the first ballot; if M loses vote for L on the second ballot.

These four pure strategies exhaust the possibilities, and each provides a complete prescription for voting. There are also four pure strategies available to each voter in the amendment procedure (given three alternatives), and just three pure strategies in the plurality procedure with the obvious labels L, M, and R.

The classical solution to successive voting games proposed by Farquharson (1969) is arrived at by successive elimination of dominated strategies, that is, by examining the game from the perspective of each player in turn and eliminating the player's dominated strategies. A reduced version of the game from which the dominated strategies have been eliminated is then examined to see whether any strategies that were undominated in the original game are dominated in this first reduction. If so, then they are deleted and the analysis proceeds to a second reduction. The process of eliminating dominated strategies continues until further reduction becomes impossible. Farquharson showed that this method leads to determinate solutions, in which only one ultimately admissible strategy survives for each player, in most cases. It is closely analogous to the method of solving certain two-person zero-sum games with saddle points by successively eliminating dominated strategies (see section 4.5), and the equilibria to which it leads are subgame perfect (Sloth, 1993). Farquharson's method is extremely cumbersome, but it is worth showing how it works in the simplest case of the plurality procedure. This will incidentally justify the solution that was arrived at informally above.

Table 10.9 shows the plurality procedure from the viewpoint of the left-wing voters. The 27 possible combinations of pure strategies are shown in the table together with their corresponding outcomes. The left-wingers choose one of the rows: they vote for L, M, or R. The choices of the other voting blocs are shown by columns: if the moderates vote for L and the right-wingers vote for R, for example, the final outcome is in column L/R. The body of the table thus shows the final outcome for all possible combinations of choices by the three voting blocs. The sincere strategies and

Table 10.9 Plurality voting outcomes from left-wingers' viewpoint (left-wingers are most numerous)

Left-wingers vote for	Moderates/right-wingers vote for								
	L/L	L/M	L/R^s	M^s/L	M^s/M	M^s/R^s	R/L	R/M	R/R^s
*L^s	L^e	L	L	L	M^e	L^s	L	L	R
M	L	M	M	M	M^e	M	M	M	R
R	L	R	R	R	M	R	R	R	R^e

s Sincere strategy or outcome
e Equilibrium point
* Primarily admissible strategy for left-wingers

outcome are indicated by footnotes; and the Nash equilibria are also shown.

The Nash equilibria in Table 10.9 offer an *embarras de choix*. The L^e in the top left-hand corner of the table, for example, denotes the outcome in which the left-wingers vote sincerely for L, the moderates vote insincerely for L, and the right-wingers vote insincerely for L: the final outcome is obviously L. But there are altogether four Nash equilibria, and they offer little guidance to the voters because each voting bloc has at least one Nash equilibrium corresponding to each of its pure strategies.

It is possible to deduce from Table 10.9, however, that the left-wingers have only one *admissible* strategy. Let us first compare the top two rows of the table, which correspond to the first two strategies of the left-wingers, bearing in mind that their preference order is LMR. It turns out that in every contingency, that is, in every column representing a combination of strategies of the other players, the outcome is either the same or better from the left-wingers' viewpoint if they choose L rather than M. If the moderates and right-wingers both choose L (column L/L), for example, the outcome is the same whether the left-wingers choose L or M. If the moderates choose L and the right-wingers choose M (column L/M), then the left-wingers do better by choosing L than by choosing M, because L wins instead of M and they prefer L to M. In every column, the left-wingers achieve an equal or preferable outcome by choosing the first row rather than the second. In other words, the left-wingers' strategy L dominates their strategy M.

Comparing each pair of rows in Table 10.9 in this way, we can quickly establish that the left-wingers' strategy M is dominated by L, and R is dominated by both L and M; the only undominated strategy available to the left-wingers is L. An undominated strategy such as this is called *primarily admissible* (the reason for the qualifying adverb will emerge shortly). The left-wingers, if they are rational, will choose this primarily admissible strategy, because to choose one of the dominated strategies would be to invite the possibility of an outcome that would in no contingency be preferable and could in some be worse. It is worth noting that the left-wingers can reach this conclusion without any knowledge of the preferences of the other voters; it emerges from examining all logically possible outcomes from their own point of view alone.

The left-wingers have only one primarily admissible strategy, and in fact it dominates each of the others (it can be shown that it necessarily does so). In the classical theory of strategic voting, a dominant strategy of this kind is called a *straightforward* strategy, and a voting procedure that offers a voter a straightforward strategy is said to be a straightforward voting procedure for that voter. A straightforward strategy, being dominant, is a "sure thing" (unconditionally best) strategy in game theory terms. It does not guarantee that a voter's favourite alternative will be chosen, but it ensures that a failure to choose that alternative will not be the result of any strategic error on the part of that voter. But, as we shall see, a primarily admissible strategy is not necessarily straightforward: it is possible for a strategy to be undominated without itself dominating all of the others, though this is possible only if there are other undominated strategies as well. It is easy to prove (see Brams, 1975, pp. 69–70) that a voter under any voting procedure always has at least one primarily admissible strategy, namely sincere voting. If the voter has only one primarily admissible strategy, in other words if it is a straightforward strategy, then it must be sincere. But a primarily admissible strategy may not be unique and may therefore not be straightforward. This is illustrated in Table 10.10, in which we examine the plurality procedure from the viewpoint of the moderates.

Table 10.10 Plurality voting outcomes from moderates' viewpoint (left-wingers are most numerous)

Moderates vote for	Left-wingers/right-wingers vote for								
	L^s/L	L^s/M	L^s/R^s	M/L	M/M	M/R^s	R/L	R/M	R/R^s
*L	L^e	L	L	L	M	M	L	R	R
*M^s	L	M^e	L^s	M	M^e	M	R	M	R
R	L	L	R	M	M	R	R	R	R^e

^{s} Sincere strategy or outcome
^{e} Equilibrium point
* Primarily admissible strategy for moderates

Bearing in mind that the moderates' preference order is MLR, we can search Table 10.10 for their admissible strategies. A comparison of row L with row M reveals that they result in identical outcomes in some contingencies (for example, column L/L), row M is preferable in some (for example, column L/M), and row L is preferable in one contingency (column R/L). Clearly neither strategy dominates the other. A comparison of each pair of rows reveals that strategies L and M are primarily admissible: neither is dominated by any other strategy. Strategy R is not primarily admissible, because it is dominated by M (though not by L). The moderates have two primarily admissible strategies, L and M. Neither, however, is straightforward, because neither dominates all of the others. One of the primarily admissible strategies, L, does not in fact dominate any of the others, although it is also not dominated by any. It is impossible at this stage to reach a decisive conclusion about which strategy the moderates will choose if they are rational. But they will obviously not choose their primarily inadmissible strategy *R*, because the outcomes that result from doing so are in no cases better and sometimes worse from their point of view than if they choose *M*. We may therefore delete the moderates' strategy *R* from the game, but first we must examine the situation from the viewpoint of the right-wingers (see Table 10.11).

The right-wingers' preference order, it will be recalled, is *RML*. With this information, an analysis of Table 10.11 reveals that they have two primarily admissible strategies: *M* and *R*. Like the moderates, they have no straightforward strategy. If they are rational, however, they will not vote for *L* because *R* dominates *L* and they achieve outcomes at least as preferable, and sometimes more so, by voting for *R*.

Table 10.11 Plurality voting outcomes from right-wingers' viewpoint (left-wingers are most numerous)

Right-wingers vote for	Left-wingers/moderates vote for								
	L^s/L	L^s/M^s	L^s/R	M/L	M/M^s	M/R	R/L	R/M^s	R/R
L	L^e	*L*	*L*	*L*	*M*	*M*	*L*	*R*	*R*
*M	*L*	M^e	*L*	*M*	M^e	*M*	*R*	*M*	*R*
*R	*L*	L^s	*R*	*M*	*M*	*R*	*R*	*R*	R^e

[s] Sincere strategy or outcome
[e] Equilibrium point
[*] Primarily admissible strategy for right-wingers

We have so far found a unique rational strategy for the left-wingers and reasons for ruling out certain inadmissible strategies of the other voting blocs or players. This has been achieved without any assumptions about the players' knowledge of one another's preference orders. It is obviously an exaggeration to say, as Brams (1975, 1976) among others have, that "if the voters have no information on each other's preference orders, they would have *no* basis on which to ... formulate strategies" (Brams, 1975, p. 59, my emphasis). But the game has not yet been fully solved, and to make further progress we do need to assume complete information.

10.8 Sophisticated voting

If each player has complete information about the preferences of the others, then each is in a position to examine a reduced version of the game constructed by assuming that only primarily admissible strategies will be chosen. This reflects an assumption on the part of each player about the likely behaviour of the others, and the assumption that the others will avoid using dominated strategies seems reasonable enough: players with sufficient common sense to avoid the strategies that can only be to their own disadvantage ought to credit their co-players with equal common sense – this is the standard game theory assumption of common knowledge of rationality introduced in section 9.2.

It is possible to search for admissible strategies in the reduced game from which all primarily inadmissible strategies have been deleted. A strategy that is admissible for a player in this first reduction is called, for obvious reasons, a *secondarily admissible* strategy. A secondarily admissible strategy is premised on the assumption that all players will use only primarily admissible strategies. The analysis can be repeated, if necessary, by deleting secondarily inadmissible strategies from the first reduction of the game, and searching in the resulting second reduction for 3-arily admissible strategies. Farquharson's (1969) classical approach proceeds in this way, searching for *m*-arily admissible strategies for each player on the assumption that the others will choose only (*m* − 1)-arily admissible strategies, until a determinate solution is found, if it exists. Farquharson was the first to suggest this, and he called it *sophisticated voting*. In the simple plurality procedure that we are analysing, a determinate solution emerges from the first reduction, which is shown in Table 10.12.

No choice of strategies for the left-wingers is shown in Table 10.12, because they have no choice to make after their primarily inadmissible strategies have been deleted: it is assumed that they choose their straightforward strategy *L*. The game has been further reduced by deleting the primarily inadmissible strategies of the moderates and right-wingers.

Table 10.12 Plurality procedure after deleting primarily inadmissible strategies (left-wingers are most numerous)

Moderates (MLR) vote for	Right-wingers (*RML*) vote for	
	**M	R^s
L	L	L
**M^s	M^e	L^s

[s] Sincere strategy or outcome
[e] Equilibrium point
** Secondarily admissible strategy

On the assumption that only the primarily admissible strategies will be chosen, it is clear that the game can be completely solved. From the moderates' viewpoint, row M represents the only undominated – and hence secondarily admissible – strategy. The right-wingers, for their part, have only one undominated column, namely M. The secondarily admissible strategies of these players are in fact *ultimately admissible*, because further reduction of the game is unnecessary. The straightforward strategy of the left-wingers, together with the secondarily admissible strategies of the moderates and right-wingers, converge on a unique and subgame perfect equilibrium point LMM.

We may therefore conclude that if the members of the committee or electorate are rational, then the left-wingers will vote straightforwardly for Leftwich, and the moderates and right-wingers will vote for Middleton. This means that Middleton will be elected to the vacant post in spite of the fact that the left-wingers command the largest bloc of votes, or that the additional casting vote belongs to a left-winger if the blocs are of equal size. If voting were sincere, of course, Leftwich would be elected; the sophisticated outcome, even in this extremely simple example, is rather unexpected.

Farquharson's classical method of solution can, at least in principle, be applied to any voting game, but it has two major drawbacks. First, it is extremely cumbersome to apply, even to the simple game above. Other voting procedures are much more complicated to analyse, and when there are more than three alternatives or candidates the classical method becomes unmanageable without the use of a computer. Second, the classical method fails to produce a determinate solution in a significant minority of cases under the plurality procedure: there comes a point beyond which the game cannot be reduced by eliminating dominated strategies. If the preference orders of the three voting blocs are LMR, MRL, and RML, for example, Farquharson's method fails to produce a determinate solution. It never fails in this way with successive or amendment procedures, however.

These problems have been partly overcome by the discovery of more efficient methods of solving voting games. The difficulties that arise in dealing with complicated voting procedures involving a large number of alternatives, voting blocs, and ballots can be circumvented by multistage game analyses, in which the entire voting game is broken down into a number of smaller games that are solved very easily, and methods have been devised for producing determinate solutions in some (though not all) plurality voting games that cannot be solved by classical methods. I shall outline each of these contributions separately.

Miller (1977) made some headway towards simplifying the analysis of complicated voting games via graph theory. McKelvey and Niemi (1978) and Bjurulf and Niemi (1981) went further in providing a simple and efficient method of analysis that works for all binary voting procedures, no matter how complicated. Binary voting procedures are those like successive and amendment voting in which each voter has to choose between two alternatives on each ballot. Apart from plurality voting and preferential voting procedures, that is, procedures such as the single transferable vote in which voters have to rank-order the alternatives, most procedures in common use are binary. McKelvey and Niemi's solution is based on a representation of the voting game as a hierarchy of minor games, which can be depicted in the form of a decision tree. Typical decision trees for the successive and amendment voting procedures are shown in Figure 10.1.

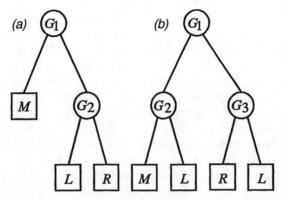

Figure 10.1 *Decision trees representing (a) the successive procedure with M presented in the first ballot, and (b) the amendment procedure with the first ballot between M and R. Non-terminal nodes G_1, G_2, and G_3 correspond to minor games.*

The terminal nodes in Figure 10.1 are labelled with the appropriate outcomes. The non-terminal nodes are labelled G_1, G_2, and (in the amendment procedure) G_3: these nodes represent particular ballots and they are treated by McKelvey and Niemi (1978), and by Bjurulf and Niemi (1981) as minor games embedded in a larger voting game. For example, in the successive procedure (Figure 10.1a) node G_1 corresponds to the first ballot for or against M; if a majority favour M, then the corresponding terminal node is reached, otherwise the outcome of the first minor game G_1 is a second minor game G_2, which represents a ballot between L and R. In the amendment procedure (Figure 10.1b), the first minor game G_1 is always followed by a second minor game, either G_2 or G_3 depending on the outcome of G_1.

Consider the minor game G_1 under the successive procedure. The outcomes of this game are shown in Table 10.13. This minor game could obviously equally well be represented from the moderates' or right-wingers' viewpoints; this simply entails a rearrangement of the labels. It is obvious

Table 10.13 The minor game G_1 under the successive procedure: voting for or against M from the left-wingers' viewpoint

Moderates	For		Against	
Right-wingers	For	Against	For	Against
Left-wingers				
For	M	M	M	G_2
Against	M	G_2	G_2	G_2

from this representation of G_1 that if the left-wingers prefer M to G_2, then they have only one rational (dominant) strategy, namely voting for M; conversely if they prefer G_2 to M, then they will vote against M if they are rational. But G_2 is a game, not an outcome. In order to determine their preference of M *vis-à-vis* G_2 the players have first to solve G_2; they can then substitute this *anticipated decision* (Miller, 1977) or *sophisticated equivalent* (McKelvey and Niemi, 1978) in the payoff matrix of G_1.

The multistage solution therefore begins at the terminal nodes of the decision tree and works backwards in steps. At the lowest, minor games, the outcomes of which are all determinate social choices and not further minor games, can be solved at a glance from a knowledge of the voters' preferences. Whichever of the two outcomes is preferred by a majority of the voters – or by the voter with the additional casting vote if opinions are split evenly – is bound to be chosen at this point; there is no scope for strategic voting on a ballot with only two alternatives. For example, under the successive procedure at G_2, L is bound to be chosen because a majority of the voters (the left-wingers and moderates) prefer L to R. And because the minor game G_2 has the inevitable outcome L, this anticipated decision can be substituted for G_2 in Table 10.13 (which represents G_1), and it is immediately obvious that the left-wingers will vote against M if they are rational in view of the fact that M is a straightforward strategy.

The computation of the anticipated decisions at each node is easy, and it is not necessary to set out the corresponding payoff matrices as in Table 10.13. The anticipated decisions at the lowest level are found by determining which of the corresponding pair of outcomes is preferred to the other by a majority of the voters (taking into account casting votes if necessary). These anticipated decisions are then placed in their correct positions at the next level up the decision tree and the whole process is repeated for the minor games immediately above them, and so on. However complicated the decision tree may be, and however many voting blocs there are, this method of solution rapidly produces an anticipated decision for each non-terminal node in the tree. In Figure 10.1(a), for example, G_2 is replaced by L because a majority prefers L to R. Then G_2 can be replaced by M because a majority prefers M to L. In Figure 10.1(b), G_2 becomes M and G_3 becomes L, then G_1 becomes M. Having filled in the nodes of the decision tree in this way, the optimal strategies for each player are immediately obvious: at each node rational players will always vote for the outcomes or anticipated decisions that they prefer.

The multistage solution of binary voting games is vastly simpler than the classical method, and it has the added virtue of reflecting more realistically the way rational voters probably think. Strategic voters probably think in something like the following manner: "Should I vote for or against M? Well, what is likely to happen if I vote against M and all the other voters pursue their own interests rationally? Clearly L will win on the second ballot, so I'm better off voting against M on the first". In this hypothetical soliloquy, "what is likely to happen" corresponds to the multistage notion of the "anticipated decision".

Theoretical aspects of strategic voting under the plurality procedure have been investigated by Farquharson (1969), Joyce (1976), Niemi and Frank (1982, 1985), Felsenthal and Maoz (1988), Felsenthal, Rapoport, and Maoz (1988), Felsenthal and Maoz (1992), Myerson and Weber (1993), and Cox (1994). In plurality voting games Farquharson's classical solution is not only cumbersome but also sometimes indeterminate. The Niemi–Frank approach is much more limited in scope than Farquharson's, because it applies only to the plurality procedure when there are three alternatives, but it yields determinate solutions in all instances in which the classical method does so and in a proportion of cases in which Farquharson's method fails. Using a computer simulation, Niemi and Frank (1985) showed that their method is effective in the overwhelming majority of cases involving three alternatives and that when there is a Condorcet winner it elects that alternative more often than Farquharson's, but contrary to Niemi and Frank's (1982, 1985) claim, when both methods are determinate they do not always yield the same outcome (Felsenthal, Rapoport, and Maoz, 1988).

With three alternatives, the essential ideas can be sketched as follows. Each voting bloc (player) examines the sincere outcome and determines whether it can obtain a preferable outcome by switching unilaterally to some insincere strategy. If not, the sincere outcome is in fact the sophisticated equilibrium. If one player can unilaterally improve on the sincere outcome by adopting an insincere strategy, then that insincere strategy and outcome are substituted in the game and the analysis reverts to the beginning. If two players can each unilaterally improve on the sincere outcome, then Niemi and Frank show that these two players may be locked in a Battle of the Sexes game, and the solution may therefore be indeterminate in pure strategies. This approach to sophisticated voting under the plurality procedure has certain advantages over the classical method, but it lacks the simplicity and intuitive persuasiveness of the multistage solution to binary procedures.

Farquharson (1969) examined the results of sincere and sophisticated voting among three alternatives and three approximately equal voting blocs under the successive, amendment, and plurality procedures (and a few less common ones). Under the successive procedure, he found that sincere and sophisticated voting lead to different social choices in one-half of all cases (different preference orders and voting orders). The order of voting always influences the final outcome under this procedure if voting is sincere: the alternative voted on first never wins. But if voting is sophisticated, the order of the successive ballots seldom makes any difference, and the alternative voted on first wins in one-half of all cases.

With three alternatives and three voting blocs under the amendment procedure, Farquharson showed that the sincere and sophisticated outcomes are different in one-quarter of all cases. If voting is sincere, the order of balloting makes a difference to the final outcomes only when there are cyclic majorities (see section 10.4), and an alternative presented in the first ballot wins in three cases out of four. If voting is sophisticated, the order of balloting is critical only in the same special cases, and an alternative presented in the first ballot wins in five cases out of eight.

Under the plurality procedure, restricting himself again to three alternatives and three voting blocs, Farquharson found that the sincere and sophisticated outcomes differ in three cases out of four. The largest voting bloc – or the voter with an additional casting vote in the case of equal-sized blocs – always obtains its favourite outcome when voting is sincere. But if sophisticated voting is used, then the favourite alternative of the strongest voting bloc wins in only one case out of four, and in two further cases the classical method of solution produces an indecisive result: any of the alternatives might win.

Using more efficient methods of analysis, several researchers extended and refined Farquharson's preliminary results. To begin with, Kramer (1972) proved that the sincere and sophisticated outcomes are identical under any binary voting procedure such as successive or amendment voting if the preference order of each voter is *separated* at each ballot. The idea of separability, first introduced by Farquharson, is extremely simple. In Figure 10.1(b), for example, the first ballot G_1 is between M or L on the one hand and R or L on the other. This ballot separates a preference order such as MLR because the preference order can be divided into the appropriate pairs (M, L), (L, R) without disturbing the original order. The order LMR, on the other hand, cannot be separated into the required sets without disturbing the preference order. Because this procedure fails to separate the left-wingers' preference order on the first ballot, the sincere and sophisticated outcomes may not be identical according to Kramer's theorem, and they are indeed different as was shown earlier. In complicated binary voting procedures with numerous ballots, alternatives, and voting blocs, this result enables a rapid check to be made to discover whether sophisticated voting may lead to a different outcome from sincere voting.

Miller (1977), McKelvey and Niemi (1978), and Bjurulf and Niemi (1981) extended Farquharson's preliminary conclusions about the effects of voting orders under binary procedures. Although the order of voting is frequently critical if voting is sincere, McKelvey and Niemi proved that this is not so for sophisticated voting: in that case the same outcomes arise from all possible voting orders unless a cyclic majority exists in the profile of voters' preferences. In the absence of a cyclic majority, McKelvey and Niemi showed that the alternative that is preferred to each of the others by a majority of the voters is invariably the final outcome of sophisticated voting, although sincere voting may lead to one of the other alternatives being chosen, that is, to what was called plurality-majority disagreement in section 10.4. Plurality-majority disagreement never occurs under binary voting procedures if voting is sophisticated, but if voting is sincere it may occur. If a cyclic majority exists, Bjurulf and Niemi established that it is always possible to find a voting order under successive or amendment procedures that ensures that a particular alternative will win under sincere voting, and a voting order that ensures that it will win under sophisticated voting. They also refined Farquharson's preliminary findings regarding the effect of the position of an alternative in the voting order on its likelihood of being chosen. It turns out to be not strictly true that an alternative voted on late under a binary procedure is *always* at an advantage if voting is sincere, and an alternative is not *always* at an advantage if it is voted on early by sophisticated voters, but these generalizations are approximately correct. The same is true under the successive procedure, but in this case an alternative presented in the very first ballot has an advantage if voting is sophisticated. The order-of-voting effects were further refined by Jung (1990).

Turning now to the plurality procedure, a (smaller) number of general conclusions are justified. First, there is the *paradox of the chairman's vote*. If voting is sincere, then the favourite alternative of the largest voting bloc, or the chairman's favourite alternative in the event of a tie, is bound to win. It is therefore rational to seek extra power in sincere decision-making bodies. But if voting is sophisticated, then the largest voting bloc or the chairman may be positively disadvantaged, as in the example discussed earlier in this section. Depending on the profile of preferences among the voters, it may be prudent to shun extra power in a sophisticated decision-making body (Niemi, 1983). There is often a tendency for strategic voters to "gang up" against and frustrate the wishes of the most powerful voter or voting bloc. This paradox provides a vivid and simple refutation of the dogma that the strongest always survive; a more incisive refutation, also based on game theory, will be discussed in section 11.2, and see also section 8.8 for a discussion of the closely related *power inversion paradox* in coalition formation.

For at least two centuries the view seems to have prevailed that strategic voting is somehow deceitful, unfair, and contrary to the spirit of democratic collective decision making. Shortly before the outbreak of the French Revolution, Jean-Charles de Borda suggested a new voting procedure that was designed to avoid certain undesirable paradoxes. When it was pointed out to him that his new procedure was vulnerable to strategic voting, he exclaimed "My scheme is intended only for honest men!" (quoted in Kelly, 1978, p. 65). During Victorian times, C. L. Dodgson (Lewis Carroll) lamented the tendency of voters to adopt a "principle of voting which makes an election more of a game of skill than a real test of the wishes of the electors" (quoted by Farquharson, 1969, p. 17), and he thought it would be better that "elections be decided according to the wish of the majority than of those who happen to have most skill at the game" (ibid.). The well-known American political scientist William H. Riker (1961) expressed the view that "there may be nothing wrong with lying as a political strategy, but one would not, I assume, wish to give a systematic advantage to liars" (p. 905). In the light of what is now known about the consequences of strategic voting, it is worth pausing to consider whether it deserves such a bad press, and whether honest, irrational sincerity is really more desirable from either an ethical or a democratic standpoint.

Consider first the problem of a plurality vote that chooses a Condorcet loser – that is, an alternative to which each of the losing alternatives is preferred by a majority of the voters to the winner. Sophisticated voting rules this possibility out (Niemi and Frank, 1982) and guarantees that no such unsuitable alternative can ever become the social choice under any voting procedure in common use. Second, computer simulations reported by Niemi and Frank (1985) and Felsenthal, Maoz, and Rapoport (cited in Felsenthal and Maoz, 1988, p. 128) indicate that sophisticated plurality voting is more likely than sincere plurality voting to select a Condorcet winner when one exists. A third powerful argument in favour of strategic voting relates to order-of-voting effects under binary procedures. In a fair voting procedure, the order in which the ballots are held ought not to determine the social choices yet it very frequently does if the voters are sincere. This is extremely rare, however, if voting is sophisticated, and can happen only if a cyclic majority exists. Brams (1975, pp. 83–85) proved that an alternative that fails to be chosen by sincere voters, but that would have been chosen under a different order of voting favoured by the majority, will win under the original "unfavourable" voting order provided that sophisticated voting is used. Thus again, sophisticated voting ensures that the will of the majority prevails. These considerations surely argue strongly in favour of the ethical and democratic desirability of strategic voting.

Those who disapprove of strategic voting sometimes try to devise strategy-proof voting procedures. For example, Brams and Fishburn (1983), Steen (1980), and others argued vigorously in favour of *approval voting* on these grounds among others. This is a relatively new voting procedure, described by its leading promoter as "the election reform of the 20th century" (Brams, 1980a, p. 105), in which voters vote for as many alternatives as they consider acceptable. But theorems have been proved to the effect that no voting procedure can be strategy-proof, in the sense of offering the voters no incentive to vote insincerely, without violating some more fundamental condition of democratic acceptability. Gibbard (1973) and Satterthwaite (1973, 1975) were the first to obtain this important result; they showed independently that any strategy-proof voting procedure is necessarily dictatorial. Further theorems along the same lines were proved by Zeckhauser (1973), Pattanaik (1976), Gärdenfors (1976), Barbera (1977), and Kelly (1978, chap. 6). If voters' preferences are *dichotomous*, that is, if the voters divide the alternatives or candidates into those they approve of and those they disapprove of, and if in addition they do not distinguish among the alternatives within each of these two groups, then approval voting is indeed uniquely strategy-proof, and furthermore in the absence of a cyclic majority an alternative wins if and only if it is a Condorcet winner, but both of these undoubted virtues evaporate under the more realistic assumption of nondichotomous voters' preferences (Felsenthal and Maoz, 1988; Niemi, 1984). Felsenthal and Maoz showed that approval voting violates a number of other conditions of acceptability also, although it may be preferable in some respects to plurality voting.

It is not entirely clear why so many people disapprove of strategic voting. In most spheres of social life people's attempts to choose strategies rationally are taken for granted and are seldom considered devious or underhand. It seems strange that myopic and irrational maximax strategies, in other words sincere voting, should be expected of intelligent voters, or that people should be slandered for trying to pursue their interests rationally. A business executive, political leader, or military general who habitually chose maximax strategies would justifiably be regarded as a dangerous fool.

10.9 Empirical evidence of strategic voting

Most empirical examples of strategic voting that have been reported are taken from real-life decision-making bodies. These examples depend on conjectures about the voters' preference orders and assumptions about the voting strategies underlying their observed behaviour, but some are persuasive none the less. The following example, originally cited by

Farquharson (1969), is taken from the letters of Pliny the Younger and refers to an incident in the ancient Roman Senate:

> The consul Afranius Dexter had been found slain, and it was uncertain whether he had died by his own hand or at those of his freedmen. When the matter came before the Senate, Pliny wished to acquit them; another senator moved that they should be banished to an island; and a third, that they should be put to death. (Farquharson, 1969, pp. 6–7; Pliny's letter is reproduced in full, op. cit., pp. 57–60)

There appear to have been three opinion blocs within the Senate. The acquitters' preference order was (obviously) ABC, that is, acquit, banish, condemn to death. The banishers' order was BAC, and that of the condemners CBA. Pliny insisted that the decision should be reached by simple plurality voting. The outcome of sincere voting would have been A, because the acquitters constituted the largest voting bloc. The decision actually reached, however, was B, which corresponds to the outcome of sophisticated voting. If the preference orders were the ones (very plausibly) assumed by Farquharson, then there is every reason to believe that the senators voted strategically. This example is formally identical to the one introduced near the beginning of section 10.7.

One of the best known examples of strategic voting occurred in the United States House of Representatives in 1956 in relation to the so-called Powell amendment to a bill authorizing the distribution of federal funds to the states for building schools "open to all children without regard to race". After examining the votes taken on the bill and the public records of the legislators involved, Riker (1982) concluded that some 97 Republican representatives who were opposed to school aid in general voted strategically in favour of the amendment, recognizing that it would be anathema to southern Democrats, and as a result of this the amendment was adopted and the bill thus amended was duly defeated (see also Denzau, Riker, and Shepsle, 1985). In a similar vein, Enelow and Koehler (1980) provided evidence that representatives in the United States Congress have sometimes voted strategically for amendments that they do not favour in order to save or to kill the associated bills. Krehbiel and Rivers (1990) reconsidered in detail the anecdotal evidence of strategic voting in Congress, especially the case of the Powell amendment, and concluded that it was less than convincing. On the other hand, Calvert and Fenno (1994) provided evidence for sophisticated voting in the United States Senate resolution on the televising of Senate debates in 1986.

Riker and Ordeshook (1973, p. 98) and Brams (1975, chap. 2) argued that sincere voting could have determined the outcome of the 1912 United States presidential election. Although voting was apparently sincere in this case, the preference orders that the authors postulate imply that Roosevelt rather than Woodrow Wilson *would* have been elected had the voters chosen sophisticated strategies. In the 1948 presidential election, on the other hand, strategic voting seems to have occurred. According to Downs (1957), "some voters who preferred the Progressive candidate to all others nevertheless voted for the Democratic candidate", because sincere voting "ironically increased the probability that the one they favored least [the Republican candidate] would win" (p. 47). Their stratagem may have succeeded, because in the event Truman (Democrat) narrowly defeated Dewey (Republican), and Wallace (Progressive) got only 2.4 per cent of the popular vote.

During the 1970 election for a senator in New York, Ottinger (Democrat), Goodell (Republican), and Buckley (Conservative) were the three candidates. The Goodell supporters, who were in a minority, probably preferred Ottinger to Buckley. Had they all voted strategically for their second preference, Ottinger, then he would probably have won the election. Some Goodell supporters did vote strategically in this way (Niemi and Riker, 1976, pp. 24–25), but most voted sincerely, and Buckley was therefore elected.

Rasch (1987) searched for evidence of strategic voting in the Norwegian *Storting* (parliament) over a 15-year period and concluded that it hardly ever occurred: "the parliamentarians simply vote directly in accordance with their preferences over the alternatives at hand" (p. 63), although strategic manipulation of the order of voting may occur occasionally under the successive voting procedure that is used in the *Storting*.

Galbraith and Rae (1989) and Johnston and Pattie (1991) cited indirect evidence of strategic voting by about 4 per cent of voters in the 1983 British general election and about 6 per cent in the 1987 general election. Strategic voting appears to have been most common in marginal seats where the chances of influencing the outcome appeared to be high, especially in constituencies held by the ruling Conservatives where one of the main opposition parties was much stronger than the other. There is evidence that in the most compelling circumstances, up to 50 per cent of British voters may have had strategic considerations in mind when deciding how to vote in 1987 (Niemi, Whitten, and Franklin, 1992), although this is controversial. Similar research in the United States reported by Abramson, Aldrich, Paolino, and Rhode (1992) found indirect evidence for strategic voting by 13–14 per cent of voters in the 1988 presidential primaries, and in French labour elections, which are held under proportional representation, there is indirect evidence (Rosenthal, 1974) of strategic voting.

A number of experimental investigations of strategic voting have been undertaken. Krehbiel (1986) reported three experimental studies of "sophisticated and myopic" voting, the results of which showed that "with only minor exceptions, committees composed of individually self-interested decision makers did exercise collective sophistication" (p. 555). Wilson and Pearson (1987) studied the effects of two separate experimental treatments and found only very limited evidence of sophisticated voting, probably because "the agendas for the experiments reported here were comparatively lengthy and the strategic choices were obscured" (p. 270), in other words the problems were probably too difficult for the experimental subjects to work out. Herzberg and Wilson (1988) performed an experiment using slightly easier voting problems and found that just under 30 per cent of the subjects' voting strategies were fully sophisticated.

Felsenthal, Rapoport, and Maoz (1988) reported the results of an experiment in which groups of four voters were asked to elect one of three alternatives using the plurality procedure. The striking finding of this study was that Condorcet winners were elected whenever they existed, whether or not they were predicted by Farquharson's (1969) or Niemi and Frank's (1982, 1985) models, and when there were no Condorcet winners, the experimental subjects tended to elect different alternatives from the ones predicted by the models. Felsenthal, Rapoport, and Maoz therefore devised a new model of sophisticated voting under the plurality procedure that was designed to reflect the behaviour of real voters more accurately. The new model predicts that a Condorcet winner will always be elected if one exists and that if a cyclic majority exists but there is a unique maximin alternative, then that alternative will be elected.

Eckel and Holt (1989) reported the results of committee voting experiments involving binary votes under the amendment procedure based on earlier experiments by Levine and Plott (1977) and Plott and Levine (1978). In all three studies, myopic (non-strategic) voting was generally exhibited by the participant subjects. But in the Eckel and Holt experiment strategic voting began to emerge after a number of decisions had been made by the same subjects with the same voter preferences and agenda; and "once a strategic outcome is achieved, future strategic outcomes with a given profile are virtually assured" (p. 771). In other words, it seems that people find it difficult to grasp the strategic principles of voting, but once understanding dawns they begin to vote strategically and continue to do so indefinitely.

10.10 Summary

At the beginning of this chapter a particular class of multi-person games governed by rules enshrined in social choice functions was identified, and the primitive terms and axioms of social choice theory were outlined in section 10.2. Section 10.3 focused on three of the most widely used voting procedures, namely the successive, amendment, and plurality (first-past-the-post) voting procedures, and showed that if voting is sincere they can lead to different social choices in simple and natural cases involving the same alternatives and individual preferences, and that different orders of voting can also affect the outcomes. Section 10.4 discussed a number of important voting paradoxes, including Condorcet's paradox of cyclic majorities, and showed that the most common voting procedures are liable to produce anomalous outcomes, and section 10.5 outlined Arrow's impossibility theorem, a consequence of Condorcet's paradox that establishes that no social choice function or voting procedure can satisfy certain minimal conditions of fairness and workableness. Section 10.6 was devoted to proportional voting schemes in general and the single transferable voting procedure (STV) in particular, and STV was shown to violate certain basic requirements of fairness. In section 10.7 the ideas behind strategic or tactical voting were explained in detail, and it was shown how strategic voting can alter the outcomes. Section 10.8 focused on Farquharson's theory of sophisticated voting, which is the most highly developed solution concept for voting games, and section 10.9 reviewed the empirical evidence of strategic voting in general and sophisticated voting in particular.

—— 11 ——

Theory of evolution: strategic aspects

11.1 Historical background

This chapter focuses on applications of game theory to problems of biological evolution. The basic ideas were first set forth in an unpublished paper on ritualized fighting in animals by George Price and subsequently developed by John Maynard Smith (1972; Maynard Smith and Price, 1973), but they can be traced back through the work of Hamilton (1967) on the evolution of sex ratios, and Lewontin (1961) on speciation and extinction, to Fisher's (1930) discussion of various evolutionary phenomena, including sexual selection. The theoretical principles and supporting empirical evidence have been reviewed several times (e.g., Axelrod and Dion, 1988; Dawkins, 1976, 1989; Hines, 1987; Krebs and Davies, 1991; Lazarus, 1982, 1987, 1994; Maynard Smith, 1974, 1976a, 1978a, 1978b, 1979, 1982, 1984; Parker, 1978). One influential biologist has expressed the view that this work may represent "one of the most important advances in evolutionary theory since Darwin" (Dawkins, 1976, p. 90).

Only a few of the simplest evolutionary games and a selection of the empirical evidence will be discussed in this chapter, because fuller accounts are readily accessible in the publications listed above. In the following section the fundamental principles of strategic evolution will be introduced and the relevance of game theory to natural selection will be explained. Section 11.3 will be devoted to Maynard Smith's two-person models of animal conflicts and the notion of an evolutionarily stable strategy, and section 11.4 will present an improved multi-person game model. Some relevant empirical evidence will be discussed in section 11.5, and the chapter will be summarized in section 11.6.

11.2 Strategic evolution and behavioural ecology

The English philosopher Herbert Spencer popularized the phrase the *survival of the fittest* to describe the theory of evolution, but it is important to understand that fitness is a subtle concept and it is not necessarily the *strongest* who survive. Section 10.8 included a discussion of the *paradox of the chairman's vote*, which is a refutation, based on the theory of strategic voting, of the dogma that the strongest are always most successful in competitive encounters, and in section 8.8 the closely related *power inversion paradox* in coalition formation was discussed. The following even more incisive refutation is based on a remarkable paradox discovered by the game theorist Martin Shubik (1954).

Suppose that Alex, Bernie, and Chris agree to fight a triangular pistol duel or "truel" under the following rules. After drawing lots to determine the order in which they will fire, they start firing one at a time in the prescribed order and continue until there is only one survivor. All three truellists know that every shot that hits its target will be instantly fatal, and that Alex hits the target every time, Bernie 80 per cent of the time, and Chris 50 per cent of the time, so that their shooting strengths correspond to their alphabetical order. Assuming that all three are rational and have common knowledge of rationality (know that they are all rational, know that they all know this, and so on), who has the best chance of survival?

The surprising answer is Chris, the worst shot. The proof relies on elementary probability theory, according to which, if the probabilities of two *independent* events are p and q respectively, then the probability that they will *both* occur is pq, and if the probabilities of two *mutually exclusive* events are r and s respectively, then the probability that *either* one *or* the other of the events will occur is $r + s$. The two key insights that unlock the proof are that it is rational for Alex and Bernie to ignore Chris and to aim only at each other as long as they are both still alive, because Chris is less dangerous to them, and that Chris's best strategy is to aim deliberately to miss the other two and to let them fight what amounts to a duel until one of them is killed, because Chris will then face only one opponent and will have the advantage of the first shot in that duel. In the initial duel between Alex and Bernie, the probability is $1/2$ that Alex will get the first shot and certainly kill Bernie with it. The probability that Bernie will get the first shot is also $1/2$, in which case the probability is $1/5$ that Alex will survive and kill Bernie in the next round. So the probability that Alex will survive the duel with Bernie is $1/2 + (1/2)(1/5) = 3/5$. If Alex does survive, there follows a duel between Alex and Chris in which Chris shoots first and has a probability of $1/2$ of killing Alex, failing which Alex will certainly kill Chris with the following shot. Alex's overall probability of survival (probability of killing both Bernie and Chris) is therefore $(3/5)(1/2) = 3/10$.

If Bernie survives the duel with Alex, a Bernie versus Chris duel ensues. The probability that Chris, who has the first shot, will kill Bernie in the first round of this duel is $1/2$, failing which the probability that Bernie will kill Chris is $4/5$, so the probability that Bernie will kill Chris in this first round is $(1/2)(4/5) = 4/10$. But if Bernie misses and Chris gets another shot, the probability that Bernie will kill Chris in the second round is the probability of Chris missing, then Bernie missing, then Chris missing again, then Bernie killing Chris, which is $(1/2)(1/5)(1/2)(4/5) = 4/100$. If Bernie misses again, the probability that Bernie will kill Chris in the third round is $4/1000$, and so on. The probability that Bernie will survive the duel with Chris is the probability of one of these mutually exclusive events occurring, which is the sum of the infinite series $(4/10) + (4/100) + (4/1000)$. ... This is the same as $0.4 + 0.04 + 0.004 \ldots$, which is obviously $0.444 \ldots$, the decimal expansion of $4/9$. Remembering that the probability of Bernie's surviving the earlier Alex versus Bernie duel is $2/5$, the overall probability that Bernie will survive the complete truel is $(2/5)(4/9) = 8/45$. Because one of the three truellists must survive, and because the probabilities that Alex and Bernie will survive are $3/10$ and $8/45$ respectively, the probability that Chris will survive is $1 - (3/10) - (8/45) = 47/90$, which is over 50 per cent and is much higher than the probabilities of survival of the other two women. The moral of this game is that things are not always what they seem. One should be wary of jumping to premature conclusions, and in particular one should not automatically assume that the "survival of the fittest" means simply the survival of the most powerful.

In fact, "survival of the fittest" has a much more specific meaning. In its modern neo-Darwinian form, the theory of evolution rests on two key premises:

(a) that evolution consists of changes in the frequencies of genes in populations of plants and animals;
(b) that the frequency of a particular gene increases if it increases the *Darwinian fitness* of its possessors. The Darwinian fitness of an individual with a particular genotype (genetic make-up) is defined simply as its *lifetime reproductive success*, that is, the number of offspring that it produces in its lifetime, which in turn determines the number of gene copies that it transmits to future generations.

The logical structure of the theory is as follows (Lazarus, 1994). A population of plants or animals, if unchecked, increases at a geometric rate, but food, habitat, and other resources are limited. There is therefore a *struggle for existence*, and because individuals vary, the struggle takes the form of the *survival of the fittest*. Some individual *phenotypic characters* are *heritable*, in other words some differences in individuals' anatomy, physiology, and behaviour are due (at least partly) to genetic differences. Individuals with phenotypic characters that result in their surviving and producing more offspring therefore increase in numbers relative to individuals without those characters, and this process is called *natural selection*. It is the mechanism that drives the process of evolution.

The basic concepts of game theory can be mapped to the elements of the theory of natural selection as follows. The players correspond to individual organisms – animals, plants, viruses, and so on. Each organism's strategy or set of strategies is simply its behavioural phenotype determined by its genotype, and its payoffs are the changes in its Darwinian fitness that result from strategic interactions with other organisms. No assumption needs to be made that the players (organisms) *choose* their strategies (genotypes) rationally or even deliberately. But different strategies can result in different payoffs, and it is well known that natural selection sometimes mimics deliberate choice. In view of the fact that Darwinian fitness is defined numerically and unambiguously, one of the most serious problems of game theory applications in other fields – the problem of assigning numbers to the payoffs – is conveniently avoided in evolutionary applications. A human decision-maker's preferences among the outcomes of a game can often be quantified only by making arbitrary assumptions, but an organism's lifetime reproductive success is inherently quantitative.

Classical evolutionary models are usually non-strategic in character. The fitness of a phenotype is traditionally assumed to depend solely on its own intrinsic characteristics, and the characteristics of other individuals in the population are assumed to be either fixed or irrelevant to the model. In the terminology of game theory, classical evolutionary models assume that an individual's expected payoffs are determined solely by its own strategy choices and that the corresponding games are therefore one-person games against Nature (see chapter 2). Lewontin (1961) was the first to formulate evolutionary problems explicitly in terms of game theory, when he suggested that species should, and do, adopt minimax strategies in one-person games against Nature. The same non-strategic assumptions are implicit in most of the literature on natural selection.

It is obvious, however, that the fitness of a phenotype sometimes depends on the genetic composition of the population or, in the terminology of modern population genetics, it is sometimes *frequency-dependent*. This is typically the case with behavioural dispositions – for example, the consequences of different types of courtship behaviour obviously depend on how others behave – but in principle it can also apply to anatomical and physiological characteristics. The study of behaviour in terms of its history of evolutionary forces favouring adaptation is called *behavioural ecology* (Krebs and Davies, 1991; Lazarus, 1994). Whenever the fitness of a particular phenotype depends on the genetic composition of the population, we may translate into the language of game theory and say that the payoff resulting from a particular strategy depends on the strategies of the other players, and in such cases game theory is clearly relevant. Natural selection poses genuinely strategic problems to organisms with regard to certain kinds of traits, but this fact was virtually ignored by evolutionary theorists for more than a century.

Strategic aspects of natural selection were first recognized in the evolution of sex ratios. The strategies available to individuals are simply the proportions of male and female offspring that they are genetically programmed to produce. Most animals and plants with distinct sexes have evolved to stable equilibria in which approximately equal numbers of males and females are produced. Once it is recognized that this requires explanation, the solution is not difficult to find. Fisher (1930) was the first to understand that in a population with a preponderance of females, an individual that produced only sons would end up with the most grandchildren, because all offspring need fathers, and that genes predisposing parents to produce sons would therefore increase in frequency. In a population consisting mostly of males, on the other hand, an individual would maximize its payoff by producing only daughters. In either case, the sexual imbalance in the population would be corrected by natural selection. The population would therefore evolve to the stable equilibrium point at which equal numbers of males and females were being produced and the production of sons and daughters was yielding the same fitness payoff.

This type of analysis was taken a step further by Hamilton (1967), who used the methods of game theory to explain the unequal sex ratios found in certain parasitic wasps and other insects. The females of this group of insects store sperm and can determine the sex of each egg they lay by fertilizing it or leaving it unfertilized; fertilized eggs develop into females and unfertilized eggs into males. Some parasitic wasps lay their eggs in the larvae of other insects such as caterpillars. The wasps mate immediately on hatching, and after mating the males die and the females disperse. If only one wasp lays her eggs in each larva, her optimal strategy is obviously to leave just one unfertilized egg in each cluster, because one male can mate with all of the females when the eggs hatch, and if more than one female lays eggs in the same larva, then the optimal ratio of female to male eggs may be even higher. It is essential to leave an unfertilized egg if none of the others is likely to do so, but even one unfertilized egg may be unnecessary otherwise. A large predominance of females is in fact found in these species, and Hamilton (1967) was able to show that the observed sex ratios are usually optimal, or very nearly so, from a game theory standpoint.

11.3 Animal conflicts and evolutionarily stable strategies

Many species of animals avoid escalated no-holds-barred fights with one another and engage instead in relatively harmless forms of *conventional fighting* to settle conflicts over valuable resources such as food, mates, territory, and positions in dominance hierarchies. The large carnivores, for example, refrain from attacking one another with the ferocity with which they attack their prey. Bighorn rams leap at each other head-on, although more damage could be inflicted on an adversary by charging him in the flank. In many species of fish the combatants seize each other by the jaws, which are protected by leathery skin, rather than biting elsewhere where more injury would be inflicted. Male fiddler crabs fighting over possession of a burrow never injure each other, although the enlarged claws that they use are powerful enough to crush the abdomens of their opponents. Rattlesnakes often wrestle with each other but never bite; male deer lower their heads and lock their branched antlers together but seldom use them to pierce each other's bodies; and some antelopes actually kneel down while engaging in combat. Many other examples could be given (see, e.g., Lorenz, 1966) of animal conflicts that are settled by ritualized displays without any physical contact at all.

Although escalated fighting is by no means unknown in the animal kingdom (Geist, 1966), and for that matter among human beings, conventional fighting is sufficiently common to require an explanation. Animals do not use their weapons to maximal effect in conventional combats. In a contest between two animals, *A* and *B*, if *A* adopts a conventional fighting strategy and *B* an escalated strategy, it would seem that *B* would gain the advantage and in the long run would pass more of its genes on to its offspring, on average, than *A*. How, then, can conventional fighting be explained within the logical framework of natural selection outlined above?

Non-strategic explanations up until the early 1970s were traditionally based on appeals to "the good of the species" (e.g., Eibl-Eibesfeldt, 1970; Lorenz, 1960). A typical argument ran as follows. If the members of a population were to engage in escalated fighting, serious injuries would be common, and the survival of the population as a whole would be placed in jeopardy. A population in which conventional fighting is the norm has a better chance of survival. Natural selection has therefore favoured conventional fighting. This argument is based on the (often hidden) assumption of *group selection*. It assumes that the fittest populations (rather than the fittest individuals) survive in the process of natural selection. But group selectionist arguments are regarded with suspicion by most contemporary evolutionary theorists (see, e.g., Dawkins, 1989; Lazarus, 1994; Maynard Smith, 1976b). The fundamental theoretical problem is to explain how a population of conventional fighters could arise in the first place. Imagine a population of escalated fighters in which a mutation occurs causing a few animals to fight conventionally. Provided that the advantage of winning outweighs the risk of injury resulting from escalated fighting, the conventional fighting mutants would fare badly against the escalated fighting majority in terms of Darwinian fitness, and their genes would soon be eradicated by selective pressures operating within the population. On the other hand, in a population of conventional fighters, a mutation that caused escalated fighting would spread through the population because it would increase the Darwinian fitness of its possessors even if it reduced the prospects of survival of the population as a whole.

The group selectionist argument is therefore unconvincing except in certain rather unusual circumstances outlined by Maynard Smith (1976b). What is required is an explanation of conventional fighting showing how it increases the Darwinian fitness of the individuals manifesting it. This requirement is fulfilled by Maynard Smith and Price's (1973) application of game theory to the problem.

Suppose that there are two pure fighting strategies available to each individual: Hawk and Dove (Maynard Smith, 1976a, 1978a; Maynard Smith and Price, 1973). The Hawk (H) strategy involves escalated fighting until the individual adopting it is injured and is forced to withdraw or its opponent gives way. The Dove (D) strategy involves conventional fighting, and the individual adopting it retreats before getting injured if its opponent escalates. An animal's genotype, we shall assume, determines the strategy that it adopts. After each contest the animals receive their payoffs. The expected (average) payoff to a Hawk in a contest with a Dove is written $E(H, D)$, the expected payoff to a Dove in a contest with another Dove is $E(D, D)$, and so on. The payoff is a measure of the change in Darwinian fitness of the contestant, that is, the increase or decrease in its expected lifetime reproductive success relative to some baseline measure, and it depends on three factors. The first is the advantage of winning: the resource over which the contest takes place is assumed to be worth V (for victory) units of Darwinian fitness to the winner. The second is the disadvantage of being injured: injury alters an animal's fitness by $-W$ (for wounds) units. The third is the time and energy wasted in a long contest, which alters the fitness of each contestant by $-T$ (for time) units in conventional fights.

The payoffs associated with every possible combination of strategies can be worked out quite easily from these components. If a pair of contestants both adopt Hawk strategies, we may assume that, on average, their chances of winning are equal, their chances of being injured are also equal, and the contest will be short so neither will waste unnecessary time and energy, so that an individual's expected payoff will be $(V - W)/2$. If both adopt Dove strategies, their chances of winning are once again equal, there will be no chance of injury to either, and the contest will be a long one in which time and energy are wasted by both contestants, so an individual's expected payoff will be $(V/2) - T$. A Dove in conflict with a Hawk will flee as soon as the Hawk escalates and will therefore receive a zero payoff. Finally, a Hawk in conflict with a Dove will win the resource without risk of injury or wastage of time and energy and will therefore receive a payoff of V.

Matrix 11.1a summarizes these payoffs in the form of a generalized payoff matrix for the Hawk-Dove game. Matrix 11.1b shows the same game with the following numerical values suggested for illustrative purposes by Maynard Smith (1978a): $V = 10$, $W = 20$, and $T = 3$.

Note that the payoffs shown in the matrices are those to Player I, following the convention with evolutionary game matrices of omitting the payoffs to Player II, even when (as is usual) the games are not zero-sum. But the games shown in Matrices 11.1 are the same from both players' points of view, so Player II's payoffs can easily be filled in if required.

Matrices 11.1 *The Hawk-Dove Game*

	II				II	
	H	D			H	D
I	$(V - W)/2$	V		I	-5	10
	0	$(V/2) - T$			0	2
	(a)				(b)	

Maynard Smith and Price (1973) introduced the concept of an *evolutionarily stable strategy* to handle games of this type. Suppose that the members of a population play the Hawk-Dove game in random pairs and that the animals then produce offspring that use the same strategies as their parents. The following question can then be asked: Is there a strategy with the property that if most members of the population adopt it, no mutant strategy can invade the population by natural selection? Such a strategy is called an evolutionarily stable strategy, or ESS for short, because no mutant strategy confers a higher Darwinian fitness on the individuals adopting it, and the ESS is consequently invulnerable to invasion by the available alternative strategies. It is therefore the strategy that we would expect to see commonly in nature.

The game shown in Matrix 11.1b turns out, on examination, to be a game of Chicken (see section 6.6). The cooperative (or cautious or maximin) strategy is Dove, and unilateral defection from it benefits the defector and harms the cooperator, whereas joint defection results in the worst possible payoffs for both players. The game does not have a symmetric equilibrium point in pure strategies, and a consequence of this is that neither of the pure strategies is an ESS. This can be shown quite easily. A population of Hawks can be invaded by Doves, because the payoff to a Hawk in such a population is $E(H, H) = -5$ and the payoff to a Dove is $E(D, H) = 0$. It follows that a Dove mutant would produce more offspring than a Hawk. A similar argument can be used to show that the Dove strategy is not an ESS: in a population of Doves a Hawk mutant would produce more offspring than a Dove.

Maynard Smith (1974, 1978a, 1978b, 1982) specified the mathematical requirements of an ESS. The computations are rather cumbersome, and a much simpler analysis will be given in section 11.4, but let us examine the standard approach first. Suppose a population consists mostly of individuals adopting some arbitrary strategy I, but a small fraction p of mutants adopt strategy J. An individual adopting strategy I will receive a payoff of $E(I, I)$ with probability $1 - p$ and a payoff of $E(I, J)$ with probability p. The payoff to an individual adopting strategy J will be $E(J, I)$ with probability $1 - p$ and $E(J, J)$ with probability p. If the Darwinian fitness of each member of the population before a series of contests is C, then after the contests the fitness of an individual adopting strategy I, denoted by $W(I)$, will be

$$W(I) = C + (1 - p)E(I, I) + pE(I, J),$$

and the fitness of an individual adopting strategy J, denoted by $W(J)$, will be

$$W(J) = C + (1 - p)E(J, I) + pE(J, J).$$

If I is an ESS, then by definition $W(I) > W(J)$. Because p is assumed to be small, this implies that either

$$E(I, I) > E(J, I) \tag{1}$$

or

$$E(I, I) = E(J, I), \text{ and } E(I, J) > E(J, J) \tag{2}$$

Conditions (1) and (2) are Maynard Smith's definitions of an ESS. The computation of actual values for an ESS from these definitions is straightforward and will be explained later. In the Hawk-Dove game shown in Matrix 11.1b, the ESS turns out to be a mixed strategy of $(8/13)H$ and $(5/13)D$. Either $8/13$ of the population will consistently adopt the Hawk and $5/13$ the Dove strategy, leading to a *genetic polymorphism*, or every individual will play a *mixed strategy* composed of Hawk $8/13$ of the time and Dove $5/13$ of the time. (For variations of these possibilities, see Mealey, 1995.) To prove that this mixed strategy is an ESS, it is necessary to show that it is invulnerable to invasion by either Hawks or Doves.

Denoting the mixed strategy by M, it will be shown first that $E(M, M) = E(H, M)$, and $E(M, H) > E(H, H)$, confirming that M is evolutionarily stable against H according to Definition (2) above. The calculation is as follows:

$$E(H, M) = (8/13)E(H, H) + (5/13)E(H, D),$$

$$E(D, M) = (8/13)E(D, H) + (5/13)E(D, D),$$

$$E(M, H) = (8/13)E(H, H) + (5/13)E(D, H),$$

$$E(M, M) = (8/13)E(H, M) + (5/13)E(D, M).$$

The values of $E(H, H)$, $E(H, D)$, $E(D, H)$, and $E(D, D)$ are the numbers in Matrix 11.1b; they are -5, 10, 0, and 2 respectively. Substituting these values in the above equations, we arrive finally at

$$E(M, M) = 10/3 = E(H, M),$$

and

$$E(M, H) = -40/13 > E(H, H) = -5,$$

which establishes that M is evolutionarily stable against H according to Definition (2). The same method of analysis can be used to show that M is evolutionarily stable against D. In other words, because H and D are by hypothesis the only alternative strategies available, M is an ESS in the Hawk-Dove game shown in Matrix 11.1b.

In the generalized Hawk-Dove game shown in Matrix 11.1a, in which no assumptions are made about the fitness equivalents of victory (V), wounds ($-W$), and time and energy wastage ($-T$), the algebraic conditions that an ESS must satisfy are as follows.

For Hawk to be a pure ESS according to Definition (1), it must be the case that $E(H, H) > E(D, H)$. Substituting the expressions given in Matrix 11.1a, we have

$$(V - W)/2 > 0,$$

that is,

$$V > W.$$

Alternatively, according to Definition (2), Hawk is a pure ESS if $E(H, H) = E(D, H)$ and $E(H, D) > E(D, D)$. Substituting as before, we have

$$(V - W)/2 = 0,$$

that is,

$$V = W,$$

and

$$V > V/2 - T.$$

This inequality immediately above is necessarily true because V and T are both positive numbers.

By a similar method of calculation – working straight from the definitions – it can be shown that Dove can never be a pure ESS, because the definitions cannot be satisfied for any values of V, W, and T. The only other possibility is a mixed ESS, and by elimination this must be the result when $V < W$. So we have proved that Hawk is a pure ESS when $V \geq W$ and that there is a mixed ESS when $V < W$.

All of this looks (and in fact is) unnecessarily complicated. The awkwardness arises from Maynard Smith's use of a two-person game to model what is, in fact, a multi-person strategic interaction. A more natural and straightforward analysis is presented in the following section.

11.4 An improved multi-person game model

A natural way to model the Hawk-Dove problem is to construct a compound multi-person game in which the players engage in a series of two-person contests with one another according to payoff structures such as those shown in Matrices 11.1. The theory of compound games, which was outlined in section 9.6, can be adapted to the problem as follows.

If each animal adopts either a Hawk or a Dove strategy (or a mixture of the two) in a series of contests with other animals, its expected payoff will be a linear function of the proportion of other members of the population playing Hawk or Dove. It does not make any difference whether each animal plays with all the others or whether each encounters a random sample of opponents, but it is assumed that all animals are, on average, involved in the same number of contests. Because we are concerned only with the relative fitness of the genotypes, we can ignore the total number of contests and concentrate instead on the expected payoffs per contest.

Suppose the members of a population play the two-person game shown in Matrix 11a in pairs. The expected payoff to an individual in each contest depends on its own strategy and the proportion of other animals in the population that adopt the Hawk strategy. If that proportion is represented by k, subject only to the restriction $0 \leq k \leq 1$ (because k is a proportion), it follows that the proportion of Dove opponents is $1 - k$. If an individual plays Hawk, then its expected payoff E(H) is simply

$$E(H) = k(V - W)/2 + (1 - k)V,$$

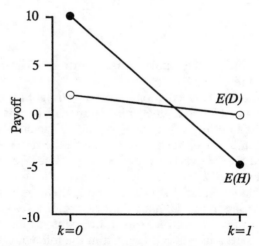

Figure 11.1 *A compound version of the Hawk-Dove game shown in Matrix 11.1b. The vertical coordinate represents an animal's expected payoff in units of Darwinian fitness, and the horizontal axis represents the proportion k, ($0 \leq k \leq 1$) of other members of the population playing Hawk. The E(H) function shows the expected payoff to the animal if it plays Hawk, and the E(D) function shows its expected payoff if it plays Dove.*

and if it plays Dove, its expected payoff $E(D)$ is

$$E(D) = (1 - k)(V/2 - T).$$

With the values shown in Matrix 11.1b, the resultant compound game is depicted in Figure 11.1.

When the Hawk-Dove problem is modelled by a compound game in this way, the ESS corresponds to the Nash equilibrium of the n-person version of the game. It is possible to see at a glance that there is no pure ESS. In a population consisting mostly of Doves (when k is small towards the left of the graph), the expected payoff to a Hawk $E(H)$ is higher than the expected payoff to a Dove $E(D)$. In such a population Hawks will therefore produce more offspring than Doves, and the proportion k of Hawks will therefore increase by natural selection, shifting the outcomes to the right until the point is reached at which the $E(H)$ and $E(D)$ payoff functions intersect. At this point the payoffs to Hawks and Doves are equal and the proportions will remain stable. In a population consisting mostly of Hawks, that is, when k is large towards the right of the graph, the expected payoff to a Dove $E(D)$ is higher than the expected payoff to a Hawk $E(H)$, so the proportion k of Hawks will decrease until the intersection point is reached. It is clear that, whatever the starting proportions of Hawks and Doves, the population will evolve to the ESS equilibrium point at the intersection of the payoff functions.

What is the proportion of Hawks at the ESS equilibrium point? Because the payoffs to a Hawk and a Dove are equal where the payoff functions intersect, the value of k can be found very simply by equating the payoff functions and solving for k. With the figures shown in Matrix 11.1b, for example, the payoff functions $E(H)$ and $E(D)$ are equated as follows:

$$-5k + 10(1 - k) = 2(1 - k),$$

$$k = 8/13,$$

indicating an equilibrium when $8/13$ of the population (strictly speaking, the population minus one individual) consists of Hawks. This confirms the result given in the previous section. It is possible, of course, to interpret the mixed ESS to mean that each individual plays a mixed strategy with Hawk occurring $8/13$ of the time.

This compound game model has several advantages over the two-person models used by Maynard Smith and his colleagues. First, the computation involved in finding an ESS is much easier, as the Hawk-Dove example shows. Second, the model clarifies the underlying strategic structure of the evolutionary process by showing that it is a multi-person game involving a whole population of players and that the critical parameter is k, the relative frequency of a particular genotype in the population. Third, the directions of evolutionary change from different starting conditions (values of k) can be seen at a glance. Last, the compound game model makes it possible to

Matrix 11.2

	A	B
A	w	x
B	y	z

provide a typology of binary (two-strategy) evolutionary games, revealing the full range of theoretical possibilities and generating testable hypotheses, as will now be shown. Multiple-strategy evolutionary games can be dealt with by breaking them down into their binary constituent parts.

A generalized payoff matrix for binary evolutionary games is shown in Matrix 11.2. The expected payoff to an A type in competition with another A type is w units of Darwinian fitness, the expected payoff to an A type in competition with a B type is x units, and so on. If the members of the population compete with one another in random pairs, either simultaneously or sequentially, the resultant compound multi-person game can be represented graphically by means of a pair of payoff functions. The expected payoff to an A type is written $E(A)$ and the expected payoff to a B type is $E(B)$. When the proportion of A types in the population is k, the expected payoff to an A type is

$$E(A) = wk + x(1 - k),$$

and the expected payoff to a B type is

$$E(B) = yk + z(1 - k).$$

The equation of the $E(A)$ payoff function defines a straight line that extends from a payoff of x when $k = 0$ to a payoff of w when $k = 1$. The $E(B)$ function is a straight line from z when $k = 0$ to y when $k = 1$. There are eight non-degenerate types of cases and their ESSs *relative to the two specified strategies* are shown diagrammatically in Figure 11.2, and listed below.

(i)   The $E(A)$ function lies above the $E(B)$ function throughout its length. In this case Strategy A dominates Strategy B, so the ESS is A.

(ii)   The $E(B)$ function lies above the $E(A)$ function throughout its length. The ESS is B.

(iii) The functions intersect with $E(A) > E(B)$ when $k = 0$ and $E(A) < E(B)$ when $k = 1$. In this case the ESS is a mixed strategy located at the intersection point. It can be found by solving the following equation (derived by equating the payoff functions and simplifying)

$$k = (z - x)/(w - x - y + z).$$

(iv) The functions intersect with $E(A) < E(B)$ when $k = 0$ and $E(A) > E(B)$ when $k = 1$. There are two pure ESSs in this interesting case, and the final result depends on the starting condition. The population will evolve to the ESS A when $k > (z - x)/(w - x - y + z)$ and to the ESS B when $k < (z - x)/(w - x - y + z)$. There is also an unstable ESS at the intersection point where $k = (z - x)/(w - x - y + z)$.

(v) $E(A) = E(B)$ when $k = 0$, and $E(A) > E(B)$ when $k = 1$. The ESS is A.

(vi) $E(A) = E(B)$ when $k = 0$, and $E(A) < E(B)$ when $k = 1$. The ESS is B.

(vii) $E(A) = E(B)$ when $k = 1$, and $E(A) > E(B)$ when $k = 0$. The ESS is A.

(viii) $E(A) = E(B)$ when $k = 1$, and $E(A) < E(B)$ when $k = 0$. The ESS is B.

There is at least one ESS in every case (in the restricted sense of evolutionary stability relative to the specified strategies). A stable mixed-strategy ESS occurs in only one case (iii), and in one other (iv) there is an unstable mixed-strategy ESS and two stable pure-strategy ESSs. The model can be used to compare a specified genotype with several alternative forms, one at a time, in order to see whether populations composed in various ways will evolve to new ESSs. No genotype is evolutionarily stable in an absolute sense, because

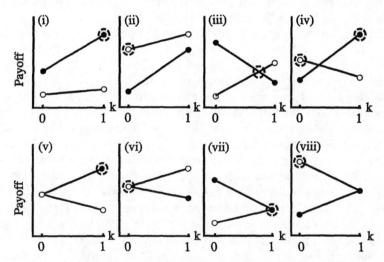

Figure 11.2 *The eight qualitatively different types of compound multi-person evolutionary games. The vertical axes represent an individual's expected payoffs in units of Darwinian fitness, and the horizontal axes represent the proportions k of A types in the population. The expected payoffs to an individual A type are shown by the lines connecting filled dots and the expected payoffs to an individual B type by the lines connecting open dots. Evolutionarily stable compositions are indicated by dashed circles.*

it is impossible to conceive of all the mutant forms that might arise. But an existing population, pure or mixed, can be examined for stability against invasion by any *specified* mutant form, and this analysis can be repeated for other specified mutants. In most cases the order in which the comparisons are made is immaterial. It occasionally happens, however, that A dominates B, B dominates C, and C dominates A. If A, B, and C are all present in the population, endless cycling will occur without an ESS ever being attained. This is closely related to Condorcet's paradox of cyclic majorities, discussed in section 10.4. An example of such a game without an ESS is given in Maynard Smith (1982, pp. 199–202) and in the appendix to Maynard Smith (1974).

Maynard Smith and Price (1973) analysed a number of animal conflict games in which more than two pure strategies are available to each player. One of their best known models is the Hawk-Dove-Retaliator game. This is an extension of the Hawk-Dove game, with the additional strategy available to an individual animal of fighting conventionally and escalating only if its adversary escalates. In other words, a Retaliator normally plays Dove but responds to a Hawk opponent by playing Hawk. Maynard Smith and Price's analysis is based on a two-person game with three rows and three columns, and it is possible to show that the ESS is Retaliator. This can be shown more easily with the help of the compound game model.

Suppose that the proportion of Hawks in a population is h, the proportion of Doves is d, and the proportion of Retaliators is r, with the natural restriction $h + d + r = 1$. The expected payoff to a Hawk in a contest with another Hawk is $E(H, H)$, and if opponents are encountered at random, the probability that a Hawk will receive this payoff is h because the proportion of potential Hawk opponents in the population is h. The expected payoff to a Hawk in a contest with a Dove is $E(H, D)$ and its corresponding probability of occurrence is d. Retaliators adopt the Hawk strategy against Hawks, so the expected payoff to a Hawk in a contest with a Retaliator is $E(H, H)$, with probability r. In a contest with an opponent chosen at random from the population, the overall expected payoff $E(H)$ to a Hawk is therefore $Eh(H, H) + Ed(H, D) + Er(H, H)$. It can be shown analogously that a Dove's expected payoff $E(D)$ in a random encounter is $Eh(D, H) + Ed(D, D) + Er(D, D)$, and a Retaliator's expected payoff $E(R)$ is $Eh(H, H) + Ed(D, D) + Er(D, D)$. Substituting the values of $E(H, H)$, $E(H, D)$, $E(D, H)$, and $E(D, D)$ shown in Matrix 11.1a, the Hawk, Dove, and Retaliator payoff functions can be rewritten as follows:

$$E(h) = h(V - W)/2 + dV + r(V - W)/2,$$

$$E(d) = h(0) + d(V/2 - T) + r(V/2 - T),$$

$$E(r) = h(V - W)/2 + d(V/2 - T) + r(V/2 - T).$$

Each of the three fighting strategies can now be tested for evolutionary stability as follows. The Hawk strategy is an ESS if, when most of the population adopt it, rare Dove or Retaliator mutants cannot invade the population and spread through it at the expense of the Hawks. If most of the population adopt the Hawk strategy, then h is close to 1 and d and r are close to zero. We can accordingly compare the payoffs to Hawks, Doves, and Retaliators as h approaches 1 while d and r approach zero. Under these conditions it is obvious by inspection of the payoff functions that $E(D) > E(H)$ provided that $V < W$ as in the numerical example of Matrix 11.1b. With this constraint, therefore, if most of the population are Hawks, Dove mutants will multiply faster than the Hawks, so the Hawk strategy is not an ESS.

To see whether the Dove strategy is an ESS, we compare the payoffs to Hawks, Doves, and Retaliators as d approaches 1 while h and r approach zero. In this case it is clear that $E(H) > E(D)$; this means that Hawk mutants will multiply faster than Doves, so the Dove strategy is not an ESS.

Turning finally to the Retaliator strategy, as r approaches 1 while h and d approach zero, neither $E(H)$ nor $E(D)$ is greater than $E(R)$, provided that $W/2 > T$ as in the numerical example of Matrix 11.1b. Under this constraint, neither Hawk nor Dove mutants will multiply faster than Retaliators, so the Retaliator strategy is an ESS. We may conclude that, with the specified constraints on the relative values of V, W, and T, the ESS of the Hawk-Dove-Retaliator game is the Retaliator strategy. A similar conclusion was reached by Maynard Smith and Price (1973) via much more cumbersome calculations. A complete solution of the game is as follows. If $V < W$ and $W/2 > T$, then Retaliator is the only ESS; but if $V \geq W$, then Hawk is also an ESS, and if $W/2 \leq T$, then Retaliator is not an ESS.

The compound game model suggests some refinements of the definition of an ESS. Maynard Smith (1978a) defined an ESS as "a strategy with the property that if most members of a large population adopt it, then no mutant strategy can invade the population" (p. 142). But this is not entirely clear. To begin with, an ESS appears to be defined in an all-or-none fashion, whereas the underlying concept of evolutionary invasion is evidently a matter of degree. In the Hawk-Dove game analysed earlier, in which the ESS is mixed, if the population consists mostly of Hawks, can Dove mutants invade it? The answer seems to be yes and no, because Doves can *partly* invade it. The invasion proceeds until 5/13 of the population are Doves, and the extent of invasion could be made arbitrarily small by a suitable choice of payoff functions. Second, if a mixed ESS consists of a large proportion of the population always playing Hawk and the rest always playing Dove, then, strictly speaking, there is no ESS according to Maynard Smith's definition, because there is no strategy with the property that if *most* adopt it no mutant can invade the population. If most adopt Hawk in a type (iii) game, then Doves invade (up to a point), if most adopt Dove, then Hawks invade (up to a point), and no other strategy is ever played.

A third objection to the classical definition of an ESS is the possibility of a game such as type (iv) in which a population containing individuals of type *A* will be completely invaded if and only if the proportion of *A*-type individuals falls below a critical value. Thus *A* is stable against *B* unless the proportion playing *A* falls below the value of *k* at the intersection point; when the proportion is smaller than this the population evolves to *B*. In Figure 11.2(iv), if "most" of the population are *B* types, with *k* less than 1/2 but not as small as at the intersection point, then *A* types will invade the population and the result will be a pure *A* ESS. The intersection point can, of course, be arbitrarily close to either of the end-points of the graph. The classical definition of an ESS is inappropriate in these cases, first because there are two pure ESSs, and second because either of them is an ESS in spite of the fact that "if most members of a large population adopt it" another strategy can invade the population and replace it.

It seems preferable to define evolutionary stability as a property of the *composition of a population*, rather than as a *property of a strategy*. An *evolutionarily stable composition* (ESC) can be defined informally as one that tends to regain its prior proportions if perturbed. More correctly, one should specify the strategies to which this stable composition refers. An evolutionarily stable composition (ESC) of strategies *A* and *B* is one in which either (a) if the proportion of *A* types in the population increased marginally, then *A* types would not be fitter than *B* types; or (b) if the proportion of *A* types decreased marginally, then *B* types would not be fitter than *A* types.

This definition of an ESC can be formalized as follows. Suppose a proportion *k* of the population adopt strategy *A* and the remainder adopt strategy *B*. The expected payoff to each individual adopting *A* may be written $E(A, k)$ and the expected payoff to each individual adopting *B* is $E(B, k)$. Now suppose that *k* increases by an arbitrary small amount *t* or decreases by an arbitrary small amount $-t$. Then *k* is an ESC if either

$$E(A, k + t) \leq E(B, k + t),$$

or

$$E(B, k - t) \leq E(A, k - t).$$

This concept of an ESC seems to avoid many of the problems associated with the original ESS approach.

11.5 Empirical evidence

A number of explicit and implicit simplifying assumptions are built into the game models described above and into others like them (see, e.g., Hines, 1987; Krebs and Davies, 1991; Maynard Smith, 1978b, 1982, 1984; Parker, 1978). Whether or not the models provide adequate accounts of strategic evolutionary processes in nature is ultimately an empirical question, but the evidence is rather scanty for two main reasons. First, it is extremely difficult to design a stringent test of an evolutionary game model because the payoffs, although fully numerical and rigorously defined, are not normally known in specific instances. Investigators have usually had to rely on indirect and partial indices of Darwinian fitness such as the number of eggs laid or the number of matings observed at a certain time and place. A second reason for the relative sparseness of the empirical evidence is that no one sought the relevant data until the pertinent questions were posed by theoretical analyses in the 1970s. Maynard Smith (1978b) has remarked that "there is a real danger that the search for functional explanations in biology will degenerate into a test of ingenuity. An important task, therefore, is the development of an adequate methodology of testing" (p. 52). Such evidence as there is has been reviewed by Parker (1978); Maynard Smith (1982, 1984); Axelrod and Dion (1988); Dawkins (1989); Krebs and Davies (1991); Lazarus (1982, 1987, 1994); and others; in this section only a few of the more striking examples will be discussed.

A fairly weak prediction of the Hawk-Dove-Retaliator model is that retaliation ought to be a common feature of animal combat, because a population of Retaliators is evolutionarily stable against Hawk and Dove mutants, and the available evidence (reviewed by Geist, 1974, 1978) confirms this prediction. The following example is typical: a rhesus monkey that loses a contest over a resource will passively submit to relatively harmless incisor bites from the victor, but it will retaliate with great ferocity if the victor uses its canines (Bernstein and Gordon, 1974).

Several examples of populations with mixed strategies (or mixtures of pure strategies) have come to light, and in a few cases there is evidence of evolutionary stability. Parker (1970) provided such evidence in a study of male dung flies, *Scatophaga stercoraria*. The females lay their eggs in cow pats, so groups of males tend to hover around cow pats in order to meet females with which to mate. A stale cow pat attracts fewer females than a fresh one. When a cow pat becomes stale, a male is therefore faced with a straightforward strategic choice: he can leave early in search of females elsewhere, or he can stay. His payoff, indexed by the expected number of female captures, clearly depends on the number of other males that leave early. If most of the other males leave early, he is better off staying because there will be very little competition for the females that arrive even though the females will be relatively few in number. But if most of the other males stay, he does better by leaving early in search of females elsewhere.

The game is type (iii) in Figure 11.2, and the ESS or ESC is therefore a mixture in which some males leave early and some stay. According to game theory, early leavers and stayers should receive the same fitness payoffs, which can be roughly estimated from the average number of female captures. Female captures are an index of fertilization rates in the short term rather than *lifetime* reproductive success, but the two things must be highly correlated. Parker showed that the predicted and observed distributions of the stay times of male flies, based on 15 942 field observations, were in very close agreement. He also showed – and this is a much more stringent test of the theory – that the average frequency of female captures was almost identical for males that left early and for those that remained on the cow pat (see also Parker, 1978, 1984).

Very clear evidence for the existence of a mixed ESS or ESC was provided by Brockmann, Grafen, and Dawkins (1979) in a study of the great golden digger wasp, *Sphex ichneumoneus*. The males of this species, apart from mating with the females, spend most of their time drinking nectar from flowers. The females dig underground burrows in the summer and provision them with grasshoppers that they have captured and paralysed. The grasshoppers provide food for the wasps' offspring when they hatch. Each female lays a single egg in each burrow and seals it if she gets a chance to do so, but ant invasions and other natural disasters often force her to abandon a burrow, for a while at least, before laying an egg in it. An individual female therefore has two alternative strategies: to dig her own burrows or to enter burrows abandoned by other females. It is clearly better for her to enter burrows prepared by others if most of the others dig their own burrows, but equally clearly at least some of the females have to do the work of preparing burrows. In other words, the underlying strategic structure of the problem is once again of type (iii) in Figure 11.2, and a mixture of digging and entering is predicted by the theory. Among 30 female wasps in Brockmann's New Hampshire study area a mixture of digging and entering was indeed observed. This was shown to be a probable ESS or ESC because the rates of egg laying, which provide a reasonable index of payoffs, were approximately equal for the two strategies. In a different colony, however, the observed frequencies of digging and entering did not appear to be in equilibrium.

An interesting example of the Concorde fallacy turned up in the same species of digger wasps, *Sphex ichneumoneus* (Dawkins and Brockmann, 1980). The Concorde fallacy, discussed in section 9.3, is the tendency to continue investing in a project because of past expenditure on it rather than expected future payoff, and female digger wasps often commit it. A female digger wasp cannot distinguish between an abandoned burrow and one whose owner is away on a provisioning trip. Occasionally two females meet at the same burrow, and the consequence is invariably a fight that continues until one of the wasps is driven off. The prize to the victor is a burrow, often already well provisioned with grasshoppers, in which to lay an egg. How hard ought a wasp to fight over a disputed burrow? If the burrow is empty, it is hardly worth fighting for, and the female would be better off giving up and spending a few hours digging a new one for herself. But if the burrow is already well provisioned it is worth fighting harder, because many days of hunting will be saved by gaining possession of it. The larger the total prize, the greater the justification for fighting over it. Dawkins and Brockmann observed 23 fights, and they were surprised to discover that the length of time a wasp was prepared to fight depended not on how much food there was in the burrow, but on how much she herself had contributed to it. The wasp that had carried the largest amount of prey into the burrow was generally the least willing to give up fighting. This is a striking example of the Concorde fallacy, as the authors pointed out.

It would seem that the wasps' behaviour is not evolutionarily stable against a mutant form that fights according to the total contents of the burrow. A wasp that regulated its fighting in this improved manner would lay more eggs, on average, than one that commits the Concorde fallacy. Why, then, has such a mutant form not invaded the population? The answer may lie in the limited intellectual capacities of the great golden digger wasp, which possibly mean that the improved behavioural pattern is simply not an available alternative. A wasp may be unable to count the number of grasshoppers in a burrow, although she can evidently judge how many she herself has carried there. Natural selection can operate only on an existing gene pool, and these wasps may not have the necessary genes for evolving an optimal strategy. In this case the observed composition of the wasp population is nevertheless an ESC, defined in relation to the available alternative strategies, and will remain so unless the mutations occur that make the superior strategy possible. Another species of digger wasp (*Ammophila campestris*) is known to have the requisite genes.

Other similar empirical examples of evolutionary stability have been reported, but they fall short of convincing scientific evidence because they are essentially anecdotal rather than experimental. It is possible to find examples in nature that appear to corroborate even mistaken theories. For example, Maynard Smith (1984, p. 99) and Axelrod and Hamilton (in Axelrod, 1984, p. 96) both stated that, in encounters with the strategic structure of the Prisoner's Dilemma game (discussed in section 6.7) iterated many times between the same players, the strategy tit for tat or TFT is an ESS, provided that the probability of repetition is sufficiently high. In an iterated Prisoner's Dilemma game, TFT is a programmed strategy in which a player cooperates on the first trial and then on every subsequent trial simply copies the other player's previous choice (section 7.5). In the light of this, Maynard Smith drew attention to empirical observations of reciprocal altruism among olive baboons and cited them as evidence for the ESS theory: "males that most often came to the help of others when solicited were also those that most often received help from others. This suggests that baboons can adopt the strategy TFT" (p. 99). But unfortunately this is all wrong.

In reality the empirical evidence is beside the point. Following Axelrod's original computer tournaments with the Prisoner's Dilemma game (Axelrod, 1980a, 1980b, 1984; Axelrod and Hamilton, 1981), which were discussed in detail in section 7.6, Selten and Hammerstein (1984) pointed out that TFT could not be an ESS, because a mutant that cooperated unconditionally (one that played ALL C) would receive the same payoff as a TFT player against both TFT players and unconditional cooperators (ALL C players), which means that TFT meets neither of Maynard Smith's definitions (1) nor (2) of an ESS. In fact, unconditional cooperators (ALL C players) would be behaviourally indistinguishable from TFT players in a population consisting mostly of TFT players; random genetic drift would allow unconditional cooperation (ALL C) to spread through the population, and this would soften up the population and make it vulnerable to evolutionary invasion by Hawk exploiters. A serious defect of TFT is its instability under the assumption of *trembling hands* (see section 6.2). A population consisting entirely of TFT players would cooperate with one another on every encounter, but if just one member of the population had a trembling hand and played a *D* strategy by mistake, everything would unravel, because it would set off a chain reaction of retaliation. Boyd and Lorberbaum (1987) proved that neither TFT nor any other pure strategy is an ESS in the iterated Prisoner's Dilemma game, and Lorberbaum (1994) eventually managed to prove that no strategy, whether pure or mixed, is an ESS.

A computer simulation incorporating mutation and selection, reported by Nowak and Sigmund (1993) and commented on briefly in section 7.6, showed that the *win-stay, lose-change* strategy (see section 3.3) is more evolutionarily stable than TFT and many other strategies in encounters with the strategic structure of the Prisoner's Dilemma game. The win-stay, lose-change strategy, sometimes called Pavlov because of its reflex-like properties (Kraines and Kraines, 1989), involves repeating a strategy choice on move *t* following a "good" payoff on move *t* −1 and switching to the other strategy on move *t* following a "bad" payoff on move *t* − 1. In this context, a "good" payoff is either the "reward" following joint cooperation or the "temptation" following unilateral defection, and a "bad" payoff is either of the other less attractive payoffs, namely the "punishment" for joint defection or the "sucker's payoff" for unilateral cooperation. It is easily verified that a player using this strategy cooperates if and only if both players chose the same strategy on the previous move. It fares poorly against unconditional defection (ALL *D*) and unlike TFT cannot invade a population of unconditional defectors, because it switches to cooperation on every other move, but it has two important advantages over TFT: it is not vulnerable to trembling hands in the way that TFT is but can correct occasional mistakes, and it can exploit unconditional cooperators (ALL C players). It may be important biologically, because it seems to be a widespread strategy in nature (Domjan and Burkhard, 1986). In terms of evolutionary survival over 10 million generations it clearly outperformed TFT and many other strategies in Nowak and Sigmund's study. For further discussions of the evolutionary implications of the iterated Prisoner's

Dilemma game, see Bartholdi, Butler, and Trick (1986), Bendor (1993), Swistak (1989), and Thomas and Feldman (1988).

Various rigorous experimental tests of ESC theory suggest themselves. In populations of plants or animals in which two (or more) clearly distinguishable alternative genotypes, A and B, are present, the relative payoffs at the endpoints of the graphs could be estimated by forming isolated breeding populations with artificially extreme compositions (mostly A and mostly B) and comparing the reproductive successes of the two types during the first few generations. Once these estimates have been made, the ESC can be predicted; it will be a uniform composition of A types or a uniform composition of B types, as shown in Figure 11.2, except in cases belonging to type (iii). In type (iii) cases the composition of the experimental population should eventually stabilize at a value of k similar to that found in the wild population, because the ESC is independent of the number of individuals.

A different kind of experiment might capitalize on differences between wild populations. Forms that exist in isolated breeding populations in different uniform compositions (all A in one population and all B in another) are strongly suggestive of type (iv) games. This theoretical interpretation could be tested rigorously by creating mixed experimental groups from the wild populations in predetermined ways, that is, by choosing different values of k. According to the theory, two opposite processes of evolutionary change to different ESCs should occur depending on the starting value of k.

11.6 Summary

The chapter began with a brief historical outline of applications of game theory to evolution. In section 11.2 the existence of strategic processes in evolution was pointed out, and a paradoxical game was described to show that the weakest can sometimes survive best in the struggle for life. The logic of the theory of evolution was explained, and it was shown how the concepts of game theory can be mapped to those of natural selection: players correspond to individual organisms, strategies to genotypes, and payoffs to changes in Darwinian fitness. In section 11.3 the problem of conventional fighting in animals was raised. Group selection provides a dubious explanation, but the theory of evolutionarily stable strategies explains how conventional fighting can arise by individual selection alone in some members of a population all the time, or in all members some of the time. An improved compound multi-person game model, leading to a typology of evolutionary games and a new concept of evolutionarily stable population compositions was outlined in section 11.4. Some relevant empirical evidence and some new experimental methods of testing the theory were discussed in section 11.5.

─── *12* ───

Game theory and philosophy

12.1 Relevance of game theory to practical problems

The publication of von Neumann and Morgenstern's *Theory of Games and Economic Behavior* in 1944 was greeted enthusiastically by many who thought they saw in it a method of solving virtually all strategic problems (see, e.g., the review of von Neumann and Morgenstern's book by Copeland, 1945). But, alas, game theory seldom provides clear and feasible solutions to practical problems of everyday life. There are three major reasons for this.

(1) Persuasive formal solutions exist only for strictly competitive (two-person zero-sum) games, but real strategic interactions are seldom strictly competitive even when they involve only two decision makers.
(2) Human beings have *bounded rationality* (March, 1986; Simon, 1957, 1976, 1978, 1985) and cannot be expected to solve any but the simplest games. Chess, for example, is a strictly competitive game, no more complex than many everyday strategic problems, and the minimax theorem tells us that it has a definite solution; but knowing this is of no help in actually playing the game or even in programming a computer to play it. The most powerful chess computers conduct minimax searches for the "best" moves according to certain very restricted criteria, although they evaluate many millions of positions for each move that they make, but this "brute force" approach enables them to "think" only a few moves ahead (Hsu, Anantharaman, Campbell, and Nowatzyk, 1990; *Scientific American*, 1981). The average number of legal moves in a chess position is about 30, and a game of chess involves about 40 moves from each player, therefore the number of possible chess games is in the region of 30^{80} or 10^{120}, far more than the number of particles in the universe (estimated to be between 10^{78} and 10^{80}), which means that no chess computer will ever be able to find the optimal strategy by brute force. A computer programmed to solve the game, even if it could analyse a billion positions per second, would still be calculating its first move after billions of years. The information-processing capacity of human beings

is modest by comparison, and brute force calculation is out of the question in most positions, but in spite of this grandmasters play remarkably strongly using methods that are not well understood by cognitive psychologists.

(3) Two characteristic features of everyday strategic interactions are, first, that the players often have incomplete information about the games that they are playing (Harsanyi and Selten, 1988, pp. 9–12), and second, that the rules and payoff functions of the games often change – and are deliberately changed by the players – while the interactions are in progress (Colman, 1975). An ingenious method has been devised for incorporating incomplete information into game theory at a formal level (Harsanyi, 1967, 1968a, 1968b), but the possibility of variable rules and payoff functions can be incorporated only at the price of vastly increased complexity, making the theory as a guide to practical action all the more vulnerable to (2).

How, then, do human beings handle strategic problems that are too complex to solve, or how ought they to handle them? The most influential theory bearing on this question was originally formulated by Herbert Simon (1957, pp. 241–273) to explain organizational decision making. Rejecting the assumption of neoclassical economics that decision makers invariably act to optimize their payoffs, Simon put forward the concept of *satisficing*. Instead of searching for the optimum strategy in every situation, a process that consumes an undue amount of time and energy and is in any event often impossible to complete, the wise decision maker, according to this theory, searches just long enough to find a strategy that is satisfactory, or that suffices; in other words one that "satisfices". For example, a newly married couple looking for a house to buy usually settle for the first one they find that is acceptable according to certain minimal requirements – price, location, number of rooms, amenities, and so on – without attempting to examine every available alternative to ensure an optimal choice. Human chess players also usually adopt satisficing moves, something that computers cannot be programmed to do effectively on account of their lack of positional judgement. It is partly because of this that chess-playing computers are weakest in certain types of "non-tactical" positions, as chess players call them, in which positional judgement is at a premium.

Strategic choices in everyday life, because they affect other people, often raise moral problems, and game theory can sometimes help to elucidate these problems without "solving" them in any formal sense. The first moral philosopher to apply game theory in this area was Richard Braithwaite (1955), who had this to say:

> The algebra I enlist for this purpose is the new mathematical Theory of Games; and I hope, by showing how it can yield results, to encourage others as well as myself to pursue and apply it further. ... Perhaps in

another three hundred years' time economic and political and other branches of moral philosophy will bask in radiation from a source – the theory of games of strategy – whose prototype was kindled round the poker tables of Princeton. (pp. 54–55)

Joseph Fletcher (1966), the originator of *situation ethics* was equally sanguine: "Moral choices need intelligence as much as they need concern. ... To be 'good' we have to get rid of innocence ... [perhaps] by learning how to assign numerical values to the factors at stake in problems of conscience" (pp. 114, 118).

It has been argued, most forcefully by Martin (1978), that game theory has various built-in biases that predispose it to handle certain kinds of problems and to generate certain kinds of conclusions. There is undoubtedly a measure of truth in this argument, although it is worth bearing in mind that it applies equally to other mathematical theories such as probability theory and statistics. According to Martin, "applying a game theory framework to ethical situations is more likely to obscure satisfactory solutions [such as changing the rules] than reveal them" (p. 98). But this would appear to be prejudging the issue: the usefulness or otherwise of a theory when applied to a particular class of problems is best determined by trying it out in practice.

If we accept the usual distinction between means and ends, perhaps the major limitation of game theory when applied to ethical problems is that it takes the players' ends as given and examines only the rationality of particular means to achieve these ends; in the terminology of Max Weber (1921) it deals only with *Zweckrationalität* (instrumental rationality) to the exclusion of *Wertrationalität* ("value" rationality). Rationality as conceived by eighteenth-century rationalist philosophers, and by many present-day non-philosophers, is concerned partly with the ends themselves, that is, with *Wertrationalität*. Game theory is completely neutral with regard to the players' values or preferences (payoff functions), provided that they are internally consistent, but it can draw certain conclusions about rational choice once these preferences are specified. The predilections and limitations of game theory in the study of practical decision problems have been discussed in more detail by Schelling (1968), Harsanyi (1976), and Mackie (1977).

Applications of game theory to philosophical problems fall into three major classes. The first class of applications have their origins within game theory itself: for example, a number of solutions (or solution concepts) have been developed to define arbitration schemes or fair and workable outcomes for two-person cooperative games. The most important of these solution concepts were discussed in section 6.10.

A second class of applications involves the use of game theory to elucidate existing philosophical problems. Among the issues to which game theory has had something to contribute are the nature and functions of rationality (discussed below in section 12.2), Kant's categorical imperative (section 12.4), and social contract theories (section 12.5).

The third and perhaps the most interesting class of applications are entirely new philosophical problems that were discovered by following the implications of game theory in particular cases. These problems were not recognized as such – and in some cases cannot even be clearly formulated – without the conceptual framework of game theory. Arrow's impossibility theorem, which shows that attempts to combine disparate individual preferences into a "fair" and "democratic" social choice are foredoomed to failure, was dealt with at length in section 10.5 and will not be discussed again in this chapter. Newcomb's problem, which also falls into this class, will be discussed in section 12.3, and the problem of the evolution and stability of moral principles, which was discovered through the application of game theory to ethics, will be discussed in section 12.6. A brief summary of the chapter will be given in section 12.7.

12.2 Rationality in games

The instrumental (*Zweckrationalität*) conception of rationality was strongly propounded by Scottish Enlightenment thinkers such as Adam Smith and David Hume. According to Hume (1739–1740), "reason is, and ought to be the slave of the passions" (p. 415), and "a passion can never, in any sense, be call'd unreasonable, but when founded on a false supposition, or when it chuses means insufficient for the design'd end" (p. 416). Two centuries later, Bertrand Russell (1954), clearly influenced by Hume, claimed that "'reason' has a perfectly clear and precise meaning. It signifies the choice of the right means to an end that you wish to achieve" (p. 8). This instrumental interpretation of rationality is favoured by many contemporary philosophers and game theorists, but we shall see that its meaning is not as clear and precise as Russell implied. First, philosophers have been struck by the mysterious way in which people manage to choose effectively in coordination games and have discussed the possibility that they may be using some mode of reasoning that enables them to achieve their ends by transcending the strictures of conventional rational choice theory. Second, a number of philosophers have drawn attention to the way in which the concept of rationality appears to break down in social dilemmas with the underlying strategic structure of the Prisoner's Dilemma game and the N-person Prisoner's Dilemma game.

12.2.1 Coordination games

Coordination games are problems of interdependent decision making in which there is agreement among the decision makers as to their preferences for the possible outcomes, so that their sole objective is to coordinate their strategies in such a way as to obtain an outcome that they both (or all) favour (see section 3.2). How rational decision makers should set about achieving their ends in these games raises deep philosophical problems that have been addressed (among others) by Lewis (1969, pp. 24–36); Gauthier (1975); Heal (1978); Gilbert (1989); Sugden (1991, pp. 774–778); and Bicchieri (1993, chap. 2).

Consider the game Head On, introduced in section 1.1.1. Two people (Players I and II), walking briskly towards each other along a narrow corridor, heading for a collision that they would both prefer to avoid, have to decide simultaneously whether to swerve left, swerve right, or keep going straight ahead. If both keep going straight ahead, or if both swerve to the same side of the corridor, then they will collide; all other strategy combinations lead to non-collision outcomes, which they both prefer. To make things easier for the players, and to clarify the discussion that follows, let us suppose that the players are able to discuss the problem in advance, although they cannot make binding and enforceable agreements (the game is *non-cooperative* in the technical sense). It may seem obvious that they should agree on a pair of strategies designed to avert a collision and that they should then both honour the agreement by doing what they agreed to do. But, on reflection, it is by no means obvious that this is a *rational* way to behave.

Because we are seeking a rational basis for action, we must accept the standard game theory assumption of *common knowledge of rationality*. That is, we must assume not only that the description of the game, including the players' preferences, is known by both of them, but also that both are rational in the sense of always acting to maximize their own expected utilities, and (crucially) that each player not only knows all this but also knows that the other player knows it, and so on. But under this assumption it turns out that the players have no reason to honour any agreement that they might reach, which means that they are in reality unable to reach any meaningful agreement in the first place.

The fact that a player may have *agreed* to swerve left (for example) does not on its own provide any rational reason why that player should *in fact* swerve left when the time comes to move. The only rational reason for action is expected utility maximization, and honouring an agreement to swerve left maximizes expected utility only if the other player also honours the agreement. It would certainly be rational for Player I to honour the agreement if Player II were likely to honour it, but under the assumption of common knowledge of rationality Player II would have reason to honour it only if Player I were likely to honour it, and we are stuck in an infinite regress without either player having any adequate basis for rational choice. Rationality is self-defeating in this game, because it is obvious that if Player I knew that Player II had an *irrational* propensity to honour non-binding agreements unconditionally, then Player I would have a *rational* reason for honouring the agreement, and coordination would be achieved without difficulty.

Empirical evidence (summarized in section 3.2) shows that, although coordination failures are by no means unknown, players often succeed in coordinating their strategies without apparent difficulty. For example, in the game Heads or Tails two people are invited to choose heads or tails independently, knowing that if and only if they both call heads or both call tails they will both win. Schelling (1960, chap. 3) found that no fewer than 86 per cent of his American subjects chose heads, and Mehta, Starmer, and Sugden (1994) found that 87 per cent of their British subjects chose heads. The above discussion suggests that the players must be using some mode of thought that transcends our current conceptions of rationality. The widely accepted explanation for their successful coordination is Schelling's concept of *salience*: heads has some kind of conventional priority over tails that enables players to recognize heads as a *focal point,* and the evidence suggests that most coordination games have focal points that the players recognize as salient, expect their co-player(s) to recognize as salient, expect their co-player(s) to expect them to recognize as salient, and so on. In Head On the salient strategy is probably swerving to the left in the United Kingdom and its former colonies and swerving to the right in most other countries, because of the obvious analogy with the rule of the road for vehicular traffic. The fact of the matter is that people often succeed in choosing effective strategies without apparent difficulty in coordination games, even in vastly more difficult games than Head On or Heads or Tails, even when they can coordinate only by choosing appropriately from among very many available strategies (see section 3.2).

Jane Heal (1978) pointed out that choosing a salient strategy seems intuitively to be the rational thing to do. The players "know that they can co-ordinate their choices only if they can single out one [strategy] from the rest". They also know that "by choosing a [strategy] which does stand out for both of them, and *only* by doing this, can they hope to co-ordinate. This provides a reason for each to make the choice of the outstanding [strategy], which is reinforced by knowledge that the other also has that reason" (p. 129, italics in original). Various commentators (e.g., Gilbert, 1989; Sugden, 1991) pointed out that the problem with this line of argument is to explain why it is rational for a player to choose a salient strategy without any reason for assuming that the other player will also choose the salient strategy, aside from the knowledge that the other player confronts the same dilemma. The fact that choosing a salient strategy has a powerful intuitive appeal does not, in itself, constitute a rational reason for choosing it.

Margaret Gilbert (1989) argued vigorously that "mere salience is *not* enough to provide rational agents with a reason for action (though it would obviously be nice, from the point of view of rational agency, if it did)" (p. 69, Gilbert's italics). Gilbert admitted that she was quite surprised when she found herself driven to this conclusion, but the conclusion is correct. The point is that although it is obviously true that the players succeed in coordinating if they both choose the same salient strategy, and although it is true by definition that successful coordination is a good outcome for them, that does not provide them with any rational grounds for behaving in that way. As Gilbert put it, "the fact that a good outcome would be reached if *both* did something cannot by itself be a reason for either one individually why he should do it. For his doing it cannot ensure that the other does it" (p. 72, Gilbert's italics). Thus, "if human beings are – happily – guided by salience, it appears that this is not a consequence of their rationality" (p. 61). David Lewis (1969, pp. 35–37) also concluded that there is no rational basis for choosing a salient strategy, but he argued that people have a natural tendency to choose salient strategies as a last resort, when they have no stronger grounds for choice.

12.2.2 Prisoner's Dilemma games

A number of philosophers, including Rescher (1975); Davis (1977); Hollis (1979); Tuck (1979); Williams (1979); Parfit (1979a, 1979b, 1984, chaps 2–5); Campbell (1985); McClennen (1985, 1994); Watkins (1985); Gauthier (1986); and Bicchieri (1993, chap. 5), have discussed the untoward consequences of rational utility maximization in social interactions with the underlying strategic structure of the Prisoner's Dilemma game (section 6.7), the *N*-person Prisoner's Dilemma (section 9.5), or social dilemmas in general. In these games, rationality seems once again to be self-defeating.

A brief resumé of the story from which the Prisoner's Dilemma game (PDG) derives its name is as follows. Two people, arrested and charged with involvement in a serious crime that they did, in fact, commit, are held in separate cells and prevented from communicating with each other. The police can obtain a conviction only if at least one of the them discloses certain incriminating evidence. Each prisoner is faced with a choice between concealing the evidence (*C*) and disclosing it (*D*). If both conceal the evidence (or cooperate), both will be acquitted; if both disclose it (or defect), both will be convicted; if only one prisoner discloses it, that prisoner will be acquitted and given a reward, and the prisoner who conceals it will receive an especially heavy sentence. The best outcome from each prisoner's point of view is acquittal plus reward, the second best is acquittal without reward, the third best is conviction, and the worst is conviction coupled with an especially heavy sentence. These payoffs are assumed to take into account the players' moral attitudes towards obstructing the course of justice, betraying a comrade, and so on; for some people the payoffs would not correspond to the Prisoner's Dilemma game.

The ends that the prisoners wish to achieve are the best possible outcomes from their own points of view, but what are the right means to these ends? Or, to put it differently, what would be a rational choice for each of the prisoners in this situation? Each might reason as follows: "If my partner chooses *C*, then the right means to the end that I wish to achieve is to choose *D*, because I shall get the best possible payoff by choosing it. If, on the other hand, my partner chooses *D*, then the right means to my end is again for me to choose *D*, because in that case I shall avoid the worst possible payoff by choosing it. Therefore, whatever strategy my partner chooses, it must be rational for me to choose *D*." But if both prisoners reason in this way (on the basis of strategic *dominance*) they will both be convicted, whereas if both opt "irrationally" for *C* they will both be acquitted and will achieve their desired ends more effectively. There is evidently a genuine problem of interpreting rationality in this game, which can, of course, crop up in many different two-person and multi-person contexts in which there is a choice between cooperation (*C*) and defection (*D*), apart from the hypothetical story outlined above (see sections 6.7, 9.4, and 9.5).

Some philosophers have offered spurious solutions to the problem. Rescher (1975), for example, discussed the dilemma at considerable length and concluded that "the parties were entrapped in the 'dilemma' because they did not internalize the welfare of their fellows sufficiently. If they do this, and do so in sufficient degree, they can escape the dilemmatic situation" (p. 48). This is the gist of Rescher's argument:

> The PDG presents a problem for the conventional view of rationality only when we have been dragooned into assuming the stance of the theory of games itself (p. 34). ... To *disregard* the interests of others is not rational but inhuman. And there is nothing *irrational* about construing our self-interest in a larger sense that also takes the interests of others into account (p. 39). ... Looked upon in its proper perspective, the prisoner's dilemma offers the moral philosopher nothing novel. Its shock-effect for students of political economy inheres solely in their ill-advised approach to *rationality* in terms of prudential pursuit of selfish advantage (p. 40). ... When we *internalize* the interests of others, the calculations of self-interest will generally lead to results more closely attuned to the general interests of the group. (p. 46, Rescher's italics throughout)

This argument rests on a fundamental misunderstanding of the nature and role of the payoffs in game theory, and it contains, in addition, an important *non sequitur*. First, the correction of the misunderstanding will be quite instructive. There is no assumption in game theory that the players' utilities, represented by the payoffs in the matrix, are based on a disregard of each other's interests. On the contrary, the utilities are assumed to reflect the players' preferences taking all things (including the "welfare of their fellows") into account as their tastes, consciences, and moral principles dictate. The PDG represents a particular pattern of preferences that can arise from altruism or selfishness or any other dispositions or motives. Rescher treats the payoffs in the PDG matrix as "raw, first-order utilities" and then proceeds to transform them into "'cooked', other-considering, second-order ones" (p. 46) in order to neutralize the dilemma. But "raw" utilities do not exist; the payoff matrix always serves them ready-cooked.

The *non sequitur* is that, even if "cooking" the utilities in a particular matrix could eliminate the PDG structure (as Rescher demonstrates mathematically), it does not follow that such cooking, if thorough enough, would "generally" allow the players to "escape the dilemmatic situation". It could easily be shown, in fact, that many non-dilemma payoff matrices would become PDGs only after the utilities have been thoroughly cooked, whereupon the problem of defining rationality would be back with a vengeance.

Tuck (1979) tried to exorcize the *N*-person Prisoner's Dilemma (NPD), which he calls the "free-rider problem", in a different way. His solution is also illusory, though for quite different reasons from those that apply to Rescher. A simple example of an NPD, applicable to people with gardens, will suffice for the discussion that follows. During a drought, one has to decide whether to water one's garden or to exercise restraint. One is better off as an individual (we may assume) watering one's garden, all things considered, whether all, or some, or none of the other members of the community water their own gardens, so watering one's garden is the "right means to an end" that one wishes to achieve. Restraint on the part of one person is unnecessary if most of the others exercise restraint, and it is futile if they do not. But if all members of the community reason in this way, then everyone ends up worse off than if all "irrationally" exercise restraint, because the water supply then dries up completely. This is obviously a multi-person generalization of the PDG in which there is once again a cooperative (C) strategy and a defecting (D) one, and it too arises in a wide variety of other contexts (see sections 9.4 and 9.5).

According to Tuck (1979), the dilemma is connected with the ancient *Sorites paradox*. A simple version of the Sorites paradox goes as follows. One stone is clearly not a heap of stones, and the addition of one stone to something that is not a heap can never transform it into a heap; therefore there can never be a heap of stones and it would be futile to try to build one. A similar argument can be used to prove that all men are bald or that all men are hairy. Tuck pinpointed what he claimed to be the crux of the NPD in the following version of the Sorites paradox. The water consumption of one person cannot transform a non-critical shortage into a critical one, and no matter how much water is being used by other members of the community the consumption of one more person cannot make all the difference. It *seems*, therefore, that the water shortage can never become critical and that there is no point in exercising restraint, just as it *seems* that a heap of stones can never be built and that it is futile to try to build one. Tuck's conclusion is that the NPD "is not one that should be taken seriously; we have seen that it is connected with a *paradox*, and the essence of paradoxes is that their conclusions should not be believed (for if they were, they would cease to be paradoxes, and become merely good arguments)" (p. 154, Tuck's italics). In Tuck's view, logicians have not yet developed the necessary formal equipment for dealing with the Sorites paradox (and therefore also the NPD), but that is a problem that need not detain a busy philosopher.

There are two comments worth making about this plausible argument. The first is that it is debatable, to say the least, whether the Sorites is genuinely paradoxical or merely sophistical. A more important point is that the whole argument collapses in the two-person (PDG) version of the dilemma, or for that matter in NPDs with very few players. With just one other player or only a few, it clearly does (or is quite likely to) make all the difference whether the individual cooperates or defects, but the dilemma is in no way diminished. Even if the Sorites is genuinely paradoxical, therefore, its relevance to the NPD is evidently tenuous.

Martin Hollis (1979) attempted to sharpen and clarify the concept of rationality in the light of the NPD. He argued that rationality ought to be defined in terms of what is objectively the best way to achieve a certain end, and not in terms of what a person may believe is the best way. According to Hollis, a person P acts rationally in choosing a course of action x if and only if the following three conditions are satisfied: (a) of all the possible courses of action available, x is likeliest to realize a goal g; (b) it is in P's objective interest to realize g; and (c) P's reasons for choosing x are the conditions labelled (a) and (b). It would not be rational for P to choose x merely because of an internal *belief* that x is the best way of achieving g, or because P had an internal *desire* to achieve g; P must choose x for the specified external reasons, because if we do not have external criteria of rationality, then the basis for classifying certain deluded people as mentally ill falls away. It follows from Hollis's argument that a person P acts rationally in the NPD if P chooses to defect (to ignore the call for restraint during the drought) and P's reason for doing so is that defecting is likeliest to realize the desired goal. If this conclusion is accepted, then a community of rational individuals ends up worse off than a community of irrationalists, but the argument sidesteps the central problem of the NPD, namely the tension between individual and collective rationality.

Bernard Williams (1979) took issue with Hollis's theory of rationality. The attempt to define rationality according to external objective criteria fails, according to Williams, because a person's reasons for performing an action are necessarily internal. If a person P believes that the liquid in a certain bottle is gin when in fact it is petrol, and if P wants a gin and tonic, then P acts rationally, relative to the false belief, by mixing the liquid with tonic and drinking it, in spite of the fact that it is not in P's objective interest to do so. Hollis tried to specify external reasons for actions, but external reason statements, "when definitely isolated as such, are false, incoherent, or really something else misleadingly expressed" (p. 19). Williams concluded that it is not necessarily irrational to cooperate in an NPD. It is rational for a person to cooperate even for purely selfish reasons in some NPDs when "reaching the critical number of those doing C is sensitive to his doing C, or he has reason to think this" (p. 27). A small NPD or a PDG would presumably meet this requirement. According to Williams, it can be rational to choose cooperatively even if this requirement is not met, and it is rational for a society to educate people to have cooperative motivations in strategic interactions of the NPD type.

Derek Parfit (1979a, 1979b, 1984, chaps 2–5) approached the problem from a different angle but came to the same conclusion as Williams, that cooperation in the PDG or NPD can be a rational course of action. He focused on the central problem, namely that principles of action such as "self-interest theory", "common-sense morality", and "consequentialism", which all involve performing those acts that best achieve the ends we feel we ought to achieve, are self-defeating in two-person and multi-person social dilemmas. If all people successfully follow any of these principles, their ends are worse achieved than if none do so. Parfit outlined various possible solutions to social dilemmas. One class of solutions would involve changing the rules of the game or the players' payoff functions to make defection impossible or unprofitable. Heavy fines for watering one's garden during a drought, coupled with intensive policing, could change the strategic structure of the underlying game so that it ceased to be an NPD. These are "political" solutions, and in Parfit's view they are often undesirable. Sometimes they are infeasible: in the case of the international nuclear arms race there is no government with the power to change the rules or the payoff structure of the game or to enforce cooperation. But Parfit argued that it is better, where possible, to find ways of making people want to cooperate for moral reasons in spite of the existence of the dilemma and an absence of coercion; these he called "moral" solutions. How, then, are we to achieve moral solutions? "Prisoner's Dilemmas need to be explained. So do their moral solutions. Both have been too little understood" (1979b, p. 544). A unified theory based on common-sense morality and consequentialism "would be more demanding than Common-sense Morality, as it now is", but "its demands may not be either unreasonable or unrealistic" (1984, p. 114).

12.3 Newcomb's problem

Newcomb's problem (or Newcomb's paradox), which first appeared in print in 1969, is one of the most perplexing problems of rational choice, and many philosophers believe that it has important implications for our under-standing of the much older problem of free will and determinism. It is named after William A. Newcomb, a theoretical physicist who discovered it in 1960 while pondering the paradox of the Prisoner's Dilemma game. It was published several years later by the Harvard University philosopher Robert Nozick (1969), who admitted in a footnote that he felt diffident about publishing it in view of the fact that he did not discover it and had not made much progress in working through it, but he added: "It is a beautiful problem. I wish it were mine".

Publication of Newcomb's problem stirred a wide-ranging philosophical debate, among the most interesting contributions to which have been the following: Nozick (1969, 1973, 1993); Bar-Hillel and Margalit (1972); Schlesinger (1974); Cargile (1975); Levi (1975); Brams (1976, chap. 8); Locke (1978); Lewis (1979); Eells (1984); Campbell (1985); Campbell and Sowden (1985); Sobel, (1991a, 1991b); Jacobi (1993); Malinas (1993); Hurley (1991, 1994). Only a few of the central issues can be sketched in the space available here.

In its clearest form, the problem is as follows. On the table in front of you are two boxes. One of them is transparent and in it you can see $1000; the other is opaque and may or may not contain $1 million. You are offered the choice of taking either just the opaque box, or both it and the transparent box. Whether or not the opaque box contains $1 million depends on a predictor of human behaviour, which we may assume to be a highly sophisticated computer, although it could just as well be a psychologist who has made a detailed study of your behaviour patterns, a psychic with precognitive powers, or even God. You are told, and you believe, that the predictor has already put either $1 million or nothing into the opaque box depending on its prediction of whether you will take both boxes or only the opaque one. It has put $1 million in the opaque box if and only if it has predicted that you will take that box only and not the transparent box as well, and that you will not use a mixed strategy of randomizing by spinning a coin, for example. Finally, you know from the predictor's past record in predicting people's behaviour in this situation that it is correct in most cases – let us assume that is right in 95 per cent of cases, although the exact figure is immaterial. The two alternatives from which the choice is to be made and the possible payoffs associated with each are shown in Matrix 12.1. What is the rational strategy in this situation? The problem is that both alternatives can be supported by simple and apparently irrefutable arguments, and decision theorists are split over which is the rational solution.

The argument for taking only the opaque box is based on the principle of *expected utility maximization* (or more simply *expected payoff maximization*). If you take both boxes, the predictor will probably have predicted that you would do that and therefore have left the opaque box empty, so you will probably get only $1000, whereas if you take only the opaque box, the predictor will probably have predicted that and have left $1 million in it. Therefore, you will probably receive a much higher payoff by taking the opaque box only.

Matrix 12.1 *Newcomb's Problem*

Predictor

	Only opaque box will be taken	Both boxes will be taken
Taken only opaque box	$1m	$0
Take both boxes	$1m + $1000	$1000

Chooser

The argument for taking both boxes is based on the *dominance* principle, or more specifically on the fact that the strategy of taking both boxes is strictly dominant. The predictor has already made its prediction, so there either is or is not $1 million in the opaque box, and if it is there, your choice cannot make it disappear. In either case your payoff is $1000 higher if you take both boxes than if you take only the opaque box. If there is $1 million in the opaque box, you get $1,001,000 by taking both boxes but $1000 less if you take the opaque box only. If the opaque box is empty, you get $1000 by taking both boxes but nothing if you take the opaque box only. In other words, you are certain to be $1000 better of by taking both boxes rather than just the opaque box whether or not there is $1 million in the opaque box.

According to some philosophers (e.g., Hurley, 1994; Sobel, 1991b), the two principles of reasoning should not be described as expected utility versus dominance, but as maximizing *evidential* expected utility versus maximizing *causal* expected utility. On the evidential view, people who take just the opaque box tend to get rich, whereas people who take both do not. It would be good news to discover that you are the kind of person who takes just the opaque box, because this would mean that the predictor had probably put $1 million in it and that you were probably about to become rich. The causal argument is that refraining from taking the transparent box cannot cause $1 million to appear in the opaque box, so you may as well take both. This is clarified in the *smoking gene case*: if, as a few experts believe, smoking behaviour is caused by a gene that also causes lung cancer, it would be bad news to discover that you are a smoker, because this would mean that you are probably going to contract lung cancer, but it would be futile to give up smoking on that account because doing so cannot cause you to escape your fate, so you may as well continue to enjoy smoking, because smoking is merely symptomatic of having the cancer gene. The evidential argument has no force in this case, and in Newcomb's problem taking both boxes could be considered symptomatic in essentially the same sense that smoking is symptomatic in the smoking gene case.

However they are labelled, both arguments seem irresistible, but logically they cannot both be right because they are mutually contradictory. Nozick (1969) commented that most people who think about this problem consider the rational strategy to be perfectly clear and obvious, but they are divided as to which strategy they see as obviously rational and which one obviously irrational. A few years later, Nozick (1974) pointed out that, because both arguments are so powerful, the real problem is not to show why one of them is right but to show why one of them is wrong. He also revealed that, out of 148 letters received by the *Scientific American* magazine after the problem was discussed there (Gardner, 1973), 60 per cent were in favour of taking only the opaque box.

It has been pointed out many times (e.g., Brams, 1975; Campbell, 1985; Davis, 1977; Hurley, 1991; Lewis, 1979; Nozick, 1969, 1993; Sobel, 1991b) that Newcomb's problem is closely related to the Prisoner's Dilemma game. David Lewis went as far as to say that "to call them 'related' is an understatement. Considered as puzzles about rationality, or disagreements between two conceptions thereof, they are one and the same problem" (p. 235). But this is clearly an overstatement, because the Prisoner's Dilemma game is by definition a two-person strategic interaction in which both players' payoffs are specified according to a particular ordinal pattern (see section 6.7), whereas Newcomb's problem is really a one-person game against Nature. Steven Brams showed that in order to convert Newcomb's problem into a Prisoner's Dilemma game, certain extra assumptions have to be made. But it is true that the two problems share a strong family resemblance. In particular, they are both highly paradoxical and they are the only two instances (that I am aware of) in which a dominant strategy exists but its choice is not obviously rational, and the pattern of payoffs of Newcomb's problem (see Matrix 12.1) conforms to the ordinal structure of one player's side of a Prisoner's Dilemma game.

No universally acceptable solution to Newcomb's problem has emerged from the voluminous debate that has surrounded it. If no flaw can be found in either the expected utility or the dominance argument, then it may be necessary to conclude that the assumptions built into the problem are incoherent. Nozick (1974) reported that 11 per cent of correspondents to the *Scientific American* believed that the problem's conditions were impossible or inconsistent or that the predictor could not exist because the assumption that it does leads to a logical contradiction. Certain classes of events may be unpredictable *in principle* when the predictions interact with the events predicted. This conclusion would have important implications for philosophical conceptions of determinism and free will, which have been controversial for centuries and are unlikely to be resolved in the near future.

12.4 Kant's categorical imperative

In modern philosophy, the most prominent alternative to Humean instrumental rationality is the conception of rationality put forward by Immanuel
Kant (1785). Kant's categorical imperative greatly clarifies the paradox at the
heart of social dilemmas and even suggests a possible rational and moral
solution to them. Game theory, for its part, can help to clarify the ideas
behind the categorical imperative, which has generated seemingly endless
debates among philosophers about its precise meaning (see, for example, the
critical essays reprinted in Wolff, 1968, pp. 211–336).

Kant accepted the Humean conception of instrumental rationality, which
he identified with his *hypothetical imperatives*, but he argued for the existence
of an additional and quite separate form of rationality that leads to
categorical imperatives. In Kant's writings, a maxim is a personal rule of
conduct (equivalent to an "ought" statement), and it is a hypothetical
imperative if it takes the form "If you want X, then do Y" (equivalent to "If
you want X, then you ought to do Y"), assuming that Y is the only or the
best means of obtaining X. Notice that the reason for doing Y is contingent
on your desire for X. A maxim is a categorical imperative if it takes the form
"Always do Y" (or "You ought always to do Y"), where the reason for doing
Y is not contingent on any desire, that is to say, Y is not your means of
obtaining some end that you desire. A categorical imperative is intended not
only to be rational, but also to serve as a fundamental principle of morality.
Kant gave various different formulations of his categorical imperative, but
his first formulation, which is the one most often quoted, is this: "Act only
on such a maxim that you can at the same time will to become a universal
law" (Kant, 1785, p. 52).

In his earlier *Critique of Pure Reason*, Kant scorned concrete examples as
the "go-carts of philosophy", but in his *Grundlegung* and his *Critique of
Practical Reason* he supplied some examples to illustrate his categorical
imperative. The clearest is a negative example of a maxim that is irrational
and therefore cannot be a categorical imperative: "Always borrow money
when in need and promise to pay it back without any intention of keeping
the promise" (1785, p. 54). One cannot rationally will this maxim to be a
universal law, because it cannot be universalized without generating a
contradiction. If everybody habitually broke promises, then there could be
no promises because nobody would believe them. People could utter the
words "I promise" but these words would express only an intention, not a
true promise, because a promise needs a promisee as well as a promiser, and
there would be no promisees. To will the maxim to be a universal law thus
leads to a logical contradiction: if everybody habitually broke promises then
nobody could do so because promises would have ceased to exist.

All of Kant's other examples are regarded as obscure. Is it rational, for
example, to adopt the maxim of always refusing to help others who are in

need or distress, provided one does not (inconsistently) demand help from others? A state of affairs in which this is a universal law is certainly possible in theory – and it is not difficult to imagine – but according to Kant it is impossible for a person to will this maxim to be a universal law, because "a will that decided in this way would be at variance with itself. ... By such a law of nature sprung from his own will, he would rob himself of all hope of the help he wants for himself" (1785, p. 56). Kant clearly perceived some kind of inconsistency here, but what exactly he meant by "a will at variance with itself" is not transparent. Why does a person's will become inconsistent when universalized in cases of this type?

When formulated in game theory terms, Kant's remarks become somewhat clearer. The players in a game are, by definition, motivated to achieve what each considers to be the best outcome. For games that are symmetric – games that are the same from the point of view of both or every player – a categorical imperative can be formulated as follows: "Assuming that you could will a single strategy to be chosen by all of the players, choose the one that would yield the best outcome". In a social dilemma, only a cooperative choice is rational according to the categorical imperative, because the alternative defecting choice, if universalized, is at variance with everyone's interests, and the outcome would be recognized as bad by any rational person. In other words, although it is better from the perspective of each individual player to defect (for example by making false promises) whether or not the other player(s) defect(s), it would be irrational to will that *every* player should defect, because a universally cooperative outcome is clearly better for everyone than a universally defecting one, irrespective of any individual's desires. This nicely captures the inconsistency that Kant probably had in mind, and incidentally shows how difficult it was for him to formulate an essentially strategic problem without the conceptual framework of game theory.

An unexpected and neglected feature of the categorical imperative is that it prescribes selfish rather than altruistic behaviour in some types of strategic interactions. An unambiguous example is the Battle of the Sexes game (see section 6.5). A man and a woman have to choose between two options for an evening's entertainment. The man prefers one of the options and the woman the other, but each would rather go out together than alone. If both opt altruistically for their less preferred alternatives, then each ends up attending a disliked entertainment alone, whereas if both choose selfishly, then each has a somewhat more enjoyable evening out. According to the categorical imperative, the players ought to adopt a selfish maxim in the Battle of the Sexes, because the only other rule that could be universalized would be an altruistic maxim, which would yield an obviously worse joint outcome. But this example also reveals a limitation of the categorical imperative, because the outcome would be better still, from both players' viewpoints, if one player acted on an altruistic maxim and the other on a selfish one, so that they could spend the evening together rather than alone, but this outcome is asymmetric and therefore could not be a universal law, quite apart from its obvious unfairness. Would it be irrational for the man or the woman to act on an altruistic maxim and at the same time will that the other person should choose selfishly? The categorical imperative seems persuasive from a rational and a moral perspective only in games with symmetric equilibrium points in which strategies can therefore be sensibly universalized.

Kant's ideas, especially his concept of universalizability, have been developed and modified in many ways by linguistic philosophers, rule utilitarians and others. For discussions of these developments, see Gewirth (1984) and Singer (1963, 1988).

12.5 Plato, Hobbes, Rousseau: social contract theories

The awful outcomes of the pursuit of individual self-interest in social dilemmas could be avoided if the rules were amended to turn them into cooperative games with binding and enforceable agreements. This would be in everyone's interest, because mutually cooperative behaviour would then be virtually assured and every player's payoffs would be improved. A number of influential philosophers have tried to solve social dilemmas in this way through *social contracts*.

The first philosophical discussion of a social contract theory can be found in a brief passage in *The Republic* of Plato, written about 380 BC, near the beginning of Book II, where Glaucon maintains that "self-interest [is] the motive that all men naturally follow if they are not forcibly restrained by law and made to respect each other's claims" (Bk. II, para. 359). As a consequence of this, Plato (through Glaucon) argues that "laws and mutual agreements" are necessary:

> This is the origin and nature of justice. It is a compromise between what is most desirable, to do wrong and avoid punishment, and what is most undesirable, to suffer wrong without redress; justice and right lie between these two and are accepted not as being good in themselves, but as having a relative value through preventing us from doing wrong. For anyone who had the power to do wrong and called himself a man would never make such an agreement with anyone – he would be mad if he did. (Bk. II, para. 359)

One of the most influential proponents of the social contract was Thomas Hobbes, especially in chapters 13 to 17 of *Leviathan*, first published in 1651, in which he discussed the unhappy consequences of an unregulated society: "Hereby it is manifest, that during the time men live without a common Power to keep them all in awe, they are in that condition which is called Warre; and such a warre, as is of every man, against every man" (chap. 13).

According to Hobbes, the natural desire for self-preservation and a decent life gives people a reason so seek cooperative solutions to social dilemmas. But in what we would now call social dilemmas, in which selfish motives lead to defecting choices, there is insufficient incentive to cooperate unless there is a general agreement to cooperate, and even if such an agreement exists, no one has a reason to abide by it unless it is binding and is backed up by some coercive mechanism of enforcement. This, Hobbes argued, must be a political sovereign whom everyone undertakes to obey and who is invested with the necessary power to punish non-cooperators. Hobbes imagined a state of nature in which there is no industry, no agriculture, no arts, literature, or society, "and which is worst of all, continuall feare, and danger of violent death; And the life of man, solitary, poore, nasty, brutish, and short" (chap. 13). In this state of nature, people come together to improve the lamentable state of affairs by setting up a civil society based on a social contract backed by a sovereign power.

There is a continuing debate in the literature of rational choice theory in general and game theory in particular about Hobbes's social contract, although one contributor to this debate felt that "rational choice theory reaps a good deal less than Hobbes attempted to sow and serves to obscure more than illuminate his teaching" (Neal, 1988, p. 635). For more positive contributions, see McLean (1981), Hampton (1986), Kavka (1986), Taylor (1987), and especially Slomp and La Manna (1993), who interpret Hobbes's state of nature as a multi-person game of Chicken.

Jean-Jacques Rousseau's *The Social Contract*, first published in 1762, pursued social contract theory a good deal further, but some of the pivotal ideas in it are generally considered to be opaque or inconsistent. The "fundamental problem to which the social contract provides a solution", according to Rousseau, is "to find a form of association that defends and protects, with the whole common force, the person and goods of each member, and in which each, by uniting with all, obeys only himself and remains as free as before" (Bk. I, chap. vi).

Great confusion has arisen from Rousseau's emphatic distinction between the *general will*, which the social contract is intended to promote, and the *will of all*, which he says is frequently in opposition to it: "There is often a great difference between the will of all and the general will; the latter regards only the common interest; the former regards private interests, and is merely the sum of particular desires" (Bk. II, chap. iii). Commentators have had difficulty explaining how the common interest can be anything other than the sum of private interests. As Runciman and Sen (1965) were apparently the first to point out, the distinction becomes transparent when couched in the framework of game theory. In a social dilemma, it is in the "private interest" of each player to defect, but it is in their "common interest" to cooperate. If the players have regard only to their private interests, then the result is joint defection, which reflects "merely the sum of particular desires". But if they form a social contract through which joint cooperation can be ensured, then "each, by uniting with all" enjoys the better outcome.

But this is not as straightforward as it seems. If a purely voluntary agreement is reached, then it may still be in the interest of an individual to defect, provided that the act of breaking the agreement is not too disagreeable; a person may prefer the outcome of defecting irrespective of how few or how many of the others cooperate. In other words, the voluntary agreement may leave the underlying strategic structure of the social dilemma intact. And if all players pursue their private interests by defecting in spite of the agreement, the agreement will collapse.

It follows from this that the players may be willing to enter into a binding contract in which joint cooperation is enforced by coercive means, as Hobbes suggested. To return to an earlier example, even if most people are disposed to defect from a voluntary agreement by watering their gardens during a drought, they may realize that each of them would be better off under a system of enforced cooperation, because universal cooperation is better for each person than universal defection. It is presumably this idea that lies behind Rousseau's seemingly paradoxical remarks about enforcement:

> Man is born free, and everywhere he is in chains (Bk I, chap. i). ... In order that the social contract should not be a vain formula, it tacitly includes an undertaking, which alone can give force to the others, that whoever refuses to obey the general will shall be constrained by the whole body: this means nothing other than that one forces him to be free (Bk. I, chap. vii). ... The undertakings that bind us to the social body are obligatory only because they are mutual, and their nature is such that in fulfilling them we cannot work for others without working also for ourselves. (Bk. II, chap. iv)

Interpreted with the help of game theory and especially social dilemmas, Rousseau's remarks about enforcement become perfectly lucid. A binding agreement among the players to cooperate, with coercive means of enforcement, seems the only way to protect the interests of all players when moral solutions cannot be relied on, that is to say when all or many would otherwise be disposed to defect. The players would actively desire to be constrained in this way if they were rational, because the constraint would guarantee a better outcome for everyone. People can improve the quality of their lives by freely choosing to put themselves in chains. "Mutual coercion mutually agreed upon" (Hardin, 1968, p. 1247) is in the rational self-interest of the participants in social dilemmas, which are ubiquitous in everyday life (see sections 9.4 and 9.5). Enforced cooperation improves the payoffs of the players; by fulfilling their obligations they serve their own interests as well as the interests of others. The many translators who have rendered Rousseau's opening sentence "Man is born free, *but* everywhere he is in chains" (italics added) are not the only readers to have misunderstood his subtle point.

One of the most perplexing aspects of Rousseau's views on the social contract is his opposition to political parties and other interest groups within the community: "It is important, therefore, in order to have a good expression of the general will, that there should be no partial association within the state, and that each citizen should think of himself alone" (Bk. II, chap. iii). Farquharson (1969, pp. 77–80) provided a rationale, based on the theory of coalition formation in cooperative games and strategic voting, by which Rousseau's hostility to political parties might be explained. A simpler rationale than Farquharson's will now be given in terms of coalition formation in a cooperative version of the Dollar Auction game, although one of the multi-person cooperative games discussed in chapter 8 could just as well have been chosen.

The rules of the Dollar Auction game, discussed in detail in section 9.3, are (briefly) as follows. Several players bid for a dollar bill according to the usual conventions of auctions, except that the highest bidder and the second-highest bidder have to pay the auctioneer amounts corresponding to their last bids and only the highest bidder receives the dollar bill in return. In a "state of nature", as Rousseau calls it, when there is no social contract, it is impossible for any player to enter the bidding without running the risk of substantial loss. But, by popular vote, the players might adopt a social contract, according to which one player, nominated in advance, bids 1 cent while the others are forbidden to bid, and the resulting 99-cent prize is divided equally among all the players. This reflects the general will in so far as there is no other outcome that is better for everyone, so the social contract would be supported by all rational players. (In conventional auctions in Britain, coordinated bidding by prior arrangement is illegal in terms of the Auction Bidding Agreements Act of 1937, precisely because it gives the bidders a big advantage.)

Suppose, however, that the players split into political parties or factions, each proposing to modify the social contract to enable their own members to distribute the 99-cent prize among themselves alone. If the various proposals were put to a popular vote, then one of the parties would gain a majority and would be able to impose its will on the others. Its members would clearly benefit from this change, and the excluded players, being bound by the social contract, would be powerless to do anything about it; but it would evidently not reflect the general will. In Rousseau's words, when "partial associations form at the expense of the whole, the will of each of these associations becomes general in relation to its members, and particular in relation to the State" (Bk. II, chap. iii). The sense in which the social contract may be said to promote the general will, and partial associations to undermine it, is given a precise interpretation in this example, and the apparent inconsistencies in Rousseau's thinking are reconciled. (For a different interpretation of Rousseau's hostility to factions, see Grofman and Field, 1988.)

12.6 Evolution and stability of moral principles

In two important publications, John Mackie (1978, 1982) showed how the theory of evolutionary games (discussed in depth in chapter 11) can be used to explain the nature and evolution of existing moral principles and to indicate constraints that must be taken into account in proposing new moral principles that are intended to be workable in practice.

Moral principles are cultural rather than physical traits, and they are transmitted through human communication rather than through genetic inheritance. But there are some cultural traits that share certain dynamic properties in common with genes and are therefore subject to evolution through a kind of natural selection. This idea can be traced back to Karl Popper (1961), but its best known proponent is Richard Dawkins (1976, 1989). Dawkins called cultural traits that are subject to natural selection *memes* – a word designed to resemble "genes" – because they are sustained by memory and mimicry. Apart from moral principles, typical examples of memes are tunes, fashions, recipes, traditions, and theories.

Genes and memes are alike in the following respects. First, they are self-replicators: in suitable environments they produce multiple copies of themselves. But second, in the process of replication errors occur, and the new forms (mutants) also produce copies of themselves. Finally, a new form may be fitter or less fit than an established one, as measured by the number of copies that it produces, and only the fittest survive in the struggle for existence (compare the discussion of natural selection in section 11.2). Cultural evolution can, of course, proceed much more rapidly than biological evolution, because it is not limited by the reproduction rate of the species.

A meme will spread through a population rapidly if there is something about it that makes it better able than the available alternatives to infect people's minds, just as germs spread when they are able to infect people's bodies. This analogy draws attention to the fact that the fittest memes are not necessarily ones that benefit society as a whole. This distinguishes meme theory sharply from functionalist theories in sociology and social anthropology, which are based on the assumption that elements of a culture that are beneficial to the society are the only ones that can survive.

One of Mackie's key arguments can be summarized roughly as follows. Consider the altruistic moral principle of always helping other people who are in need or distress, which was discussed earlier in connection with Kant's categorical imperative. We may assume that the costs associated with helping others – in terms of time and energy expenditure, inconvenience, and so forth outweigh any direct and immediate benefits, such as feelings of satisfaction for having acted altruistically, but that these costs to the helper are generally less than the benefits to the person helped. A third necessary assumption is that people are rational in the instrumental sense discussed earlier: they try to choose the best means to the ends that they wish to achieve. Now in a society in which indiscriminate altruism was the ethical norm, an individual who adopted a purely selfish principle of accepting help but never offering it would receive a higher expected payoff, enjoying all the benefits but incurring none of the costs of indiscriminate altruism. This new selfish morality would therefore tend to be imitated by others and would spread until it had infected the whole population. In the terminology of evolutionary games, indiscriminate altruism would not be an *evolutionarily stable strategy* (ESS).

Intermediate between indiscriminate altruism and selfishness is the moral principle of *reciprocal altruism*: reciprocal altruists are willing to help only those who have not acted in a selfish manner towards them in the past. Mackie recognized that this principle corresponds to the tit for tat (TFT) programmed strategy in the PDG (see sections 7.5 and 11.5). In a society consisting initially of selfish individuals only, if the new moral principle of reciprocal altruism arose, it would spread through the population and wipe out the selfish morality. The expected payoffs to the reciprocal altruists would be higher because they would fare no worse in interactions with the selfish individuals but would do better than selfish individuals in interactions with their own kind. Natural selection therefore favours an ESS in which reciprocal altruism is the norm, and this, according to Mackie, is the moral principle that is in fact adopted by most people.

Christian teaching, of course, advocates indiscriminate altruism. It is therefore interesting to investigate the logical consequences, according to Mackie's theory, of indiscriminate altruism in a mixed population of reciprocal altruists and selfish individuals, a population perhaps in the process of evolving to a pure ESS of reciprocal altruism. It turns out that the introduction of indiscriminate altruists into this population would tend to shift the direction of evolution towards selfishness. This is because selfish individuals would get more out of interactions with the indiscriminate altruists than reciprocal altruists would; they would enjoy the benefits without incurring the costs. In other words, the presence of indiscriminate altruists endangers the healthy reciprocal altruist morality by enabling selfishness to prosper, and if the indiscriminate altruists were sufficiently numerous, the selfish strategy would be an ESS and both kinds of altruists would be wiped out. Selfishness is a relatively ineffective strategy in a population of reciprocal altruists, but it pays better than reciprocal altruism when there are enough indiscriminately altruistic "suckers" to take advantage of. According to Mackie (1978):

> This seems to provide fresh support for Nietzche's view of the deplorable influence of moralities of the Christian type. But in practice there may be little danger. After two thousand years of contrary moral teaching, reciprocal altruism is still dominant in all human societies. ... Saintliness is an effective topic for preaching, but with little practical persuasive force. (p. 464)

The evolutionary consequences of Christian morality in Mackie's theory provide a vivid illustration of what Popper (1969) described as "the *main task of the theoretical social sciences. It is to trace the unintended social repercussions of intentional human actions*" (p. 342, Popper's italics).

A considerable body of literature has developed around issues associated with the evolution and stability of cooperation, selfishness, and so on: see, for example, Gauthier (1986); Caporael, Dawes, Orbell, and van de Kragt (1989); Schssler (1990a, 1990b); Nowak and Sigmund (1993). If reciprocal altruism is interpreted as the TFT programmed strategy in PDG-type interactions, then it is clear that it is not, in fact, evolutionarily stable, although Mackie was correct in assuming that it is more robust than unconditional cooperation and unconditional defection (see section 11.5).

12.7 Summary

At the beginning of this chapter, several reasons were put forward to explain the fact that formal game theory seldom provides straightforward solutions to practical problems of strategy and that there are also important limitations to what can be said about moral problems within the conceptual framework of game theory, but it was argued that the theory can throw light on existing problems in philosophy and can also draw attention to previously unrecognized problems. In section 12.2, the concept of rationality was examined in the light of game theory. As it is normally interpreted by contemporary philosophers, rationality appears to break down in coordination games and social dilemmas with the strategic structure of the Prisoner's Dilemma or N-person Prisoner's Dilemma games. Several attempts by philosophers to come to grips with this and other related problems were critically reviewed. Section 12.3 centred on a paradox of rational choice with profound philosophical implications, namely Newcomb's problem, which was shown to be closely related to the Prisoner's Dilemma game. Section 12.4 dealt with Kant's categorical imperative as a principle of morality. Game theory elucidates Kant's essentially strategic ideas and also reveals some of their limitations. In section 12.5, the ideas of Plato, Hobbes, and Rousseau about the social contract were discussed. Game theory has been applied to these theories and in some cases has illuminated their fundamental ideas. Section 12.6 discussed the use of evolutionary games to explain the nature and development of existing moralities and to indicate certain constraints on any new moralities that might evolve.

Appendix: A simple proof of the minimax theorem

A.1 Introductory remarks

The minimax theorem lies at the heart of formal game theory; in fact, the genesis of game theory is often traced to its original proof by John von Neumann (1928). It is a remarkable mathematical discovery that is mentioned in most books on game theory but seldom proved, except in the more mathematical ones. In common with many people, I first encountered game theory in non-mathematical books, and I soon became intrigued by the minimax theorem but frustrated by the way the books tiptoed around it without proving it.

It seems reasonable to suppose that I am not the only person who has encountered this problem, but I have not found any source to which mathematically unsophisticated readers can turn for a proper understanding of the theorem, so I have attempted in the pages that follow to provide a simple, self-contained proof with each step spelt out as clearly as possible both in symbols and in words. The proof, which is very much shorter and simpler than von Neumann's, was worked out in collaboration with my mathematical colleague Roy Davies, who pointed out that it is really a variation on a well-known theme (see, e.g., Blackwell and Girshick, 1954). Non-mathematicians will find the argument much more explicit and therefore easier to follow than the standard presentations in mathematical textbooks; but elementary algebra and geometry are assumed, and a complete understanding requires some knowledge of the rudiments of probability theory and mathematical analysis.

A.2 Preliminary formalization

A finite, two-person, zero-sum game is specified by a rectangular array of numbers $[a_{ij}]$, called a *payoff matrix*, with m rows and n columns. The numbers are the payoffs to Player I, and because the game is zero-sum, Player II's payoffs are simply the negatives of these numbers. According to the rules of the game, Player I chooses a strategy corresponding to one of the rows, and simultaneously – or, what amounts to the same thing, in ignorance of I's choice – Player II chooses a strategy corresponding to one of the columns. The number at the intersection of the chosen row and column is the payoff to Player I. Thus if Player I chooses row i and Player II chooses column j, then the number a_{ij} at the intersection is the amount gained by Player I and lost by Player II; in other words, the amount a_{ij} is transferred from Player II to Player I. The payoff matrix and the rules of the game are assumed to be common knowledge: each player knows the specification of the game, and each knows that the other knows it, and so on.

Instead of deliberately selecting a *pure* strategy – a specific row or column – a player may use a randomizing device to choose among the strategies. A player with two pure strategies, for example, may choose one of them by tossing a coin. A player who chooses in this way is said to be using a *mixed strategy*. In general, a mixed strategy assigns a predetermined probability to each available pure strategy; in the coin-tossing example, for example, the assigned probabilities are $1/2$ and $1/2$. A mixed strategy can be represented by a string of non-negative numbers of length m (for Player I) or n (for Player II) that sum to 1. A mixed strategy for Player I can accordingly be written

$$(x) = (x_1, x_2, \ldots, x_m)$$

and a mixed strategy for Player II

$$(y) = (y_1, y_2, \ldots, y_n),$$

where $x_1 \geq 0, x_2 \geq 0, \ldots, x_m \geq 0; y_1 \geq 0, y_2 \geq 0, \ldots, y_n \geq 0; x_1 + x_2 + \ldots + x_m = 1$; and $y_1 + y_2 + \ldots + y_n = 1$. A pure strategy can be viewed as a special case of a mixed strategy in which a probability of 1 is assigned to one of the x_i or y_j and 0 to each of the others.

If Player I uses a mixed strategy (x) and Player II uses a mixed strategy (y), then row i will be chosen with probability x_i and column j with probability y_j. Because these events are independent, the payoff a_{ij} will occur with probability $x_i y_j$. The *expected payoff* is then simply a weighted average of all the payoffs a_{ij}, each one occurring with probability $x_i y_j$, and it can be written $\Sigma a_{ij} x_i y_j$, where $i = 1, 2, \ldots, m$, and $j = 1, 2, \ldots, n$.

A.3 The minimax theorem

Because the expected payoff represents Player I's average gain and Player II's average loss, Player I wants to maximize it and Player II wants to minimize it. If Player I knew in advance that Player II was going to use a specific mixed strategy (y'), then Player I's best counter-strategy would be one that maximizes the expected payoff against (y'); the expected payoff would then be

$$\max_{(x)} \Sigma a_{ij} x_i y_j'.$$

Similarly, if Player II knew Player I's mixed strategy (x') in advance, Player II could use a counter-strategy that minimizes the expected payoff, yielding

$$\min_{(y)} \Sigma a_{ij} x_i' y_j.$$

These counter-strategies cannot be implemented in practice, because neither player has foreknowledge of the other's intentions. Player I can none the less ensure a maximum *security level* by assuming that Player II will meet any strategy x with the counter-strategy that minimizes the payoff in that event and by choosing (x) so as to maximize the expected payoff under this pessimistic assumption. Player I thus ensures that the expected payoff will be no less than

$$\max_{(x)} \min_{(y)} \Sigma a_{ij} x_i y_j.$$

A similar argument shows that Player II's security level is maximized by the use of a strategy (y) that minimizes the expected payoff against Player I's maximizing counter-strategy against it; the expected payoff will then be no more than:

$$\min_{(y)} \max_{(x)} \Sigma a_{ij} x_i y_j.$$

THEOREM. *If $[a_{ij}]$ is any $m \times n$ payoff matrix, then*

$$\max_{(x)} \min_{(y)} \Sigma a_{ij} x_i y_j = \min_{(y)} \max_{(x)} \Sigma a_{ij} x_i y_j, \tag{1}$$

where $(x) = (x_1, x_2, \ldots, x_m)$ and $(y) = (y_1, y_2, \ldots, y_n)$ represent all strings of non-negative numbers of length m, n, and sum 1.

A.4 Proof

Step 1. Denote the left-hand side of Equation (1) by v and the right-hand side by w. Assume that the payoff matrix $[a_{ij}]$ is given, and let $(x') = (x_1', x_2', \ldots, x_m')$ be that (x) for which the left-hand maximum is attained and $(y') = (y_1', y_2', \ldots, y_n')$ be that (y) for which the right-hand minimum is attained. Because the minimum of a variable quantity is less than or equal to any particular value of it, and the opposite holds for a maximum,

$$v = \min_{(y)} \Sigma a_{ij} x_i' y_j \leq \Sigma a_{ij} x_i' y_j' \leq \max_{(x)} \Sigma a_{ij} x_i y_j' = w. \tag{2}$$

We have proved that $v \leq w$, and it will now suffice to establish that $v \geq w$. First, after providing a geometrical model of a game in Step 2, we shall prove in Steps 3 to 6 that if $w > 0$, then $v > 0$.

Step 2. If Player I chooses row 1 and Player II uses a mixed strategy (y), then the expected payoff will be the following weighted average of the n numbers in row 1:

$$a_{11}y_1 + a_{12}y_2 + \ldots + a_{1n}y_n = \Sigma a_{1j}y_j.$$

The same mixed strategy (y) in combination with Player I's row 2 would yield an expected payoff of $\Sigma a_{2j}y_j$, and so on for each of the m rows. Any of Player II's mixed strategies (y) therefore determines a point in m-dimensional space, each coordinate of the point corresponding to the expected payoff of (y) in combination with one of Player I's pure strategies (rows). The coordinates of the point determined by (y) are then

$$(\Sigma a_{1j}y_j, \Sigma a_{2j}y_j, \ldots, \Sigma a_{mj}y_j).$$

Let C be the set of all these points, where as before $(y) = (y_1, y_2, \ldots, y_n)$ represents all strings of non-negative numbers of length n satisfying $y_1 + y_2 + \ldots + y_n = 1$.

If $m = 2$, C is two-dimensional and can be shown pictorially; if $m = 3$, it is three-dimensional. For $m > 3$, C does not correspond to any object in ordinary space, but it can be handled algebraically by generalizing straightforwardly from the two-dimensional and three-dimensional cases. The game shown in Matrix A.1, with $m = 2$, will suffice to give a geometrical

Matrix A.1

II

		1	2	3
	1	2	5	1
I	2	3	1	−1

interpretation to C. The representation of this game in two-dimensional space is shown in Figure A.1.

Every point in C corresponds to a strategy for Player II. The first coordinate of the point is the payoff if Player I simultaneously chooses row 1, and the second coordinate is the payoff if Player I chooses row 2. The vertices of C correspond to Player II's pure strategies, and all other points on the edges or in the interior of C are weighted averages of its vertices and correspond to Player II's mixed strategies. As an illustration, the point $(3, 1)$ in C corresponds to $(y) = (2/7, 3/7, 2/7)$, because the expected payoff against row 1 is then

$$\Sigma a_{1j}y_j = (2)(2/7) + (5)(3/7) + (1)(2/7) = 3,$$

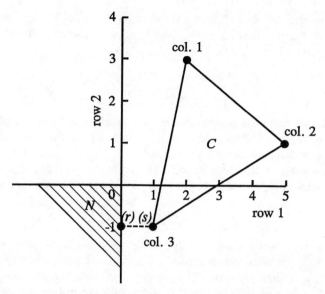

Figure A.1 *Geometric interpretation of the game specified by Matrix A.1, showing the sets C and N discussed in the text and the line segment between (s) and (r) (dashed)*

and against row 2 the expected payoff is

$$\Sigma a_{2j}y_j = (3)(2/7) + (1)(3/7) + (-1)(2/7) = 1,$$

so the coordinates of the corresponding point are (3, 1). If Player I uses a mixed strategy (x), the expected payoff will be a weighted average of the coordinates of the point in C corresponding to Player II's strategy. Thus if Player I uses (x) and Player II uses (y), the expected payoff is

$$x_1(\Sigma a_{1j}y_j) + x_2(\Sigma a_{2j}y_j) + \ldots + x_m(\Sigma a_{mj}y_j) = \Sigma a_{ij}x_iy_j.$$

Step 3. Now suppose that $w > 0$. According to the definition of w, for any (y') there exists (x) such that

$$\Sigma a_{ij}x_iy'_j > 0,$$

which implies that for any point in C, at least one of its coordinates must be positive. The point cannot, therefore, lie in the region N consisting of points with all coordinates negative or zero. We have established that C and N have no common point.

Step 4. Let $(r) = (r_1, r_2, \ldots, r_m)$ be the point in N nearest to C, and let $(s) = (s_1, s_2, \ldots, s_m)$ be the point in C nearest to (r). Now if r_1 is replaced by any negative or zero number r'_1, then the point $(r'_1, r_2, \ldots, r_m)$ is also in N and is therefore no nearer than (r) to (s). This is easy to visualize in two or three dimensions (see Figure A.1); in m dimensions:

$$(s_1 - r'_1)^2 + (s_2 - r_2)^2 + \ldots + (s_m - r_m)^2 \geq$$
$$\geq (s_1 - r_1)^2 + (s_2 - r_2)^2 + \ldots + (s_m - r_m)^2.$$

Generalizing from the three-dimensional case, the repeated application of Pythagoras' theorem shows that the left-hand side of this inequality is the square of the distance between (s) and $(r'_1, r_2, \ldots, r_m)$, and the right-hand side is the square of the distance between (s) and (r) – this is a well-known result in elementary coordinate geometry or vector algebra. The inequality simplifies to

$$(s_1 - r'_1)^2 \geq (s_1 - r_1)^2. \tag{3}$$

Now if $s_1 \leq 0$, then a possible value of r'_1 is $r'_1 = s_1$, in which case the left-hand side of (3) is zero and therefore $r_1 = s_1$. If, on the other hand, $s_1 > 0$, and we take $r'_1 = 0$, then (3) becomes $s_1^2 \geq (s_1 - r_1)^2$, which simplifies to $2s_1r_1 \geq r_1^2$. In that case, because $r_1 \leq 0$ and s_1 is a positive number, the inequality is satisfied only if $r_1 = 0$. It follows from these two results that $s_1 \geq r_1$ and, because either $r_1 = s_1$ or $r_1 = 0$, that $(s_1 - r_1)r_1 = 0$. The same argument can be used to show that $s_2 \geq r_2$ and $(s_2 - r_2)r_2 = 0$, and so on. Thus

$$s_1 \geq r_1, s_2 \geq r_2, \ldots, s_m \geq r_m.$$

and

$$(s_1 - r_1)r_1 + (s_2 - r_2)r_2 + \ldots + (s_m - r_m)r_m = 0. \tag{4}$$

The lines from (r) to (s) and to the origin $(0, 0, \ldots, 0)$ are thus at right angles.

Step 5. For any number t between 0 and 1 and any point (a) in C, the point

$$t(a) + (1 - t)(s) = (ta_1 + (1 - t)s_1, \ldots, ta_m + (1 - t)s_m)$$

on the straight line between (a) and (s) is a weighted average of the points (a) and (s). Because (a) and (s) belong to C, they in turn are weighted averages of the vertices of C, and therefore so is the point $t(a) + (1 - t)(s)$. This means that the point $t(a) + (1 - t)(s)$ also belongs to C, and it is therefore no nearer than (s) to (r):

$$[ta_1 + (1 - t)s_1 - r_1]^2 + \ldots + [ta_m + (1 - t)s_m - r_m]^2 \geq$$
$$\geq (s_1 - r_1)^2 + \ldots + (s_m - r_m)^2.$$

This simplifies to:

$$2(a_1 - s_1)(s_1 - r_1) + \ldots + 2(a_m - s_m)(s_m - r_m) \geq$$
$$\geq -t[(a_1 - s_1)^2 + \ldots + (a_m - s_m)^2].$$

Because t can be arbitrarily close to zero, it follows that

$$(a_1 - s_1)(s_1 - r_1) + \ldots + (a_m - s_m)(s_m - r_m) \geq 0.$$

This can be rewritten

$$a_1(s_1 - r_1) + \ldots + a_m(s_m - r_m) \geq$$

$$\geq [(s_1 - r_1)^2 + \ldots + (s_m - r_m)^2] + [(s_1 - r_1)r_1 + \ldots + (s_m - r_m)r_m]$$

In view of (4), we may conclude that

$$a_1(s_1 - r_1) + \ldots + a_m(s_m - r_m) \geq (s_1 - r_1)^2 + \ldots + (s_m - r_m)^2.$$

The right-hand side of this inequality is a sum of squares and cannot, therefore, be negative, so

$$a_1(s_1 - r_1) + \ldots + a_m(s_m - r_m) \geq 0. \tag{5}$$

Thus, by (4), the lines from (r) to (a) and to (s) make an acute angle or a right angle.

Step 6. Each of the numbers $s_1 - r_1, \ldots, s_m - r_m$ is positive or zero according to Step 4, and not all are zero because (s) and (r) are different points, so their sum q is positive. Let $x_1^0 = (s_1 - r_1)/q, \ldots, x_m^0 = (s_m - r_m)/q$. Then $x_1^0, \ldots, x_m^0$ are each the result of dividing a positive or zero number by a positive number. It follows that $x_1^0, \ldots, x_m^0$ are each non-negative, and it is clear that $x_1^0 + \ldots + x_m^0 = 1$ because $(s_1 - r_1) + \ldots + (s_m - r_m) = q$ and $q/q = 1$. Therefore $(x^0) = (x_1^0, \ldots, x_m^0)$ satisfies the requirements of a mixed strategy for Player I.

Dividing each term of (5) by the positive quantity q, and bearing in mind that $(s) \neq (r)$,

$$a_1 x_1^0 + \ldots + a_m x_m^0 > 0$$

for every point (a) in C. According to the definition of C in Step 2, the coordinates of (a) are $(\Sigma a_{1j}y_j, \ldots, \Sigma a_{mj}y_j)$. We have therefore found a mixed strategy (x^0) for Player I such that

$$x_1^0(\Sigma a_{1j}y_j) + \ldots + x_m^0(\Sigma a_{mj}y_j) > 0$$

for every (y), so that

$$\min_{(y)} \Sigma a_{ij} x_i^0 y_j > 0.$$

Because this holds for (x^0), it must hold for the mixed strategy (x) that maximizes

$$\min_{(y)} \Sigma a_{ij} x_i y_j.$$

This means that

$$\max_{(x)} \min_{(y)} \Sigma a_{ij} x_i y_j > 0.$$

This completes the proof that if $w > 0$, then $v > 0$.

Step 7. Now let k be any number, and consider the $m \times n$ payoff matrix that has $a_{ij} - k$ in place of a_{ij} for every i and j. All payoffs for pure strategies in this game are evidently reduced by k, and therefore so are those for mixed strategies, so that v and w are replaced by $v - k$ and $w - k$ respectively. By what we have just proved, if $w - k > 0$, then $v - k > 0$. This implies that if $w > k$, then $v > k$. Because k can be arbitrarily close to w, it follows that $v \geq w$. But we have seen in Step 1 that $v \leq w$. It follows that $v = w$, that is,

$$\max_{(x)} \min_{(y)} \Sigma a_{ij} x_i y_j = \min_{(y)} \max_{(x)} \Sigma a_{ij} x_i y_j.$$

This completes the proof of the minimax theorem.

A.5 Remark

Because the outer two numbers in Equation (2) are equal, their common value is also equal to the term in the middle. This implies that (x') and (y') are mixed strategies that provide the same security level to both players. In other words, mixed strategies providing the same security level to both players are bound to exist in any finite, two-person, zero-sum game; that is, every finite, strictly competitive game has an equilibrium point or saddle point in mixed strategies.

Mathematically trained readers may have noticed that reference was made several times in the proof to the minimum or maximum of a set of numbers on the assumption that such an extreme value is attained within the set. It is possible, however, for a set to be "open-ended" in the sense that a presumed minimum or maximum value does not in fact belong to the set – for example, the set of all positive numbers has no minimum, because zero is not itself a positive number, and the set of all negative numbers has no maximum for the same reason. It is crucial to the proof of the minimax theorem that the various minima and maxima are attained, but proving this is a routine technical exercise in analysis that would have interrupted and obscured the line of argument of the main proof. Moreover, it is intuitively obvious, at any rate in simple, geometrically visualizable cases.

References

Abramson, P. R., Aldrich, J. H., Paolino, P., & Rhode, D. W. (1992). "Sophisticated" voting in the 1988 presidential primaries. *American Political Science Review,* **86**(1), 55–69.

Alcock, J. E. (1974). Cooperation, competition and the effects of time pressure in Canada and India. *Journal of Conflict Resolution,* **18**, 171–197.

Alcock, J. E. (1975). Motivation in an asymmetric bargaining situation: A cross-cultural study. *International Journal of Psychology,* **10**, 69–81.

Alcock, J. E. & Mansell, D. (1977). Predisposition and behavior in a collective dilemma. *Journal of Conflict Resolution,* **21**, 443–457.

Apfelbaum, E. (1974). On conflicts and bargaining. *Advances in Experimental Social Psychology,* **7**, 103–156.

Argyle, M. (1991). *Cooperation: The Basis of Sociability.* London: Routledge.

Arickx, M. & Van Avermaet, E. (1981). Interdependent learning in a minimal social situation. *Behavioral Science,* **26**, 229–242.

Arrow, K. J. (1951). *Social Choice and Individual Values.* New York: Wiley.

Arrow, K. J. (1963). *Social Choice and Individual Values* (2nd ed.). New York: Wiley.

Atkinson, R. C. & Suppes, P. (1958). An analysis of two-person game situations in terms of statistical learning theory. *Journal of Experimental Psychology,* **55**, 369–378.

Aumann, R. J. (1987). Correlated equilibrium as an expression of Bayesian rationality. *Econometrica,* **55**, 1–18.

Avedon, E. M. & Sutton-Smith, B. (1971). *The Study of Games.* New York: Wiley.

Axelrod, R. (1980a). Effective choice in the Prisoner's Dilemma. *Journal of Conflict Resolution,* **24**, 3–25.

Axelrod, R. (1980b). More effective choice in the Prisoner's Dilemma. *Journal of Conflict Resolution,* **24**, 379–403.

Axelrod, R. (1984). *The Evolution of Cooperation.* New York: Basic Books.

Axelrod, R. & Dion, D. (1988). More on the evolution of cooperation. *Science,* **242**, 1385–1390.

Axelrod, R. & Hamilton, W. D. (1981). The evolution of cooperation. *Science,* **211**, 1390–1396.

Bacharach, M. O. L. (1992). Backward induction and beliefs about oneself. *Synthese,* **91**, 217–284.

Bacharach, M. O. L. (1994). Variable universe games. In K. Binmore, A. Kirman, & P. Tani (Eds), *Frontiers of Game Theory* (pp. 255–275). Cambridge, MA: MIT Press.

Barbera, S. (1977). Manipulation of social decision functions. *Journal of Economic Theory*, **15**, 266–278.

Bar-Hillel, M. & Margalit, A. (1972). Newcomb's paradox revisited. *British Journal for the Philosophy of Science*, **23**, 295–304.

Bartholdi, J. J. III, Butler, C. A., & Trick, M. A. (1986). More on the evolution of cooperation. *Journal of Conflict Resolution*, **30**, 129–140.

Bartos, O. J. (1974). *Process and Outcome of Negotiations*. New York: Columbia University Press.

Beer, F. A. (1986). Games and metaphors: Review article. *Journal of Conflict Resolution*, **30**, 171–191.

Beggan, J. K. & Messick, D. M. (1988). Social values and egocentric bias: Two tests of the might over morality hypothesis. *Journal of Personality and Social Psychology*, **55**, 606–611.

Bell, D. E., Raiffa, H., & Tversky, A. (Eds). (1988). Descriptive, normative, and prescriptive interactions in decision making. In D. E. Bell, H. Raiffa, & A. Tversky (Eds), *Decision Making: Descriptive, Normative, and Prescriptive Interactions* (pp. 9–30). Cambridge: Cambridge University Press.

Bendor, J. (1993). Uncertainty and the evolution of cooperation. *Journal of Conflict Resolution*, **37**, 709–734.

Bendor, J., Kramer, R., & Stout, S. (1991). When in doubt: Cooperation in a noisy Prisoner's Dilemma. *Journal of Conflict Resolution*, **35**, 691–719.

Berlekamp, E. R., Conway, J. H., & Guy, R. K. (1985). *Winning Ways for Your Mathematical Plays* (2 vols, 3rd ed.). London: Academic Press.

Bernoulli, D. (1738). Specimen theoriae novae de mensura sortis. *Comentarii Academii Scientarum Imperialis Petropolitanae*, **5**, 175–192. [Trans. L. Sommer, *Econometrica*, 1954, **22**, 23–26.]

Bernstein, I. S. & Gordon, T. P. (1974). The function of aggression in primate societies. *American Scientist*, **62**, 304–311.

Bertilson, H. S. & Lien, S. K. (1982). Comparison of reaction time and interpersonal communication tasks to test effectiveness of a matching strategy in reducing attack-instigated aggression. *Perceptual and Motor Skills*, **55**, 659–665.

Bertilson, H. S., Wonderlich, S. A., & Blum, M. W. (1983). Withdrawal, matching, withdrawal-matching, and variable-matching strategies in reducing attack-instigated aggression. *Aggressive Behavior*, **9**, 1–11.

Bertilson, H. S., Wonderlich, S. A., & Blum, M. W. (1984). Withdrawal and matching strategies in reducing attack-instigated aggression. *Psychological Reports*, **55**, 823–828.

Bethlehem, D. W. (1975). The effect of Westernization on cooperative behaviour in central Africa. *International Journal of Psychology*, **10**, 219–224.

Bethlehem, D. W. (1982). Anthropological and cross-cultural perspectives. In A. M. Colman (Ed.), *Cooperation and Competition in Humans and Animals* (pp. 250–268). Wokingham: Van Nostrand Reinhold.

Bicchieri, C. (1993). *Rationality and Coordination*. Cambridge: Cambridge University Press.

Binmore, K. & Dasgupta, P. (Eds). *The Economics of Bargaining*. Oxford: Blackwell.

Binmore, K., Swierzbinski, J., Hsu, S., & Prolux, C. (1993). Focal points in bargaining. *International Journal of Game Theory, 22,* 381–409.

Bixenstine, V. E. & O'Reilly, E. F., Jr. (1966). Money vs. electric shock as payoff in a Prisoner's Dilemma game. *Psychological Record, 16,* 251–264.

Bjurulf, B. H. & Niemi, R. G. (1981). Order-of-voting effects. In M. J. Holler (Ed.), *Power, Voting, and Voting Power*. Würzburg: Physica-Verlag.

Black, D. (1948a). The decisions of a committee using a special majority. *Econometrica, 16,* 245–261.

Black, D. (1948b). On the rationale of group decision making. *Journal of Political Economy, 56,* 23–34.

Black, D. (1958). *The Theory of Committees and Elections*. Cambridge: Cambridge University Press.

Blackwell, D. & Girshick, M. A. (1954). *Theory of Games and Statistical Decisions*. New York: Wiley.

Blair, D. H., Bordes, G., Kelly, J. S., & Suzumura, K. (1976). Impossibility theorems without collective rationality. *Journal of Economic Theory, 13,* 361–379.

Blau, J. H. (1957). The existence of a social welfare function. *Econometrica, 25,* 302–313.

Blau, J. H. (1972). A direct proof of Arrow's theorem. *Econometrica, 40,* 61–67.

Blin, J.-M. (1973). Intransitive social orderings and the probability of the Condorcet effect. *Kyklos, 26,* 25–35.

Bogdanor, V. (1984). *What is Proportional Representation? A Guide to the Issues*. Oxford: Martin Robertson.

Bogdanor, V. (1992). *Proportional Representation*. London: Electoral Reform Society.

Bonacich, P., Shure, G. H., Kahan, J. P., & Meeker, R. J. (1976). Cooperation and group size in the N-person Prisoners' Dilemma. *Journal of Conflict Resolution, 20,* 687–706.

Borda, J.-C. de (1781). Mémoire sur les élections au scrutin par M. de Borda. *Mémoires de l'Académie Royale des Sciences anée 1781,* 657–665. [Trans. A. de Grazia, *Isis,* 1953, **44,** 42–51.]

Border, K. C. & Segal, U. (1994). Dutch books and conditional probability. *The Economic Journal, 104,* 71–75.

Boring, E. G. (1950). *A History of Experimental Psychology* (2nd ed.). New York: Appleton-Century-Crofts.

Bornstein, G. (1992). The free-rider problem in intergroup conflicts over step-level and continuous public goods. *Journal of Personality and Social Psychology,* **62**, 597–606.

Bornstein, G., Rapoport, Am., Kerpel, L., & Katz, T. (1989). Within- and between-group communication in intergroup competition for public goods. *Journal of Experimental Social Psychology,* **25**, 422–436.

Bowen, B. D. (1972). Occurrence of the paradox of voting in U.S. senate roll call votes. In R. G. Niemi & H. F. Weisberg (Eds.), *Probability Models of Collective Decision Making* (pp. 181–203). Columbus, OH: Charles E. Merrill.

Boyd, R. & Lorberbaum, J. P. (1987). No pure strategy is evolutionarily stable in the repeated Prisoner's Dilemma game. *Nature,* **327**(6117), 58–59.

Braiker, H. B. & Kelley, H. H. (1979). Conflict in the development of close relationships. In R. L. Burgess & T. L. Huston (Eds), *Social Exchange in Developing Relationships* (pp. 135–168). New York: Academic Press.

Braithwaite, R. B. (1955). *Theory of Games as a Tool for the Moral Philosopher.* Cambridge: Cambridge University Press.

Brams, S. J. (1975). *Game Theory and Politics.* New York: Free Press.

Brams, S. J. (1976). *Paradoxes in Politics: An Introduction to the Nonobvious in Political Science.* New York: Free Press.

Brams, S. J. (1977). Deception in 2 × 2 games. *Journal of Peace Science,* **2**, 171–203.

Brams, S. J. (1978). *The Presidential Election Game.* New Haven, CT: Yale University Press.

Brams, S. J. (1980a). Approval voting in multicandidate elections. *Policy Studies Journal,* **9**, 102–108.

Brams, S. J. (1980b). *Biblical Games: A Strategic Analysis of Stories in the Old Testament.* Cambridge, MA: The MIT Press.

Brams, S. J. (1994). Game theory and literature. *Games and Economic Behavior,* **6**, 32–54.

Brams, S. J. & Fishburn, P. C. (1983). *Approval Voting.* Boston, MA: Birkhauser.

Brayer, A. R. (1964). An experimental analysis of some variables in minimax theory. *Behavioral Science,* **9**, 33–44.

Brewer, M. B. & Kramer, R. M. (1986). Choice behavior in social dilemmas: Effects of social identity, group size, and decision framing. *Journal of Personality and Social Psychology,* **50**, 543–549.

Brewer, M. B. & Schneider, S. K. (1990). Social identity and social dilemmas: A double-edged sword. In D. Abrams & M. A. Hogg (Eds), *Social Identity Theory: Constructive and Critical Advances* (pp. 169–184). Hemel Hempstead: Harvester Wheatsheaf.

Brockmann, H. J., Grafen, A., & Dawkins, R. (1979). Evolutionarily stable nesting strategy in a digger wasp. *Journal of Theoretical Biology,* **77**, 473–496.

Brockner, J. & Rubin, J. Z. (1985). *Entrapment in Escalating Conflicts: A Social Psychological Analysis*. New York: Springer-Verlag.

Brockner, J., Rubin, J. Z., & Lang, E. (1981). Face-saving and entrapment. *Journal of Experimental Social Psychology, 17*, 68–79.

Brockner, J., Shaw, M. C., & Rubin, J. Z. (1979). Factors affecting withdrawal from an escalating conflict: Quitting before it's too late. *Journal of Experimental Social Psychology, 15*, 492–503.

Bull, P. & Frederikson, L. (1994). Non-verbal communication. In A. M. Colman (Ed.), *Companion Encyclopedia of Psychology* (Vol. 2, pp. 852–872). London: Routledge.

Burhans, D. T., Jr. (1973). Coalition game research: A reexamination. *American Journal of Sociology, 79*, 389–408.

Caldwell, M. D. (1976). Communication and sex effects in a five-person Prisoner's Dilemma Game. *Journal of Personality and Social Psychology, 33*, 273–280.

Calvert, R. L. & Fenno, R. F. (1994). Strategy and sophisticated voting in the Senate. *Journal of Politics, 56*, 349–376.

Campbell, R. (1985). Background for the uninitiated. In R. Campbell & L. Sowden (Eds), *Paradoxes of Rationality and Cooperation: Prisoner's Dilemma and Newcomb's Problem* (pp. 3–41). Vancouver: University of British Columbia Press.

Campbell, R. & Sowden, L. (Eds). (1985). *Paradoxes of Rationality and Cooperation: Prisoner's Dilemma and Newcomb's Problem*. Vancouver: University of British Columbia Press.

Caplow, T. (1956). A theory of coalitions in the triad. *American Sociological Review, 21*, 489–493.

Caplow, T. (1959). Further development of a theory of coalitions in the triad. *American Sociological Review, 64*, 488–493.

Caporael, L. R., Dawes, R. M., Orbell, J. M., & Van de Kragt, A. J. C. (1989). Selfishness examined: Cooperation in the absence of egoistic incentives. *Behavioral and Brain Sciences, 12*, 683–699.

Carey, M. S. (1980). Real life and the dollar auction. In A. I. Teger, *Too Much Invested to Quit* (pp. 117–133). New York: Pergamon.

Cargile, J. (1975). Newcomb's paradox. *British Journal for the Philosophy of Science, 26*, 234–239.

Carment, D. W. (1974). Indian and Canadian choice behaviour in a Maximizing Difference game and a game of Chicken. *International Journal of Psychology, 9*, 213–221.

Carment, D. W. & Alcock, J. E. (1984). Indian and Canadian behavior in two-person power games. *Journal of Conflict Resolution, 28*, 507–521.

Chammah, A. M. (1969). *Sex Differences, Strategy, and Communication in Mixed-Motive Games*. Unpublished doctoral dissertation, University of Michigan.

Chaney, M. V. & Vinacke, W. E. (1960). Achievement and nurturance in triads varying in power distribution. *Journal of Abnormal and Social Psychology*, **60**, 175–181.

Chernoff, H. (1954). Rational selection of decision functions. *Econometrica*, **22**, 423–443.

Chertkoff, J. M. (1966). The effects of probability of success on coalition formation. *Journal of Experimental Social Psychology*, **2**, 265–277.

Chertkoff, J. M. (1970). Social psychological theories and research in coalition formation. In S. Groennings, E. W. Kelley, & M. Lieserson (Eds), *The Study of Coalition Behaviors* (pp. 297–322). New York: Holt.

Chertkoff, J. M. (1971). Coalition formation as a function of differences in resources. *Journal of Conflict Resolution*, **15**, 371–383.

Chertkoff, J. M. & Braden, J. L. (1974). Effects of experience and bargaining restrictions on coalition formation. *Journal of Personality and Social Psychology*, **30**, 169–177.

Chun, Y. (1989). A new axiomatization of the Shapley value. *Games and Economic Behavior*, **1**, 119–130.

Cohen, J. M. & Cohen, M. J. (1980). *The Penguin Dictionary of Modern Quotations*. Harmondsworth: Penguin.

Coleman, A. A., Colman, A. M., & Thomas, R. M. (1990). Cooperation without awareness: A multiperson generalization of the minimal social situation. *Behavioral Science*, **35**, 115–121.

Collard, D. (1978). *Altruism and Economy: A Study in Non-Selfish Economics*. Oxford: Martin Robertson.

Colman, A. M. (1975). The psychology of influence. In B. Frost (Ed.), *The Tactics of Pressure* (pp. 11–24). London: Stainer & Bell.

Colman, A. M. (1979). The Borda effect: Evidence from small groups and from a British general election. *Bulletin of the British Psychological Society*, **32**, 221. [Abstract]

Colman, A. M. (1980). The likelihood of the Borda effect in small decision-making committees. *British Journal of Mathematical and Statistical Psychology*, **33**, 50–56.

Colman, A. M. (Ed.). (1982a). *Cooperation and Competition in Humans and Animals*. Wokingham: Van Nostrand Reinhold.

Colman, A. M. (1982b). Experimental games. In A. M. Colman (Ed.), *Cooperation and Competition in Humans and Animals* (pp. 113–140). Wokingham: Van Nostrand Reinhold.

Colman, A. M. (1982c). *Game Theory and Experimental Games: The Study of Strategic Interaction* (1st ed.). Oxford: Pergamon.

Colman, A. M. (1984). The weak Borda effect and plurality-majority disagreement. *British Journal of Mathematical and Statistical Psychology*, **37**, 288–292.

Colman, A. M. (1986). Rejoinder to Gillett. *British Journal of Mathematical and Statistical Psychology*, **39**, 87–89.

Colman, A. M. (1992). Arguments against proportional representation.

Politics Review, **2**(2), 14–15.

Colman, A. M. & Pountney, I. (1975a). Voting paradoxes: A Socratic dialogue. I. *Political Quarterly,* **46**(2), 186–190.

Colman, A. M. & Pountney, I. (1975b). Voting paradoxes: A Socratic dialogue. II. *Political Quarterly,* **46**(3), 304–309.

Colman, A. M. & Pountney, I. (1978). Borda's voting paradox: Theoretical likelihood and electoral occurrences. *Behavioral Science,* **23**, 15–20.

Condorcet, M. J. A. N. C. Marquis de (1785). *Essai sur l'application de l'analyse à la probabilité des décisions rendues à la pluralité des voix.* Paris: l'Imprimerie Royale.

Conway, J. H. (1976). *On Numbers and Games.* London: Academic Press.

Coombs, C. H. (1964). *A Theory of Data.* New York: Wiley.

Cooper, R., De Jong, D. V., Forsythe, R., & Ross, T. W. (1992a). Communication in coordination games. *Quarterly Journal of Economics,* **107**, 739–771.

Cooper, R., De Jong, D. V., Forsythe, R. & Ross, T. W. (1992b). Forward induction in coordination games. *Semiotics Letters,* **40**, 167–172.

Copeland, A. H. (1945). Review of von Neumann and Morgenstern's *Theory of Games and Economic Behavior. Bulletin of the American Mathematical Society,* **51**, 498–504.

Costanza, R. (1984). Review essay: The nuclear arms race and the theory of social traps. *Journal of Peace Research,* **21**, 79–86.

Costanza, R. & Shrum, W. (1988). The effects of taxation on moderating the conflict escalation process: An experiment using the Dollar Auction game. *Social Science Quarterly,* **69**, 416–432.

Cox, G. W. (1994). Strategic voting equilibria under the single non-transferable vote. *American Political Science Review,* **88**, 608–621.

Cox, T. H., Lobel, S., & McLeod, P. L. (1991). Effects of ethnic group cultural differences on cooperative and competitive behavior on a group task. *Academy of Management Journal,* **34**, 827–847.

Crawford, V. P. & Haller, H. (1990). Learning how to cooperate: Optimal play in repeated coordination games. *Econometrica,* **58**, 571–595.

Crosbie, P. V. & Kullberg, V. K. (1973). Minimum resource or balance in coalition formation. *Sociometry,* **36**, 476–493.

Crumbaugh, C. M. & Evans, G. W. (1967). Presentation format, other-person strategies, and cooperative behavior in the Prisoner's Dilemma. *Psychological Reports,* **20**, 895–902.

Darwin, C. (1859). *The Origin of Species by Means of Natural Selection, or the Preservation of Favoured Races in the Struggle for Life.* London: John Murray.

Davenport, W. (1960). Jamaican fishing: A game theory analysis. In S. W. Mintz (Ed.), *Papers in Caribbean Anthropology* (Nos. 57–64, pp. 3–11). New Haven, CT: Yale University Publications in Anthropology.

David, F. N. (1962). *Games, Gods and Gambling: A History of Probability and Statistical Ideas.* London: Griffin.

Davis, J. H., Laughlin, P. R., & Komorita, S. S. (1976). The social psychology of small groups. *Annual Review of Psychology, 27*, 501–542.

Davis, L. H. (1977). Prisoners, paradox, and rationality. *American Philosophical Quarterly, 14*, 319–327. [Reprinted in R. Campbell & L. Sowden (Eds), *Paradoxes of Rationality and Cooperation: Prisoner's Dilemma and Newcomb's Problem* (pp. 45–59). Vancouver: University of British Columbia Press]

Davis, M. & Maschler, M. (1965). The kernel of a cooperative game. *Naval Research Logistics Quarterly, 12*, 223–259.

Davis, M. D. (1970). *Game Theory: A Nontechnical Introduction.* New York: Basic Books.

Dawes, R. M. (1973). The commons dilemma game: an *n*-person mixed-motive game with a dominating strategy for defection. *Oregon Research Institute Research Bulletin, 13*(2).

Dawes, R. M. (1975). Formal models of dilemmas in social decision making. In M. Kaplan & S. Schwartz (Eds), *Human Judgement and Decision Processes: Formal and Mathematical Approaches* (pp. 87–107). New York: Academic Press.

Dawes, R. M. (1980). Social dilemmas. *Annual Review of Psychology, 31*, 169–193.

Dawes, R. M. (1988). *Rational Choice in an Uncertain World.* Orlando, FL: Harcourt Brace Jovanovich.

Dawes, R. M. & Orbell, J. (1981). Social dilemmas. In G. Stephenson & J. Davis (Eds), *Progress in Applied Social Psychology* (Vol. 1). Chichester: Wiley.

Dawes, R. M., McTavish, J., & Shaklee, H. (1977). Behavior, communication, and assumptions about other people's behavior in a Commons Dilemma situation. *Journal of Personality and Social Psychology, 35*, 1–11.

Dawkins, R. (1976). *The Selfish Gene.* Oxford: Oxford University Press.

Dawkins, R. (1989). *The Selfish Gene* (2nd ed.). Oxford: Oxford University Press.

Dawkins, R. & Brockmann, H. J. (1980). Do digger wasps commit the Concorde fallacy? *Animal Behaviour, 28*, 892–896.

Dawkins, R. & Carlisle, T. R. (1976). Parental investment, mate desertion, and a fallacy. *Nature, 262*, 131–133.

De Jong, D. V., Forsythe, R., & Ross, T. W. (1992). Forward induction in coordination games. *Economics Letters, 40*, 167–172.

DeMeyer, F. & Plott, C. (1970). The probability of a cyclical majority. *Econometrica, 38*, 345–354.

Denzau, A., Riker, W., & Shepsle, K. (1985). Farquharson and Fenno: Sophisticated voting and home style. *American Political Science Review, 79*, 1117–1134.

Deutsch, M. (1958). Trust and suspicion. *Journal of Conflict Resolution, 2*, 265–279.

Deutsch, M. (1969). Socially relevant science: Reflections on some studies of interpersonal conflict. *American Psychologist*, **24**, 1076–1092.

Deutsch, M. (1982). Interdependence and psychological orientation. In V. J. Deregla & J. Grzelak (Eds), *Cooperation and Helping Behavior*. New York: Academic Press.

Deutsch, M. & Krauss, R. M. (1960). The effect of threat upon interpersonal bargaining. *Journal of Abnormal and Social Psychology*, **61**, 181–189.

Deutsch, M. & Krauss, R. M. (1962). Studies of interpersonal bargaining. *Journal of Conflict Resolution*, **6**, 52–76.

Dimand, R. W. & Dimand, M. A. (1992). The early history of the theory of strategic games from Waldegrave to Borel. In E. R. Weintraub (Ed.), *Toward a History of Game Theory: Annual Supplement to Volume 24 History of Political Economy* (pp. 15–27). Durham, NC & London, England: Duke University Press.

Dodgson, C. L. (1876). *A Method of Taking Votes on More Than Two Issues*. Oxford: Clarendon Press. [Reprinted in Black, D., 1958, *The Theory of Committees and Elections*. Cambridge: Cambridge University Press.]

Domjan, M. & Burkhard, B. (1986). *The Principles of Learning and Behavior*. Monterey, CA: Brooks/Cole.

Donninger, C. (1986). Is it always efficient to be nice? A computer simulation of Axelrod's computer tournament. In A. Deikmann & P. Mitter (Eds), *Paradoxical Effects in Social Behavior: Essays in Honor of Anatol Rapoport*. Heidelberg: Physica-Verlag.

Doron, G. (1979). The Hare voting system is inconsistent. *Political Studies*, **27**, 283–286.

Doron, G. & Kornick, R. (1977). Single transferrable vote: An example of a perverse social choice function. *American Journal of Political Science*, **21**, 303–311.

Downs, A. (1957). *An Economic Theory of Democracy*. New York: Harper & Row.

Druckman, D. (1994). Determinants of compromising behavior in negotiation: A meta-analysis. *Journal of Conflict Resolution* **38**, 507–556.

Dummett, M. (1984). *Voting Procedures*. Oxford: Clarendon Press.

Eckel, C. & Holt, C. A. (1989). Strategic voting in agenda-controlled committee experiments. *American Economic Review*, **79**, 763–773.

Edgeworth, F. Y. (1881). *Mathematical Psychics*. London: Kegan Paul.

Eells, E. (1984). Newcomb's many solutions. *Theory and Decision*, **16**, 59–105.

Eibl-Eibesfeldt, I. (1970). *Ethology: The Biology of Behavior*. New York: Holt, Rinehart & Winston.

Einhorn, H. J. & Hogarth, R. M. (1988). Behavioral decision theory: Processes of judgment and choice. In D. E. Bell, H. Raiffa, & A. Tversky (Eds), *Decision Making: Descriptive, Normative, and Prescriptive Interactions* (pp. 113–146). Cambridge: Cambridge University Press.

Eiser, J. R. (1980). *Cognitive Social Psychology: A Guidebook to Theory and*

Research. Maidenhead: McGraw-Hill.

Eiser, J. R. & Bhavnani, K.-K. (1974). The effect of situational meaning on the behaviour of subjects in the Prisoner's Dilemma Game. *European Journal of Social Psychology*, **4**, 93–97.

Eiser, J. R. & Tajfel, H. (1972). Acquisition of information in dyadic interaction. *Journal of Personality and Social Psychology*, **23**, 340–345.

Elster, J. & Hylland, A. (Eds). (1986). *Foundations of Social Choice Theory*. Cambridge: Cambridge University Press.

Enelow, J. M. & Koehler, D. H. (1980). The amendment in legislative strategy: Sophisticated voting in the U.S. Congress. *Journal of Politics*, **5**, 396–413.

Evans, G. (1964). Effect of unilateral promise and value of rewards upon cooperation and trust. *Journal of Abnormal and Social Psychology*, **69**, 587–590.

Evans, G. & Crumbaugh, C. M. (1966). Effects of Prisoner's Dilemma format on cooperative behavior. *Journal of Personality and Social Psychology*, **3**, 486–488.

Farquharson, R. (1968). *Drop Out!* Harmondsworth: Penguin.

Farquharson, R. (1969). *Theory of Voting*. New Haven, CT: Yale University Press.

Faucheux, C. (1976). A critique of cross-cultural social psychology. *European Journal of Social Psychology*, **6**, 269–322.

Felsenthal, D. S. & Maoz, Z. (1988). A comparative analysis of sincere and sophisticated voting under the plurality and approval procedures. *Behavioral Science*, **33**, 116–130.

Felsenthal, D. S. & Maoz, Z. (1992). Normative properties of four single-stage multi-winner electoral procedures. *Behavioral Science*, **37**, 109–127.

Felsenthal, D. S., Rapoport, Am., & Maoz, Z. (1988). Tacit cooperation in three-alternative non-cooperative voting games: A new model of sophisticated behaviour under the plurality procedure. *Electoral Studies*, **7**, 143–161.

Festinger, L. (1957). *A Theory of Cognitive Dissonance*. New York: Row, Peterson.

Fischhoff, B. (1983). Predicting frames. *Journal of Experimental Psychology: Learning, Memory and Cognition*, **9**, 103–116.

Fishburn, P. C. (1970). Arrow's impossibility theorem: Concise proof and finite voters. *Journal of Economic Theory*, **2**, 103–106.

Fishburn, P. C. (1973a). *The Theory of Social Choice*. Princeton, NJ: Princeton University Press.

Fishburn, P. C. (1973b). Voter concordance, simple majorities, and group decision methods. *Behavioral Science*, **18**, 361–376.

Fishburn, P. C. (1974a). Simple voting systems and majority rule. *Behavioral Science*, **19**, 166–176.

Fishburn, P. C. (1974b). Single-peaked preferences and probabilities of cyclical majorities. *Behavioral Science*, **19**, 21–27.

Fishburn, P. C. (1977). An analysis of voting procedures with nonranked voting. *Behavioral Science*, **22**, 178–185.

Fishburn, P. C. (1988). Normative theories of decision making under risk and under uncertainty. In D. E. Bell, H. Raiffa, & A. Tversky (Eds), *Decision Making: Descriptive, Normative, and Prescriptive Interactions* (pp. 78–98). Cambridge: Cambridge University Press.

Fishburn, P. C. & Brams, S. J. (1983). Paradoxes of preferential voting. *Mathematics Magazine*, **56**(4), 207–214.

Fishburn, P. C. & Gehrlein, W. V. (1976). An analysis of simple two-stage voting systems. *Behavioral Science*, **21**, 1–12.

Fisher, R. A. (1930). *The Genetical Theory of Natural Selection*. Oxford: Oxford University Press.

Fisher, R. A. (1934). Randomisation, and an old enigma of card play. *Mathematical Gazette*, **18**, 294–297.

Fleishman, J. A. (1988). The effects of decision framing and other's behavior on cooperation in a social dilemma. *Journal of Conflict Resolution*, **32**, 162–180.

Fletcher, J. (1966). *Situation Ethics: The New Morality*. Philadelphia, PA: Westminster Press.

Flood, M. M. (1958). Some experimental games. *Management Science*, **5**, 5–26.

Flood, M., Lendenmann, K, & Rapoport, An. (1983). 2 × 2 games played by rats: Different delays of reinforcement as payoffs. *Behavioral Science*, **28**, 65–78.

Fox, J. (1972). The learning of strategies in a simple, two-person zero-sum game without saddlepoint. *Behavioral Science*, **17**, 300–308.

Fox, J. & Guyer, M. (1973). Equivalence and stooge strategies in zero-sum games. *Journal of Conflict Resolution*, **17**, 513–533.

Fox, J. & Guyer, M. (1977). Group size and others' strategy in an N-person game. *Journal of Conflict Resolution*, **21**, 323–338.

Fox, J. & Guyer, M. (1978). "Public" choice and cooperation in N-person Prisoner's Dilemma. *Journal of Conflict Resolution*, **22**, 469–81.

Fréchet, M. (1953). Emile Borel, initiator of the theory of psychological games and its application. *Econometrica*, **21**, 95–96.

Friedman, J. W. (1991). *Game Theory With Applications to Economics* (2nd ed.). New York: Oxford University Press.

Frisch, D. & Clemen, R. T. (1994). Beyond expected utility: Rethinking behavioral decision research. *Psychological Bulletin*, **116**, 46–54.

Furnham, A. & Quilley, R. (1989). The Protestant work ethic and the Prisoner's Dilemma game. *British Journal of Social Psychology*, **28**, 79–87.

Galbraith, J. W. & Rae, N. C. (1989). A test of the importance of tactical voting: Great Britain 1987. *British Journal of Political Science*, **19**, 126–136.

Gale, A. (1994). Ethical issues in psychological research. In A. M. Colman (Ed.)., *Companion Encyclopedia of Psychology* (Vol. **2**, pp. 1156–1176).

London: Routledge.

Galeotti, G. (1994). On proportional nonrepresentation. *Public Choice,* **80,** 359–370.

Gallo, P. S. (1966). Effects of increased incentives upon the use of threat in bargaining. *Journal of Personality and Social Psychology,* **4,** 14–20.

Gallo, P. S. & McClintock, C. G. (1965). Cooperative and competitive behavior in mixed-motive games. *Journal of Conflict Resolution,* **9,** 68–78.

Gamson, W. A. (1961a). An experimental test of a theory of coalition formation. *American Sociological Review,* **26,** 565–573.

Gamson, W. A. (1961b). A theory of coalition formation. *American Sociological Review,* **26,** 373–382.

Gamson, W. A. (1962). Coalition formation at presidential nominating conventions. *American Journal of Sociology,* **68,** 157–171.

Gamson, W. A. (1964). Experimental studies of coalition formation. In L. Berkowitz (Ed.), *Advances in Experimental Social Psychology,* **1,** 82–110. New York: Academic Press.

Gärdenfors, P. (1976). Manipulation of social choice functions. *Journal of Economic Theory,* **13,** 217–228.

Gardner, M. (1980). Mathematical games: From counting votes to making votes count: The mathematics of elections. *Scientific American,* **243**(4), 16–26.

Gardner, M. (1988). Nontransitive paradoxes. In M. Gardner, *Time Travel and Other Mathematical Bewilderments* (pp. 55–69). New York: W. H. Freeman.

Gardner, R. M., Corbin, T. L., Beltramo, J. S., & Nickell, G. G. (1986). The Prisoner's Dilemma Game and cooperation in the rat. *Psychological Reports,* **55,** 687–696.

Garman, M. & Kamien, M. (1968). The paradox of voting: Probability calculations. *Behavioral Science,* **13,** 306–316.

Gauthier, D. (1975). Coordination. *Dialogue,* **14,** 195–221.

Gauthier, D. (1986). *Morals by Agreement.* Oxford: Clarendon Press.

Geist, V. (1966). The evolution of horn-like organs. *Behaviour,* **27,** 175–214.

Geist, V. (1974). On fighting strategies in animal combat. *Nature,* **250,** 354.

Geist, V. (1978). On weapons, combat, and ecology. In L. Krames, P. Pliner, & T. Alloway (Eds), *Aggression, Dominance, and Individual Spacing.* New York: Plenum.

Gewirth, A. (1984). *Reason and morality.* Chicago, IL: University of Chicago Press.

Gibbard, A. (1973). Manipulation of voting schemes: A general result. *Econometrica,* **41,** 587–601.

Gibbons, R. (1992). *A Primer in Game Theory.* Hemel Hempstead: Harvester Wheatsheaf.

Gibbs, J. (1982). *Sex and Communication Effects in a Mixed-Motive Game.* Unpublished doctoral dissertation, University of Durham.

Gilbert, M. (1989). Rationality and salience. *Philosophical Studies*, **57**, 61–77.

Gillett, R. T. (1984). The weak Borda effect is an unsatisfactory index of plurality/majority disagreement. *British Journal of Mathematical and Statistical Psychology*, **37**, 128–130.

Gillies, D. B. (1953). *Some Theorems on N-person Games*. Unpublished doctoral dissertation, Princeton University.

Glance, N. S. & Huberman, B. A. (1994). The dynamics of social dilemmas. *Scientific American*, **270**(3), 58–63.

Gleser, L. J. (1969). The paradox of voting: Some probabilistic results. *Public Choice*, **7**, 47–64.

Goehring, D. J. & Kahan, J. P. (1976). The uniform N-Person Prisoner's Dilemma game: Construction and test of an index of cooperation. *Journal of Conflict Resolution*, **20**, 111–128.

Good, D. A. (1991). Cooperation in a microcosm: Lessons from laboratory games. In R. A. Hinde & J. Groebel (Eds), *Cooperation and Prosocial Behaviour* (pp. 224–237). Cambridge: Cambridge University Press.

Goodnow, J. J. (1955). Determinants of choice-distribution in two-choice situations. *American Journal of Psychology*, **68**, 106–116.

Grodzins, M. (1957). Metropolitan segregation. *Scientific American*, **197**(4), 33–41.

Grofman, B. (1972). A note on some generalizations of the paradox of cyclical majorities. *Public Choice*, **12**, 113–114.

Grofman, B. & Field, S. L. (1988). Rousseau's general will: A Condorcetian perspective. *American Political Science Review*, **82**, 567–576.

Grzelak, J. (1988). Conflict and cooperation. In M. Hewstone, W. Stroebe, J.-P. Codol, & G. M. Stephenson (Eds), *Introduction to Social Psychology: A European Perspective* (pp. 288–312). Oxford: Basil Blackwell.

Guilbaud, G. T. (1952). Les théories de l'interêt général et la problème logique de l'aggregation. *Economie Appliquée*, **5**, 501–584. [Trans. and reproduced in P. F. Lazarsfeld & N. W. Henry (Eds), *Readings in Mathematical Social Sciences* (pp. 262–307), Chicago: Science Research Associates.]

Guinier, L. (1994). *The Tyranny of the Majority: Fundamental Fairness in Representative Democracy*. New York: Free Press.

Gumpert, P., Deutsch, M., & Epstein, Y. (1969). Effects of incentive magnitude on cooperation in the Prisoner's Dilemma game. *Journal of Personality and Social Psychology*, **11**, 66–69.

Guyer, M. & Perkel, B. (1972). *Experimental Games: A Bibliography (1945–1971)*. Ann Arbor, MI: Mental Health Research Institute, Communication 293.

Guyer, M. & Rapoport, An. (1972). 2 × 2 games played once. *Journal of Conflict Resolution*, **16**, 409–431.

Haldeman, H. R. & DiMona, J. (1978). *The Ends of Power*. New York: Times Books.

Hamburger, H. (1973). N-person Prisoner's Dilemma. *Journal of Mathematical Sociology,* **3,** 27–48.

Hamburger, H. (1977). Dynamics of cooperation in take-some games. In W. H. Kempf & B. H. Repp (Eds), *Mathematical Models for Social Psychology.* Bern: Hans Huber.

Hamburger, H. (1979). *Games as Models of Social Phenomena.* San Francisco: W. H. Freeman.

Hamburger, H., Guyer, M., & Fox, J. (1975). Group size and cooperation. *Journal of Conflict Resolution,* **19,** 503–531.

Hamermesh, D. S. (1973). Who "wins" in wage bargaining? *Industrial and Labor Relations Review,* **26,** 146–149.

Hamilton, W. D. (1967). Extraordinary sex ratios. *Science,* **156,** 477–488.

Hampton, J. (1986). *Hobbes and the Social Contract Tradition.* Cambridge: Cambridge University Press.

Hardin, G. (1968). The tragedy of the commons. *Science,* **162,** 1243–1248.

Harford, T. C. & Solomon, L. (1967). 'Reformed sinner' and 'lapsed saint' strategies in the Prisoner's Dilemma game. *Journal of Conflict Resolution,* **11,** 104–109.

Harris, R. J. (1969a). A geometric classification system for 2 × 2 interval-symmetric games. *Behavioral Science,* **14,** 138–146.

Harris, R. J. (1969b). Note on Howard's theory of meta-games. *Psychological Reports,* **24,** 849–850.

Harris, R. J. (1972). An interval-scale classification system for all 2 × 2 games. *Behavioral Science,* **17,** 371–383.

Harsanyi, J. C. (1967, 1968a, 1968b). Games with incomplete information played by "Bayesian" players. *Management Science,* **14,** 159–182, 320–334, 486–502.

Harsanyi, J. C. (1973a). Games with randomly distributed payoffs: A new rationale for mixed-strategy equilibrium points. *International Journal of Game Theory,* **2,** 1–23.

Harsanyi, J. C. (1973b). Oddness of the number of equilibrium points: A new proof. *International Journal of Game Theory,* **2,** 235–250.

Harsanyi, J. C. (1976). *Essays on Ethics, Social Behavior, and Scientific Explanation.* Dordrecht: D. Reidl.

Harsanyi, J. C. & Selten, R. (1988). *A General Theory of Equilibrium Selection in Games.* Cambridge, MA: MIT Press.

Harvey, J. H. & Smith, W. P. (1977). *Social Psychology: An Attributional Approach.* St Louis, MI: Mosby.

Haywood, O. G., Jr. (1954). Military decision and game theory. *Journal of the Operations Research Society of America,* **2,** 365–385.

Heal, J. (1978). Common knowledge. *The Philosophical Quarterly,* **28,** 116–131.

Heckathorn, D. (1978). A paradigm for bargaining and a test of two bargaining models. *Behavioral Science,* **23,** 73–85.

Herzberg, R. Q. & Wilson, R. K. (1988). Results on sophisticated voting in an experimental setting. *Journal of Politics*, **50**, 471–486.

Hillinger, C. (1971). Voting on issues and on platforms. *Behavioral Science*, **16**, 564–566.

Hines, W. (1987). Evolutionarily stable strategies: A review of basic theory. *Theoretical Population Biology*, **31**, 195–272.

Hobbes, T. (1651). *Leviathan, or the Matter, Forme and Power of a Commonwealth, ecclesiasticall and civill* (Ed. M. Oakeshott, Oxford: Basil Blackwell, 1946).

Hofstadter, D. R. (1983). Metamagical themas: Computer tournaments of the Prisoner's Dilemma suggest how cooperation evolves. *Scientific American*, **248**(5), 14–20.

Hollis, M. (1979). Rational man and social science. In R. Harrison (Ed.), *Rational Action: Studies in Philosophy and Social Science*. Cambridge: Cambridge University Press.

Hottes, J. & Kahn, A. (1974). Sex differences in a mixed-motive conflict situation. *Journal of Personality*, **42**, 260–275.

Howard, N. (1971). *Paradoxes of Rationality: Theory of Metagames and Political Behavior*. Cambridge, MA: MIT Press.

Howard, N. (1974). "General" metagames: An extension of the metagame concept. In A. Rapoport (Ed.), *Game Theory as a Theory of Conflict Resolution* (pp. 261–83). Dordrecht: D. Reidel.

Howard, N. (1987). The present and future of metagame analysis. *European Journal of Operational Research*, **32**, 1–25.

Hsu, F., Anantharaman, T., Campbell, M., & Nowatzyk, A. (1990). A grandmaster chess machine. *Scientific American*, **263**(4), 18–24.

Hume, D. (1739–1740). *A Treatise of Human Nature: Being an Attempt to Introduce the Experimental Method of Reasoning Into Moral Subjects*. London: Thomas Longman. [Edited by L. A. Selby-Bigge, Oxford: Clarendon Press, 1888, 2nd ed. 1978]

Humphreys, L. G. (1939). Acquisition and extinction of verbal expectations in a situation analogous to conditioning. *Journal of Experimental Psychology*, **25**, 294–301.

Hurley, S. L. (1991). Newcomb's problem, Prisoner's Dilemma, and collective action. *Synthese*, **86**, 173–196.

Hurley, S. L. (1994). A new take from Nozick on Newcomb's problem and Prisoner's Dilemma. *Analysis*, **54**, 65–72.

Isenberg, D. J. (1986). Group polarization: A critical review and meta-analysis. *Journal of Personality and Social Psychology*, **50**, 1141–1151.

Jacobi, N. (1993). Newcomb paradox: A realist resolution. *Theory and Decision*, **35**, 1–17.

Jerdee, T. H. & Rosen, B. (1974). Effects of opportunity to communicate and visibility of individual decisions on behavior in the common interest. *Journal of Applied Psychology*, **59**, 712–716.

Johnston, R. J. & Pattie, C. J. (1991). Tactical voting in Great Britain in 1983 and 1987: An alternative approach. *British Journal of Political Science,* **21**, 95–128.

Jones, A. J. (1980). *Game Theory: Mathematical Models of Conflict.* Chichester: Ellis Horwood.

Jones, G. G. (1986). *Factors Affecting Escalation in Auction Games.* Unpublished doctoral dissertation, University of Leicester.

Jorgenson, D. O. & Papciak, A. S. (1981). The effects of communication, resource feedback, and identifiability on behavior in a simulated commons. *Journal of Experimental Social Psychology,* **17**, 373–385.

Joyce, R. C. (1976). *Sophisticated Voting for Three Candidate Contests Under the Plurality Rule.* Unpublished doctoral dissertation, University of Rochester.

Jung, J. P. (1990). Black and Farquharson on order-of-voting effects: An extension. *Social Choice and Welfare,* **7**, 319–329.

Kahan, J. P. (1973). Noninteraction in an anonymous three-person Prisoner's Dilemma Game. *Behavioral Science,* **18**, 124–127.

Kahan, J. P. & Goehring, D. J. (1973). Responsiveness in two-person zero-sum games. *Behavioral Science,* **18**, 27–33.

Kahan, J. P. & Rapoport, Am. (1974a). Decisions of timing in bipolarized conflict situations with complete information. *Acta Psychologica,* **38**, 183–203.

Kahan, J. P. & Rapoport, Am. (1974b). Test of the bargaining set and kernel models in three-person games. In Am. Rapoport (Ed.), *Game Theory as a Theory of Conflict Resolution* (pp. 119–160). Dordrecht: D. Reidl.

Kahan, J. P. & Rapoport, Am. (1977). When you don't need to join: The effects of guaranteed payoffs on bargaining in three-person cooperative games. *Theory and Decision,* **8**, 97–126.

Kahan, J. P. & Rapoport, Am. (1984). *Theories of Coalition Formation.* Hillsdale, NJ: Erlbaum.

Kahn, H. (1965). *On Escalation.* New York: Praeger.

Kahneman, D. & Tversky, A. (1982). The psychology of preferences. *Scientific American,* **246**(1), 136–142.

Kahneman, D. & Tversky, A. (1984). Choices, values, and frames. *American Psychologist,* **39**, 341–350.

Kalai, E. & Smorodinsky, M. (1975). Other solutions to Nash's bargaining problem. *Econometrica,* **43**, 513–518.

Kalisch, G. K., Milnor, J. W., Nash, J. F., & Nering, E. D. (1954). Some experimental n-person games. In R. M. Thrall, C. H. Coombs, & R. L. Davis (Eds), *Decision Processes* (pp. 301–27). New York: Wiley.

Kandori, M., Mailath, G. J., & Rob, R. (1993). Learning, mutation, and long run equilibria in games. *Econometrica,* **61**, 29–56.

Kanouse, D. E. & Wiest, W. M. (1967). Some factors affecting choice in the Prisoner's Dilemma. *Journal of Conflict Resolution,* **11**, 206–213.

Kant, I. (1785). *Grundlegung zur Metaphysik der Sitten*. In E. Cassirer (Ed.), 1912–1922, Immanuel Kants Werke (Vol. IV). Berlin. [English translation by L. W. Beck entitled *Foundations of the Metaphysics of Morals*, Chicago: University of Chicago Press]

Karlin, S. (1959). *Mathematical Models and Theory in Games, Programming, and Economics* (Vol. 2). Reading, MA: Addison-Wesley.

Kaufman, H. & Becker, G. M. (1961). The empirical determination of game-theoretical strategies. *Journal of Experimental Psychology,* **61**, 462–468.

Kaufman, H. & Lamb, J. C. (1967). An empirical test of game theory as a descriptive model. *Perceptual and Motor Skills,* **24**, 951–960.

Kaufman M. & Tack, W. H. (1975). Koalitions-bildung und Gewinnaufteilung bei strategisch äquivalenten 3-Personen-Spielen. *Zeitschrift für Sozialpsychologie,* **6**, 227–245.

Kavka, G. (1986). *Hobbesian Moral and Political Theory*. Princeton, NJ: Princeton University Press.

Kelley, H. H. (1965). Experimental studies of threats in interpersonal negotiations. *Journal of Conflict Resolution,* **9**, 79–105.

Kelley, H. H. & Arrowood, A. J. (1960). Coalitions in the triad: Critique and experiment. *Sociometry,* **23**, 231–244.

Kelley, H. H. & Grzelak, J. L. (1972). Conflict between individual and common interest in an n-person relationship. *Journal of Personality and Social Psychology,* **21**, 190–7.

Kelley, H. H. & Stahelski, A. J. (1970a). Errors in perception of intentions in a mixed-motive game. *Journal of Experimental Social Psychology,* **6**, 379–400.

Kelley, H. H. & Stahelski, A. J. (1970b). The inference of intentions from moves in the Prisoner's Dilemma game. *Journal of Experimental Social Psychology,* **6**, 401–419.

Kelley, H. H. & Stahelski, A. J. (1970c). Social interaction basis of cooperators' and competitors' beliefs about others. *Journal of Personality and Social Psychology,* **16**, 66–91.

Kelley, H. H., Thibaut, J. W., Radloff, R., & Mundy, D. (1962). The development of cooperation in the "minimal social situation". *Psychological Monographs,* **76**, Whole No. 19.

Kelly, J. S. (1974). Voting anomalies, the number of voters, and the number of alternatives. *Econometrica,* **42**, 239–251.

Kelly, J. S. (1978). *Arrow Impossibility Theorems*. New York: Academic Press.

Kerr, N. L. (1989). Illusions of efficacy: The effects of group size on perceived efficacy in social dilemmas. *Journal of Experimental Social Psychology,* **25**, 287–313.

Kerr, N. L. (1992). Efficacy as a causal and moderating variable in social dilemmas. In W. B. G. Liebrand, D. M. Messick, & H. A. M. Wilke (Eds), *Social Dilemmas: Theoretical Issues and Research Findings* (pp. 59–80). Oxford: Pergamon.

Kerr, N, L. & Kaufman-Gilliland, C. M. (1994). Communication, commitment, and cooperation in social dilemmas. *Journal of Personality and Social Psychology*, **66**, 513–529.

Keynes, J. M. (1936). *The General Theory of Employment Interest and Money.* London: Macmillan.

Keynes, J. M. (1937). The general theory of employment. *Quarterly Journal of Economics*, **51**, 209–223.

Kirman, A. P. & Sondermann, D. (1972). Arrow's theorem, many agents, and invisible dictators. *Journal of Economic Theory*, **5**, 267–277.

Komorita, S. S. (1979). An equal excess model of coalition formation. *Behavioral Science*, **24**, 369–381.

Komorita, S. S. (1984). Coalition bargaining. *Advances in Experimental Social Psychology*, **18**, 183–245.

Komorita, S. S. (1987). Cooperative choice in decomposed social dilemmas. *Personality and Social Psychology Bulletin*, **13**, 53–63.

Komorita, S. S. & Barth, J. M. (1985). Components of reward in social dilemmas. *Journal of Personality and Social Psychology*, **48**, 364–373.

Komorita, S. S. & Carnevale, P. (1992). Motivational arousal vs. decision framing in social dilemmas. In W. B. G. Liebrand, D. M. Messick, & H. A. M. Wilke (Eds), *Social Dilemmas: Theoretical Issues and Research Findings* (pp. 209–223). Oxford: Pergamon.

Komorita, S. S. & Chertkoff, J. M. (1973). A bargaining theory of coalition formation. *Psychological Review*, **80**, 149–162.

Komorita, S. S. & Ellis, A. L. (1988). Level of aspiration in coalition bargaining. *Journal of Personality and Social Psychology*, **54**, 421–431.

Komorita, S. S. & Kravitz, D. A. (1983). Coalition formation: A social psychological approach. In P. B. Paulus (Ed.), *Basic Group Processes* (pp. 179–203). New York: Springer-Verlag.

Komorita, S. S. & Lapworth, C. W. (1982). Cooperative choice among individuals versus groups in an N-person dilemma situation. *Journal of Personality and Social Psychology*, **42**, 487–496.

Komorita, S. S. & Miller, C. E. (1986). Bargaining strength as a function of coalition alternatives. *Journal of Personality and Social Psychology*, **51**, 325–332.

Komorita, S. S., Parks, C. D., & Hulbert, L. G. (1991). Reciprocity and the induction of cooperation in social dilemmas. *Journal of Personality and Social Psychology*, **62**, 607–617.

Komorita, S. S., Sweeny, J., & Kravitz, D. A. (1980). Cooperative choices in the n-person dilemma situation. *Journal of Personality and Social Psychology*, **38**, 504–516.

Kozelka, R. (1969). A Bayesian approach to Jamaican fishing. In I. R. Buchler & H. G. Nutini (Eds), *Game Theory in the Behavioral Sciences* (pp. 117–125). Pittsburgh, PA: University of Pittsburgh Press.

Kraines, D. & Kraines, V. (1989). Pavlov and the Prisoner's Dilemma. *Theory and Decision,* **26**, 47–79.

Kramer, G. H. (1972). Sophisticated voting over multidimensional choice spaces. *Journal of Mathematical Sociology,* **2**, 165–180.

Kramer, G. H. (1973). On a class of equilibrium conditions for majority rule. *Econometrica,* **41**, 285–297.

Kramer, R. M. & Brewer, M. B. (1984). Effects of group identity on resource use in a simulated commons dilemma. *Journal of Personality and Social Psychology,* **46**, 1044–1057.

Kramer, R. M. & Brewer, M. B. (1986). Social group identity and the emergence of cooperation in resource conservation dilemmas. In H. Wilke, D. M. Messick, & C. G. Rutte (Eds), *Experimental Social Dilemmas.* Frankfurt am Main: Verlag Peter Lang.

Kramer, R. M., McClintock, C. G., & Messick, D. M. (1986). Social values and cooperative response to a simulated resource conservation crisis. *Journal of Personality,* **54**, 576–592.

Krebs, J. R. & Davies, N. B. (1991). *Behavioural Ecology: An Evolutionary Approach* (3rd ed.). Oxford: Basil Blackwell.

Krehbiel, K. (1986). Sophisticated and myopic behavior in legislative committees: An experimental study. *American Journal of Political Science,* **30**, 542–561.

Krehbiel, K. & Rivers, D. (1990). Sophisticated voting in Congress: A reconsideration. *Journal of Politics,* **52**, 548–578.

Kreps, D. M. & Wilson, R. (1982). Reputation and imperfect information. *Journal of Economic Theory,* **27**, 253–279.

Kuhlman, D. M. & Marshello, A. J. F. (1975). Individual differences in game motivation as moderators of preprogrammed strategy effects in Prisoner's Dilemma. *Journal of Personality and Social Psychology,* **32**, 922–931.

Kuhlman, D. M. & Wimberley, D. L. (1976). Expectations of choice behavior held by cooperators, competitors, and individualists across four classes of experimental game. *Journal of Personality and Social Psychology,* **34**, 69–81.

Lacey, O. L. & Pate, J. C. (1960). An experimental test of game theory as a descriptive model. *Psychological Reports,* **7**, 527–530.

Laplace, P.-S. (1814). *Théorie Analytique des Probabilités.* 2nd ed. Paris. In P.-S. Laplace, 1878–1912, *Oeuvres Complètes* (Vol. 7, Supplement 1). Paris.

Lazarus, J. (1982). Competition and conflict in animals. In A. M. Colman (Ed.), *Cooperation and Competition in Humans and Animals* (pp. 26–56). Wokingham: Van Nostrand Reinhold.

Lazarus, J. (1987). The concepts of sociobiology. In H. Beloff & A. M. Colman (eds), *Psychology Survey 6* (pp. 192–217). Leicester: The British Psychological Society.

Lazarus, J. (1994). Behavioural ecology and evolution. In A. M. Colman (Ed.), *Companion Encyclopedia of Psychology* (Vol. 1, pp. 69–87). London: Routledge.

Leininger, W. (1989). Escalation and cooperation in conflict situations: The

Dollar Auction revisited. *Journal of Conflict Resolution*, **33**, 231–254.

Leonard, R. J. (1992). Creating a context for game theory. In E. R. Weintraub (Ed.), *Toward a History of Game Theory: Annual Supplement to Volume 24 History of Political Economy* (pp. 29–76). Durham, NC & London, England: Duke University Press.

Levi, I. (1975). Newcomb's many problems. *Theory and Decision*, **6**, 161–175.

Levin, I. P. & Gaeth, G. J. (1988). How consumers are affected by the framing of attribute information before and after consuming the product. *Journal of Consumer Research*, **15**, 374–378.

Levine, M. E. & Plott, C. R. (1977). Agenda influence and its implications. *Virginia Law Review*, **63**, 561–604.

Levinsohn, J. R. & Rapoport, Am. (1978). Coalition formation in multistage three-person cooperative games. In H. Sauermann (Ed.), *Beiträge zur experimentellen Wirtschaftsforschung. Vol. III: Coalition Forming Behavior.* Tübingen: J. C. B. Mohr.

Lewis, D. K. (1969). *Convention: A Philosophical Study.* Cambridge, MA: Harvard University Press.

Lewis, D. K. (1979). Prisoner's Dilemma is a Newcomb problem. *Philosophy and Public Affairs*, **8**, 235–240.

Lewontin, R. C. (1961). Evolution and the theory of games. *Journal of Theoretical Biology*, **1**, 382–403.

Lichtenberger, J. (1975). *Drei-Personen-Spiele mit Seitenzahlungen.* Unpublished doctoral dissertation, Universität des Saarlandes.

Lieberman, B. (1959). *Human Behavior in a Strictly Determined 2 × 2 Matrix Game.* Research Memorandum, Department of Social Relations, Harvard University.

Lieberman, B. (1960a). *A Failure of Game Theory to Predict Human Behavior.* Memo SP-101, Laboratory of Social Relations, Harvard University.

Lieberman, B. (1960b). Human behavior in a strictly determined 3 × 3 matrix game. *Behavioral Science*, **5**, 317–322.

Lieberman, B. (1962). Experimental studies of conflict in some two-person and three-person games. In J. H. Criswell, H. Solomon, & P. Suppes (Eds), *Mathematical Models in Small Group Processes* (pp. 203–220). Stanford, CA· Stanford University Press.

Liebrand, W. B. G. (1984). The effect of social motives, communication and group size on behaviour in *n*-person multistage mixed-motive games. *European Journal of Social Psychology*, **14**, 239–264.

Liebrand, W. B. G., Jansen, R. W. T. L., Rijken, V. M., & Shure, C. J. M. (1986). Might over morality: Social values and the perception of other players in experimental games. *Journal of Experimental Social Psychology*, **22**, 293–215.

Liebrand, W. B. G. & Van Run, G. J. (1985). The effects of social motives on behavior in social dilemmas in two cultures. *Journal of Experimental Social Psychology*, **21**, 86–102.

Liebrand, W. B. G., Wilke, H. A. M., Vogel, R., & Wolters, F. J. M. (1986). Value orientation and conformity: A study using three types of social dilemma games. *Journal of Conflict Resolution, 30,* 77–97.

Lindskold, S., Betz, B., & Walters, P. (1986). Transforming competitive or cooperative climates. *Journal of Conflict Resolution, 30,* 99–114.

Lloyd, W. F. (1833). *Two Lectures on the Checks to Population.* Oxford: Oxford University Press.

Locke, D. (1978). How to make a Newcomb choice. *Analysis, 38,* 17–23.

Lorberbaum, J. (1994). No strategy is evolutionarily stable in the repeated Prisoner's Dilemma. *Journal of Theoretical Biology, 168,* 117–130.

Lorenz, K. (1966). *On Aggression.* London: Methuen.

Lucas, R. E. (1981). *Studies in Business Cycle Theory.* Cambridge, MA: MIT Press.

Lucas, W. F. (1968). *The Proof That a Game May Not Have a Solution.* Memorandum RM-5543-PR. Santa Monica, CA: The Rand Corporation.

Luce, R. D. & Raiffa, H. (1957). *Games and Decisions: Introduction and Critical Survey.* New York: Wiley.

Lumsden, M. (1973). The Cyprus conflict as a Prisoner's Dilemma Game. *Journal of Conflict Resolution, 17,* 7–32.

Mack, D. (1975). Skirting the competition. *Psychology Today, 8,* 39–41.

Mackie, J. L. (1977). *Ethics: Inventing Right and Wrong.* Harmondsworth: Penguin.

Mackie, J. L. (1978). The law of the jungle: Moral alternatives and principles of evolution. *Philosophy, 53,* 455–464.

Mackie, J. L. (1982). Cooperation, competition, and moral philosophy. In A. M. Colman (Ed.), *Cooperation and Competition in Humans and Animals* (pp. 271–284). Wokingham: Van Nostrand Reinhold.

Malcolm, D. & Lieberman, B. (1965). The behavior of responsive individuals playing a two-person, zero-sum game requiring the use of mixed strategies. *Psychonomic Science, 2,* 373–374.

Malinas, G. (1993). Reflective coherence and Newcomb problems: A simple solution. *Theory and Decision, 35,* 151–166.

March, J. G. (1986). Bounded rationality, ambiguity, and the engineering of choice. In J. Elster (Ed.), *Rational Choice* (pp. 142–170). Oxford: Basil Blackwell. [Originally published in *Bell Journal of Economics,* 1978, *9,* pp. 587–608]

Martin, D. (1978). The selective usefulness of game theory. *Social Studies of Science SAGE, 8,* 85–110.

Marwell, G. & Ames, R. E. (1979). Experiments on the provision of public goods I: Resources, interest, group size, and the free rider problem. *American Journal of Sociology, 84,* 1335–1360.

Marwell, G. & Schmitt, D. (1972). Cooperation in a three-person Prisoner's Dilemma. *Journal of Personality and Social Psychology, 21,* 376–383.

Maschler, M. (1978). Playing an n-person game: An experiment. In H.

Sauermann (Ed.), *Beiträge zur experimentellen Wirtschaftsforschung. Vol. III: Coalition Forming Behavior.* Tübingen: J. C. B. Mohr.

May, R. M. (1971). Some mathematical remarks on the paradox of voting. *Behavioral Science,* **16,** 143–151.

May, R. M. (1983). Preference and paradox. *Nature,* **303**(5), 16–17.

Maynard Smith, J. (1972). Game theory and the evolution of fighting. In J. Maynard Smith, *On Evolution* (pp. 8–28). Edinburgh: Edinburgh University Press.

Maynard Smith, J. (1974). The theory of games and the evolution of animal conflicts. *Journal of Theoretical Biology,* **47,** 209–221.

Maynard Smith, J. (1976a). Evolution and the theory of games. *American Scientist,* **64**(1), 41–45.

Maynard Smith, J. (1976b). Group selection. *Quarterly Review of Biology,* **51,** 277–283.

Maynard Smith, J. (1978a). The evolution of behavior. *Scientific American,* **239**(3), 136–145.

Maynard Smith, J. (1978b). Optimization theory in evolution. *Annual Review of Ecology and Systematics,* **9,** 31–56.

Maynard Smith, J. (1979). Game theory and the evolution of behaviour. *Proceedings of the Royal Society of London B,* **205,** 475–488.

Maynard Smith, J. (1982). *Evolution and the Theory of Games.* Cambridge: Cambridge University Press.

Maynard Smith, J. (1984). Game theory and the evolution of behavior. *Behavioral and Brain Sciences,* **7,** 95–101.

Maynard Smith, J. & Price, G. R. (1973). The logic of animal conflict. *Nature,* **246,** 15–18.

McClennen, E. F. (1985). Prisoner's dilemma and resolute choice. In R. Campbell & L. Sowden (Eds), *Paradoxes of Rationality and Cooperation: Prisoner's Dilemma and Newcomb's Problem* (pp. 94–104). Vancouver: University of British Columbia Press.

McClennen, E. F. (1994). *Rationality and rules.* Unpublished manuscript, Department of Philosophy, Bowling Green State University.

McClennen, E. F. & Found, P. (1995). Dutch books and money pumps. *Theory and Decision,* in press.

McClintock, C. G. (1972). Game behavior and social motivation in interpersonal settings. In C. G. McClintock (Ed.), *Experimental Social Psychology* (pp. 271–297). New York: Holt, Rinehart, & Winston.

McClintock, C. G. & Liebrand, W. B. G. (1988). The role of interdependence structure, individual value orientation and other's strategy in social decision making: A transformational analysis. *Journal of Personality and Social Psychology,* **55,** 396–409.

McClintock, C. G. & McNeel, C. P. (1966). Cross-cultural comparisons of interpersonal motives. *Sociometry,* **29,** 406–427.

McClintock, C. G. & McNeel, S. P. (1967). Prior dyadic experience and monetary reward as determinants of cooperative behavior. *Journal of Personality and Social Psychology,* 5, 282–94.

McClintock, C. G. & Nuttin, J. M. (1969). Development of competitive game behavior in children across two cultures. *Journal of Experimental Social Psychology,* 5, 203–219.

McDaniel, W. C. & Sistrunk, F. (1991). Management dilemmas and decisions: Impact of framing and anticipated responses. *Journal of Conflict Resolution,* 35, 21–42.

McKelvey, R. D. & Niemi, R. G. (1978). A multistage game representation of sophisticated voting for binary procedures. *Journal of Economic Theory,* 18, 1–22.

McLean, I. S. (1981). The social contract in *Leviathan* and the Prisoner's Dilemma supergame. *Political Studies,* 29, 339–351.

McLean, I. S. (1988). Ships that pass in the night: Electoral reform and social choice theory. *Political Quarterly,* 59, 63–71.

McLean, I. S. (1989). *Democracy and New Technology.* Cambridge: Polity Press.

McNeel, C. P., McClintock, C. G., & Nuttin, J. (1972). Effects of sex-role in a two-person mixed-motive game. *Journal of Personality and Social Psychology,* 24, 372–378.

McNeil, B. J., Pauker, S. G., & Tversky, A. (1988). On the framing of medical decisions. In D. E. Bell, H. Raiffa, & A. Tversky (Eds), *Decision Making: Descriptive, Normative, and Prescriptive Interactions* (pp. 562–568). Cambridge: Cambridge University Press.

McVicar, J. (1981). Postscript. In S. Cohen & L. Taylor, *Psychological Survival: The Experience of Long-Term Imprisonment* (2nd ed., pp. 221–229). Harmondsworth: Penguin.

Mealey, L. (1995). The sociobiology of sociopathy: An integrated evolutionary model. *Behavioral and Brain Sciences,* in press.

Medlin, S. M. (1976). Effect of grand coalition payoffs on coalition formation in 3-person games. *Behavioral Science,* 21, 48–61.

Meeker, B. F. (1970). An experimental study of cooperation and competition in West Africa. *International Journal of Psychology,* 5, 11–19.

Mehta, J., Starmer, C., & Sugden, R. (1994). Focal points in pure coordination games: An experimental investigation. *Theory and Decision,* 36, 163–185.

Messick, D. M. (1967). Interdependent decision strategies in zero-sum games: A computer-controlled study. *Behavioral Science,* 12, 33–48.

Messick, D. M. (1973). To join or not to join: An approach to the unionization decision. *Organizational Behavior and Human Performance,* 10, 145–156.

Messick, D. M. & Brewer, M. B. (1983). Solving social dilemmas: A review. In L. Wheeler & P. Shaver (Eds), *Review of Personality and Social Psychology,* 4, 11–41. Beverly Hills: Sage.

Messick, D. M. & Rutte, C. G. (1992). In W. B. G. Liebrand, D. M. Messick, & H. A. M. Wilke (Eds), *Social Dilemmas: Theoretical Issues and Research*

Findings (pp. 101–107). Oxford: Pergamon.

Michener, H. A., Fleishman, J. A., Vaske, J. J., & Statza, G. R. (1975). Minimum resource and pivotal power theories: A competitive test in 4-person coalition situations. *Journal of Conflict Resolution*, **19**, 89–107.

Milgrom, P. & Roberts, J. (1982). Predation, reputation, and entry deterrence. *Journal of Economic Theory*, **27**, 280–312.

Miller, C. E. & Crandall, R. (1980). Experimental research on the social psychology of bargaining and coalition formation. In P. Paulus (Ed.), *Psychology of Group Influence* (pp. 333–374). Hillsdale, NJ: Erlbaum.

Miller, C. E. & Komorita, S. S. (1986). Changes in outcomes in coalition bargaining. *Journal of Personality and Social Psychology*, **51**, 721–729.

Miller, D. T. & Holmes, J. G. (1975). The role of situational restrictiveness on self-fulfilling prophecies: A theoretical and empirical extension of Kelley and Stahelski's triangle hypothesis. *Journal of Personality and Social Psychology*, **31**, 661–673.

Miller, N. R. (1977). Graph-theoretic approaches to the theory of voting. *American Journal of Political Science*, **21**, 769–803.

Milnor, J. (1954). Games against nature. In R. M. Thrall, C. H. Coombs, & R. L. Davis (Eds.), *Decision Processes* (pp. 49–59). New York: Wiley.

Mintz, A. (1951). Non-adaptive group behavior. *Journal of Abnormal and Social Psychology*, **46**, 150–159.

Mitchell, C. R. (1991). Ending conflicts and wars: Judgement, rationality and entrapment. *International Social Science Journal*, **43**, 35–55.

Molander, P. (1985). The optimal level of generosity in a selfish, uncertain world. *Journal of Conflict Resolution*, **29**, 611–618.

Molm, L. D. (1981). A contingency change analysis of the disruption and recovery of social exchange and cooperation. *Social Forces*, **59**, 729–751.

Moore, P. G. (1980). *Reason by Numbers*. Harmondsworth: Penguin.

Morin, R. E. (1960). Strategies in games with saddle-points. *Psychological Reports*, **7**, 479–483.

Morley, I. E. & Stephenson, G. M. (1977). *The Social Psychology of Bargaining*. London: George Allen & Unwin.

Muir, H. C. & Marrison, C. (1989). Human factors in cabin safety. *Aerospace*, April, 18–21.

Murnighan, J. K. (1978). Models of coalition behavior: Game theoretic, social psychological, and political perspectives. *Psychological Bulletin*, **85**, 1130–1153.

Myers, D. G. & Lamm, H. (1976). The group polarization phenomenon. *Psychological Bulletin*, **83**, 602–627.

Myerson, R. B. (1991). *Game Theory: Analysis of Conflict*. Cambridge, MA: Harvard University Press.

Myerson, R. B. & Weber, R. J. (1993). A theory of voting equilibria. *American Political Science Review*, **87**, 102–114.

Nail, P. & Cole, S. G. (1985). Three theories of coalition behaviour: A probabilistic extension. *British Journal of Social Psychology*, **24**, 181–190.

Nanson, E. J. (1882). Methods of elections. *Transactions and Proceedings of the Royal Society of Victoria*, **18**.

Nash, J. F. (1950a). Equilibrium points in n-person games. *Proceedings of the National Academy of Sciences, U.S.A.*, **36**, 48–49.

Nash, J. F. (1950b). The bargaining problem. *Econometrica*, **18**, 155–162.

Nash, J. F. (1951). Non-cooperative games. *Annals of Mathematics*, **54**, 286–295.

Nash, J. F. (1953). Two-person cooperative games. *Econometrica*, **21**, 128–140.

Neal, P. (1988). Hobbes and rational choice theory. *Western Political Quarterly*, **41**, 635–652.

Nemeth, C. (1970). Bargaining and reciprocity. *Psychological Bulletin*, **74**, 297–308.

Nemeth, C. (1972). A critical analysis of research utilizing the Prisoner's Dilemma paradigm for the study of bargaining. *Advances in Experimental Social Psychology*, **6**, 203 34.

Nemeth, C. (Ed.). (1974). *Social Psychology: Classic and Contemporary Integrations*. Chicago, IL: Rand McNally.

Niemi, R. G. (1969). Majority decision-making with partial unidimensionality. *American Political Science Review*, **63**, 488–497.

Niemi, R. G. (1970). The occurrence of the paradox of voting in university elections. *Public Choice*, **8**, 91–100.

Niemi, R. G. (1983). An exegesis of Farquharson's Theory of Voting. *Public Choice*, **40**, 323–328.

Niemi, R. G. (1984). The problem of strategic behavior under approval voting. *American Political Science Review*, **78**, 952–958.

Niemi, R. G. & Frank, A. Q. (1982). Sophisticated voting under the plurality procedure. In P. C. Ordeshook & K. A. Shepsle (Eds), *Political Equilibrium*. Boston, MA: Kluwer Nijhoff.

Niemi, R. G. & Frank, A. Q. (1985). Sophisticated voting under the plurality procedure: A test of a new definition. *Theory and Decision*, **19**, 151–162.

Niemi, R. G. & Riker, W. H. (1976). The choice of voting systems. *Scientific American*, **234**(6), 21–27.

Niemi, R. G. & Weisberg, H. F. (1968). A mathematical solution for the probability of the paradox of voting. *Behavioral Science*, **13**, 317–323.

Niemi, R. G. & Weisberg, H. F. (Eds). (1972). *Probability Models of Collective Decision Making*. Columbus, OH: Charles E. Merrill.

Niemi, R. G. & Weisberg, H. F. (1973). A pairwise probability approach to the likelihood of the paradox of voting. *Behavioral Science*, **18**, 109–118.

Niemi, R. G., Whitten, G., & Franklin, M. N. (1992). Constituency characteristics, individual characteristics and tactical voting in the 1987 British general election. *British Journal of Political Science*, **22**, 229–254.

Nowak, M. & Sigmund, K. (1993). A strategy of win-stay, lose-shift that outperforms tit-for-tat in the Prisoner's Dilemma game. *Nature*, **364**, 56–58.

Nozick, R. (1969). Newcomb's problem and two principles of choice. In N. Rescher (Ed.), *Essays in Honor of Carl Hempel* (pp. 114–146). Dordrecht: D. Reidl.

Nozick, R. (1974). Reflections on Newcomb's paradox. *Scientific American*, **230**(3), 102–108.

Nozick, R. (1993). *The Nature of Rationality*. Princeton, NJ: Princeton University Press.

Nurmi, H. (1983). Voting procedures: A summary analysis. *British Journal of Political Science*, **13**, 181–208.

Nydegger, R. V. (1977). Independent utility scaling and the Nash bargaining model. *Behavioral Science*, **22**, 283–289.

Ofshe, L. & Ofshe, R. (1970). *Utility and Choice in Social Interaction*. Englewood Cliffs, NJ: Prentice-Hall.

Olson, M., Jr. (1965). *The Logic of Collective Action: Public Goods and the Theory of Groups*. Cambridge, MA: Harvard University Press.

Olson, M. (1982). *The Rise and Decline of Nations*. New Haven, CT: Yale University Press.

O'Neill, B. (1986). International escalation and the Dollar Auction. *Journal of Conflict Resolution*, **30**, 33–50.

Orbell, J. M., Van de Kragt, A. J. C., & Dawes, R. M. (1988). Explaining discussion-induced cooperation. *Journal of Personality and Social Psychology*, **54**, 811–819.

Ordeshook, P. C. (1986). *Game Theory and Political Theory: An Introduction*. Cambridge: Cambridge University Press.

Ordeshook, P. C. & Zeng, L. (1994). Some properties of Hare voting with strategic voters. *Public Choice*, **78**, 87–101.

Orwant, C. J. & Orwant, J. E. (1970). A comparison of interpreted and abstract versions of mixed-motive games. *Journal of Conflict Resolution*, **14**, 91–97.

Oskamp, S. (1971). Effects of programmed strategies on cooperation in the Prisoner's Dilemma and other mixed-motive games. *Journal of Conflict Resolution*, **15**, 225–259.

Oskamp, S. & Kleinke, C. (1970). Amount of reward as a variable in the Prisoner's Dilemma game. *Journal of Personality and Social Psychology*, **16**, 133–140.

Owen, G. (1968). *Game Theory*. Philadelphia, PA: W. B. Saunders.

Papadimitriou, C. H., & Steiglitz, K. (1982). *Combinatorial Optimization: Algorithms and Complexity*. Englewood Cliffs, NJ: Prentice-Hall.

Parfit, D. (1979a). Is common-sense morality self-defeating? *Journal of Philosophy*, **76**, 533–545.

Parfit, D. (1979b). Prudence, morality, and the Prisoner's Dilemma. *Proceedings of the British Academy*, **65**, 539–564.

Parfit, D. (1984). *Reasons and Persons*. Oxford: Clarendon Press.

Parker, G. A. (1970). The reproductive behaviour and nature of sexual selection in *Scatophaga stercoraria* L. II. *Journal of Animal Ecology*, **39**, 205–228.

Parker, G. A. (1978). Selfish genes, evolutionary games, and the adaptiveness of behaviour. *Nature*, **274**, 849–855.

Parker, G. A. (1984). Evolutionarily stable strategies. In J. R. Krebs & N. B. Davies (Eds), *Behavioural Ecology: an Evolutionary Approach* (2nd ed.). Oxford: basil Blackwell.

Pate, J. L. (1967). Losing games and their recognition. *Psychological Reports*, **20**, 1031–1035.

Pate, J. L. & Broughton, E. D. (1970). Game-playing behavior as a function of incentive. *Psychological Reports*, **27**, 36.

Pate, J. L., Broughton, E. D., Hallman, L. K., & Letterman, A. N. L. (1974). Learning in two-person zero-sum games. *Psychological Reports*, **34**, 503–510.

Pattanaik, P. K. (1976). Counter-threats and strategic manipulation under voting schemes. *Review of Economic Studies*, **43**, 11–18.

Payne, W. (1965). Acquisition of strategies in gaming situations. *Perceptual and Motor Skills*, **20**, 473–479.

Pettit, P. & Sugden, R. (1989). The backward induction paradox. *The Journal of Philosophy*, **86**, 169–182.

Pinter, H. (1960). *The Caretaker*. London: Methuen.

Pinter, H. (1972). Harold Pinter: An interview. In A. Ganz (Ed.), *Pinter: A Collection of Critical Essays* (pp. 19–33). Englewood Cliffs, NJ: Prentice-Hall.

Plon, M. (1974). On the meaning of the notion of conflict and its study in social psychology. *European Journal of Social Psychology*, **4**, 389–436.

Plott, C. R. (1986). Rational choice in experimental markets. *Journal of Business*, **59**, S301-S327.

Plott, C. R. & Levine, M. E. (1978). A model of agenda influence on committee decisions. *American Economic Review*, **68**, 146–160.

Popper, K. R. (1961). *Evolution and the Tree of Knowledge*. Herbert Spencer Lecture delivered in Oxford, 30 October. [Reprinted in K. R. Popper, *Objective Knowledge: An Evolutionary Approach* (pp. 256–284). Oxford: Clarendon, 1972.]

Popper, K. R. (1969). *Conjectures and Refutations: The Growth of Scientific Knowledge* (3rd ed.). London: Routledge & Kegan Paul.

Poulton, E. C. (1994). *Behavioral Decision Theory: A New Approach*. Cambridge: Cambridge University Press.

Poundstone, W. (1993). *Prisoner's Dilemma*. Oxford: Oxford University Press.

Pruitt, D. G. (1967). Reward structure and cooperation: The decomposed Prisoner's Dilemma game. *Journal of Personality and Social Psychology*, **7**,

21–27.

Pruitt, D. G. (1970). Motivational processes in the decomposed Prisoner's Dilemma game. *Journal of Personality and Social Psychology,* **14,** 227–238.

Pruitt, D. G. (1993). *Negotiation in Social Conflict.* Pacific Grove, CA: Brooks/ Cole.

Pruitt, D. G. & Kimmel, M. J. (1977). Twenty years of experimental gaming: Critique, synthesis, and suggestions for the future. *Annual Review of Psychology,* **28,** 363–392.

Psathas, G. & Stryker, S. (1965). Bargaining behavior and orientations in coalition formation. *Sociometry,* **28,** 124–144.

Rabbie, J. M. (1991). Determinants of instrumental intra-group cooperation. In R. A. Hinde & J. Groebel (Eds), *Cooperation and Prosocial Behaviour* (pp. 238–262). Cambridge: Cambridge University Press.

Rabbie, J. M., Schot, J. C., & Visser, L. (1989). Social identity theory: A conceptual and empirical critique from the perspective of a behavioural interaction model. *European Journal of Social Psychology,* **19,** 171–202.

Rabinowitz, K., Kelley, H. H., & Rosenblatt, R. M. (1966). Effects of different types of interdependence and response conditions in the minimal social situation. *Journal of Experimental Social Psychology,* **2,** 169–197.

Raiffa, H. (1953). Arbitration schemes for generalized two-person games. In H. Khun & A. W. Tucker (Eds), *Contributions to the Theory of Games* (Annals of Mathematics Studies, Vol. **2,** pp. 361–387). Princeton, NJ: Princeton University Press.

Riaffa, H. (1992). Game theory at the University of Michigan, 1948–1952. In E. R. Weintraub (Ed.), *Toward a History of Game Theory: Annual Supplement to Volume 24 History of Political Economy* (pp. 165–175). Durham, NC & London, England: Duke University Press.

Ramsey, F. P. (1931). Truth and probability. In R. B. Braithwaite (Ed.), *Foundations of Mathematics and Other Logical Essays* (pp. 156–198). London: Routledge & Kegan Paul.

Rapoport, Am. (1987). Comparison of theories of payoff disbursement of coalition values. *Theory and Decision,* **22,** 13–47.

Rapoport, Am., Bornstein, G., & Erev, I. (1989). Intergroup competition for public goods: Effects of unequal resources and relative group size. *Journal of Personality and Social Psychology,* **56,** 748–756.

Rapoport, Am. & Kahan, J. P. (1976). Where three isn't always two against one: Coalitions in experimental three-person games. *Journal of Experimental Social Psychology,* **12,** 253–273.

Rapoport, Am., Kahan, J. P., & Stein, W. E. (1976). Decisions of timing in experimental probabilistic duels. *Journal of Mathematical Psychology,* **13,** 163–191.

Rapoport, An. (1962). The use and misuse of game theory. *Scientific American,* **207**(6), 108–118.

Rapoport, An. (1967a). Escape from paradox. *Scientific American,* **217**(1),

50–56.

Rapoport, An. (1967b). Exploiter, Leader, Hero, and Martyr: The four archetypes of the 2 × 2 game. *Behavioral Science,* **12**, 81–84.

Rapoport, An. (1970). Conflict resolution in the light of game theory and beyond. In P. Swingle (Ed.), *The Structure of Conflict* (pp. 1–42). New York: Academic Press.

Rapoport, An. (1971). *The Big Two: Soviet-American Perceptions of Foreign Policy.* Indianapolis, IN: Pegasus.

Rapoport, An. (1984). Game theory without rationality. *Behavioral and Brain Sciences,* **7**, 114–115.

Rapoport, An. (1989). *Decision Theory and Decision Behaviour: Normative and Descriptive Approaches.* Dordrecht: Kluwer.

Rapoport, An. & Chammah, A. M. (1965). *Prisoner's Dilemma: A Study in Conflict and Cooperation.* Ann Arbor, MI: University of Michigan Press.

Rapoport, An. & Chammah, A. M. (1969). The game of Chicken. In I. R. Buchler & H. G. Nutini (Eds), *Game Theory in the Behavioral Sciences* (pp. 151–175). Pittsburgh, PA: University of Pittsburgh Press.

Rapoport, An. & Guyer, M. (1966). A taxonomy of 2 × 2 games. *General Systems,* **11**, 203–214.

Rapoport, An. & Orwant, C. (1962). Experimental games: A review. *Behavioral Science,* **7**, 1–37.

Rasch, B. E. (1987). Manipulation and strategic voting in the Norwegian parliament. *Public Choice,* **52**, 57–73.

Rasmusen, E. (1989). *Games and Information: An Introduction to Game Theory.* Oxford: Blackwell.

Reeve, A. & Ware, A. (1992). *Electoral Systems: A Comparative and Theoretical Introduction.* London: Routledge.

Rescher, N. (1975). *Unselfishness: The Role of the Vicarious Affects in Moral Philosophy and Social Theory.* Pittsburgh, PA: University of Pittsburgh Press.

Reychler, L. (1979). The effectiveness of a pacifist strategy in conflict resolution: An experimental study. *Journal of Conflict Resolution,* **23**, 228–260.

Rhinehart, L. (1972). *The Dice Man.* Frogmore: Panther.

Richelson, J. T. (1981). A comparative analysis of social choice functions, IV. *Behavioral Science,* **26**, 346–353.

Riker, W. H. (1961). Voting and the summation of preferences: An interpretative bibliographical review of selected developments during the last decade. *American Political Science Review,* **55**, 900–911.

Riker, W. H. (1962). *The Theory of Political Coalitions.* New Haven, CT: Yale University Press.

Riker, W. H. (1965). Arrow's theorem and some examples of the paradox of voting. In J. M. Claunch (Ed.), *Mathematical Applications in Political Science* (pp. 41–60). Dallas, TX: Southern Methodist University Press.

Riker, W. H. (1967a). Bargaining in a three-person game. *American Political Science Review,* **61,** 642–656.

Riker, W. H. (1967b). A new proof of the size principle. In J. L. Bernd (Ed.), *Mathematical Applications in Political Science* (Vol. **11,** pp. 167–174). Dallas, TX: Southern Methodist University Press.

Riker, W. H. (1971). An experimental examination of formal and informal rules of a three-person game. In B. Lieberman (Ed.), *Social Choice.* New York: Gordon and Breach.

Riker, W. H. (1982). *Liberalism Against Populism.* San Francisco: Freeman.

Riker, W. H. & Ordeshook, P. C. (1973). *An Introduction to Positive Political Theory.* Englewood Cliffs, NJ: Prentice-Hall.

Robinson, J. (1951). An iterative method of solving a game. *Annals of Mathematics,* **54,** 296–301.

Robinson, M. (1975). Prisoner's Dilemma: Metagames and other solutions. *Behavioral Science,* **20,** 201–205.

Robinson, T. W. (1970). Game theory and politics: Recent Soviet views. *Studies in Soviet Thought,* **10,** 291–315.

Rosenthal, H. (1974). Game-theoretic models of bloc-voting under proportional representation: Really sophisticated voting in French labor elections. *Public Choice,* **18,** 1–23.

Rosenthal, R. W. (1981). Games of perfect information, predatory pricing and the chain-store paradox. *Journal of Economic Theory,* **25,** 92–100.

Roth, A. E. (Ed.). (1988). *The Shapley Value: Essays in Honor of Lloyd S. Shapley.* New York: Cambridge University Press.

Rousseau, J.-J. (1762). Du Contrat Social ou Principes du Droit Politique. In J.-J. Rousseau, *Oeuvres Complètes* (Vol. III). Dijon: Éditions Gallimard, 1964.

Rubin, J. Z. & Brockner, J. (1975). Factors affecting entrapment in waiting situations: The Rosencrantz and Guildenstern effect. *Journal of Personality and Social Psychology,* **31,** 1054–1063.

Rubin, J. Z., Brockner, J., Small-Weil, S., & Nathanson, S. (1980). Factors affecting entry into psychological traps. *Journal of Conflict Resolution,* **24,** 405–426.

Runciman, W. G. & Sen, A. K. (1965). Games, justice and the general will. *Mind,* **74,** 554–562.

Russell, B. (1954). *Human Society in Ethics and Politics.* London: George Allen & Unwin.

Rustow, D. (1955). *The Politics of Compromise: A Study of Parties and Cabinet Government in Sweden.* Princeton, NJ: Princeton University Press.

Sakaguchi, M. (1960). Reports on experimental games. *Statistical Applied Research JUSE,* **7,** 156–165.

Samuelson, C. D. & Allison, S. T. (1994). Cognitive factors affecting the use of social decision heuristics in resource-sharing tasks. *Organizational Behavior and Human Decision Processes,* **58,** 1–27.

Samuelson, C. D., Messick, D. M., Rutte, C. G., & Wilke, H. A. M. (1984). Individual and structural solutions to resource dilemmas in two cultures. *Journal of Personality and Social Psychology, 47,* 94–104.

Satterthwaite, M. A. (1973). *The Existence of a Strategy Proof Voting Procedure: A Topic in Social Choice Theory.* Unpublished doctoral dissertation, University of Wisconsin.

Satterthwaite, M. A. (1975). Strategy-proofness and Arrow's conditions: Existence and correspondence theorems for voting procedures and social welfare functions. *Journal of Economic Theory, 10,* 187–217.

Savage, L. J. (1951). A theory of statistical decision. *Journal of the American Statistical Association, 46,* 55–67.

Schellenberg, J. A. (1988). A comparative test of three models for solving "the bargaining problem". *Behavioral Science, 33,* 81–96.

Schelling, T. C. (1960). *The Strategy of Conflict.* Cambridge, MA: Harvard University Press.

Schelling, T. C. (1966). *Arms and Influence.* New Haven, CT: Yale University Press.

Schelling, T. C. (1967). What is game theory? In J. C. Charlesworth (Ed.), *Contemporary Political Analysis* (pp. 224–232). New York: Free Press.

Schelling, T. C. (1968). Game theory and the study of ethical systems. *Journal of Conflict Resolution, 12,* 34–44.

Schelling, T. C. (1971a). Dynamic models of segregation. *Journal of Mathematical Sociology, 1,* 143–186.

Schelling, T. C. (1971b). On the ecology of micromotives. *The Public Interest, 25,* 61–98.

Schelling, T. C. (1972). A process of segregation: Neighbourhood tipping. In A. H. Pascal (Ed.), *Racial Discrimination in Economic Life* (pp. 157–184). Lexington, MA: Lexington Books.

Schelling, T. C. (1973). Hockey helmets, concealed weapons, and daylight saving: A study of binary choices with externalities. *Journal of Conflict Resolution, 17,* 381–428.

Schelling, T. C. (1978). *Micromotives and Macrobehavior.* New York: W. W. Norton.

Schlenker, B. R. & Bonoma, T. V. (1978). Fun and games: The validity of games for the study of conflict. *Journal of Conflict Resolution, 22,* 7–38.

Schlesinger, G. (1974). The unpredictability of free choices. *British Journal for the Philosophy of Science, 25,* 209–221.

Schick, F. (1986). Dutch bookies and money pumps. *Journal of Philosophy, 83,* 112–119.

Schmeidler, D. (1969). The nucleolus of a characteristic function game. *SIAM Journal of Applied Mathematics, 17,* 1163–1170.

Schroeder, D. A. (1995). *Social Dilemmas: Perspectives on Individuals and Groups.* New York: Praeger.

Schulz, U. (1986). The structure of conflict and preferences in experimental games. In R. Scholz (Ed.), *Current Issues in West German Decision Research.* Frankfurt: Lang.

Süchssler, R. (1990a). *Kooperation unter Egoisten.* München: Oldenbourg.

Schüssler, R. (1990b). Die Möglichkeit der Kooperation unter Egoisten. *Zeitschrift für philosophische Forschung,* **44**, 292–304.

Scientific American (1981). Program Power, **244**(4), 71A-72.

Scodel, A., Minas, J. S., Ratoosh, P., & Lipetz, M. (1959). Some descriptive aspects of two-person non-zero-sum games. *Journal of Conflict Resolution,* **3**, 114–119.

Selten, R. (1965). Spieltheoretische Behandlung eines Oligopolmodells mit Nachfrageträgheit. *Zeitschrift für die gesamte Staatswissenschaft,* **121**, 301–324, 667–689.

Selten, R. (1975). Re-examination of the perfectness concept for equilibrium points in extensive games. *International Journal of Game Theory,* **4**, 25–55.

Selten, R. (1978). The chain store paradox. *Theory and Decision,* **9**, 127–159.

Selten, R. & Hammerstein, P. (1984). Gaps in Harley's argument on evolutionarily stable learning rules and in the logic of "tit for tat". *Behavioral and Brain Sciences,* **7**, 115–116.

Sen, A. K. (1970). *Collective Choice and Social Welfare.* Edinburgh: Oliver & Boyd.

Séris, J.-P. (1974). *La Théorie des Jeux.* Paris: Presses Universitaires de France, Dossiers Logos.

Sermat, V. (1967a). The effect of initial cooperative or competitive treatment upon a subject's response to conditional cooperation. *Behavioral Science,* **12**, 301–313.

Sermat, V. (1967b). The possibility of influencing the other's behavior and cooperation: Chicken vs. Prisoner's Dilemma. *Canadian Journal of Psychology,* **27**, 204–219.

Sermat, V. (1970). Is game behavior related to behavior in other interpersonal situations? *Journal of Personality and Social Psychology,* **16**, 92–109.

Shapley, L. S. (1953). A value for n-person games. In H. W. Kuhn & A. W. Tucker (Eds), *Contributions to the Theory of Games II. Annals of Mathematical Studies 28* (pp. 307–317). Princeton, NJ: Princeton University Press.

Shapley, L. S. & Shubik, M. (1954). A method of evaluating the distribution of power in a committee system. *American Political Science Review,* **48**, 787–792.

Shapley, L. S. & Snow, R. N. (1950). Basic solutions of discrete games. *Annals of Mathematical Studies,* **24**, 27–35.

Shepsle. K. A. (1972). Parties, voters, and the risk environment: A mathematical treatment of electoral competition under uncertainty. In R. G. Niemi & H. F. Weisberg (Eds), *Probability Models of Collective Decision Making* (pp. 273–297). Columbus, OH: Charles E. Merrill.

Shubik, M. (1954). Does the fittest necessarily survive? In M. Shubik (Ed.), *Readings in Game Theory and Political Behavior* (pp. 43–46). New York:

Doubleday.

Shubik, M. (Ed.). (1964). *Game Theory and Related Approaches to Social Behavior.* New York: Wiley.

Shubik, M. (1971). The Dollar Auction game: A paradox in noncooperative behavior and escalation. *Journal of Conflict Resolution,* **15**, 109–111.

Shure, G. H., Meeker, R. J., & Hansford, E. A. (1965). The effectiveness of pacifist strategies in bargaining games. *Journal of Conflict Resolution,* **9**, 106–117.

Sidowski, J. B. (1957). Reward and punishment in a minimal social situation. *Journal of Experimental Psychology,* **54**, 318–326.

Sidowski, J. B., Wyckoff, L. B., & Tabory, L. (1956). The influence of reinforcement and punishment in a minimal social situation. *Journal of Abnormal and Social Psychology,* **52**, 115–119.

Siegel, S. & Goldstein, D. A. (1959). Decision-making behavior in a two-choice uncertain outcome situation. *Journal of Experimental Psychology,* **57**, 37–42.

Siegel, S., Siegel, A. E., & Andrews, J. M. (1964). *Choice, Strategy, and Utility.* New York: McGraw-Hill.

Simon, H. A. (1957). *Models of Man: Social and Rational.* New York: Wiley.

Simon, H. A. (1976). *Administrative Behavior: A Study of Decision-making Processes in Administrative Organizations* (3rd ed.). New York: Free Press.

Simon, H. A. (1978). Rationality as process and as product of thought. *American Economic Review,* **68**, 1–16.

Simon, H. A. (1985). Human nature in politics: The dialogue of psychology with political science. *American Political Science Review,* **79**, 293–304.

Singer, M. G. (1963). *Generalization in Ethics.* London: Eyre and Spottiswoode.

Singer, M. G. (1988). Morality and universal law. In G. H. R. Parkinson (Ed.), *An Encyclopedia of Philosophy* (pp. 568–589). London: Routledge.

Singleton, R. R. & Tyndall, W. F. (1974). *Games and Programs: Mathematics for Modeling.* San Francisco: W. H. Freeman.

Skotko, V., Langmeyer, D., & Lundgren, D. (1974). Sex differences as artifacts in the Prisoner's Dilemma game. *Journal of Conflict Resolution,* **18**, 707–713.

Slomp, G. & La Manna, M. M. A. (1993). *The Impossibility of Rational Choice: Hobbes vs Game Theory.* Leicester: Leicester University Faculty of Social Sciences Discussion Papers in Economics No. 93/10.

Sloth, B. (1993). The theory of voting and equilibria in noncooperative games. *Games and Economic Behavior,* **5**, 152–169.

Slovic, P., Fischhoff, B., & Lichtenstein, S. (1977). Behavioral decision theory. *Annual Review of Psychology,* **28**, 1–39.

Slovic, P., Fischhoff, B., & Lichtenstein, S. (1982). Response mode, framing, and information processing effects in risk assessment. In R. M. Hogarth (Ed.), *New Directions for Methodology of Social and Behavioral Science: The*

Framing of Questions and the Consistency of Responses (pp. 21–36). San Francisco: Jossey-Bass.

Slovic, P. & Lichtenstein, S. (1983). Preference reversals: A broader perspective. *American Economic Review*, **73**, 596–605.

Smith, A. (1776). *An Inquiry Into the Nature and Causes of the Wealth of Nations.* [Reprinted in an edition edited by E. Cannan, 1904. London: Methuen. Vol. 1.]

Smith, P. B. & Bond, M. H. (1993). *Social Psychology Across Cultures: Analysis and Perspectives.* Hemel Hempstead: Harvester Wheatsheaf.

Smith, V. L. (1992). Game theory and experimental economics: Beginnings and early influences. In E. R. Weintraub (Ed.), *Toward a History of Game Theory: Annual Supplement to Volume 24 History of Political Economy* (pp. 241–282). Durham, NC & London, England: Duke University Press.

Smith, W. P. & Anderson, A. J. (1975). Threats, communication and bargaining. *Journal of Personality and Social Psychology,* **32**, 76–82.

Sobel, J. H. (1991a). Non-dominance, third person and non-action Newcomb problems, and metatickles. *Synthese,* **86**, 143–172.

Sobel, J. H. (1991b). Some versions of Newcomb's problem are Prisoners' Dilemmas. *Synthese,* **86**, 197–208.

Stahelski, A. J. & Kelley, H. H. (1969). *The Effects of Incentives on Cooperators and Competitors in a Prisoner's Dilemma Game.* Paper presented at the Western Psychological Association Convention, Vancouver. [Cited in Wrightsman, O'Connor, & Baker, 1972, pp. 51–52.]

Stavely, E. S. (1972). *Greek and Roman Voting and Elections.* Ithaca, NY: Cornell University Press.

Steen, L. A. (1980). From counting votes to making votes count: The mathematics of elections. *Scientific American*, **243**(4), 16–26.

Steunenberg, B. (1992). Coalition theories: Empirical evidence for Dutch municipalities. *European Journal of Political Research*, **22**, 245–278.

Straffin, P. (1980). The Prisoner's Dilemma. *UMAP Journal*, **1**, 101–103.

Strube, M. J. & Lott, C. L. (1984). Time urgency and the Type A behavior pattern: Implications for time investment and psychological traps. *Journal of Research in Personality*, **18**, 395–409.

Stryker, S. (1972). Coalition behavior. In C. G. McClintock (Ed.), *Experimental Social Psychology* (pp. 338–380). New York: Holt, Rinehart & Winston.

Stryker, S. & Psathas, G. (1960). Research on coalitions in the triad: Findings, problems, and strategy. *Sociometry,* **23**, 217–230.

Sugden, R. (1991). Rational choice: A survey of contributions from economics and philosophy. *The Economic Journal*, **101**, 751–785.

Sullivan, M. P. & Thomas, W. (1972). Symbolic involvement as a correlate of escalation: The Vietnam case. In R. M. Russett (Ed.), *Peace, War, and Numbers.* Beverly Hills, CA: Sage.

Suppes, P. & Atkinson, R. C. (1960). *Markov Learning Models for Multiperson Interactions.* Stanford, CA: Stanford University Press.

Swingle, P. G. (1970a). Dangerous games. In P. G. Swingle (Ed.), *The Structure of Conflict* (pp. 235–276). New York: Academic Press.

Swingle, P. G. (Ed.) (1970b). *The Structure of Conflict*. New York: Academic Press.

Swistak, P. (1989). How to resist invasion in the repeated Prisoner's Dilemma game. *Behavioral Science*, **34**, 151–153.

Taylor, M. (1987). *The Possibility of Cooperation*. Cambridge: Cambridge University Press.

Tedeschi, J. T., Bonoma, T. V., & Novinson, N. (1970). Behavior of a threatener: Retaliation vs. fixed opportunity costs. *Journal of Conflict Resolution*, **14**, 69–76.

Tedeschi, J. T., Schlenker, B. R., & Bonoma, T. V. (1973). *Conflict, Power, and Games*. Chicago, IL: Aldine.

Teger, A. I. (1980). *Too Much Invested to Quit*. New York: Pergamon.

Teger, A. I. & Carey, M. S. (1980). Stages of escalation. In A. I. Teger, *Too Much Invested to Quit* (pp. 45–60). New York: Pergamon.

Teger, A. I., Carey, M. S., Hillis, J., & Katcher, A. (1980). Physiological and personality correlates of escalation. In A. I. Teger, *Too Much Invested to Quit* (pp. 61–81). New York: Pergamon.

Thibaut, J. W. & Kelley, H. H. (1959). *The Social Psychology of Groups*. New York: Wiley.

Thomas, E. A. C. & Feldman, M. W. (1988). Behavior-dependent contexts for repeated plays of the Prisoner's Dilemma. *Journal of Conflict Resolution*, **32**, 699–726.

Thomas, L. C. (1984). *Games, Theory and Applications*. Chichester: Ellis Horwood.

Thorndike, R. L. (1911). *Animal Intelligence: Experimental Studies*. New York: Macmillan.

Toda, M., Shinotsuka, H., McClintock, C. G., & Stech, F. J. (1978). Development of competitive behavior as a function of culture, age, and social comparison. *Journal of Personality and Social Psychology*, **36**, 825–839.

Tognoli, J. (1975). Reciprocation of generosity and knowledge of game termination in the decomposed Prisoner's Dilemma game. *European Journal of Social Psychology*, **5**, 297–312.

Tropper, R. (1972). The consequences of investment in the process of conflict. *Journal of Conflict Resolution*, **16**, 97–98.

Trussler, S. (1973). *The Plays of Harold Pinter: An Assessment*. London: Victor Gollancz.

Tuck, R. (1979). Is there a free-rider problem, and if so, what is it? In R. Harrison (Ed.), *Rational Action: Studies in Philosophy and Social Science*. Cambridge: Cambridge University Press.

Turner, J. C., Hogg, M. A., Oakes, P. J., Reicher, S. D., & Wetherall, M. (1987). *Rediscovering the Social Group: A Self-Categorization Theory*. Oxford:

Blackwell.

Tversky, A. (1969). Intransitive preferences. *Psychological Review, 76*, 31–48.

Tversky, A. & Kahneman, D. (1981). The framing of decisions and the psychology of choice. *Science, 211*, 453–458.

Tversky, A. & Kahneman, D. (1982). Rational choice and the framing of decisions. In R. M. Hogarth (Ed.), *New Directions for Methodology of Social and Behavioral Science: The Framing of Questions and the Consistency of Responses*. San Francisco: Jossey-Bass.

Tversky, A. & Kahneman, D. (1988). Rational choice and the framing of decisions. In D. E. Bell, H. Raiffa, & A. Tversky (Eds), *Decision Making: Descriptive, Normative, and Prescriptive Interactions* (pp. 167–192). Cambridge: Cambridge University Press.

Tysoe, M. (1982). Bargaining and negotiation. In A. M. Colman (Ed.), *Cooperation and Competition in Humans and Animals* (pp. 141–172). Wokingham: Van Nostrand Reinhold.

Tyszka, T. & Grzelak, J. L. (1976). Criteria of choice in non-constant zero-sum games. *Journal of Conflict Resolution, 20*, 357–376.

Van Huyck, J., Battalio, R. C., & Beil, R. O. (1990). Tacit coordination games, strategic uncertainty and coordination failure. *American Economic Review, 80*, 234–248.

Van Lange, P. A. M. (1992). Rationality and morality in social dilemmas: The influence of social value orientations. In W. B. G. Liebrand, D. M. Messick, & H. A. M. Wilke (Eds), *Social Dilemmas: Theoretical Issues and Research Findings* (pp. 133–146). Oxford: Pergamon.

Van Lange, P. A. M. & Liebrand, W. B. G. (1989). On perceiving morality and potency: Social values and the effects of person perception in a give-some dilemma. *European Journal of Personality, 3*, 209–225.

Van Lange, P. A. M., Liebrand, W. B. G., & Kuhlman, D. M. (1990). Causal attribution of choice behavior in three-person Prisoner's Dilemmas. *Journal of Experimental Social Psychology, 26*, 34–48.

Van Lange, P. A. M., Liebrand, W. B. G., Messick, D. M., & Wilke, H. A. M. (1992). Social dilemmas: The state of the art. In W. B. G. Liebrand, D. M. Messick, & H. A. M. Wilke (Eds), *Social Dilemmas: Theoretical Issues and Research Findings* (pp. 3–28). Oxford: Pergamon.

Vinacke, W. E. (1969). Variables in experimental games: Toward a field theory. *Psychological Bulletin, 71*, 293–318.

Vinacke, W. E. & Arkoff, A. (1957). An experimental study of coalitions in the triad. *American Sociological Review, 22*, 406–414.

von Neumann, J. (1928). Zur Theorie der Gesellschaftsspiele. *Mathematische Annalen, 100*, 295–320.

von Neumann, J. & Morgenstern, O. (1944). *Theory of Games and Economic Behavior.* Princeton, NJ: Princeton University Press. [2nd ed., 1947; 3rd ed., 1953.]

Vorob'ev, N. N. (1977). *Game Theory: Lectures for Economists and Systems*

Scientists. New York: Springer-Verlag. [Original Russian ed., *Teoriya Igr,* 1974, Leningrad University Press.]

Wald, A. (1945). Statistical decision functions which minimize maximum risk. *Annals of Mathematics,* **46,** 265–280.

Walker, M. (1977). The Jamaican fishing study reinterpreted. *Theory and Decision,* **8,** 265–272.

Watkins, J. (1985). Second thoughts on self-interest and morality. In R. Campbell & L. Sowden (Eds), *Paradoxes of Rationality and Cooperation: Prisoner's Dilemma and Newcomb's Problem* (pp. 59–74). Vancouver: University of British Columbia Press.

Webb, J. M. & Krus, D. J. (1993). Modeling society as a zero-sum game: An empirical demonstration. *Psychological Reports,* **72,** 415–418.

Weber, M. (1921). *Wirtschaft und Gesellschaft.* Tübingen: J. C. B. Mohr.

Wichman, H. (1972). Effects of isolation and communication on cooperation in a two-person game. In L. S. Wrightsman, J. O'Connor, & N. J. Baker (Eds), *Cooperation and Competition: Readings on Mixed-Motive Games* (pp. 197–205). Belmont, CA: Brooks/Cole.

Wilke, H. & Mulder, M. (1971). Coalition formation on the gameboard. *European Journal of Social Psychology,* **1,** 339–356.

Williams, B. (1979). Internal and external reasons. In R. Harrison (Ed.), *Rational Action: Studies in Philosophy and Social Science.* Cambridge: Cambridge University Press.

Williams, J. D. (1966). *The Compleat Strategyst* (2nd ed.). New York: McGraw-Hill.

Willis, R. H. (1962). Coalitions in the tetrad. *Sociometry,* **25,** 358–376.

Wilson, R. (1975). On the theory of aggregation. *Journal of Economic Theory,* **10,** 89–99.

Wilson, R. K. & Pearson, A. (1987). Evidence of sophisticated voting in a committee setting: Theory and experiments. *Quality and Quantity,* **21,** 255–273.

Wolff, R. P. (1968). *Kant: A Collection of Critical Essays.* London: Macmillan.

Wrightsman, L. S. (1966). Personality and attitudinal correlates of trusting and trustworthy behaviors in a two-person game. *Journal of Personality and Social Psychology,* **4,** 328–332.

Wrightsman, L. S., O'Connor, J., & Baker, N. J. (Eds). (1972). *Cooperation and Competition: Readings in Mixed-Motive Games.* Belmont, CA: Brooks/Cole.

Yamagishi, T. (1988). The provision of a sanctioning system in the United States and Japan. *Social Psychology Quarterly,* **51,** 264–270.

Young, H. P. (1993). The evolution of conventions. *Econometrica,* **61,** 57–84.

Young, J. W. (1977). Behavioral and perceptual differences between structurally equivalent, two-person games: A rich versus poor context comparison. *Journal of Conflict Resolution,* **21,** 299–322.

Zeckhauser, R. (1973). Voting systems, honest preferences, and Pareto optimality. *American Political Science Review,* **67,** 934–946.

Zermelo, E. (1912). Über eine Anwendung der Mengenlehre auf die Theorie des Schachspiels. *Proceedings of the Fifth International Congress of Mathematicians, Cambridge,* **2**, 501–510.

Index

Abramson, P. R., 269
admissible strategy, 69–71, 82, 256, 257, 259, 260
see also dominant strategy
Afranius Dexter, 268
agenda voting paradox, 234
Alcock, J. E., 151, 221, 225
Aldrich, J. H., 269
Allison, S. T., 184
Ames, R. E., 214, 221
Anantharaman, T., 294
Anderson, A. J., 157
Andrews, J. M., 23
Angelo and Isabella (game), 5, 7, 8, 9, 11, 20, 21–22
animal conflicts, 276–293
antelopes, 277
Antilochos, 111
Apfelbaum, E., 98, 135
approval voting, 267
arbitration scheme, 126
archery, 15
Argyle, M., 97, 135, 151, 156, 213
Arickx, M., 42, 48
Arkoff, A., 180, 182, 183
arms races, 118, 192, 198
Arrow, K. J., 14, 238, 244, 245, 250
Arrow's impossibility theorem, 238, 244–246
Arrowood, A. J., 182, 183, 184
Atkinson, R. C., 87, 92
attribution effects, 152–154, 221–223
auction games, 187, 191–200, 313
Aumann, R. J., 65
Avedon, E. M., 64
Axelrod, R., 144, 145, 146, 147, 148, 272, 289, 291

baboons, 291
Bacharach, M. O. L., 34, 36, 191
backgammon, 180
backward induction, 63, 104–107, 187, 189–191
bad apple theory, 216
Baker, N. J., 13, 98, 135

bandwagon effect, 36
Bar-Hillel, M., 305
Barbera, S., 267
bargaining, 126–132, 161–185
Barth, J. M., 223, 224, 225
Bartholdi, J. J., 144, 293
Bartos, O. J., 132
Battalio, R. C., 34, 37
Battle of Bismarck Sea, 54–60, 101
Battle of the Sexes game, 110–111, 116–117, 119–121, 135, 136, 211, 309–310
Bayes, T., 25
Becker, G. M., 89, 92
Beer, F. A., 144
Beggan, J. K., 143
behavioural ecology, 275
Beil, R. O., 34, 37
Bell, D. E., 22, 94
Beltramo, J. S., 137
Bendor, J., 144, 148, 293
Berlekamp, E. R., 63
Bernoulli, D., 18
Bernstein, I. S., 289
Bertilson, H. S., 42, 48
Bethlehem, D. W., 151
Betz, B., 142
Bhavnani, K.-K., 158, 159
Bicchieri, C., 9, 10, 37, 105, 187, 298, 300
bighorn rams, 276
Binmore, K., 86, 131
Bixenstine, V. E., 151
Bjurulf, B. H., 233, 235, 236, 260, 261, 265
Black, D., 229, 240, 241, 242
Blackwell, D., 317
Blair, D. H., 246
Blau, J. H., 244
Blin, J.-M., 240
Blum, M. W., 42, 48
Bogdanor, V., 246, 250
Bonacich, P., 215, 223
Bond, M. H., 151, 152
Bonoma, T. V., 98, 135, 149, 180
Borda effect, 242–243
Borda, J.-C. de, 229, 242, 266
Border, K. C., 232

Bordes, G., 246
Borel, E., 13
Boring, E. G., 19
Bornstein, G., 217, 219
bounded rationality, 294–295
Bowen, B. D., 242
Boyd, R., 292
Braden, J. L., 183
Braiker, H. B., 45
Braithwaite, R. B., 132, 295
Brams, S. J., 81, 114, 118, 125, 171, 174, 182,
    183, 238, 242, 250, 257, 258, 266, 267,
    268, 305, 307
Brayer, A. R., 93, 94, 96
Brewer, M. B., 212, 219, 220, 223, 224
Brockmann, H. J., 290, 291
Brockner, J., 200, 201
Broughton, E. D., 89
Bull, P., 142
Burhans, D. T., Jr., 180
Burkhard, B., 43, 48, 292
Butler, C. A., 144, 293
bystander apathy, 217

Caldwell, M. D., 205, 215, 218, 219, 223
Calvert, R. L., 268
Campbell, M., 294
Campbell, R., 300, 305, 307
Caplow, T., 179
Caporael, L. R., 214, 219, 220, 316
Carey, M. S., 197, 198
Cargile, J., 305
Carlisle, T. R., 191
Carment, D. W., 151
Carnevale, P., 224
Carroll, L., *see* Dodgson, C. L.
categorical imperative, 117, 308–310
Centipede game, 104–105, 106–107
certainty, decision making under, 10, 15–17
Chain-store game, 187–191
Chammah, A. M., 137, 138, 139, 140, 144, 149
Chaney, M. V., 183
characteristic function, 163–167, 172, 194–195
charades (game), 35
Chernoff, H., 30
Chertkoff, J. M., 180, 182, 183, 184
chess, 3, 7, 9, 13, 56, 63, 294–295
Chicken game, 111–115, 117, 119–121, 135,
    138, 139–140
    cross-cultural studies of, 151
    framing effects, 154, 157–158, 159, 225
    Hawk-Dove game isomorphic with, 279

Hobbes's state of nature as, 311
    metagame approach to, 125
    multi-person, 211–212
    programmed strategies in, 143
    sex differences in, 149
Chun, Y., 172
Clemen, R. T., 23
coalitions, 161–185 *passim*, 186, 193, 195, 266
    experiments on, 180–185
cognitive dissonance, 200
Cohen, J. M., 114, 201
Cohen, M. J., 114, 201
cold war, 118, 125
Cole, S. G., 184
Coleman, A. A., 48, 49
Colman, A. M., 40, 48, 49, 93, 94, 95, 96, 111,
    158, 159, 193, 209, 212, 215, 225, 238,
    243, 250, 295
common knowledge, 9, 62, 80, 189, 273, 298
common language, 40
commons dilemma, 214
    see also social dilemmas
communication effects, 141–142, 218–221
commuters' problem, 41–42, 47–48
complete information, 9, 78, 80
compound games, 208, 209–212, 281–288
computer tournaments of Prisoner's
    Dilemma, 144–149
Concorde fallacy, 191, 290–291
Condorcet, M. J. A. N. C. Marquis de, 229,
    237
Condorcet's paradox, 235, 237–242, 244, 286
Confucius, 116
conservation, 203–205
constant-sum games, 53–84
    see also strictly competitive games
conventional fighting, 276–277
Conway, J. H., 63
Coombs, C. H., 242
Cooper, R., 34, 37
cooperation index, 139
cooperative games, 126–132, 161–185,
    194–195
    see also bargaining
coordination games, 11, 33–40, 161–162,
    297–300
Copeland, A. H., 294
Corbin, T. L., 137
core, 167–168, 171, 174, 181
    see also least core
Costanza, R., 192, 199
courtship behaviour, 275

Cox, G. W., 263
Cox, T. H., 151
crabs, 276–277
Crandall, R., 180
Crawford, V. P., 34, 40
Crosbie, P. V., 183, 184
cross-cultural studies, 151–152
cross-wired train, 41–42, 47–48
crossword puzzles, 15
Crumbaugh, C. M., 144, 156
Cuban missile crisis, 114, 125
cyclic majorities, 237–242, 250, 264, 286
Cyprus conflict, 117

Darwinian fitness, 274, 277, 278, 282 (fig.),
    289
  see also evolution
Dasgupta, P., 131
Davenport, W., 69
David, F. N., 12
Davies, N. B., 272, 275, 288, 289
Davies, R. O. 317
Davis, J. H., 135, 144
Davis, L. H., 300, 307
Davis, M., 174, 176
Davis, M. D., 63
Dawes, R. M., 22, 205, 212, 214, 215, 218,
    219, 220, 221, 222, 316
Dawkins, R., 191, 272, 277, 289, 290, 291, 314
DD lock-in effect 136–137
de-individualtion, 217–218
De Jong, D. V., 34, 37
Dean, J., 111
decomposed Prisoner's Dilemma, 154–156,
    208–209, 224
DeMeyer, F., 240
Denzau, A., 268
depth, strategic, 36
Deutsch, M., 137, 140, 141, 142, 156, 222
diet problem, 16
digger wasps, 290–291
Dimand, M. A., 13
Dimand, R. W., 13
DiMona, J., 113
Dion, D., 272, 289
Dodgson, C. L., 229, 266
Dollar Auction game, 187, 191–200
  characteristic function, 194–195
  Rousseau's philosophy and, 313
dominant imputation, 168, 169
dominant strategy, 69–71, 82, 255, 286
  experiments involving, 87, 90, 92,

Newcomb's problem, 306–307
social dilemmas, 205, 207
two-person mixed-motive games, 108, 112,
    116, 120
voting games, 256, 257, 259, 261
Domjan, M., 43, 48, 292
Donninger, C., 144, 149
Doron, G., 249, 250
Downs, A., 239, 269
Doyle, Sir A. C., 62, 67
Dresher, M., 115
Droop, H., 247
Druckman, D., 87
duels, 91, 92, 273–274
Dummett, M., 246, 250
dung flies, 289–290
Dutch book, 232–233

Eckel, C., 270
Edgeworth, F. Y., 204
Eells, E., 305
efficacy, *see* personal efficacy
Eibl-Eibesfeldt, I., 277
Einhorn, H. J., 23
Eiser, J. R., 135, 154, 158, 159
electoral reform, 250
Ellis, A. L., 182
Ellsberg, D., 113
Elster, J., 229
Enelow, J. M., 268
Epstein, Y., 140
equal excess theory, 177–179, 182
equilibrium point, 57–61, 64, 66, 67, 68–69,
    70, 71, 81, 107
  defined, 58–61
  see also Nash equilibrium
Erev, I., 217
escalation, 191–201
escape panics, 212–213
ESS, *see* evolutionarily stable strategy
essential games, 164
Euclidian geometry, 6
evaluation apprehension, 150–151
Evans, G., 141, 156
Evans, G. W., 144
evolution, 148, 272–293
  moral principles, 314–316
evolutionarily stable composition, 288, 290,
    291, 292–293
evolutionarily stable strategy, 279–292
    passim
  definition, 279–280

evolutionarily stable strategy – *continued*
  moral principles and, 315, 316
  see also evolutionarily stable composition
expected utility, 15, 19–23, 32, 305–307
  passim
expected value, 17–19, 32
experimental gaming, 85–99, 134–160,
  212–226
  critique of, 97–99
  popularity of, 86
extensive form, 9, 54–60, 101, 103–104, 193

Farquharson, R., 251, 255, 259, 260, 263, 264,
  265, 266, 268, 270, 313
Faucheux, C., 151
Fechner, G. T., 19
Feldman, M. W., 293
Felsenthal, D. S., 236, 238, 263, 266, 267, 270
Fenno, R. F., 268
Fermat P. de, 12
Festinger, L., 200
fictitious play, 75–77
fiddler crabs, 276–277
Field, S. L., 313
Fields, W. C., 200
first past the post voting, *see* voting proce-
  dures, plurality
Fischhoff, B., 23, 94
Fishburn, P. C., 20, 229, 233, 238, 240, 243,
  249, 250, 267
Fisher, R. A., 13, 272, 276
fitness, Darwinian, *see* Darwinian fitness
Fleishman, J. A., 182
Fletcher, J., 296
Flood, M., 90, 92, 115, 136
focal point, 37–40
  see also salience
Forsythe, R., 34, 37
Found, P., 232
Fox, J., 89, 215, 216, 217, 218
framing effects, 40, 87, 94–96, 154–160,
  214–215, 224–225
Frank, A. Q., 263, 266, 270
Franklin, B., 35
Franklin, M. N., 269
Fréchet, M., 13
Frederikson, L., 142
free-rider problems, 204, 214, 302
  see also social dilemmas
Friedman, J. W., 61, 131, 187
Frisch, D., 23
Furnham, A., 159

Gaeth, G. J., 94
Galbraith, J. W., 269
Gale, A., 195
Galeotti, G., 250
Gallo, P. S., 134, 140
gambling, 17–23, 191
game theory
  basic terminology, 6–9
  definition, 3, 10
  elements of, 3–14
  history, 12–14
  principal objective, 3–4
  rationality in, 297–304
game tree, 55, 63, 101
games
  Angelo and Isabella, 5, 7, 8, 9, 11, 20,
    21–22
  Battle of the Sexes, 110–111, 116–117,
    119–121, 135, 136, 211, 309–310
  Centipede, 104–105, 106–107
  Chain-store game, 197–191
  chess, 3, 7, 9, 13, 56, 63, 294–295
  Chicken, *see* Chicken game
  coordination, 11, 33–40, 161–162, 297–300
  Dollar Auction, 187, 191–200, 313
  handy-dandy, 64
  Hawk-Dove, 278–283
  Hawk-Dove-Retaliator, 286–287
  Head On, 4–5, 7, 8, 9, 11, 20, 34, 35, 37–38,
    298
  Heads or Tails, 299
  Holmes v. Moriarty, 62–67, 72, 82–83
  journalist's dilemma, 23–32
  Leader, 108–110, 119–121, 135, 136, 211
  Maximizing Difference, 135, 138–139, 140,
    151, 211, 212
  mixed-motive, 12, 34, 86, 97, 100–101, 162,
    194
  morra, 65–69
  Mr and Mrs, 35, 36
  N-person Prisoner's Dilemma, 202,
    213–214, 217, 222, 225, 302–304
  pachisi, 180
  Predatory Pricing, 101–103, 106, 187, 189
  Price War, 5, 7, 8, 9, 11, 20
  Prisoner's Dilemma, *see* Prisoner's
    Dilemma game
  Rendezvous, 34, 39
  Research and Development, 28, 30
  roulette, 17–18
  Russian roulette, 11, 17, 20
  Saul and David, 81–82

Shareholders', 165–167, 173–174, 180
St Petersburg, 18–19
strictly competitive, 12–13, 34, 53–99, 129,
    131, 132, 164, 187, 255
strictly determined, 13, 53–84
trucking, 156–157
zero-sum, 11–12, 129, 131, 132, 162,
    164–165, 187, 194, 255
see also under names of specific games
games of chance, 10–11, 12
games of skill, 10, 15–17
Gamson, W. A., 180, 181, 183, 184
Gärdenfors, P., 267
Gardner, M., 242, 307
Gardner, R. M., 137
Garman, M., 240
Gauthier, D., 298, 300, 316
Gehrlein, W. V., 243
Geist, V., 277, 289
Gewirth, A., 310
Gibbard, A., 267
Gibbons, R., 65, 104
Gibbs, J., 150
Gilbert, M., 39, 298, 299
Gillett, R. T., 243
Gillies, D. B., 167
Girshick, M. A., 317
give-some games, 214, 224
    see also social dilemmas
Glance, N. S., 205
Gleser, L. J., 240
Goehring, D. J., 89, 215
Golden Rule, 116, 136
Goldstein, D. A., 23
golf, 15
Good, D. A., 135
Goodnow, J. J., 23
Gordon, D., 132
Gordon, T. P., 289
Grafen, A., 290
Grodzins, M., 36
Grofman, B., 313
group identity, 220–221
group polarization phenomenon, 199
group selection, 277
group size effects, 215–218
group solidarity, 220–221
Grzelak, J. L., 140, 141, 143, 156, 221, 222
Guilbaud, G. T., 240
Guinier, L., 246, 250
Gumpert, P., 140
Guy, R. K., 63

Guyer, M., 13, 89, 107, 135, 215, 216, 217, 218

Haldeman, H. R., 113
Haller, H., 34, 40
Hallman, L. K., 89
Hamburger, H., 97, 118, 205, 212, 215, 216,
    217, 218
Hamermesh, D. S., 132
Hamilton, W. D., 144, 272, 276, 291
Hammerstein, P., 144, 146, 148, 292
Hampton, J., 311
handy-dandy (game), 64
Hansford, E. A., 143
Hardin, G., 204, 214, 312
Hare voting system, *see* single transferable
    vote
Harford, T. C., 144
Harris, R. J., 107, 125
Harsanyi, J. C., 14, 40, 65, 79, 80, 100, 126,
    186, 296
Harsanyi transformation, 80
Harvey, J. H., 156
Hawk-Dove game, 278–283
Hawk-Dove-Retaliator game, 286–287
Haywood, O. G., Jr., 54, 57
Head On game, 4–5, 7, 8, 9, 11, 20, 34,
    37–38, 298
Heads or Tails game, 299
Heal, J., 9, 37, 298
Heckathorn, D., 132
Herzberg, R. Q., 270
hide-and-seek, 34
Hillinger, C., 239
Hillis, J., 197
Hines, W., 272, 288
Hitler, 114
Ho Chi Minh, 113
Hobbes, T., 310, 311
Hofstadter, D. R., 116, 144, 148
Hogarth, R. M., 23
Hogg, M. A., 220
Hollis, M., 204, 300, 303
Holmes, J. G., 154
Holmes v. Moriarty game, 62–67, 72, 82–83
Holt, C. A., 270
Homer, 111
Hottes, J., 149, 150
Howard, N., 114, 121, 124, 125, 171
Hsu, F., 294
Hsu, S., 86
Huberman, B. A., 205
Hulbert, L. G., 217

Hume, D., 40, 297
Humphreys, L. G., 23
Hurley, S. L., 305, 306, 307
Hylland, A., 229

Imamura, H., 55, 56, 57, 58
imperfect information, 56, 57, 80, 189
imputation, 166, 167, 169, 174, 176
   defined, 166–167
incentive effects, 139–140, 223
incomplete information, 33, 79–83, 85, 87,
   190, 295
independence of irrelevant alternatives,
   30–32, 128–129, 245
inertia selling, 201
inessential games, 164
infinite games, 54, 91
inflation, 202–203
information sets, 56, 101
insufficient reason, 25–26
insurance, 18, 21
interdependent decision making, 3–4
interpersonal control theory, 216–217
intransitive preferences, 231, 232–233, 237
   see also cyclic majorities, single-peakedness
investment, 37
invisible hand, 202–203, 205
Isenberg, D. J., 199

Jacobi, N., 305
Jamaican fishermen, 69
Jansen, R. W. T. L., 143
Jerdee, T. H., 214, 218, 219
Johnson, L. B. 198
Johnston, R. J., 269
Jones, A. J., 137
Jones, G. G., 198, 199
Jorgenson, D. O., 217, 219, 223
journalist's dilemma (game), 23–32
Joyce, R. C., 263
Jung, J. P., 265

Kahan, J. P., 87, 89, 91, 92, 161, 178, 180, 181,
   185, 215, 218, 223
Kahn, A., 149, 150
Kahn, H., 113
Kahneman, D., 23, 94, 95
Kalai, E., 131
Kalisch, G. K., 180, 185
Kamien, M., 240
Kandori, M., 34
Kanouse, D. E., 149

Kant, I., 117, 205, 308, 314
Karlin, S., 91
Katcher, A., 197
Katz, T., 219
Kaufman-Gilliland, C. M., 217, 219, 220, 223
Kaufman, H., 88, 89, 91
Kaufman M., 181
Kavka, G., 311
Kelley, H. H., 42, 43, 45, 46, 47, 48, 140, 152,
   153, 157, 182, 183, 184, 221, 222
Kelly, J. S., 229, 240, 246, 266, 267
Kenney, General George C., 54, 55, 56, 57,
   58, 59
kernel, 174–176, 181
Kerpel, L., 219
Kerr, N. L., 217, 219, 220, 223
Keynes, J. M., 10, 25, 36, 37
Kimmel, M. J., 97, 135, 144, 155
Kleinke, C., 140
Koehler, D. H., 268
Komorita, S. S., 135, 144, 161, 177, 180, 182,
   183, 215, 217, 223, 224, 225
Kornick, R., 249, 250
Kozelka, R., 69
Kraines, D., 292
Kraines, V., 292
Kramer, G. H., 264
Kramer, R., 144, 148, 220, 221, 224
Krauss, R. M., 156
Kravitz, D. A., 161, 223
Krebs, J. R., 272, 275, 288, 289
Krehbiel, K., 250, 268, 269
Kreps, D. M., 187, 190
Krus, D. J., 87
Kuhlman, D. M., 144, 154, 221, 222
Kullberg, V. K., 183, 184

La Manna, M. M. A., 311
Lacey, O. L., 89
Lamb, J. C., 88
Lang, E., 201
Langmeyer, D., 149
lapsed saint strategy, 144
Lapworth, C. W., 215
Laughlin, P. R., 135, 144
law of effect, 43
Lazarus, J., 272, 274, 275, 277, 289
Leader (game), 108–110, 119–121, 135, 136,
   211
least core, 177, 181
   see also core
Leininger, W., 192, 193

Lendenmann, K., 90, 92
Leonard, R. J., 13
Letterman, A. N. L., 89
Levi, I., 305
Levin, I. P., 94
Levine, M. E., 270
Levinsohn, J. R., 181
Lewis, D. K., 9, 37, 298, 299, 305, 307
Lewontin, R. C., 272, 275
Lichtenberger, J., 181
Lichtenstein, S., 23, 94, 232
Lieberman, B., 88, 89, 92, 94
Liebrand, W. B. G., 143, 212, 215, 216, 219, 221, 222
Lien, S. K., 42, 48
light-guessing experiment, 23
Lindskold, S., 142
linear programming, 16, 75
Lipetz, M., 137
Lloyd, W. F., 204
Lobel, S., 151
Locke, D., 305
Lorberbaum, J. P., 149, 292
Lorenz, K., 277
Lott, C. L., 201
lotteries, 20–23
Lucas, R. E., 10
Lucas, W. F., 169
Luce, R. D., 13, 30, 34, 61, 110, 111, 136, 137, 161
Lumsden, M., 117
Lundgren, D., 149

Macbeth effect, 197, 198
Mack, D., 149
Mackie, J. L., 296, 314, 315, 316
Mailath, G. J., 34
Malcolm, D., 88
Malinas, G., 305
Mansell, D., 221, 225
Maoz, Z., 236, 238, 263, 266, 267, 270
March, J. G., 294
Margalit, A., 305
Marrison, C., 213
Marshello, A. J. F., 144, 221
Martin, D., 296
Marwell, G., 214, 215, 221
Maschler, M., 174, 176, 181
matrix transformations, 78–79
maximax, 26, 90, 251
maximin, 135–136, 163, 164, 194, 279
  decision principle, 26

two-person zero-sum games, 58, 59, 60, 65, 83
two-person mixed-motive games, 109, 110, 111, 120, 129–130
maximin bargaining solution, 129–130
Maximizing Difference game, 135, 136, 138–138, 140, 151
  multi-person, 211–212
May, R. M., 238, 240
Maynard Smith, J., 144, 272, 277, 278, 279, 280, 281, 286, 287, 288, 289, 291
McClennen, E. F., 232, 300
McClintock, C. G., 134, 137, 138, 139, 140, 141, 151, 215, 221
McDaniel, W. C., 224
McKelvey, R. D., 260, 261, 262, 265
McLean, I. S., 250, 311
McLeod, P. L., 151
McNeel, C. P., 138, 140, 151
McNeil, B. J., 95
McTavish, J., 215, 218, 219, 221, 222
McVicar, J., 113
Mealey, L., 280
Medlin, S. M., 181
Meeker, R. J., 143, 151, 215, 223
Mehta, J., 38, 39, 40, 299
memes, 314–316
Menelaos, 111
Méré, Chevalier de, 12
Messick, D. M., 90, 212, 143, 205, 215, 217, 219, 221, 222, 223
metagames, 121–125
Michener, H. A., 182
Milgrom, P., 187, 190
Miller, C. E., 180, 182
Miller, D. T., 154
Miller, N. R., 236, 260, 262, 265
Milnor, J. W., 32, 180, 185
Minas, J. S., 137
minimal social situation, 33, 40–50
  multi-person, 33, 48–50
minimal winning coalition theory, 179–180, 183
minimax
  experimental evidence, 86–87, 88, 89, 90, 91, 92, 93, 94, 96
  theory, 58, 59, 60, 61, 65, 67, 78, 83
minimax regret principle, 28–32
minimax theorem, 13, 66, 70, 71, 77
  proof, 317–324
minimum resource theory, 180, 182, 184
Mintz, A., 212, 213, 218

Mitchell, C. R., 192
mixed-motive games, 12, 34, 86, 97, 100–101, 162, 194
    two-person two-strategy, 107–108, 118–121
mixed strategy, 64–66, 67, 68–69, 83, 280, 285
mob behaviour, 217
Molander, P., 144
Molm, L. D., 42, 46, 48
money pump, 232–233
Moore, P. G., 27, 30
Morgenstern, O., 13, 20, 21, 22, 26, 32, 62, 63, 121, 162, 163, 168, 169, 294, 317
Morin, R. E., 92, 93
Morley, I. E., 87
morra (game), 65–69
Mr and Mrs (game), 35, 36
Muir, H. C., 213
Mulder, M., 184
multi-person games, 33, 48–50, 161–226, 202
Mundy, D., 42
Murnighan, J. K., 161
mutual fate control, 42
Myerson, R. B., 9, 54, 129, 263

N-person Prisoner's Dilemma
    empirical research, 213–214, 216, 217, 222, 225
    philosophy, 303, 304
    theory, 202
    see also social dilemmas
Nail, P., 184
Nanson, E. J., 238
Nash bargaining solution, 130–131
Nash equilibrium
    defined, 58–61
    experimental evidence, 86–88
    minimax theorem and, 324
    mixed-motive games, 100–128 *passim*
    multi-person non-cooperative games, 162, 186–212 *passim*
    two-person zero-sum games, 57–81 *passim*
    voting games, 251–256 *passim*
Nash, J. F., 14, 58, 128, 130, 180, 184, 186
Nathanson, S., 201
natural selection, 274–276, 283
    see also evolution
Nature (player), 6–7, 10–11, 15, 17, 24–32 *passim*, 80, 275
Neal, P., 311
negotiation games, 85, 87, 126–132
Nemeth, C., 97, 135, 140, 141

Nering, E. D., 180, 185
Neumann, J. von, 13, 20, 21, 22, 26, 32, 62, 63, 66, 121, 162, 163, 168, 169, 294, 317
Newcomb, W. A., 304
Newcomb's problem, 69, 304–307
Nickell, G. G., 137
Niemi, R. G., 232, 233, 235, 236, 240, 242, 251, 260, 261, 262, 263, 265, 266, 267, 269, 270
Nixon, R. M., 113
noisy duels, 91, 92, 273–274
normal form, 9, 56–57, 103–104
noughts and crosses (game), 13
Novinson, N., 149
Nowak, M., 43, 144, 149, 292, 316
Nowatzyk, A., 294
Nozick, R., 305, 307
nucleolus, 176–177
Nurmi, H., 229, 238
Nuttin, J. M., 151
Nydegger, R. V., 132

O'Connor, J., 13, 98, 135
O'Neill, B., 192, 193
O'Reilly, E. F., Jr., 151
Oakes, P. J., 220
Ofshe, L., 23
Ofshe, R., 23
Old Testament, 81
olive baboons, 291
Olson, M., Jr., 214
one-person games, 15, 275
Orbell, J., 212, 214, 219, 220, 316
Ordeshook, P. C., 174, 179, 187, 229, 234, 236, 238, 240, 249, 268
ordinal preferences, 80–83
Orwant, C. J., 89, 134, 157
Orwant, J. E., 157
Oskamp, S., 140, 142
Owen, G., 54, 91

pachisi, 180
Paolino, P., 269
Papadimitriou, C. H., 16, 75
Papciak, A. S., 217, 219, 223
paradox of the chairman's vote, 265–266, 272–273
    see also power inversion paradox
paradoxes of voting, 229, 234, 236, 237–243, 244, 265–266
Pareto optimality, 116, 128, 205, 207, 208
Parfit, D., 300, 304

Parker, G. A., 272, 288, 289, 290
Parks, C. D., 217
Pascal, B., 12
Pate, J. C., 89
Pattanaik, P. K., 267
Pattie, C. J., 269
Pauker, S. G., 95
Pavlov strategy, 149, 292
Payne, W., 88
payoff function, 7–8
Pearson, A., 269
perfect equilibrium, *see* subgame perfect
    equilibrium
perfect information, 9, 56, 63, 70, 71, 80, 91,
    103
Perkel, B., 13
Perner, J., 132
personal efficacy, 217
perturbed game, 106, 107
Pettit, P., 105, 190
Pinter, H., 169, 171
Plato, 310
Pliny the Younger, 268
Plon, M., 14
Plott, C. R., 199, 240, 270
plurality-majority disagreement, 243, 265
plurality voting, *see* voting procedures,
    plurality
Poe, E. A., 171
poker, 3
Popper, K. R., 314, 316
Poulton, E. C., 23
Poundstone, W., 125, 144
Pountney, I., 238, 242, 243
power inversion paradox, 183–184, 266, 273
    see also paradox of the chairman's vote
Predatory Pricing (game) 101–103, 106, 187,
    189
preferential voting, 261
Price, G. R., 272, 278, 279, 286, 287
Price War (game), 5, 7, 8, 9, 11, 20
Prisoner's Dilemma game, 69, 90, 115–118,
    119–125, 291
  attribution effects in, 152–154
  characteristic function, 164–165
  computer tournaments, 144–149
  decomposed, 154–156, 208–209, 224
  evolution of cooperation and, 144–149,
    316
  experimental evidence, 134, 135, 139–140,
    141, 142, 143, 144

framing effects, 154–160
historical background, 13, 14
multi-person, 202, 205–209
Newcomb's problem and, 304, 307
rationality in, 300–304
sex differences, 149
social dilemmas, 201, 202, 205, 215, 217,
    225
programmed strategies, 85, 90–91, 93,
    142–144, 199, 216, 315
  see also tit for tat strategy
Prolux, C., 86
proportional representation, 246–250
Pruitt, D. G., 87, 98, 135, 144, 155, 156
Psathas, G., 182, 184
psychological traps, 200–201
psychophysical law, 19
public goods dilemmas, 214, 222, 224
  see also social dilemmas
Puccini, G., 117

Quilley, R., 159

Rabbie, J. M., 135, 156
Rabinowitz, K., 42, 46, 48
Radloff, R., 42
Rae, N. C., 269
Raiffa, H., 13, 22 30, 34, 61, 94, 110, 111, 115,
    131, 132, 136, 137, 161
Raiffa-Kalai-Smorodinsky bargaining solu-
    tion, 131–132
rams, 276
Ramsey, F. P., 232
randomization, 64–66, 67, 68
Rapoport, Amnon, 87, 91, 161, 178, 180, 181,
    182, 185, 217, 219, 266, 270
Rapoport, Anatol, 13, 22, 23, 54, 89, 90, 91,
    92, 97, 107, 108, 111, 117, 120, 124, 132,
    134, 135, 137, 138, 139, 140, 144, 147,
    149, 161, 198, 229, 230
Rasch, B. E., 234, 235, 269
Rasmusen, E., 9, 25, 54, 56, 71
rationality in games, 297–304
Ratoosh, P., 137
rats, 90
rattlesnakes, 277
Ray, N., 111
reciprocal altruism, 315
  see also tit for tat strategy
Reeve, A., 246, 250
reformed sinner strategy, 144
Reicher, S. D., 220

Rendezvous (game), 34, 39
Rescher, N., 300, 301, 302
Research and Development (game), 28, 30
resource management dilemma, 214, 224
　see also social dilemmas
Reychler, L., 143
Rhinehart, L., 64
Rhode, D. W., 269
Richelson, J. T., 249
Rijken, V. M., 143
Riker, W. H., 174, 179, 181, 182, 183, 229,
　232, 236, 242, 266, 268, 269
risk, decision making under, 10–11, 17–23,
　32
Rivers, D., 268
Rob, R., 34
Roberts, J., 187, 190
Robinson, J., 75
Robinson, M., 125
Rosen, B., 214, 218, 219
Rosenblatt, R. M., 42, 46, 48
Rosenthal, H., 269
Rosenthal, R. W., 101, 104, 105, 187, 189
Ross, T. W., 34, 37
Roth, A. E., 172
roulette, 17–18
Rousseau, J.-J., 311, 312, 313
Rubin, J. Z., 200, 201
Runciman, W. G., 311
Rusk, D., 114
Russell, B., 297
Russian roulette, 11, 17, 20
Rustow, D., 234
Rutte, C. G., 217, 222, 223

saddle point, 131, 255
　defined, 59
　minimax theorem, 317
　two-person zero-sum games, 57–61, 62,
　　63, 65, 66, 68, 70
Sakaguchi, M., 88
salience, 37–40, 109, 299–300
Samuelson, C. D., 184, 217, 223
sardines (game), 35
satisficing, 295
Satterthwaite, M. A., 267
Saul and David (game) 81–82
Savage, L. J., 28
Schellenberg, J. A., 132
Schelling, T. C., 34, 35, 36, 37, 38, 205, 208,
　296, 299
Schick, F., 232

Schlenker, B. R., 98, 135, 180
Schlesinger, G., 305
Schmeidler, D., 176
Schmitt, D., 215
Schneider, S. K., 220
Schot, J. C., 156
Schroeder, D. A., 212
Schulz, U., 144
Schüssler, R., 316
Scodel, A., 137
Segal, U., 232
segregation, 36
Selten, R., 14, 40, 100, 104, 105, 106, 126, 144,
　146, 148, 187, 190, 292
Sen, A. K., 229, 311
Séris, J.-P., 161
Sermat, V., 140, 143, 157
sex differences, 149–151
sex ratios, 275–276
Shakespeare, W., 8, 171
Shaklee, H., 215, 218, 219, 221, 222
Shapley, L. S., 73, 130, 172, 174
Shapley-Snow theorem, 73–74
Shapley value, 172–174, 181, 182, 184, 195
Shareholders' game, 165–167, 167–169,
　173–174, 180
Shaw, G. B., 116
Shaw, M. C., 201
Shepsle. K. A., 25, 268
Shinotsuka, H., 151
Shrum, W., 199
Shubik, M., 80, 174, 191, 194, 196, 273
Shure, G. H., 143, 215, 223
Sidowski, J. B., 40, 42, 43
Siegel, A. E., 23
Siegel, S., 23
Sigmund, K., 43, 144, 149, 292, 316
silent duels, 91
Simmel, G., 161
Simon, H. A., 294
simple games, 173
simplex algorithm, 75, 77
sincere voting, 229–230
　see also straightforward voting
Singer, M. G., 310
single-peakedness, 241–242, 249
single transferable vote, 246–250
Singleton, R. R., 56, 61, 75
Sistrunk, F., 224
size principle, 182
skill, games of, 15
Skotko, V., 149

Slomp, G., 311
Sloth, B., 254
Slovic, P., 23, 94, 232
Small-Weil, S., 201
Smith, A., 202, 203, 205, 297
Smith, P. B., 151, 152
Smith, V. L., 13
Smith, W. P., 156, 157
smoking gene, 306–307
Smorodinsky, M., 131
Snow, R. N., 73
Sobel, J. H., 305, 306, 307
social choice function, 229, 231–232
social choice rule, see social choice function
social contract, 310–313
social dilemmas, 201–226
    attribution effects, 221–223
    communication effects, 218–221
    decomposed, 224
    empirical findings, 212–225
    formalization, 205–209
    framing effects, 224–225
    group size effects, 215–218
    individual differences, 221
    Kant's categorical imperative and, 309
    rationality in, 300–304
    Rousseau's general will and, 311
social value orientations, 221
social welfare function, 244
Solomon, L., 144
sophisticated voting, 258–267
Sorities paradox, 302–303
Sowden, L., 305
Sox, H. C., 95
Spencer, H., 272
St Petersburg paradox (game), 18–19, 21
stable set, 168–169, 171, 174
Stahelski, A. J., 140, 152, 153, 221
Starmer, C., 38, 39, 40, 299
Statza, G. R., 182
Stavely, E. S., 251
Stech, F. J., 151
Steen, L. A., 267
Steiglitz, K., 16, 75
Stein, W. E., 91, 92
Stephenson, G. M., 87
Steunenberg, B., 183
Stout, S., 144, 148
Straffin, P., 115
straightforward voting, 256, 257
strategic depth, 36
strategic voting, 250–270

empirical evidence, 267–270
strategy
    admissible, 69–71, 82, 256, 257, 259, 260
    definition of, 8–9
    dominant, 69–71, 82, 205, 207, 255, 286; *see also* dominant strategy
    evolutionarily stable, 279–292 *passim*, 315, 316
    lapsed saint, 144
    maximax, 26, 90, 251
    minimax, 58, 59, 60, 61, 65, 67, 78, 83; *see also* minimax
    mixed, 64–66, 67, 68–69, 83, 280, 285
    Pavlov, 149, 292
    reformed sinner, 144
    tit for tat, 143–144, 145–149 *passim*, 158, 217, 291, 292, 315
    win-stay, lose-change, 43, 149, 292
strictly competitive games, 12–13, 34, 129, 131, 132, 164, 187, 255
    experimental evidence, 85–99
    theory, 53–83
strictly determined games, 12, 53–84
Strube, M. J., 201
Stryker, S., 180, 182, 184
subgame, definition of, 101
subgame perfect equilibrium, 66, 101–107, 186, 189, 193, 253–254, 260
subjective expected utility, 22–23, 32
Sugden, R., 9, 37, 38, 39, 40, 66, 104, 105, 190, 298
Sullivan, M. P., 198
superadditivity, 163–164, 165, 166
Suppes, P., 87, 92
survival of the fittest, 265–266, 272–273
    see also evolution
Sutton-Smith, B., 64
Suzumura, K., 246
Sweeny, J., 223
Swierzbinski, J., 86
Swingle, P. G., 111, 135
Swistak, P., 144, 148, 293

Tabory, L., 40, 43
tacit coordination, 37–40
    see also coordination games
Tack, W. H., 181
tactical voting, 250–270
    empirical evidence, 267–270
Tajfel, H., 154
take-some games, 214, 224
    see also social dilemmas

Taylor, M., 311
Tedeschi, J. T., 98, 135, 149, 180
Teger, A. I., 195, 196, 197
TFT, see tit for tat strategy
Thatcher, M., 203
Thibaut, J. W., 42, 47
Thomas, E. A. C., 293
Thomas, L. C., 121, 127, 177
Thomas, R. M., 48, 49
Thomas, W., 198
Thorndike, R. L., 43
ticktacktoe (game), 13
timing, games of, 91
tit for tat strategy, 143–144, 145–149 *passim*,
      158, 217, 291, 292
   moral principles and, 315
Toda, M., 151
Tognoli, J., 156
Tönnies, F., 152
Tosca (opera), 117–118
tragedy of the commons, 204–205, 214, 225
   see also social dilemmas
transformations of payoff matrices, 78–79
transitivity of preferences, 231, 232–233
   see also cyclic majorities, single-peakedness
travelling salesman problem, 16–17
trembling-hand equilibrium, 66, 101,
      105–107
triangle hypothesis, 153–154, 222
Trick, M. A., 144, 293
Tropper, R., 195, 196, 197
trucking game, 156–157
"truel", 273–274
Truman, H. S. 269
Trussler, S., 171
Tuck, R., 300, 302, 303
Tucker, A. W., 115
Turner, J. C., 220
Tversky, A., 22, 23, 94, 95, 232
two-person zero-sum games, 53–99, 129,
      131, 132, 255
   see also strictly competitive games
Tyndall, W. F., 56, 61, 75
Tysoe, M., 87
Tyszka, T., 221

uncertainty, decision making under, 10, 11,
      23–32
utility, 19–23, 79, 107, 301

validity, 97, 134
value of a game

multi-person games, 163, 168–169, 172
two-person zero-sum games, 59, 67, 68,
      70, 71, 74, 77, 79, 83
Van Avermaet, E., 42, 48
Van de Kragt, A. J. C., 214, 219, 220, 316
Van Huyck, J., 34, 37
Van Lange, P. A. M., 212, 215, 216, 219, 221,
      222, 223
Van Run, G. J., 221
Vaske, J. J., 182
Viet Nam war, 191, 198
Vinacke, W. E., 180, 182, 183
Visser, L., 156
Vogel, R., 222
von Neumann, J., see Neumann, J. von
von Neumann-Morgenstern solution,
      168–169, 171
Vorob'ev, N. N., 14
voting, 229–270
   paradoxes, 229, 234, 236, 237–243, 244,
      265–266
   procedures, 233–237
   proportional representation, 246–250
   sincere, 229–230
   sophisticated, 258–267
   straightforward, 256, 257
   strategic, 250–270
   tactical, 250–270
voting procedures, 233–237
   amendment, 235–236, 251, 252–253, 261,
      264–265
   approval, 267
   first past the post, see plurality
   Hare system, 246–250
   plurality, 236, 246, 248, 251, 253, 261,
      263–264, 264–265
   preferential, 261
   proportional representation, 246–250
   single transferable vote, 246–250
   successive, 233–235, 251, 252, 254–255,
      260–261, 264–265

wage bargaining, 202–203
Wald, A., 26
Waldegrave, J., 13
Walker, M., 69
Walters, P., 142
Ware, A., 246, 250
wasps, 276, 290–291
Watkins, J., 300
Webb, J. M., 87
Weber, M., 296

Weber, R. J., 263
weighted majority games, 165–167, 173–174, 180–185 passim
Weisberg, H. F., 240
Wetherall, M., 220
Whitten, G., 269
Wichman, H., 141
Wiest, W. M., 149
Wilke, H. 184, 212, 215, 217, 222, 223
Williams, B., 300, 303, 304
Williams, J. D., 67, 74
Willis, R. H., 185
Wilson, R. K., 187, 190, 269, 270
Wimberley, D. L., 154, 222
win-stay, lose-change strategy, 43, 149, 292
wine problem, 40

Wolff, R. P., 308
Wolters, F. J. M., 222
Wonderlich, S. A., 42, 48
Wrightsman, L. S., 13, 98, 135
Wyckoff, L. B., 40, 43

Yamagishi, T., 222
Young, H. P., 34
Young, J. W., 157

Zeckhauser, R., 267
Zeng, L., 249
Zermelo, E., 12, 70
zero-sum games, 11–12, 129, 131, 132, 162, 164–165, 187, 194, 255
  see also strictly competitive games